MARXISM AND INTERNATIONAL RELATIONS

Studies in Critical Social Sciences Book Series

Haymarket Books is proud to be working with Brill Academic Publishers (www.brill.nl) to republish the *Studies in Critical Social Sciences* book series in paperback editions. This peer-reviewed book series offers insights into our current reality by exploring the content and consequences of power relationships under capitalism, and by considering the spaces of opposition and resistance to these changes that have been defining our new age. Our full catalog of *SCSS* volumes can be viewed at https://www.haymarketbooks.org/series_collections/4-studies-in-critical-social-sciences.

Series Editor
David Fasenfest (York University, Canada)

Editorial Board
Eduardo Bonilla-Silva (Duke University)
Chris Chase-Dunn (University of California–Riverside)
William Carroll (University of Victoria)
Raewyn Connell (University of Sydney)
Kimberlé W. Crenshaw (University of California–LA and Columbia University)
Heidi Gottfried (Wayne State University)
Alfredo Saad-Filho (Queen's University, Belfast)
Chizuko Ueno (University of Tokyo)
Sylvia Walby (Lancaster University)
Raju Das (York University)

Marxism and International Relations

Perspectives from the Brazilian Global South

Edited by
Caio Martins Bugiato

Haymarket Books
Chicago, IL

First published in 2024 by Brill Academic Publishers, The Netherlands
© 2024 Koninklijke Brill NV, Leiden, The Netherlands

Published in paperback in 2025 by
Haymarket Books
P.O. Box 180165
Chicago, IL 60618
773-583-7884
www.haymarketbooks.org

ISBN: 979-8-88890-354-4

Distributed to the trade in the US through Consortium Book Sales and Distribution (www.cbsd.com) and internationally through Ingram Publisher Services International (www.ingramcontent.com).

This book was published with the generous support of Lannan Foundation, Wallace Action Fund, and the Marguerite Casey Foundation.

Special discounts are available for bulk purchases by organizations and institutions. Please call 773-583-7884 or email info@haymarketbooks.org for more information.

Cover design by Jamie Kerry and Ragina Johnson.

Printed in the United States.

Library of Congress Cataloging-in-Publication data is available.

Contents

Preface VII
Acknowledgements XI
Notes on Contributors XII

PART 1
Key Ideas by Marx and Engels for IR

1 Marx and the Formation of the Modern International System 3
Luis Manoel Rebelo Fernandes

2 Marx, Engels and the System of World Power in the Nineteenth Century 15
Muniz Gonçalves Ferreira

3 Revolutions and International Relations
Marxism's Contributions and Failures 34
Paulo Gilberto Fagundes Visentini

PART 2
Marxist Thinkers as IR Theorists

4 The Center-Periphery Dialectic
Lenin's Contribution to the Analysis of Contemporary International Relations 49
Rita Matos Coitinho

5 'War against War'
Rosa Luxemburg as an International Relations Theorist 76
Miguel Borba de Sá

6 The Imperialist Chain of the Interstate Relations
Nicos Poulantzas' Theory on Imperialism 105
Caio Martins Bugiato

7 Hegemonic Struggle and Populism
Agonistic Solutions to the Identity Challenge 121
Mayra Goulart da Silva

8 Imperialism as a Complex System of Domination
  An Approach from Domenico Losurdo 142
    Diego Pautasso

9 David Harvey and the International Relations
  Some Appointments 156
    Leonardo César Souza Ramos, Rodrigo Corrêa Teixeira, and Marina Scotelaro de Castro

PART 3
Marxist Theories on Imperialism

10 Notes on Imperialism, State and International Relations 173
    Luiz Felipe Brandão Osório

11 The Marxist Debate on Post-World War II Imperialism 194
    Caio Martins Bugiato and Tatiana Berringer

12 Imperialism
   The Question of System Stability 212
     Marcelo Pereira Fernandes

PART 4
Latin-American Theory on Dependency

13 The Marxist Theory of Dependency
   Contributions of Latin American Marxism to International Relations 237
     Maíra Machado Bichir

14 Imperialism and Dependence vs. Interdependence
   The Muted side of a Theoretical Clash 257
     Rejane Carolina Hoeveler

15 Brazilian Sub-imperialism and Peripheral Development
   A Critique of the Marxist Dependency Theory 278
     Tiago Soares Nogara

Index 303

Preface

Even their most active critics cannot ignore the influence on the human sciences of the thought of Karl Marx, Friedrich Engels, and of Marxists throughout history. In History, Sociology, Economics, and Linguistics, among others, the contribution of Marxists to the epistemology, ontology, and theory of these fields was intense. However, the same does not occur in the field of International Relations (IR), in Brazil, and worldwide. IR, traditionally understood as relations (generally conflictive) among states in an anarchic international system, has been systematically distanced from the thought inaugurated by the founders of modern and scientific socialism. For sure, IR is one of the few social sciences in which it has been relatively easy to avoid an encounter with Marxist thought.

Since its birth as a field of scientific knowledge in 1919 (thus more than a century), IR have insisted on ignoring Marxism, its theorizations, and its concrete analyses of international phenomena. Despite some exceptions, justifications for such disagreement appear in different and controversial arguments. From an institutional point of view, one argue that: the origin of IR at the beginning of the twentieth century, as an area of scientific knowledge, in British and US universities, was not impacted by Marxism, which was born from classical German philosophy and the European workers' movement, that means, from outside academic world; the institutional consolidation of the IR field in the West after World War II, during the Cold War period, carried with it an aversion to Marxism, identified with the Union of Soviet Socialist Republics (USSR). From the theoretical-political point of view, one argue that: Marxism would have nothing to say about international relations since it would be an economistic theory that would reduce the phenomena of international politics to the dynamics of the capitalist economy; it would not offer a theory on the state (the main agent of international relations); it would merely be a normative perspective dedicated to the socialist utopia and incapable of carrying out analyzes of concrete reality; or even it would be one more among the various Eurocentric perspectives that would not fit for analyzing the periphery.

Thus, we must consider Kees van der Pijl's (2014) argument that the formation of the IR mainstream (the theories of Realism, Liberalism and later Constructivism) is a construction of ideas that project Western supremacy in the form of an intellectual hegemony functional to the center of capitalism. In this way, it obscures the relations of domination and exploitation implicit in the liberal world. The origin of this construction is in Woodrow Wilson's reaction at the end of World War I to the internationalism of the Russian Revolution: his

Fourteen Points are a counterrevolutionary copy of the Bolshevik program. Then the nascent discipline in the second decade of the twentieth century was responsible to initiate an intellectual process to obfuscate and marginalize first the rich debate conducted by the theory on imperialism and then Marxism in general. Therefore, IR emerged to disentangle international phenomena from class struggles and from the processes of capital accumulation, which ultimately promotes capitalism as the natural and superior state of human life. Still in the course of its development, guided by its mainstream the theories and the analyzes of this field sought to ratify domination strategies of states, governments and classes by universalizing abstract concepts that would explain international relations without any link to capitalism.

However, a theoretical movement in the area has opposed this situation, especially in Europe, in the last few years with the development of Marxist perspectives pertinent to International Relations. In this sense, it is worth mentioning some of them, such as Neogramcian approaches in International Relations, studies on Unequal and Combined Development, the Political Marxism and the Amsterdam School. The authors of these perspectives have developed significant contributions that insert Marxism in IR in a relevant, singular and remarkable way.

Fortunately, this movement has also taken off in Brazil. For some years now, a series of events and publications on Marxism and International Relations have been promoted by researchers in the area with the general objective of questioning: where is Marxism in IR, and how would be its theoretical developments, its divergences and convergences and its concrete analyzes of phenomena in the field? In 2016, the Network of Studies in International Relations and Marxism (RIMA [In Portuguese: Rede de Estudos em Relações Internacionais e Marxismo]) was founded at the I Colloquium International Relations and Marxism in Rio de Janeiro. In this first event (and in the following ones), we had the participation of Brazilian intellectuals who have relevant production on the theme and the presence of the foreigner researches Beverly Silver and Leo Panitch. During the pandemic in 2020, RIMA organized the virtual seminar "Where is the 21st Century Going?" with the participation of the Argentine Atilio Borón and the II International Relations and Marxism Colloquium was held in 2022 in Rio de Janeiro, with the presence of professor Benno Teschke. In addition to these events, a textual production has been developed in Brazil, such as books, dossiers in academic journals and dissertations and PhD theses in postgraduate programs in the country. Nevertheless, we highlight a recent production that has contributed to mitigate the mentioned mismatch, "Marxismo e Relações Internacionais" (Bugiato, 2021 [In English: Marxism and International Relations]). This book prioritizes theoretical research that are fundamental to intervene in the field of International Relations Theories. Now, its research can be seen in the next pages.

It is important to affirm that such movement in Brazil is connected to another one that occurred in the second half of the twentieth century. Before the consolidation of the IR academic field in Brazilian universities in the 2000s, several Social Sciences intellectuals in Brazil and Latin America developed research and analysis on international relations from a Marxist perspective, culminating in the theory of dependency. Those theorists and analysts indicated that the process of development of capitalism in the periphery contained particularities that should be continually researched. They carried out researches on issues such as the place of Latin American economies in the global expansion of capitalism, the changes inherent to the advance of monopolistic capitalism, the entry of international capital into the countries of the region, the particularities of the dependent state, among other issues. In the academic development of International Relations in the country, several Marxist researchers rescued the theory of dependence and pointed out that the analysis made by Latin American researchers on dependent capitalism involves the adoption of the critical perspective offered by the Global South, particularly the perspective of the working class in the Global South. This analysis can be view as deepening the analysis of imperialism, seen from the perspective of the periphery.

So, this book is a collection of research developed in Brazil in recent years and our first collective publication on Marxism and International Relations in English. Its public is the academic audience interested in Marxist thought pertinent to International Relations. The authors present in 15 Chapters theories, concepts, and themes that can take the reader to theoretical developments and to promote analysis of concrete situations. We organized the book into four sections: key ideas by Marx and Engels for IR; Marxist thinkers as IR theorists; Marxist theories on imperialism; and the Latin-American theory on dependency. In the first section, the authors highlight the contributions of the "Communist Manifesto" to understanding the modern international system, the conception of international politics found in the journalistic articles by Marx and Engels published in the New York Daily Tribune, and the importance of studies on revolutions for International Security. In the second section, researchers dedicated to works of Marxist thinkers – Lenin, Luxemburg, Poulantzas, Laclau and Mouffe, Losurdo, and Harvey – present their reflections on international relations, which allows us to consider them as IR theorists. In the third section, the authors deal with the Marxist theory of imperialism and its debates at different moments: World War I, the second half of the twentieth century, and nowadays. In the fourth section, the authors present the Marxist theory on dependency, with exposition, debate, and critique. Originally from Latin America, this theory is fundamental to understanding the dynamics of global capitalism and particularly of the Global South, its contradictions, and transformations.

References

Bugiato C (2021) *Marxismo e Relações Internacionais*. Goiânia: Editora Phillos Academy.

Van der Pijl K (2014) *The Discipline of Western Supremacy: Modes of Foreign Relations and Political Economy*. Volume III. London: Pluto Press.

Acknowledgements

I want to thank everyone who made this book possible. I would like to thank all the authors who took part in this collective work, without whom this book would not exist. It represents a years-long effort to promote a subject that has been obscured for so long. I would also like to thank the masters who were part of my formation as a professor and researcher: Marcos Del Roio, Armando Boito Junior, and Ricardo Musse. Special thanks go to Professor Alfredo Saad-Filho, who put me in touch with the publisher, and to David Fasenfest, who is in charge of the series *Studies in Critical Social Science*. Finally, I would like to thank my wife, Laiane Brasil Leal, and my son, Tito Brasil Bugiato. Onwards!

Notes on Contributors

Tatiana Berringer
Adjunct Professor (C3) of International Relations at the Federal University of ABC. Professor in the Postgraduate Program in World Political Economy (EPM) and the Master's Program in International Relations (PRI) at UFABC. PhD and MA in Political Science from Unicamp, BA in International Relations from UNESP – Franca (2007). She took part in a Missión de Travaille at the Université de la Lumiére Lyon II as part of the Capes – Cofecub Project "Brazil and France in neoliberal globalization" (2014). She was a Visiting Scholar at the School of Oriental and African Studies (SOAS) in London (2016). She is the author of the book "The Brazilian bourgeoisie and foreign policy in the FHC and Lula governments", translated (and expanded) into English by Brill Publisher under the title "Brazilian bourgeoisie and foreign policy". Member of the group "Neoliberalism and Class Relations in Brazil", linked to the Center for Marxist Studies (Cemarx). Participates in the CNPQ 2021 Universal Project – The political crisis, the new right, the state and social classes in Brazil. Coordinates the CAPES/DAAD Project "Sustainable development agenda for the Greater ABC region and German investments in value chains".

Miguel Borba de Sá
Assistant Professor at Department of Political Science of the Federal University of Rio de Janeiro (UFRJ), Brazil. He is a member of the Laboratory of Interdisciplinary Studies in International Relations at the Federal Rural University of Rio de Janeiro (LIERI/UFRRJ), and also sits on the board of Political Advisors to the Institute of Alternative Policies for the Southern Cone (Instituto PACS). He has formerly taught in public, private, and catholic universities from Portugal and Brazil. His recent works include publications in the fields of International Relations Theory, Marxism, Peace Studies, International Political Economy, and Post/De/Anti-colonial Approaches. He holds a PhD and a Master of Science degree in International Relations from the Pontifical Catholic University of Rio de Janeiro and a Master of Arts in Ideology and Discourse Analysis from the University of Essex, UK.

Luiz Felipe Brandao Osório
Professor of International Relations and the Graduate Program in Social Sciences in Development, Agriculture and Society (CPDA) at UFRRJ and the Graduate Program in International Political Economy (PEPI) at UFRJ. Vice-Director of the Institute of Human and Social Sciences (ICHS/UFRRJ).

Post-Doctorate in Political and Economic Law from Universidade Presbiteriana Mackenzie/SP (2016). PhD and Master's in International Political Economy from UFRJ. Law degree from UFJF. Author of the book Imperialism, State and International Relations, published by Ideias & Letras. Researcher at the CLACSO Critical Legal Thought WG, NIEP-Marx/UFF and the Interdisciplinary Laboratory for International Relations Studies (LIERI-UFRRJ).

Rejane Carolina Hoeveler

She has a PhD in Social History from the Graduate Program in History at the Fluminense Federal University (PPGH-UFF), the same institution where she completed her master's degree, also in History, in 2013. She graduated in History from the Federal University of Rio de Janeiro (UFRJ). She is currently a post-doctoral student in Social Work at the Federal University of Alagoas (UFAL), and a collaborating professor in UFAL's Graduate Program in Social Work. She was an hourly lecturer in Brazilian History on the History and Social Sciences degree course at the Getúlio Vargas Foundation in Rio de Janeiro (FGV-RJ), and a substitute lecturer at the School of Social Work (ESS) at the Federal University of Rio de Janeiro (UFRJ) between 2020 and 2022. She spent time at the Institute for Ibero-American Studies in Berlin. Specialty topics: Neoliberalism and social policies in Latin America; Contemporary History of the Americas; Contemporary Democracies and Dictatorships; Feminism.

Rodrigo Corrêa Teixeira

Professor at the Pontifical Catholic University of Minas Gerais. He is permanent professor in the Stricto Sensu Postgraduate Program in Geography – Treatment of Spatial Information and a professor in the Department of International Relations. He holds a PhD in Geography, concentrating on Spatial Organization, from the Institute of Geosciences at UFMG. He obtained a Master's degree in History from the Faculty of Philosophy and Human Sciences of UFMG and a Specialist degree in International Relations from PUC Minas. He is a researcher at the Center for the Study of Colonialities and the South Atlantic Studies Group (Department of International Relations at PUC Minas).

Paulo Gilberto Fagundes Visentini

Full Professor of International Relations at the Federal University of Rio Grande do Sul/UFRGS. Professor of Postgraduate Studies in Political Science/UFRGS and Military Sciences/ECEME. Post-doctorate in International Relations from the London School of Economics and PUC-Rio. PhD in Economic History from USP, MA in Political Science and BA in History from UFRGS. He held the Rui Barbosa Chair at the University of Leiden/Netherlands and the Rio Branco

Chair at the University of Oxford/United Kingdom. He was Director of the Latin American Institute for Advanced Studies/UFRGS. Visiting Professor at NUPRI/USP, University of Cape Verde, Superior Institute of International Relations/Mozambique and University of Venice/Italy. Coordinator of the Brazilian Center for Strategy and International Relations/NERINT-UFRGS. Founding editor of Austral: Brazilian Journal of International Relations.

Muniz Gonçalves Ferreira

He has a degree in History from the Fluminense Federal University (1987), a master's degree in International Relations from the Pontifical Catholic University of Rio de Janeiro (1992) and a doctorate in Economic History from the University of São Paulo (1999). He is currently a professor at the Federal Rural University of Rio de Janeiro. He has experience in History, with an emphasis on International Relations, working mainly on the following subjects: military dictatorship, communist movement, far-right and international relations.

Mayra Goulart da Silva

Professor of Political Science at the Federal University of Rio de Janeiro, the Graduate Program in Social Sciences (PPGCS) at the Federal Rural University of Rio de Janeiro (UFRRJ) and Coordinator of the Laboratory of Parties, Elections and Comparative Politics (LAPPCOM). PhD in Political Science (2013) from the Institute of Social and Political Studies (IESP-UERJ). Post-doctorate at the Center for Research and Studies in Sociology (CIES-Iscte) of the University Institute of Lisbon, where she continues as a Visiting Researcher.

Maira Machado Bichir

Adjunct Professor of Political Science and Sociology – Society, State and Politics in Latin America, of the Postgraduate Program in Contemporary Integration of Latin America (PPGICAL) and of the Specialization in Human Rights in Latin America at the Federal University of Latin American Integration (UNILA). She holds a master's and doctorate in Political Science from the State University of Campinas (Unicamp), a bachelor's degree in Social Sciences from the State University of Campinas (UNICAMP) and a bachelor's degree in International Relations from the São Paulo State University "Júlio de Mesquita Filho" (UNESP), Franca. She is the coordinator of the Marxism and Politics Study Group (GEMP), linked to UNILA. She is a member of the Working Group States in Dispute, linked to the Latin American Council of Social Sciences (CLACSO). Her field of research and interest encompasses studies on Latin American political and social thought, the state, power, politics, dependency, patriarchy, colonialism, imperialism, class relations and social relations.

Caio Martins Bugiato
Graduated in International Relations from Universidade Estadual Paulista (UNESP – Marília campus). Master's and PhD in Political Science from the University of Campinas (UNICAMP). Post-doctoral student in Sociology at the University of São Paulo (USP). Professor of Political Science and International Relations at the Federal Rural University of Rio de Janeiro (UFRRJ) and the Postgraduate Program in International Relations at the Federal University of ABC (PRI-UFABC). Coordinator of the Collective of Marxist Studies on the International (CEMINAL). Researcher at the Network for Studies in International Relations and Marxism (RIMA).

Rita Matos Coitinho
PhD in Geography (2018) from the Postgraduate Program in Geography at the Federal University of Santa Catarina (UFSC). Career civil servant at the Brazilian Institute of Museums (TAC/SOCIOLOGY) since 2011. Curator and coordinator of the Research Program at the Victor Meirelles Museum /IBRAM. Researcher at the "Nino Gramsci" Historical and Geographical Materialism Studies Center at UFSC. Collaborator at CHAM – Center for Humanities at the Nova University of Lisbon. She holds a Master's degree in Sociology from the University of Brasília (2007), a degree in Social Sciences from the Federal University of Santa Catarina (2004) and is currently studying for a PhD in Political Science (UFSC).

Diego Pautasso
Post-Doctorate in International Strategic Studies (2018), PhD (2010) and Master (2006) in Political Science and BA (2003) in Geography from UFRGS. He is a collaborating professor in the Postgraduate Program in International Strategic Studies (UFRGS), the Center for Latin American and Caribbean Studies at the Southwest University of Science and Technology (Sichuan/China) and the Specialization in International Relations (UFRGS-Southern Military Command). He is currently a Geography teacher at the Military College of Porto Alegre. He is the author of the book "China and Russia in the Post-Cold War" and co-author of "International Relations Theory: Marxist Contributions".

Marcelo Pereira Fernandes
He is currently an Associate Professor III at the Federal Rural University of Rio de Janeiro (UFRRJ) and a lecturer in the Postgraduate Program in Regional Economics and Development (PPGER) at UFRRJ and the Postgraduate Program

in International Political Economy (PEPI) at UFRJ. Masters in Economics from the Pontifical Catholic University of São Paulo (PUC/SP) and PhD from the Fluminense Federal University (UFF/RJ). Member of the Advisory Board of the Brazilian Center for Solidarity with Peoples and the Struggle for Peace (CEBRAPAZ). Member of the Research Group Historical Patterns of Economic Development in South America and the Interdisciplinary Laboratory of Studies in International Relations. He is interested in Political Economy, International Political Economy, Imperialism, South American Economies, China's Economic Development, BRICS Economies and the Economy of the Sea. He is currently President of the Regional Economics Council of Rio de Janeiro (CORECON-RJ).

Luis Manoel Rebelo Fernandes

He holds a BA in International Relations from Georgetown University (1979), an MA in Political Science (Political Science and Sociology) from the University Research Institute of Rio de Janeiro – IUPERJ (1989) and a PhD in Political Science (Political Science and Sociology) from the University Research Institute of Rio de Janeiro – IUPERJ (1997). He is currently a professor at the Institute of International Relations (IRI) of the Pontifical Catholic University of Rio de Janeiro and a professor at the Federal University of Rio de Janeiro. As a public manager, he has served as Executive Secretary of the Ministry of Science and Technology, and others. He is the current Coordinator of the Political Science and International Relations Area at CAPES (2018–2022), a member of the agency's Technical-Scientific Council (CTC-ES) and a member of its Superior Council (2018–2021).

Marina Scotelaro de Castro

BA and PhD in International Relations from the Pontifical Catholic University of Minas Gerais (PUC Minas); MA in Social Policy from the Federal University of Espírito Santo. Professor of International Relations at the University Center of Belo Horizonte. Member of the Middle Powers Research Group at PUC Minas (CNPq) and the Center for Latin American Studies at the University of Brasilia (CNPq). Post-doctoral student and associate researcher at the Institute of International Relations at UnB.

Tiago Soares Nogara

He is currently affiliated with the College of Liberal Arts at Shanghai University (上海大学). He holds a PhD in Political Science from the University of São Paulo (USP). He holds a master's degree in International Relations from the University of Brasilia (UnB) and a degree in Social Sciences from the Federal University of Rio Grande do Sul (UFRGS), with a sandwich period at the Faculty of Political Science and International Relations of the National University of Rosario (UNR). He was a visiting professor on the international relations course at the University of Brasilia (UnB), teaching Theory of International Relations I and Topics in International Politics II. He is assistant coordinator of the Brazilian Strategic Environment research line at the International Security Studies and Research Group (GEPSI). His research focuses on South American politics and regionalism, Brazilian foreign policy and Chinese foreign policy.

Leonardo César Souza Ramos
He has a degree in International Relations from the Pontifical Catholic University of Minas Gerais, a master's degree in International Relations from the Pontifical Catholic University of Rio de Janeiro and a doctorate in International Relations from the Pontifical Catholic University of Rio de Janeiro. He is currently a professor in the Department of International Relations and coordinator of the Postgraduate Program in International Relations at the Pontifical Catholic University of Minas Gerais and a visiting professor at the National University of Rosario (UNR). He is a CNPq Research Productivity Fellow, level 2. He leads the Middle Powers Research Group (GPPM). He is a researcher at the National Institute for Studies on the United States (INCT-INEU/CNPq/FAPESP) and a researcher associated with the Coordination of Asian Studies (CEASIA/UFPE).

PART 1

Key Ideas by Marx and Engels for IR

∴

CHAPTER 1

Marx and the Formation of the Modern International System

Luis Manoel Rebelo Fernandes[1]

1   Introduction

Along with Adam Smith and Keynes, Marx makes up the triad of modern thinkers who most influenced our current world configuration.[2] The main theoretical approaches that shaped the academic discipline of International Relations over the last century, nonetheless, have tended to consider Marxist theory mostly irrelevant for understanding or explaining the modern international system. The neorealist Kenneth Waltz, for example, classifies Marxist approaches as the most complete expression of what he calls the 'second image' of international conflict: the one that conceives it as a result of the *internal* structures of states, disregarding the dynamics of the international *system* itself (Waltz, 1959: especially Chapter 5). Martin Wight, the main exponent of the so-called 'English School of International Relations', states that "neither Marx nor Lenin nor Stalin made any systematic contribution to the international theory" (Wight, 1966: 26). A similar assessment is supported even by authors who adopt a Marxist theoretical perspective (although they base this assessment on opposite lines of argument). Justin Rosenberg, for example, criticizes the text of the "Communist Manifesto" for painting a transnational image of the global expansion of capitalism, ignoring its international dimension (Rosenberg, 1996: 8).

In contrast with the IR discipline's orthodox bias against Marxist theory, this text argues that Marx's theoretical framework provides us with fundamental keys to unveil and understand the formation and dynamics of the modern international system. I sustain that Marx's potential contributions to IR theory have not been adequately valued even by authors within the discipline who were or are inspired by Marxist theory, including 'critical theory'

---

1   Professor at the Institute of International Relations (IRI) at PUC-Rio and Federal University of Rio de Janeiro.
2   This text is a revised and expanded version of an article originally published in the journal "Contexto Internacional": Fernandes, 1998. Translated into English by Alberto Resende Jr.

or 'world-system' approaches. I highlight, in particular, a crucial dimension of the 'dialectics of modernity' revealed by Marx: the contradictory articulation of *trans*national and *inter*national processes in the capitalist constitution of the modernity. I further argue that the theoretical identification of this contradictory articulation is key to unraveling the genesis and development of the modern international system.

2   Marx and the Study of International Relations

The mismatch between Marxism and orthodox scholars of international relations is not fortuitous. As an academic discipline that was constituted with a focus on the study of relations between states in the international system the area of 'international relations' is the result of the process of institutionalization of separate and specialized 'territories' of knowledge in the universities of the Anglo-Saxon world in the twentieth century. Marxist thought, in turn, is heir to another tradition – that of classical German philosophy, especially Hegelian – which conceives social reality as a historically produced totality (thus being averse to ontologies and analytical methods that carve social knowledge into watertight compartments). The compatibility of these theoretical traditions is problematic. When trying to position Marx's theoretical propositions in the framework of the intellectual debates which shaped the dominant narrative about the IR discipline's development, most scholars tended to present Marx's approach as subsidiary to theoretical perspectives centered on the proposition of a 'worldwide' or 'international' society[3].

As observed by Fred Halliday (1999: especially Chapter 3), Marx's theoretical approach does not fit in very well in either side of IR discipline's "founding debates". It is simultaneously 'utopian' (in formulating an alternative project of social emancipation) and 'realist' (in emphasizing the material interests that command human action and the role played by force in history); 'Scientific' (by intending to discover laws of social development) and 'normative' (by explicitly highlighting the transformative vocation of his philosophy); 'world-systemic' (by stressing the integration of the globe into a single world market) and 'state-centric' (by recognizing, theoretically and politically, the centrality

---

3   That is the key concept of the so-called 'English School'. In addition to Martin Wight, already mentioned above, it includes authors such as Manning (1975) and Bull (1977). The concept of 'international society' refers to reflections by Hugo Grotius, still in the seventeenth century. Among the authors who situate the Marxist theory as a 'world society' perspective are Kubalkova and Cruickshank (1989) and Thorndike (1988).

of state power for exercising domination both at the domestic and international levels). Despite this ambivalent and problematic relationship with dominant but disputed paradigms within their IR academic field, Marx provided crucial indications for understanding the genesis and evolution of the modern international system. That is what I intend to demonstrate next.

3   Marx and the Dialectics of Globalization in Modernity

Marx's original theoretical contributions on the subject are contained in the dense historical narrative that opens the "Communist Manifesto", written in partnership with Friedrich Engels and originally published in 1848. In addition to its mobilizing ideological appeal, and the powerful social and political movements it has inspired since then, the great strength of the text resides precisely in having intellectually captured the process of historical rupture that formed the modern world.

It would be an obvious anachronism to attribute to Marx paternity of the concept of 'modernity', as this is a contemporary concept. Even without being explicitly theorized, the 'spectrum' of this concept orders and commands the dense historical narrative that opens the "Communist Manifesto", as if by Adam Smith's invisible hand. The word "modern" appears more than a dozen times in the text's opening pages, referring alternately to "industry", "bourgeois society", "bourgeoisie", "proletariat", "productive forces", "production relations", "representative state" and "government". The key provided in the text to understand those modern manifestations is precisely the genesis, consolidation, and global expansion of capitalism. In other words, it is the historical process of constituting the capitalist mode of production that simultaneously constitutes 'modernity', unifying and shaping the world "in its image and likeness" (Marx and Engels, no date: 25).

This identification of the role played by capitalism in the constitution of the modern world allowed Marx to capture, in a unique way, its profoundly contradictory nature. As Göran Therborn rightly noted, Marxism emerged early on as a theory and practice of the "dialectics of modernity" (Therborn, 1995: 248). He simultaneously captured the emancipatory potential embedded in developments such as industrialization, urbanization, mass literacy, the dissolution of traditional values, and the orientation towards an open future (no longer conceived as a mere repetition of the past); and the oppressive/inhuman nature of the new mechanisms of exploitation, of factory despotism, and the generalization of a cold and calculating instrumental rationality with the commodification of ever broader dimensions of social life.

In the pages of the "Communist Manifesto", Marx identifies, as a constitutive process of the modern world, the global expansion of historical capitalism from its initial confines in northwest Europe. In a fulminating and overwhelming process, the new mode of production integrated, for the first time in history, the entire globe into a single market, subordinating, subverting, and supplanting various forms of pre-existing cultures and societies. Within the framework of this impressive rupture, the European powers subjugated, in a few decades, even the ancient empires of the East, which had sustained a material development superior to that of Europe for centuries (until the advent of the Industrial Revolution).[4]

Marx reveals how this historical rupture was prepared by the global expansion of merchant capital in the so-called 'Age of Discoveries' and the colonization processes that followed. The text of the "Communist Manifesto" anticipates, here, a point that Marx further developed in his famous chapter 24 of volume 1 of "Das Capital": the role of colonial dispossession in the historical process of 'primitive accumulation' that made the advent of modern (i.e., industrial) capitalism possible in northwest Europe. What Marx highlights is the impetus given to the advent of new forms of production in Europe by the intensification of global trade flows (via the exploration of new trade routes with to India and China, the colonization of America, and the establishment of colonial trade). It was precisely the need to serve these ever-expanding markets that displaced old feudal-guild system, initially by small scale independent producers, then by manufacturing processes, and finally by modern (capitalist) large scale industry. In the nineteenth century, this large-scale capitalist industry reaped the fruits sown by earlier mercantile expansion, unifying the world in a single market under British dominance.

European capitalism, thus, was born intertwined with global flows of trade and wealth. It was formed and developed as a transnational system from the very beginning. But that is only one side of the story. The other is that the increasing centralization of property, production, wealth, and population brought about by this transition to more modern economic forms led to the

---

4 The first volume of Fernand Braudel's book, "Material Civilization and Capitalism 15th–18th Centuries", contains an extremely interesting map in that respect, based on research conducted by the ethnographer Gordon W. Hewes. The map in question classifies, according to their levels of material development, the 76 main civilizations and cultures existent in the world at the beginning of Europe's westward expansion (around 1500). The six most developed civilizations at the time, according to this classification, were Japan, Korea, China, the Indonesian Plains, the Southeast Asian Plains, and India. Northwestern Europe appears only in seventh place. See Braudel, 1985: 58–9.

strengthening of a new type of bourgeoisie (initially commercial, then manufacturing, finally industrial and banking) that played a decisive role as a political and social counterpoint to the decentralized feudal power structures. The result was a process of political centralization that resulted in the formation of unified national states in northwest Europe under the aegis of absolutist secular power.[5] The fragmented powers of the old feudal society were "gathered into one nation, with one government, one law, one national class interest, one customs barrier" (Marx and Engels, no date: 25). In line with the predominant realist interpretations in academic IR theory, the mutual recognition of those sovereign territorial powers in the Peace Treaty of Westphalia in 1648 – at the end of the bloody [religious] Thirty Years War- marks the birth of the modern international system in Europe.

The transition to capitalism in northwestern Europe thus *simultaneously* constituted a transnational system (integrated into a global market in formation, within the framework of which the new mode of production was generalized) and an international system (consisting of sovereign centralized states, initially only in Europe). The very formation of colonial merchant empires – and the major trade wars this engendered – was a consequence of attempts to forcibly monopolize newly constituted global flows of trade and wealth, using the new concentrated political power of nation-states. These, in turn, triggered processes of unification and integration of their respective internal markets, expropriating the communal lands that made subsistence peasant economies possible (i.e., forcing peasants to become landless 'free workers'). In the nineteenth century, this recently consolidated European capitalism took advantage of the concentrated power of the large, centralized states to effectively subordinate the entire globe to its dynamics, initially through a universal liberalization agenda (which favored British capital) and, later, via the assembly of new competing colonial empires (imperialism). The edgy and contradictory articulation of global and national dimensions, therefore, is ingrained in capitalist modernity from its very beginning.

---

5 The "Communist Manifesto" explicitly formulates this understanding of the balance between the bourgeoisie and the nobility as the social foundation of the formation of absolutist states in Western Europe. Perry Anderson argued, in his book "Lineages of the Absolutist State", that, in addition to strengthening the bourgeoisie, political centralization was an expression of a reaction by the aristocracy to the weakening of its domination over the peasantry caused by the generalization of monetary relations in the countryside (see Anderson, 1979). These differences in interpretation do not affect the fundamental argument of this chapter, which highlights the articulation of transnational and international processes in the constitution of the modern world.

4 The Illusion of Convergence

The image of the modern world revealed by Marx is that of a bifrontal Janus, with both transnational and international faces. But it is undoubtedly the transnational face that appears most prominently in the text of the "Communist Manifesto". The reason for this can be found in a methodological footnote written by Engels himself, in which he states that he and Marx had "considered England a typical country for the economic development of the bourgeoisie" (Marx and Engels, no date: 23). As this was destined to "create the world in its image and likeness", the method adopted was based on the fact that humanity could see its future in the English mirror. But that presupposed global convergence towards unique economic, political, social, and cultural standards within the framework of capitalism.

The strength of this understanding lies in its identification of capital's insatiable expansionist drive for accumulation, which pushes it incessantly to search for new markets across the globe. In times of so-called 'globalization', the relevance of this line of argument is quite evident. But except for the most hardened globalists (in their apologetic or apocalyptic versions), several passages of the "Communist Manifesto" in this regard sound, today, a bit overblown. The world market is still far from removing its national base from industry (even in the case of multinational companies[6]). Universalist humanism is still far from replacing national narrowness and exclusivism as the main reference of identity (as attested by the resurgence of chauvinist and racist movements around the world). The countless national and local literatures are still far from being swallowed up by a single universal literature. Even concerning historical events contemporary to the text of the "Communist Manifesto", it is worth noting that an artillery with a much less figurative meaning than that of 'low prices' was necessary to bend the 'walls of China' and maintain the opium trade routes open to British traffickers in the nineteenth century.[7]

The predominant image in the text is, in fact, that of a fulminating territorial expansion of capitalism across the globe, which, like fire on the prairie, consumes all cultures and civilizations it encounters along the way and makes the borders of national political communities increasingly irrelevant. The proper

---

6 From 70 to 75% of the added value of large multinational companies in central capitalist countries continues to be produced in their countries of origin. More than 85% of its technological activity is concentrated on a national basis. See, in that regard, the studies by Patel and Pavitt (1991) and by Hirst and Thompson (1996).

7 The near-coincidence of the sesquicentennial of the "Communist Manifesto" and the end of the British occupation of Hong Kong eloquently attests to that.

international dimension of this process – for the understanding of which the text provides crucial theoretical keys – remains in the background. But this makes Marx's theoretical approach vulnerable to the same type of critique directed to Western theories of modernization in the twentieth century by development, dependency, and 'world-system' theorists: that, once the globe is economically integrated, it cannot be expected that the regions incorporated later reproduce the same pattern of development as the countries where capitalism originated.[8] This criticism was anticipated by Trotsky when he stated that, given the uneven and combined development of capitalism within the framework of the world market it created, "England, at a certain time, revealed the future of France, in a certain way that of Germany, but by no means those of Russia and India" (Trotsky, 1977: 1009) In other words, the world unified by capitalism is not homogeneously shaped in the image of its core societies.

In addition to methodological considerations, there are also historical-contextual reasons for that underestimation of the international dimension in the pages of the "Communist Manifesto". The text was written only two years after the cancellation of the Corn Laws in England (which marked the end of mercantilist practices and the triumph of the liberal agenda of British industrialists), in a period marked by the dissolution of the former Spanish and Portuguese colonial empires in the Americas (with the active support of British power structures) and the emergence of strong liberal movements in opposition to absolutism in Europe. Liberalism, with its anti-state and non-interventionist ideology, emerged as the theory and practice *par excellence* of mid-nineteenth century industrial capitalism. The full impact of the late industrialization processes in the United States, Japan and Germany which mobilized, in an openly non-liberal vein, the centralized power of their respective national states to actively promote industrialization – was only felt later in the century.[9] The practices of political control over money (via the Central Banks' emission monopoly) and the relaunching of colonial expansion by the central capitalist countries only became generalized later. All this contributed to a predominantly transnational image of capitalist modernity in the text of the "Communist Manifesto".

---

8 For a critique of modernization theories, see Baran (1977), Frank (1966), Wallerstein (1974) and Cardoso (1993).
9 Based on this impact that Engels formulated, towards the end of his life, the concept of 'state capitalism'. See Engels (1977): 53–55.

5 The Theoretical Key to Understand the Genesis of the Modern International System

In present times, when the dominant discourse on globalization has become almost 'common sense' (albeit under increasingly fierce attack from political forces both on the right and on left), the transnational dimension of capitalist modernity anticipated by Marx is one of the aspects most highlighted by commentators of his work. The central argument I present here highlights that the richest and most relevant theoretical key provided by Marx lies in another dimension that remains largely obscured: his understanding of the contradictory articulation of transnational and international processes in the capitalist constitution of the modern world.

From this angle, the great 'novelty' of the twentieth century was not so much the constitution of a global capitalist economy (this was already formed and consolidated in the nineteenth century) but the extension of the system of sovereign *political communities* to the entire planet (following the crises of the old colonial-mercantilist system in the Americas and its colonial-imperialist successor in Africa and Asia).[10] This finding does not ignore or underestimate the fact that, under the impact of important technological innovations, the integration of global markets intensified greatly in the twenty and twenty-first centuries, compressing the dimensions of time and space within them. But, according to the theoretical clue bequeathed by Marx, these developments only accelerated, in an uneven and differentiated way, a secular process inherent to (and constitutive of) capitalism since its origins. In this sense, the development and diffusion of new information and communication technologies at the end of the twentieth century played a role similar to the development and diffusion of the telegraph and telephone at the end of the nineteenth century. It is precisely the combined development of these two processes – the integration of global markets and the globalization of the political form of the sovereign state – that gives the international system its contemporary configuration, marked by an extremely unequal (but changeable) distribution of political, military, diplomatic and economic power.

---

10 The last century was also deeply marked, of course, by the attempt to constitute an alternative socialist world system to the capitalist global economy, but as this attempt failed, I will not talk about it in this article.

6   Marx and the National Question

This innovative theoretical perspective presented by Marx in the nineteenth century captured and unveiled the historical processes that formed unified national states in Europe (and structured the international system, displacing the transnational power of the Church and the local powers of nobility), revealing their connections with the genesis, consolidation, and expansion of the capitalist mode of production. Contrary to simplistic interpretations very prevalent in academic and political debates, this perspective does not abstractly oppose the 'class question' to the 'national question' (or 'socialism' to 'nationalism') but rather provides a 'class analyses' of the emergence of the 'national question' and of 'nationalism' itself. It was this theoretical key that allowed thinkers and political leaders of Marxist inspiration in the following century to identify in the national liberation struggles of peoples under colonial rule or in semi-colonial or dependent countries a fundamental vector to face and defeat imperialist domination of central capitalist powers, now under the aegis of finance capital – the most concentrated, centralized form assumed by monopoly capital.[11]

This strategic conception was at the origin of most of the socialist experiences that polarized the development of the international system in the twentieth century, especially after the constitution of the former 'socialist camp'. The fact is that, inspired by Lenin's theoretical-strategic formulations (which were based on the theoretical key provided by Marx on the relationship between the global expansion of the capitalist mode of production and the national question to situate in the struggles of its time), the Soviet Union and other socialist countries transformed the active support (military, political, economic and diplomatic) of national liberation struggles into a cornerstone of their respective foreign policies. In doing so, they profoundly transformed the international system in the twentieth century by triggering and sustaining a global decolonization process.

The theoretical-strategic formulation proposed by Lenin indicated that the constitution of sovereign national states by dominated, colonized, semi-colonial people could oppose their conquered territorial power to the domination of financial capital, enabling national development projects with an anti-imperialist content that can open pathways for longer or shorter periods of transition to socialism. The question arises again at the beginning of the 21st

---

11   For the theoretical basis of this proposition and the programmatic-strategic formulation resulting from it, see Lenin (1977b and 1977c).

century, generated by the collapse of the former 'socialist bloc' and by the relative weakening of positions of power held by the capitalist countries that were at the dominant core of the international system in the two previous centuries.

7   Conclusion

Rather than being an 'irrelevant' author for the study of international relations, the argument developed in this text sustains that Marx made a crucial theoretical contribution to this study by revealing the 'missing link' in the formation of the modern international system, which conditions and structures its contradictory development up to the present day. In contrast to realism's axiomatic understanding, which conceives the balance of power as a permanent and recurrent attribute of any states system not subordinated to a common government (i.e., under conditions of 'anarchy'), Marx revealed how the emergence of a system of sovereign states in Europe in the seventeenth century was the result of a very particular and concrete historical process, associated with the advent of new capitalist productive forms leveraged by the commercial impulse propitiated by the global expansion of merchant capital. The new social relations generated by this process constituted the central institutional link that articulates the modern world: the separate existence of autonomous political and economic spheres, both at the domestic and international levels. It is this separation that allows and enables, via a legal structure of property rights, investment flows beyond national borders.[12]

The institutionalization of academic knowledge over the past century uncritically embraced this separation of political and economic spheres, moving towards the isolated study of each (via 'political science' and 'pure economics'). Even the classic approaches of International Political Economy, which chose the interaction between both spheres in the international system as their main object of study, tended to assume their separation as a non-problematic starting point instead of theoretically explaining their emergence.[13] The historical understanding formulated by Marx makes it possible to unravel precisely this emergence, providing a crucial theoretical key for understanding the modern international system. But fully exploiting the explanatory potential of this key requires that we theoretically re-establish the contradictory balance between the transnational and international dimensions of the dialectics

---

12 This point is developed fully in the book by Rosenberg (1994).
13 See, for example, Gilpin (1987)

of globalization that accompanies the genesis, consolidation, and expansion of capitalism. It requires, in particular, that we explore, from the theoretical keys provided by Marx, the heterogeneous nature of the international system, as opposed to the logical models built on the premise of homogeneous states prevalent in realist readings of international relations. In this realm, the theoretical contributions of authors such as Lenin, Gramsci, and even our late Ignácio Rangel who conceive the combination of varied socio-economic structures in national social formations constituted in the wake of the global expansion of capitalism can add an important complement to Marx's original and innovative understanding of the origins and dynamics of the modern international system.[14]

References

Anderson P (1979) *Lineages of the Absolutist State*. Londres: Verso.
Baran P (1977) *A Economia Política do Desenvolvimento*. Rio de Janeiro: Zahar.
Braudel F (1985) *Civilization & Capitalism 15th-18th Century – Volume 1*. Londres: Fontana Press.
Bull H (1977) *The Anarchical Society*. Londres: Macmillan.
Cardoso FH (1993) Originalidade da Cópia: a CEPAL e a Idéia do Desenvolvimento. In: Cardoso FH (ed.) *As Idéias e Seu Lugar*. Petrópolis: Vozes.
Engels F (1977) Do Socialismo Utópico ao Socialismo Científico. In: *Textos – Volume 1*, São Paulo: Editora Alfa-Ômega,.
Fernandes L (1998) O *Manifesto Comunista* e o 'Elo Perdido' do Sistema Internacional. *Contexto Internacional*, Vol. 20, N°1. Rio de Janeiro: PUC-Rio.
Frank AG (1966) The Development of Underdevelopment. *Monthly Review*, Vol. 18, N° 4. New York: MR Press.
Gilpin R (1987) *The Political Economy of International Relations*. Princeton: Princeton University Press.
Gramsci A (1989) *Maquiavel, a Política e o Estado Moderno*. Rio de Janeiro: Civilização Brasileira.
Gramsci A (2004) A Questão Meridional. In: *Escritos Políticos*. Rio de Janeiro: Civilização Brasileira.
Halliday F (1999) *Repensando as Relações Internacionais*. Porto Alegre: Editora da UFRGS.

---

14 See, in this regard: Marx (2008), Lenin (1977a and 1985), Gramsci (1989 and 2004) and Rangel (2005).

Hirst P and Thompson G (1996) *Globalization in Question*. Cambridge: Polity Press.
Kubalkova V and Cruickshank A (1989) *Marxism and International Relations*. Oxford: Oxford University Press.
Lenin V (1977a) Karl Marx. In: *Obras Escolhidas*. Lisboa: Edições Avante.
Lenin V (1977b) Sobre o Direito das Nações à Autodeterminação. In: *Obras Escolhidas*. Lisboa: Edições Avante.
Lenin V (1977c) O Imperialismo, Fase Superior do Capitalismo. In: *Obras Escolhidas*. Lisboa: Edições Avante.
Lenin V (1985) *O Desenvolvimento do Capitalismo na Rússia*. São Paulo: Nova Cultural.
Manning C (1975) *The Nature of International Society*. Londres: Macmillan.
Marx K (2008) *Contribuição à Crítica da Economia Política*. São Paulo: Editora Expressão Popular.
Marx K and Engels F (no date) Manifesto do Partido Comunista. In: *Textos – Volume 3*. São Paulo: Editora Alfa-Ômega.
Patel P and Pavitt K (1991) Large Firms in the Production of the World's Technology: An Important Case of 'Non-Globalization'. *Journal of International Business Studies*, Vol. 22, N°. 1. Basingstoke: Palgrave Macmillan.
Rangel I (2005) A História da Dualidade Brasileira. In: *Obras Reunidas*. Rio de Janeiro: Editora Contraponto.
Rosenberg J (1996) Isaac Deutscher and the Lost History of International Relations. *New Left Review*, N° 215. Londres: Verso.
Rosenberg J (1994) *The Empire of Civil Society*. Londres: Verso.
Therborn G (1995) Dialética da Modernidade: A Teoria Crítica e o Legado do Marxismo do Século XX. *Dados – Revista de Ciências Sociais*, Vol. 38, N°. 2. Rio de Janeiro, IUPERJ.
Thorndike T (1998) The Revolutionary Approach: The Marxist Perspective. In: Taylor T (ed.) *Approaches and Theory in International Relations*. London: Longman.
Trotsky L (1977) *História da Revolução Russa – Vol. 3*. Rio de Janeiro: Paz e Terra.
Wallerstein I (1974) The Rise and Future Demise of the World Capitalist System: Concepts for Comparative Analysis. *Comparative Studies in Society and History*, Vol. 16, N° 4. Cambridge: Cambridge University Press.
Waltz K (1959) *Man, the State and War*. New York: Columbia University Press.
Wight M (1966) Why is There no International Theory? In: Butterfield H and Wight M (eds.) *Diplomatic Investigations*. London: George Allen and Unwin.

CHAPTER 2

Marx, Engels and the System of World Power in the Nineteenth Century

Muniz Gonçalves Ferreira[1]

1 Introduction

This chapter is concerned with the production of Karl Marx and Friedrich Engels regarding diplomatic relations among European national states during the 1950s and 1960s.[2] In the course of those years, the initiators of the Marxist tradition had the opportunity to exercise their skills as analysts of international affairs in European and North American publications, in particular in the pages of the American newspaper "New York Daily Tribune", for which they were correspondents in Europe from 1851 to 1862. "The New York Daily Tribune" was founded in 1841 and published until 1924. Until the mid-1950s, it was guided by liberal leftist positions, becoming, from then on, an organ of the Republican Party. When the American Civil War broke out, the "Tribune", consistent with the position adopted by the Republican Party, clearly sided with the abolitionist forces, supporting the northern states in their struggle against southern secession. However, due to financial difficulties suffered during the course of the war, they dismissed all their international collaborators, interrupting Marx's correspondence in 1862.

The first articles that Marx and Engels devoted to diplomatic relations among European states in the "Tribune" had, as a background, the ebb of revolutionary movements that had spread across the continent in the period 1847–1849 and the establishment of the Second French Empire under the direction of Luiz Bonaparte, in the year 1851. It was precisely the activity of this last character that the two columnists directed their first observations in matters of international diplomacy. However, in the first year of Marx and Engels' collaboration with the "Tribune", the national emergence of the populations of Central-Eastern Europe and the balance of democratic-radical movements

---

[1] Full Professor of Contemporary History at the Department of History at the Federal Rural University of Rio de Janeiro. E-mail: ferreiramuniz8@gmail.com.
[2] Chapter originally published as an article in the Brazilian journal "Crítica Marxista", volume 1, number 21, 2005. Translated into English by Alberto Resende Jr,

within the Germanic world constituted the privileged themes of the journalistic correspondence of the two revolutionary German thinkers with the American daily.

Only from the 1853–1854 biennium onwards did the political-diplomatic articulations among the main European national states become at the center of the international concerns of the two companions in struggles and letters. The international interests touched by the Italian unification movement, the fate of Turkey, and the actions of Russia, were the international themes that most catalyzed the attention of Marx and Engels in that period.

The restorationist and conservative objectives that presided over the founding of the international system of the Congress of Vienna[3] did not escape the eyes of the two German critics. Interested as they were in the fate of the European revolutionary movement, Marx and Engels did not spare criticism of the concepts and methods of the five powers (Austria, Prussia, Russia, England, and France), which constituted the hard core of that system. For the authors, behind the high-sounding verbiage of the European statesmen of that period, two unspeakable objectives were hidden: the desire for supremacy and the repudiation of the revolution. For them, therefore, such designs could not inspire other international attitudes, if not those characterized by hypocrisy and simulation between the great powers, disrespect for national sovereignty, and the systematic practice of blackmail and intimidation in the treatment given to smaller states. As a general rule, therefore, the practice of reciprocal interference in the internal affairs of other states prevailed, limited only by the balance of power in the relations between them.

Still, in that context, Marx and Engels already noticed the deepening tensions between the European powers concerning the problems of the Near East. There was then a shift in the attention of the main Western European states to the perspectives generated by the deterioration of the power of the Turkish Empire, which meant real possibilities for absorbing valuable portions of the former empire of the sultans such as those located in the Balkan region, as well as in the vicinity of the Bosporus Strait and the Dardanelles. Thus, an extensive series of articles by the two authors dealt with the so-called 'Eastern Question', the nodal point of the future Crimean War (1853–1856).

---

3 International political order agreed upon in the Austrian capital at the end of the Napoleonic wars of the early nineteenth century. It had as its main protagonists England, the Austrian Empire, Prussia, and Russia with France incorporated after the monarchical restoration. Its main objective was to constitute a collective security system that would preserve the monarchical and absolutist regimes in Europe at the time from the revolutionary threat.

2 Assessment of the Role Played by Russia in the International System

The obstinate way in which Marx and Engels dedicated themselves to denouncing and fighting tsarism brings up the theme of the alleged 'Russiaphobia' of those authors. In the writings they dedicated to the so-called "Eastern question", Marx and Engels did not limit themselves to attacking the actions of Moscow diplomacy but also sought to lay bare the conservative and anti-revolutionary purposes of the Western powers. In their views, the purpose of the foreign policy of the Euro-Western powers was to weaken Russia as a rival in the dispute for supremacy in the regions of the Near East and the Balkans, at the same time that they sought to preserve Russian power so that the country continued to play its role as the gendarme of the revolutionary-democratic movements in those same regions. According to Marx and Engels's perception, therefore, the performance of the West in the face of the 'Eastern question' was characterized by designs that were anti-revolutionary and hegemonic at the same time. Anglo-French strategic plans were interested in the existence of a policy of reciprocal containment between the Tsar and the Sultan capable of tensioning and paralyzing the two rival states without depriving them of their ability to crush by force the revolutionary movements that might insinuate themselves within the scope of the areas under its possession.

As supporters and active militants of the European revolutionary movements – which, it is good to remember, had, in continental terms, predominantly democratic-republican character – they opposed the counter-revolutionary nature of tsarism. As analysts of international relations, they fought against the expansionist and destabilizing objectives of Imperial Russia's foreign policy, aimed at the conquest and subordination of people located in the field of strategic projection of that power. The multidimensionality of such a perspective contributed to placing them at the heart of the progressive European intelligentsia alongside, simultaneously, other personalities and socialist, democratic, and liberal tendencies.

David Riazanov, whose real name was David Goldenbank, was perhaps the first Marxologist in history. Born in Russia in 1870, he joined the revolutionary movement in 1889. He worked on the recovery and organization of the unpublished manuscripts of Marx and Engels, then held by the German Social Democratic Party (SPD), being responsible for their transfer to Moscow after the Russian Revolution. He organized the first editions of texts such as "The German Ideology" and the "Economic-Philosophical Manuscripts" of 1844, work in which he had György Lukács collaboration. In his study, "Origins of Russian Hegemony in Europe" (Riazanov, 1974), the Russian scholar historicized the reasons for Marx's and Engels' irreducible opposition to tsarism. According to him, such a posture had been adopted by the demiurges of the philosophy of praxis in the course of their experiences at the head of the "New Rhine Gazette", an organ of German radical republicanism in the years 1848–1849. The revolution failure in Germany, as well as in other parts of Europe, would have crystallized in the thinking of Marx and Engels a certain interpretation of the counterrevolutionary role that was being played, at that moment, by the main European powers. As the young Friedrich Engels wrote at the time:

> Prussia, England, and Russia are the three powers that most fear the German revolution and its primordial consequence – German unification: Prussia because it would cease to exist, England because the German market would be subtracted from its exploitation, Russia, by the fact that democracy would not stop progressing not only up to the Vistula but even on the banks of the Dune and the Dniepr[4].
> ENGELS, 2020: 95

Dating from that time, therefore, not only the construction of a violently anti-czarist image but also a conviction about the inevitability of counter-revolutionary alignments in England. For Marx and Engels, there were two orders of factors that would lead the first capitalist country in the world to stand alongside the most reactionary autocracies in Europe. The first of them would be the monopoly of the formulation and execution process of British foreign policy by the representatives of the territorial aristocracy of that country. The second of these would be the fact that, for Marx and Engels, any revolutionary triumph in continental Europe, in particular in France and Germany, would immeasurably strengthen Chartism within England. The failure of German unification under the aegis of a democratic republic and each defeat of the revolution in France would, according to Marx and Engels, mean, in the eyes of the aristocracy and conservative circles of British politics, the defeats of English Chartism itself. The human embodiment of this policy would be Lord Palmerston, Henry John Temple Palmerston. (1784–1865), British statesman and one of the most prominent personalities of English politics in the nineteenth century.

Marx and Engels conceived that their tasks, first as supporters of the unification of Germany on democratic bases, and also as supporters of the

---

4 It is curious in this citation the absence of Austria the cornerstone of the international system of Vienna and pointed out by Marx and Engels in other passages as the most reactionary of the monarchies of Central-Eastern Europe.

European revolution, would consist of: a) unmasking the opportunism of English diplomacy presided over by Palmerston (who posed internationally as a champion of constitutionalism and freedoms), denouncing his reactionary and pro-autocratic character; b) to intensify the political fight against the Prussian ruling circles in favor of the unification of Germany in the form of a democratic Republic; and c) to denounce and call to combat all democratic forces against Russian tsarism, seen as the quintessence of European reaction, and sworn enemy of the German revolution. It is very significant to observe the fact that those evaluations produced in the course of the failed German revolutionary initiatives of the 1940s would profoundly mark the readings of Marx and Engels on the historical-political role played by the main European powers in the following decades. The fact that engagement in the German and European revolutionary process of the 1940s was the first experience of concrete political action by Marx and Engels explains, to a great extent, the longevity of the impressions collected in that process. This fact would determine that the themes of the German revolution and the 'lessons' taken from it would indelibly mark the political views of Marx and Engels until the end of their lives.

Riazanov (1974) observes that, despite Palmerston's disservice to the failed German revolution of the late 1940s, the British statesman still enjoyed considerable sympathy in German liberal circles. Claiming the heritage of George Canning[5], who had been a kind of liberal and constitutionalist counterpoint to the reactionary-conservative hard line of the 'Club of Vienna' in the early 1820s, Palmerston was seen by broad liberal segments as a champion of constitutionalism. 'Unmasking' Palmerston was, above all, a way of undermining his influence within important political segments inserted in the field of the German democratic revolution.

---

5   George Canning (1779–1827) was a prominent Whig politician and statesman in England in the first half of the nineteenth century. He replaced Castlereagh, a deeply conservative politician and the person responsible for structuring the Quadruple Alliance (England, Austria, Prussia and Russia) that defeated Napoleon in 1814 – at the head of the British Chancellery. He reversed the agenda of English foreign policy, replacing the emphasis on 'continental' themes with a more insular focus, which rescued the centrality of British concerns with its maritime trade to the detriment of 'policing Europe' against possible disturbances.

3 The Fate of Turkey in the Vienna System

Marx and Engels gave Ottoman Turkey complacent contempt. To them, the Turkish entity was little more than a relic of the past, a decaying and almost harmless vestige of a once aggressive and proud empire. Within their society, they identified a fusion of Asian despotism with Byzantine anachronism. Deprived of any idyll concerning Eastern or pre-capitalist formations, the two German thinkers were incapable of sharing the sympathies that certain Western intellectuals devoted to Ottoman Porte. In fact, this former Muslim state, which had once stirred Europe with its annexationist spirit, was, in the mid-nineteenth century, no more than a dying power. Divided between subjugation by the czar and political and economic dependence on the Western powers, the homeland of the Sultan of Constantinople was nothing more than a simple object of international politics. Marginalized by world political decisions and corroded by its internal conflicts, as in the issue of Balkan nationalities, this historical formation was in an advanced process of decomposition. Western ruling circles were naturally interested in taking advantage of the collapse of the Ottoman Empire, incorporating territories and populations until then subordinated to its sovereignty and its hegemonies. But it was also interesting to prevent the power vacuum left by the Ottoman ebb from generating a picture of generalized instability in the vicinity of the Mediterranean Sea. Worse still, they feared that the absorption of the former provinces by other powers – Russia in the first place, but also, to a lesser extent, Austria and Prussia – would provide conditions for an "excessive" accumulation of power by one of these powers, to the detriment of the Anglo-French hegemonistic designs themselves.

Marx and Engels gave the 'Eastern Question' a focus similar in form but different in content. They feared that the Turkish retreat would leave tsarism free to undertake an annexationist climb toward the center of the European continent. They also understood that the strengthening of Russia in Eastern Europe would reinforce the power of the most conservative social forces in that region, thus making a revolutionary-democratic solution unfeasible for the problem of German unity, as well as with regard to the national emergence of the southern Slavs. On the other hand, they assessed that, from the gem and counter-revolutionary pretensions of the western powers point of view, the jettisoning of Turkey from the Congress of Vienna constituted a certain embarrassment. Particularly after the ascension of Louis Bonaparte to the French throne, certain diplomatic circles in the West, especially English and Austrian ones, would have started to fear the results of the attempts of Tutorship of Turkey by Napoleon III. The intimacy of relations between the French Emperor and the Sultan of Constantinople before and during the Crimean War would have encouraged the managers of the Holy Alliance to seek the incorporation of Turkey into the system emanating from the Congress of Vienna. In his article "Eccentricities of politics" (Marx, 1975a), Marx, after outlining such a scenario, states that one of the consequences of the Crimean War would be the production of a supplementary clause that would guarantee Turkish inclusion in the protocols of 1815. Such a prediction, no matter how suggestive its foundation, would end up not being verified historically.

Engels and Marx defended in their articles in the "Tribune" that the western chancelleries did not consider the possibility of 'restoring' the decadent Ottoman Empire, but rather that its gradual disappearance would not engender the collapse of political stability in the regions than under their authority, nor would it allow a disproportionate increase in of power by Russia. Conversely, each following their own national goals, he sought to establish his influence as deeply and broadly as possible in the areas abandoned by the sultan's retreat. In that respect, London and Paris favored different ways of materializing the same ambitions. The British power would privilege, although not exclusively, the exercise of the role of mediator of the Russo-Turkish controversies, seeking to appear as a supposed peacemaker in the antagonisms between the two Eurasian empires. France under Napoleon III, whom Marx and Engels had already harshly stigmatized for his 'adventurism', would have opted for a policy more clearly engaged alongside the Ottoman monarchy, thus playing the role of the main instigator of the Russo-Turkish War. In the article "The London press – Napoleon's policy on the Turkish question" (Marx, 1975b), published in the "Tribune" on April 19, 1853, Marx once again invested against the postures adopted by Luiz Bonaparte regarding the Turkish question. For him, the adventurism manifested by the ruler of the Second French Empire in the face of that problem would have the objective of winning the recognition of the European monarchical powers for whom both he and his late uncle would be no more than usurpers of thrones. In addition, he also sought to give France a prominent place within the 'concert of nations'.

4   The Role of British Diplomacy

Marx, as already mentioned, devoted several writings to the examination of the Foreign Office's action in the face of the so-called 'Eastern problem'. In those articles, he attempted to characterize British diplomacy from the point of view of its social constraints. According to such a definition, the foreign policy of 'bourgeois' Great Britain would be formulated and carried out with the social interests of the 'aristocratic' circles of that society as its horizon. A conception that, in turn, was based on the following ideas: a) despite the capitalist nature of the economy and bourgeois preeminence within British society, political power in that country would rest based on an aristocratic-bourgeoisie coalition; b) given the monopoly of political power and representation by the coalition of the aforementioned ruling classes, British policy, both internally and externally, would have an essentially oligarchic character; c) the Tory and Whig perspectives in terms of foreign policy represented, respectively, an aristocratic, conservative and protectionist alternative to the other bourgeois, liberal and free-trade alternative, and traditionally, and until that moment, the aristocratic-conservative tendency had been largely dominant. Such a conception would produce two significant effects on Marxian analyzes of British diplomacy: first, it would enable Marx to develop interpretations that would accentuate the relative autonomy of the British state concerning the economic and social dimension prevailing in that country. Secondly, it would allow him to perceive the non-mechanical subordination of the movements of English diplomacy to the interests of the British capitalism. Those nuances would lead the theorist of proletarian socialism to a characterization of British foreign policy as counterrevolutionary, pro-aristocratic, and even 'harmful to the economic interests of English capitalism'. Such analyzes acquired full outline in the articles that Marx devoted to Lord Palmerston's performance in the pages of the "Tribune" and the "People's Paper".[6]

These texts were published in the form of an independent paperback in England, still during the author's lifetime. Marx based his formulations on the examination of a wide collection of diplomatic documents, parliamentary minutes, and journalistic material. The work that resulted from that has as one of its main peculiarities the acute description of the decision-making mechanisms, especially in terms of foreign policy, used by the British government in the nineteenth century. A meticulous appreciation was made of the processes for defining the behavior of British diplomacy in the face of the most important international conflicts of the period, such as the struggle for the unification of Italy, the national emergency in Poland and Hungary, the Irish problem, the liberal reforms in Greece, in Portugal and Spain. The most controversial aspect of those texts is Marx's fixation on proving Palmerston's 'russophilia' at all costs.

---

6 Those articles may be consulted in their original version in "Collected Works", volume 12, (1853–1854) pages 341–406 (Marx and Engels, 1975a), or in the Spanish translation, preceded by a presentation by Robert Payne (1975), "El desconocido Carlos Marx".

5 The Crimean War and Its Developments

The Crimean War pitted France, Great Britain, and the Ottoman Empire against Tsarist Russia. More than that, it was the result of a rapprochement between Great Britain, seen as the most liberal and constitutionalist of the powers of the International System of the Congress of Vienna, with France, an eternal outsider and supposed factor of destabilization of the same, confronting Russia, first-time guardian of the post-Napoleonic international order.

The writing that best expresses Marx's perceptions about the meaning of the Crimean War from the point of view of power relations between the managing powers of the international system of the Congress of Vienna is the aforementioned article "Eccentricities of Politics", published in the "Tribune" in July 1955 (Marx, 1975a). That article is based on the reading of two books: "Du Congrès de Vienne" (On the Congress of Vienna) by the abbot Dominique Dufour de Pradt and "Denkschrift, betreffend die Gleichgewichts-Lage Europa's, beim Zusammentritte des Wiener Congress verfasst" (Memorial concerning the situation of equilibrium of Europe, written during the meetings of the Congress of Vienna), by the Prussian Marshal K. F. Knesebeck. In the first work, the author defends the idea, supported by Marx, that the Congress of Vienna had laid the foundations for the establishment of Russian supremacy in Europe. According to that author, the war of independence of Europe against France, that is, the Napoleonic Wars ended with the subjection of Europe before Russia. Corroborating this argument, whose anti-revolutionary inspiration needs no observation, Marx stresses that

> The war against France, which was at the same time a war against the Revolution, an anti-Jacobin war, led to a transfer of influence from West to East, from France to Russia. The Congress of Vienna was the natural outcome of the Anti-Jacobin War, the Treaty of Vienna the legitimate product of the Congress of Vienna, and Russian supremacy the natural child of the Treaty of Vienna.
>
> MARX, 1975a: 283

In sequence, Marx came to the defense of Frederick William III of Prussia in the face of the accusations imputed to him of having, through his blind dedication to the Russian sovereign, undermined the foundations of the project conceived by Castlereagh, Metternich, and Talleyrand, in the sense of "raising barriers secure territories against Russian encroachments" (Marx, 1975a: 283). According to Marx, the Prussian prince should not be held solely responsible for a situation (Russian supremacy) inevitably engendered by the international system approved by Congress. For Marx, Russian supremacy in Europe was so linked to the resolutions of the Congress of Vienna that even a war against Russia that did not expressly propose to revoke the provisions of that treaty would only reinforce the current situation. It was from this perspective that he interpreted at that moment the meaning of the Crimean War, then in progress, as a conflict that, far from representing the overcoming of the status quo approved in 1815, would only make a small repair to it, to allow the introduction of Turkey in the scheme of the five managing powers of the international system.

From Knesebeck's pamphlet, Marx extracts quotes that engender a passionate defense of the strengthening of Turkey to exercise the role of barrier to the irruption of uncivilized and barbarian populations across the European continent and factor of stability of the eastern limits of Europe against the innate anarchy of the Poles and the disturbances caused by the Greeks. Marx interprets this furious libel as a simple ratification of the inspiring purposes of the Crimean War: the extension and consolidation of the Treaty of Paris of 1815.

At the conclusion of the article, Marx does not miss the opportunity to stigmatize Luiz Bonaparte, according to him, one of the central actors in the masquerade then underway, an individual who, in his opportunism, was capable of disappointing the most elementary expectations concerning coherence and fidelity to the Bonapartist legend itself:

> Throughout the period of the Restoration and the July Monarchy, there was a widespread illusion in France that Napoleonism (sic) meant the abolition of the Treaty of Vienna, which had placed Europe under the tutelage of Russia and France under the 'surveillance publique'[7] from Europe. Now the present impersonator of his uncle, haunted by the inexorable irony of his fatal position, is proving to the whole world that Napoleonism means war, not to emancipate France 'from', but to bring Turkey 'under' the Treaty of Vienna. War in the interest of the Treaty of Vienna and under the pretext of putting Russia's power in check!.
>
> MARX, 1975a: 286

Having formally extended over three years (1853–1856) but actually producing a relatively small number of military operations, the Crimean War also

---

[7] In French, in the original, public surveillance.

counted, from 1855, on the accession of the kingdom of Sardinia to the Anglo-Franco-Ottoman coalition against the Tsar's armies. Its triggering factor was an unusual reason: the disputes between the authorities of the Roman Catholic and Greek Orthodox churches for control of the sacred places of Palestine. Such a quarrel unquestionably expressed the clash between Russian expansionist aspirations concerning territories subordinated to the Ottoman Porte in the Balkan and Mediterranean regions and the Western fear of that threat. A cardinal role was played by France in the Second Napoleonic Empire, anxious to neutralize the anti-French provisions of the Congress of Vienna and seeing the Russian Empire as the greatest obstacle to such a reversal. Moreover, according to Marx and Engels, the role of the emperor of the French as an arsonist of war responded to multiple needs: a) to gain recognition of its imperial power, considered illegitimate and usurping by the other European monarchies; b) divert the attention of the French people from internal problems by undertaking adventures abroad; c) take advantage of the exceptional nature of the war to sack the French treasury and d) win the prestige of a 'liberator' among the oppressed nationalities of Europe, one day claimed by his uncle. A more contemporary translation of Luiz Bonaparte's ambitions could characterize them – abstracting their mystifying and manipulative implications concerning the French people themselves and the oppressed nationalities of Europe – as an effort to conquer the position of the protagonist of the international order of that time, reversing the situation of jettisoning decisions and consequent marginalization within the international system, relegated to France by Napoleon's victors.

Austro-Prussian neutrality was for Marx and Engels, a manifestation of cowardice and a reaffirmation of the anti-revolutionary character of the ruling classes of these two German states. For the two Germanic socialist thinkers, the main reason for the non-engagement of both Prussia and Austria in the war was the fear of their rulers that the fight against Russia would become a revolutionary war of the European people against the autocracies of the continent. This interpretation considered, above all, the revolutionary forces that a collapse of the orthodox empire would unleash in the areas occupied by the 'revolutionary' nationalities, then lacking a unified national state in Europe largely, according to them, due to the activity of Russian diplomacy and weapons: Germany, Poland, Hungary, and Italy.

Following the same theoretical framework, the European correspondents of the "Tribune" considered that the neutralization of the reactionary influences of tsarism on the European continent by weakening the conservative social forces that largely relied on their military power, would stimulate the action of revolutionary forces, including socialists, in countries such as England and

France. Therefore, it would follow from this the validity of the attitude, in the last analysis, temporizing of the ruling classes of these countries in relation to the Tsarist Empire, even in the face of its most daring undertakings. That generalized posture of temporizing would see radicalized manifestations in the action of political circles and elements that were bitterly pro-Russian, such as Lord Palmerston, a great ally of tsarism in Western Europe, according to Marx's merciless and not infrequently exaggerated accusation. That being the case, the policy of the western powers about Russia should be guided, in the interpretation of Marx and Engels, by a double approach: a) in what referred to the validity of the social concerns of their ruling classes, frightened by the possibility of revolutions political and/or social in Europe, it was about preserving, at all costs, the existence of the tsarist autocracy so that it could play, whenever necessary, its role as counter-revolutionary police on the continent and b) from the strict point of view of *raison d'État*, it was a question, however, of containing the Russian advance in the Mediterranean and Caucasian areas, making it impossible for the Russian state to accumulate an 'excess of power' that would destabilize the balance of forces in the international system to its benefit and the detriment of the western powers.

Peculiar because it combines elements that would later be shaped in often dissonant traditions of thought and action. This position was characterized by what I try to define as a 'revolutionary realist' perspective. 'Realistic' because it interpreted the evolution of international relations, observing the correlations of strength between states, the national interests of the powers, and their strategic projections. 'Revolutionary' because guided by the idea that the transformations necessary to generate a fairer and more democratic system of international relations, suitable for the full development of people, would be produced by the action of revolutionary forces. What kind of revolutions? There is no doubt that for England and France, Marx and Engels were betting, if not in the short term, at least in the medium term, on the occurrence of proletarian revolutions oriented towards socialism and communism. But as far as the German states, East Euro-Slavic nationalities, and the Russian and Ottoman empires were concerned, Marx and Engels' expectations focused on the creation of democratic republics to replace the autocratic monarchies than in existence. However, 'antediluvian' appreciations regarding a very close resumption of revolutionary movements and a strong dose of 'Germanocentrism', inheritance of its political initiations within the revolutionary upheavals that had shaken the German-speaking world are also not foreign to such considerations in the previous decade.

6   European Diplomacy after the Paris Treaty

In the articles they devoted to the development of French foreign policy in the context of the Crimean War, Marx and Engels were not very indulgent. It is also a question here of a vast repertoire of denunciations and accusations against the government headed by Louis Bonaparte (Marx, 1975c). In them, Marx discharged his batteries against what he considered the degeneracy of the French army, stimulated by the supposedly adventurous, demagogic, and corrupt character of Napoleon III. A situation exemplified by the description of the trajectory of St. Arnaud, Marshal of the French Army and Minister of War, who, according to the columnist, built his military reputation serving in the Foreign Legion in Algeria alongside bandits, mercenaries, and deserters from various countries, "the scum of the European armies". The French Emperor himself, characterized as an individual blinded by operatic illusions about his greatness, was stigmatized as the official caricature of a glorious past. The anti-Bonapartist virulence of Marx and Engels would not spare liberal and democratic political leaders, French or foreign, either, who trusted Louis Bonaparte's protests in defense of the freedom of the oppressed nationalities of Europe. As a result, with the same lack of ceremony with which they imposed on other militants of the democratic and revolutionary European left the stigma of collaborating with the tsarist autocracy, Marx and Engels imputed to personalities such as Barbès, Kosuth, and the Polish émigrés, the accusation of contributing to the legitimation of Louis Napoleon.

The domestic and foreign policies of the two largest German states at the time, Austria and Prussia, also did not escape the attention of the "Tribune" correspondents (Marx, 1975d). Through their common system of analysis of historical processualism, they considered that, after the outbreak of the Crimean War, Prussia, wishing to weaken Russian influence on its Euro-Eastern border and ensure full supremacy over most of the Polish territory shared by both, could declare war on Russia. By engaging in a confrontation with the main bastion of the European autocracies, the Prussian leaders would awaken the democratic and revolutionary energies of the German populations, dormant since the revolutionary failure of the previous decade, triggering a movement that could lead to the long-awaited republican-democratic solution to the problem of German national unification. By doing so, the Prussia of the Junker aristocrats would be playing the role of 'unconscious instrument of history' according to the historical-dialectical conception that Marx and Engels inherited and reworked from Hegel.

With regard to Austria, the perspectives were not so optimistic. In the article entitled "The Austrian Bankruptcy" (Marx, 1975e), Marx assessed that the economic debilitation the Habsburg state was going through at that moment, combined with the national emergency in Galicia, Hungary, and Italy, made it impossible for Austria to participate in any adventure beyond borders. Moreover, the growing concern of the ruling circles of this southern Germanic state with the preservation of its empire would push its diplomacy towards the most conservative positions possible. For this reason, even if they feared the spread of Russian power across the Balkan Peninsula, they did not want any more serious weakening of tsarism, according to them, because in that case, the Habsburgs would have no friend to turn to on the occasion of the next revolutionary offensive. On the other hand, according to Marx and Engels' expectation about an imminent resumption of revolutionary actions on the continent, the entry of Austria into the war could mean a displacement of military operations to the heart of Europe, generating an escalation of revolutionary insurgency on the part of the oppressed people in the region. According to them, the populations most immediately interested in the issue of Eastern complications would be, in addition to the Germans, the Hungarians, and the Italians, an appreciation that accentuated not only the revolutionary Germanocentrism of the founders of the philosophy of praxis but also their persistent appeal to the conception of the character of a potentially revolutionary approach to 'historical nationalities'.

The idea that the ruling circles of the western powers were not interested in the collapse of Russia appears reiterated in a series of articles published in the biennium 1855–1856 when the last and decisive phase of the Crimean War unfolded. Marx and Engels endeavored to demonstrate that Anglo-French military operations were conditioned by the counterrevolutionary aspirations of their governmental leadership. According to such designs, combats against the czar's forces should take place in peripheral areas, far from the main centers of Russian political and social life, thus neutralizing any prospect that once conducted in those regions, the war could become a popular uprising. From that point of view, they reinterpreted the French and British directives aimed at the development of the military operations at strictly local levels. According to the governments and military commands of those countries, it was a matter of limiting the extent of the fighting to restrict the number of losses, but, for Marx and Engels, the desired objective was to prevent the 'war of containment' from excessively weakening that bulwark of the Holy Alliance and to avoid the subversion of its internal structures. In an article signed by them, initially published in the German periodical "Neue Order Zeitung"[8] and later partially

---

8 Newspaper published by radical democratic circles in Germany. It was one of the first to appear in the atmosphere of political reaction following the failure of the German revolutions

reproduced in the "Tribune", the two authors emphasized their opinions on the paradoxical and unusual character of the Crimean War in its third year of the outbreak.

> The Anglo-French coalition war against Russia will undoubtedly go down in the annals of military history as 'the incomprehensible war'. Maximum conversations combined with minimum actions, extensive preparations, and meaningless meanings, a precaution bordering on timidity followed by rash acts bred by ignorance, more than mediocre generals at the head of more than courageous troops, almost deliberate reverses in the sequence of victories won amid mistakes, armies initially ruined by negligence later saved by the strangest of accidents – a great set of contradictions and inconsistencies.
> MARX and ENGELS, 1975b: 784

The lukewarmness of the western powers suggested in this text would be transferred, in the two author's future assessment, from the battlefields to the negotiation tables at the end of the dispute. And indeed, in the preparatory meetings for the signing of the Treaty of Paris, which put an end to the conflict, Russian diplomacy skillfully took advantage of the indecisions and disagreements of the two great Western allies to secure terms that were more favorable to them. The Treaty of Paris was signed on March 30, 1856, by representatives of the states that confronted each other in the Crimean War of 1853–1856 (Great Britain, France, Russia, Sardinia, and Turkey). Its signature is considered a turning point in international relations in the nineteenth century, as it effectively ended the system of alliances established by the Congress of Vienna in 1815. Polarized by the figures of Bismarck, Cavour, and Gorchakov, the meeting that originated the Treaty guaranteed the formal independence and territorial integrity of the Ottoman Empire, forced Russia to return the citadel of Kars to the Turks, ceded part of Bessarabia to Turkey, established the Black Sea region as a zone of neutrality. Russia on the other hand, confirmed its status as protector of the Danube principalities, formally submitted to the tutelage of the great powers, and as guardian of all Christians residing within the Ottoman Empire; moreover, it ensured free navigation across the Danube.

The period immediately following the Treaty of Paris registers an ebb in Marx and Engels' production dedicated to the themes of international politics

---

of the years 1847–1848. Marx collaborated with it from December 1854 to November 1855; during this period a significant portion of the articles produced by Marx and Engels were published, simultaneously or alternately in the "Tribune" and in the "Neue Order Zeitung".

and diplomacy in the pages of the "Tribune". It can be inferred that the aforementioned Treaty meant a restabilization of the European international order based on a certain alignment of forces. On the other hand, the unfolding of the Crimean War unequivocally provoked a certain exhaustion of the main protagonists of European politics in what referred to as the political-diplomatic movements of continental scope. Even Austria and Prussia, absent from that conflict, probably did not fail to perceive in it an opportunity to demonstrate the military power of their partners in the 'concert of nations', which may have suggested caution and concentration to them, aiming at accumulating forces to the clashes that would inevitably come.

However, apart from such contingencies, an association of political and diplomatic processes would interfere decisively in the framework of power relations among the great European powers in the immediate post-Crimean War period.

As for the behavior of the other major European powers in the period, we can see the occurrence of some very significant inflections concerning the roles played until then, or at least claimed, from the managing the international order in force point of view. Austria, one of the main continental bastions of the International System of the Congress of Vienna, would experience a marked process of political isolation and diminishing influence. That movement had begun in the 1830s, when the Austrian Empire, faithful to the non-negotiable principles of 'legitimism' that guided its international activity, allied itself with Turkey against the Greek nationalists. It was when, for the first time since the formation of the Holy Alliance, it positioned itself in a different field from its consorts Russia, and England, which, by the way, profiled in the same field as the 'dangerous' France. Later, they would see their internal stability significantly shaken as a result of the revolutionary insurrections of the 'Spring of the People' period, when its empire had been saved from an imminent dismemberment (Hungarian Revolution) by the czar's troops. However, the worst moment of its diplomacy occurred during the Crimean War, when Austria managed to displease the western powers with its refusal to fight Russia and, later, displease Russia with the pressures for it to accept the terms of the Treaty from Paris. Furthermore, relations between the Austrian Habsburgs and the Russian Romanovs tended to gradually deteriorate as their differences became evident regarding the situation of the Danube principalities and the Balkan provinces, given to Russian protection by the Treaty of Paris, but coveted with less and less ceremony by the southern Germans. The overall result of Austria's weakening as a power, its loss of international influence, and political isolation was its conversion from one of the fundamental pillars of the system into an insignificant player.

Russia emerged from the Crimean war overwhelmed by frustration, humiliation, and resentment. Frustration at not having consummated its objective of delivering a coup de grace to the uncomfortable Ottoman entity, which in its post-imperial lethargy obstructed the Russian march towards the Black Sea and the Mediterranean. Humiliation at having its centuries-old trajectory of military conquests interrupted by the Anglo-French coalition, which imposed on its respect for Turkish integrity and the evacuation of the principalities of the Danube (Moldavia and Wallachia), in addition to vetoing the construction of its much-dreamed fleet in the Black Sea, militarily stripping its southern borders. However, few sentiments must have been known more bitterly to Russian summits than Tsar Nicholas I's resentment of Prince Schwarzenberg, who reciprocated the decisive support given by the Russians in crushing the uprising of Hungarian revolutionaries led by Louis Kossuth in 1848 with the abandonment of the old ally in the confrontation with the Western powers and, even worse, acting as a Western agent in convincing Russian statesmen to accept the terms of the Treaty of Paris. The result of the process, as far as Russia's behavior is concerned, was the transformation of the main bastion of the conservative European order into a 'revisionist' international system.

The France of Napoleon III appears at that moment as the most active power in the international system. As Marx and Engels observed several times, the need to gain legitimacy within a family of aristocratic powers, the attempt to re-edit the glorious international trajectory of Napoleon I, and the effort to divert French public opinion from the internal problems experienced by the country impressed the Second French Empire the mark of 'militantism' in terms of European politics and diplomacy. Participation in the winning coalition during the Crimean War would confer appreciable diplomatic dividends on the Bonapartist empire. The most elemental of all: it was the first time since Waterloo that the French state was directly involved in a continental war alike conflagration, militarily and diplomatically triumphing over Russia, an important enemy of the past, whose victory over French forces in 1812 initiated the process of disintegration of the empire of Napoleon I. Secondly, the fact that in this war, France had as its ally England, the archenemy of yesteryear, the first world power, and the only one capable of ensuring French economic isolation on the international stage. Thirdly, the greatest of all French triumphs: the country, which had been marginalized at the Congress of Vienna, now endorsed a new international pact that dismantled the foundations of the previous system, divided its former adversaries and relegated almost all of them (Austria, Russia, and Prussia) to unequivocal political marginalization.

Now, if those successes updated the mystique of Napoleon Bonaparte's successor, restoring to France the position of manager of European affairs, which had one day been taken from them, on the other hand, it did nothing but stimulate Napoleon III to new international attacks. After all, France proclaimed itself an empire, and the way of life for empires is territorial conquest. A frequent participant in Carbonari circles in his Italian exile, a political by-product of the liberal emergence of 1848 in France, Louis Napoleon would express his political-territorial ambitions in Europe in terms of support for the national affirmation of the oppressed nationalities on that continent. A claim that, if it had already led him to dispute the protection of the Christian populations of the Ottoman Empire with Russian tsarism, would now lead him to defy the Habsburg emperor in support of the Italian national cause.

Marx, who had analyzed with singular acuity the circumstances that presided over the inauguration of the so-called Second French Empire, was never able to discern any positive trait in the political personality of Louis Bonaparte.[9] For Marx, behind the declarations of Napoleon III in defense of the rights of the oppressed nationalities of Europe, there was purely and simply hidden the intention of obtaining territorial acquisitions. In some articles published in the period 1856–1858, Marx reiterated the stigmatizing qualifications about Louis Bonaparte and his government, initially outlined in the brochure of 52.

7 Conclusion

Dialectical thinkers Engels and Marx understood the implications that the particular movement of states, driven by 'national interests' not expressly linked to the needs of capital and the economic aspirations of the European ruling classes, could produce for the historical-revolutionary development of the continent. Moreover, living in the Anglo-Saxon political and cultural context and having English and North American public opinion as privileged interlocutors, the two authors could not fail to shape their international analyzes according to themes and, in a certain way, values characteristic of Anglo-Saxon traditions. Americans in international policy and diplomacy. That, however, does not mean that the understanding of international phenomena in terms of a 'power policy' carried out by national states – and not by social classes – driven by their 'strategic' interests, developed by the "Tribune's" European collaborators, has meant only an opportunistic adjustment to the dominant standards of analysis. The specificity of the vision of Marx and Engels consists

---

9   The original reasons for the revulsion that Marx dedicated to this French statesman can be appreciated in loco in the work "The Eighteen Brumaire of Louis Bonaparte" of 1852 (Marx, 1975f).

precisely in their unique ability to articulate those two distinct dimensions, however, interconnected and located at the base of the development of international relations in their time: the sphere of conflicting social interests, the engine of class struggle and catalyst of possible political-social revolutions within states and within the European framework, and the sphere of action of national states, determined by strategic interests of power and generating configurations of international systems.

References

Engels F (2020) The danish-prussian armistice. In: Cotrim L (ed.) *Nova Gazeta Renana*. São Paulo: Expressão Popular, 292–295.

Marx K (1975a) Eccentricities of politics. In: *Collected Works*, vol. 14 – New York Daily Tribune, number 4.437, July 10, 1855. New York: International Publishers, 283–286.

Marx K (1975c) Reorganization of the British War Administration. – The Austrian Summons. – Britain's Economic Situation. – St. Arnaud. In: *Collected Works*, vol. 13 – New York Daily Tribune, number 4.144, July 24, 1854. New York: International Publishers, 227–233.

Marx K (1975e) The Austrian bankruptcy. In: *Collected Works*, vol. 13 – New York Daily Tribune, number 4.033, March 22, 1854. New York: International Publishers, 43–49.

Marx K (1975f) The Eighteen Brumaire of Louis Bonaparte. In: In: *Collected Works*, vol. 11. New York: International Publishers, 99–197.

Marx K (1975b) The london press – Policy of Napoleon on the turkish question. In: *Collected Works*, vol. 12 – New York Daily Tribune, number 3.746 of 04/19/1853. New York: International Publishers, 18–20.

Marx K (1975d) The treaty between Austria and Prussia – Parliamentary debates of May 29. In: *Collected Works*, vol. 13 – New York Daily Tribune, number 4.103, June 12, 1854. New York: International Publishers, 215–219.

Marx K and Engels F (1975a) *Collected Works*. New York: International Publishers.

Marx K and Engels F (1975b) The Anglo-French War against Russia. In: *Collected Works*, vol. 14 – Neue Order Zeitung, numbers 385 and 387 of August 20 and 21, 1855, reprinted in abbreviated form as an editorial in the New York Daily Tribune, number 4.483 of September 1, 1855. New York: International Publishers, 484–488.

Payne R (1975) *El desconocido Carlos Marx*. Barcelona: Editorial Bruguera.

Riazanov D (1974) Origine de l'hégemonie de la Russie en Europe. In: Dangeville R (ed.) *Karl Marx et Friedrich Engels, La Russie*. Paris: Union Générale D'Éditions, 15–58.

CHAPTER 3

Revolutions and International Relations
Marxism's Contributions and Failures

Paulo Gilberto Fagundes Visentini[1]

> The higher cost of academic integration with the 'real world' was a growing concentration in the aspects of 'reality' considered to be adequate by sponsors at the State and corporate levels.[2]
>
> FRED HALLIDAY

∴

1   Introduction

Since its first manifestations, Marxism had developed analytical and conceptual structural instruments for the understanding of revolutionary processes as a fundamental notion of historical disruption. More recently, the application of Marxism for International Relations analysis has experienced a considerable advance, breaking the Realism vs. Liberalism 'bipolarity' (and, the latter, which could be perceived as an inadequate philosophical denomination). The first one emphasizes conflict and power relations within an 'anarchical' international system, whereas the second focus on transnational cooperation interactions. Based on political economy and Historical Materialism, Marxism brought to light a third paradigm, which is grounded in 'the economy and domination issues at the international level'.

However, the Marxist mainstream, which considers the domestic concept of revolution as a given, as incredible as it seems, is still not able to fully integrate

---

1 Professor of International Relations at Federal University of Rio Grande do Sul (UFRGS).
2 This chapter is based on arguments originally developed in an article entitled "O Impacto das Revoluções na Ordem Mundial: uma ausência nos Estudos de Defesa" (in English, "The impact of Revolutions in the World Order: an absence in defense studies", translation note) published in the Brazilian journal "Revista Brasileira de Estudos de Defesa", vol. 3., n.2. 2016. Translated into English by the author.

to its economic and systemic view of the international dimension the concept of rupture (and renovation) that revolutions generate in the world-system. From now on, we will be presenting a brief and introductory theoretical discussion, which was originally developed as part of a research project about the impacts of the Third World (Geopolitical South) revolutions that took place in the 1970s and 1980s.

2 The Marxist International Relations Approach: War and Revolution

Whereas analyzing classical authors, Jacques Huntzinger (1987) considers Carl Von Clausewitz, Francisco de Vitoria and Karl Marx as representatives of the major International Relations paradigms. These several schools of thought reflect problems and historical moments of their framing and represent diverse standpoints that are not entirely incompatible. In this sense, orthodoxy and theoretical eclecticism are the two extreme poles to avoid, as the political prescriptive and normative use of theories. Theories are, foremost, simplifications to understand a reality that is too complex to apprehend in all its dimensions.

The Prussian General Clausewitz, alongside with Thucydides, Machiavelli, Hobbes, Vattel, Hume, the European balance thinkers, Rousseau, Espinosa and the supporters of nineteenth century European nationalism represent International Relations 'Classical' paradigm (as considered by the French perspective), also called 'Realism' (in the Anglo-Saxon stance). This school of thought considers the international system as being totally or partially anarchical, with the state as its main player. Therefore, Realism put an emphasis on the conflict and power relations amongst state actors. To these names one can add Realist thinkers of the twentieth century such as Edward Carr ("Twenty Years of Crisis"), Raymond Aron ("Peace and War Among Nations") and Hans Morgenthau ("Politics Among Nations"). Also, this school of thought shelters, together with 'Classical Realism, Neorealism, Hegemonic Stability Theory' and 'Game Theory'.

Dominican Salamanca's priest Francisco de Vitoria, alongside stoicism, Cicero, medieval Christianism, sixteenth century jusnaturalism, Kant and the eighteenth century cosmopolitism are representatives of the 'Idealist' paradigm that emphasizes the existence of an international community of 'societas inter gentes', or a universal community of mankind. In the Anglo-Saxon world, this school of thought is also referred to as Liberalism, which also embodies 'Liberal Institutionalism' ('Neoliberalism'), 'Functionalism', 'Integration Theories' and 'Constructivism'. Keohane, Kindleberger and Joseph Nye are contemporary academics linked to the Liberalism/Idealism school, which is based on 'cooperation and ethical relations', within an essentially 'transnational' framework. It is important to notice that, philosophically, Liberalism is in contradiction with the Christian matrix vision, which sheds some light on the artificial 'bipolar' perspective of International Relations theories.

Marx and Engels, as well as the Jacobins, Fichte, Hegel, Hobson, Hilferding, Lenin and Bukharin, focus on economic imperialism notions, north-south and center-periphery cleavages, as well as dependence and world-system theories. Considering contemporary and strictly academic authors, one can add Fred Halliday, Giovanni Arrighi, Immanuel Wallerstein, Justin Rosenberg and Samir Amin as internationalists with a Marxist inspiration. Although Marxism had not developed a formal theory of International Relations, Historical Materialism is capable to explain the notion of economy and domination in the international arena, within a perspective that put emphasis on the macro-processes of evolution, transformation, and disruption.

For their turn, the previously mentioned schools give priority to the functioning of the system, and value the prescriptive and normative dimension. So, the Marxist school comprises the systemic and conflictive explanations of the previous visions, even though it still had not developed, in depth, the needed methodological tools for that, considering the political dimension in particular. Although it is possible to explain war and to study it within the world-system view, the same cannot be said about revolutions, which are so well explained in their domestic dimension.

As Hannah Arendt (2011) points out, the twentieth century was defined by wars and revolutions. However, International Relations research and studies areas have been dealing with both issues differently. There are several courses, specialized centers, and journals about war, but revolution as an international theme has been neglected. As stated by Fred Halliday (1999), there are no academic journals that focus on this issue. For instance, the 'Late Revolutions' (the 1970s-1980s) took place during the crisis and transformation of the economy and world-systems, and had significant effects, but fell prey to Fukuyama's "End of History" (Fukuyama, 1989), as if the end of the Cold War made their impact null. It is curious how even some academics are unaware of processes that characterized these two decades and only consider China and Vietnam as post-Revolutionary Reformed States, and Iran, Cuba and North Korea are defined as 'Renegade States'.

The historical dimension is widely secondary in contemporary International Relations analysis and needs to be recovered. Historical and theoretical issues are the reasons for an analysis of this theme. As an area dominated by Political Science, International Relations is being characterized by theorizations not strongly based on empirical knowledge and that present an instrumental stance. China and Vietnam would not have achieved the level of development that they hold now, if not for the international autonomy gained due to their revolutions. Without a process of state building, governing elites and social transformations promoted through revolutionary processes, the situation in Angola, Mozambique, Ethiopia, and Iran for instance, would not have led them to the center of the international stage.

In just over a decade, Halliday (1983) notices that during this period, fourteen revolutions had taken place in the Third World. They had a significant regional impact, generating trends and countertrends as well as violent international conflicts and civil wars. Because of the balance power in place at that time and the changes that the world economy underwent, they ended up affecting the international system. In the second half of the 1970s decade, 'Peaceful Coexistence' ended, and a Second (or New) Cold War began in the 1980s. All of that, contributed to a deep change in International Relations, with the implosion of the Soviet side at its core, and the current power imbalances that followed and that are still a source of instability in the world-system (Fontaine, 1995).

3   Revolutions: a Neglected Dimension in International Relations

A deeper and objective historical analysis shows that the twentieth century was marked by several disruptions and revolutionary experiences in all continents, with achievements and outstanding intrinsic and diverse characteristics. Besides, they deeply affected the international agenda and framed world history and capitalism itself. Due to the defeats that characterized the Soviet supported or type of regimes, in the 1980s to the 1990s transition, silence prevailed, overshadowed by journalistic cliches (Keeran and Kenny, 2004). In Brazil, the last in-depth and large-scale publication was the 12-volume works of "História do Marxismo,"[3] organized by Eric Hobsbawm and edited in the 1980s. But, nowadays, there is a renewed interest in the theme and for academic research. In Europe and North America, strictly academic works on revolutions and socialist regimes are being released.

Revolution contemporary notion was born from the bourgeois world revolutionary experiences that emerged in the North Atlantic (the 1642 English Revolution, the 1776 American Revolution and the 1789 French Revolution). It is a tool for achieving political power, in the short term, as well as a political,

---

3   Translation note "Marxism History".

social, economic process of change in society, which includes the transformation of the power bloc, usually on a long run. The articulation of these dimensions was built by Marxism. The English Revolution was precocious and the American one peripherical (despite its impacts on Latin America). For its turn, the French experience had brought to life the ideological and social element in International Relations, with a profound systemic impact, promptly turning itself into an internationalized larger scale revolution- and a counter-revolution as well (Chan and Williams, 1994).

4 Revolutions and Their Regimes

For the theoretical and methodological purposes of this study, revolution means a sudden political change, usually (but not always) violent, that overthrows a regime, and the struggle for building another new one. This rupture of the current order seeks to make structural transformations in the ongoing political-law and socioeconomic orders. The event catalyst can be a popular riot, an armed insurrection, a *coup d'état* or even a relatively peaceful political transition. But, for these conjectural elements to be effective, domestic, and external political objective conditions are needed (Richards, 2004).

Added to the bourgeois revolutions, the democratic-bourgeois revolutions (with the active participation of the people) and the clear-cut socialist revolutions, during the second half of the twentieth century democratic popular revolutions had developed, in peripheral countries specially. They were Third World national liberation, democratic, anti-imperialism and 'anti-feudalism' revolutions, usually linked to decolonization and nationalism. Their triggers were popular riots, reformist mobilizations, *coups d'etat* (even military ones), *guerrilla* struggles, as the ones theorized and promoted by Mao Zedong, Ho Chi Minh, Fidel e Raúl Castro and Che Guevara, Amílcar Cabral, among others (Silva, 2004). They were characterized by an alliance of the small bourgeois, peasants, and sectors of the proletariat.

Explanatory theories of revolution and socialism are still strongly focused on European cases, and the knowledge and reflections about Third World experiences are more limited and recent, as less documented. In general, there is a persistence of the view that peripheral countries 'would not be prepared' for revolution and for socialism, in a very narrow interpretation. During the European Imperialist era, deeper social contradictions moved from the center to the periphery, in which the process of proletarization deepened, due to the rural exodus and market-driven agriculture. It is important to stress that the international dimension, already significant in classical revolutions, had become even more decisive in the growing internationalization frame deepened by peripheral capitalism (Davis, 1985).

Unlike capitalism, the political dimension of socialism is the predominant instance, therefore, economy is organized by the economic central planning principle (instead of the market), with the collective property of the means of production, nationalization of banks and foreign trade. Society tends to be incorporated into a single unit, with politics that search to gradually eliminate inequalities and the universalization of social policies such as education, health, housing, public transportation, employment, and leisure. In a situation of extreme tension, this process was historically materialized, through Authoritarian and repressive movements, but socially inclusive, and politically paternalists.

5 Revolutions and International Politics

Revolutions are always linked both to domestic and external factors and, following their closure, they necessarily cause an international impact as they affect the internal rules in which the international (capitalist) order is based. As Fred Halliday recalls (2007:148), "Revolutions are international events in their causes and effects." In this sense, they serve as an inspiration for political forces from other countries, either from supporters, or adversaries. Normally, revolutions lead to foreign wars, usually associated to civil internal wars, or their result.

That was the case in Russia (as its revolution took place during the World War I) and China, countries with a huge relevance on the international order. Foreign invasions, civil war and other impacts on the world were a byproduct, as well as the creation of the III International (Communist) and, later on, the more fluid existence of the International Communist Movement. That was also the case of Korea, Vietnam, Cuba and Nicaragua, smaller nations at the periphery of the world-system. Even though the first two of them, gained significant strategic relevance as they took place in China's frontiers, in which socialism was not consolidated yet.

The last two cases led to changes within the United States direct sphere of influence, namely Cuba, that also had a remarkable world performance in the Third World, mostly in the Non-Aligned Countries Movement. For its turn, North Korea was closer to the Chinese border, alongside Japan, a strategic region for Washington and the 1950–51 Korean War had a global impact. On the other hand, in the Islamic world and the African continent, this feature gained a higher complexity as the process of building a national state was still on the beginning, and, on the first case, located in a geopolitical strategic zone with valuable resources such as oil.

Also, in the African case, revolutions took place in the initial period of formation of the nation-state, following the collapse of the colonial bureaucratic and repressive apparatus. Ethiopia was an exception to the rule, as the state framework was conquered, transformed, and strengthened. Therefore, African Revolutions altered the sensitive balance that was being constructed amongst the younger and fragile states of the continent, generating a broad destabilizing effect. Finally, the Iranian Revolution showed distinct characteristics, as the prevailing side was not based on a Marxist vision, and represented a nationalist, anti-imperialist movement, and a cultural reaction to the West. Nevertheless, it is international impact was similar.

6 A Chronology: Revolutions of the Twentieth Century

Throughout the twentieth century, socialism with a Marxist orientation, was able to put forward a set of successful revolutions in successive waves. The first one had taken place in the context of the World War I, as the Russian Revolution and the Socialist agenda prevailed in the Soviet Union. The Mongolian Revolution is also a part of this period, with its own circumstances. The second one, was a product of antifascists movements and of the World War II results and affected Eastern Europe. They were both 'Revolutions from above' supported by Moscow and that would lead to the built of Popular Democracies, but also, they were autonomous revolutions such as the ones in Yugoslavia and Albania. It is important to highlight that, in the aftermath of the World War I (from 1918 till 1923) countries such as Germany, Hungary, Czechoslovakia and Bulgaria, had endured revolutions and even (short lived) socialist regimes. Later, the left was defeated, sometimes by external intervention.

The third wave, which was developing consecutively, had the Chinese Revolution at its core, beginning in the 1920s decade, and was characterized by the peasant question. After 25 years of *guerrillas* and war, the most populous nation of the planet became a socialist regime. The Korean Revolution and the first stage of Indochina's one, were a part of this period. The Marxist revolutions and the regimes built during the first half of the twentieth century had taken place in the 'periphery of the Center'. In other words, the industrial capitalist powers that were dominant at the system's center were involved in open conflicts (imperial race, World War I and World War II), as they were struggling to redefine the world-system and, within it, the hegemonic stand. Thus, the victory of these two revolutions and structuring regimes of a new world reality, the Soviet and the Chinese, were made possible, as they were at the periphery of the geopolitical space affected by huge confrontation and transformation.

Finally, at the fourth and last wave, the Third World's decolonization and nationalist movements were the main players of the triumph of several Socialist-oriented revolutions as the Cuban, Vietnamese, Afghan, South Yemen, and the African ones in the 1970s. They happened in the second half of the twentieth century, in the 'core of the periphery', in other words, at the Southern, non-industrial, part of the planet, in which 'the unequal and combined capitalist development was taking place' (Westad, 2007; Davis, 1985).

Despite its limited resources, considering this set of revolutions, two of them had become paradigmatic references and had systemic effects all over the world, the Cuban, and the Vietnamese. They were clearly linked and dependent of the two greatest foundational revolutions, but they had developed dynamics of their own. The Iranian Revolution case can be included in this category, even though its unfolding ended up being different as a post-revolutionary project. Anyway, the 'Islamization' of the revolutionary process does not overshadow its Republican, modernizing, anti-imperialism (but not anticapitalism) and internationalist base. Also, Algeria and other revolutions of the 1950s-1960s can be seen as part of this phase.

7 Revolutions and the Dialectical Contradiction of Marxism

The theoretical frame of this study is mostly anchored in the analysis developed in Fred Halliday's work "Revolution and World Politics: The Rise and Fall of the Sixth Great Power" (1999), and other studies by the same author, cited in the references. At the same time, it is inspired by elements found in the debates of several works such as the ones by Armstrong (1993), Buzan and Weaver (2003), Calvert (1984), Davis (1985), Goldstone, Gurr and Moshiri (1991), Kissinger (1973), Kolko (1994), Skocpol (1979), Schutz & Slater (1990), Toynbee (1963) and Westad (2007).

Academically, International Relations studies derived from the study of war as a rational aggressive and deliberate act, and not as an internationalization of social conflict. Even the very own United Nations Charter is concerned about world order as something apart from the internal context of states. In the same fashion, Anglo-Saxon Political Science considers revolution as a break of regular processes. Until the release of Theda Skocpol work (that, in some way, updates Barrington Moore Jr, classical book the "Social Origins of Dictatorship and Democracy", 1975), revolutions were seen as domestic phenomena. For its turn, Jack Goldstone (1991) emphasized that international factors (such as economic-fiscal pressures and political alliances of destabilization) weakened the state and provoked revolutions.

When Realists and Neorealists such as Kenneth Waltz do not relate internal and external dimensions, they ignore that most alliances envision to prevent revolutions in a member state. Revolutions cannot certainly escape the previously existing system, but they push forward their change and represent moments of transition to a new world, although International Relations perceive them as a 'collapse' (or a negative antisystemic disruption).

It should be noted that all revolutions try to internationalize, as counterrevolutions do as well (in search for homogeneity), usually without success. Thus, the limits for 'revolution export' (or counterrevolution) lead to truces, cutback of ideological rhetoric and a more 'diplomatic attitude'. However, this does not mean that revolutions had been "socialized" as Halliday (1999:187) mentions, "until the post-revolutionary orders remain intact, they continue to represent a challenge to other states system".

In the view of Historical Sociology, the 'international' created the state, and not the other way around, and when considering the revolutionary process studied here in their international dimension it is important to highlight that wars generate revolutions and vice versa.

For example, in the cases analyzed one can notice that the 1970s revolutions led to conventional wars in the periphery (with the involvement of great powers), and the international community was not prepared for them. Besides, in the regional plan, the greatest impact does not come from a deliberate action, but its example serves as a catalyst against the established order.

Even Marxism, that supposedly could explain the revolutions it inspires, has explanatory limitations. One of them is to hold few elements to analyze the differences amongst several revolutions and the persistence of the national question. An exception can be found in Brucan (1974). Another one is the emphasis on 1infrastructural elements1 that leads to an analysis that favors capitalist systemic relations in a global scale. Paradoxically, smaller attention is given to the chances of revolutions outbreaks. Wallerstein (1974), for example, bets on antisystemic social movements, and Arrighi (1996) passes by economic cycles neither finding revolutions nor dealing properly with post-revolutionary states such as China. There is some kind of 'divorce' amongst its academic-scientific work and its political proposals. So, they think the international system as a social economic global (capitalist) system overlapping secondary political structures.

Marxism, with its totalizing thought, established a dialectical contradictory connection of the global and national spheres, for instance, of the transnational and international processes. In the case of the global/transnational dimension, the dominant notions are the ones of International Political Economy and the world-system, which emphasize capitalist development structures, without exploring in the same manner the role of national states and processes of revolutionary disruption.

Considering the notion of the 'unequal and combined character of capitalist development', one can notice that its impact creates differences from within the system, which are not only represented by the notions of center and periphery of the same order. Why is the structural process of capitalism development and enlargement still linked to the existence (and resistance) of national states? One can state that as the global system evolved, at the same time, a complex system of political sovereign (or autonomous) expanded. Therefore, the nature of the international system is heterogeneous, and the current 'globalization' cycle only reduced the dimensions of time and space and 'accelerated the unequal and diverse movement' (Fernandes, 2018).

Marxist thought about the National Question (Visentini, 2018) and revolutionary processes advanced more slowly in relation to the system of International Relations. The Marxist analysis of the world-system presents itself as a 'global' science, almost determinist, while revolutions, curiously, for a theory based on the own concept of revolution, still remains at the national "political" domain or as a piece of political art. What needs to be done to overcome this deadlock so the impact of revolutions in International Relations could be fully integrated into the Marxist view?

Methodologically, Halliday (1999) suggests four needed tools as elements for theoretical reflection and empirical research: a) cause: to what extent the 'international' generates a revolution; b) foreign policy: how do revolutionary states carry their relations with other nations; c) answers: which is the reaction of other states; d) formation: how, in the long run, international factors and the world-system manage to constrain the post-revolutionary internal development of states and condition their political., social and economic evolution.

Even though Halliday, in his final works, had not been identifying himself as a Marxist anymore, this research agenda is clearly affiliated with a more mature version of Historical Materialism. He had criticized the determinist version of Marxism and had called the attention for the relevance of revolutions within the transformation of world order. Thus, not even neoliberal globalization could prevent the outbreak of disruptions and revolutionary renewals, although their character changes over time. As one can notice in a reaction generated by any diversion of the dominant political economic model, even of minimal.

References

Arendt H (2011) *Sobre a Revolução*. São Paulo: Ed. Companhia das Letras.

Armstrong D (1993) *Revolution and World Order- The Revolutionary State in International Society*. Oxford: Claredon Press.

Arrighi G (1996) *O Longo Século XX*. São Paulo: Unesp.

Brucan S (1974) *La Disolución del Poder. Sociologia de las Relaciones Internacionales y Políticas*. Mexico: Siglo XXI.

Buzan B and Waever, O (2003) *Regions and powers. The Structure of International Security*. Cambridge: Cambridge University Press.

Calvert P (1984) *Revolution and International politics*. London: Frances Pinter.

Chan S and Williams A (1994) *The Renegade States. The evolution of revolutionary foreign policy*. Manchester: Manchester University Press.

Davis M (1985) *O imperialismo nuclear e dissuasão extensiva*. In: Thompson, E. et al. *Exterminismo e Guerra Fria*. São Paulo: Brasiliense.

Fernandes L (2018) Marx e a gênese do sistema internacional moderno. In: Monteiro A and Bonicuore A (eds.) *Marx: Desbravar um Mundo Novo no Século XXI*. São Paulo: Anita Garibaldi/ Fundação Maurício Grabois.

Fontaine A (1995). *Aprés eux, lê Déluge. De Kabul a Saravejo*. Paris: Fayard.

Fukuyama, F (1989). The End of History? *The National Interest*, 16: 3–18. Available (consulted in September 15, 2023) at: http://www.jstor.org/stable/24027184.

Goldstone J and Gurr R and Moshiri F (eds.) (1991) *Revolutions of the Late Twentieth Century*. Boulder/Oxford: Westview.

Halliday F (1999) *Revolution and World Politics: The rise and fall of the sixth great power*. Durham: Duke University Press.

Halliday F (1983) *Génesis de la Segunda Guerra Fria*. Mexico: Fondo de Cultura Econômica.

Halliday F (2007) *Repensando as Relações Internacionais*. Third ed. Porto Alegre: Ed. UFRGS.

Huntzinger J (1987) *Introduction aux Relations Internationales*. Paris: Éditions du Seuil.

Keeran R and Kenny T (2004) *Socialism Betrayed: Behind the Collapse of the Soviet Union*. New York: International Publishers.

Kissinger H (1973) *O mundo restaurado*. Rio de Janeiro: José Olympio Editora.

Kolko G (1994) *Century of War*. New York: The New Press.

Moore B Jr (1975) *As Origens Sociais da Ditadura e da Democracia*. Lisboa: Cosmos.

Richards M (2004) *Revolutions in World History*. Nova York: Routledge.

Schutz B and Slater R (eds.) (1990) Revolution and Political change in the Third World. Boulder: Lynne Rienner/ London: Adamantine.

Silva F (2004) *Enciclopédia de Guerras e Revoluções do Século XX*. Rio de Janeiro: Ed. Elsevier.

Skocpol T (1979) *States and Social Revolutions*. Cambridge: Cambridge University Press.
Toynbee A (1963) *A América e a Revolução Mundial*. Rio de Janeiro: Zahar Ed.
Visentini P (2018) O poder e a fraqueza das nações: a Questão Nacional em uma perspectiva marxista. Monteiro A and Bonicuore A (eds.) *Marx: Desbravar um Mundo Novo no Século XXI*. São Paulo: Anita Garibaldi/ Fundação Maurício Grabois.
Wallerstein I (1974) *The modern world system: capitalist agriculture and the origins of the european world-system in the sixteenth century*. New York: Academic Press.
Westad O (ed.) (2007). *The Global Cold War*. Cambridge: Cambridge University Press.

PART 2

Marxist Thinkers as IR Theorists

CHAPTER 4

The Center-Periphery Dialectic
Lenin's Contribution to the Analysis of Contemporary International Relations

Rita Matos Coitinho[1]

> The mastery of nature, so the imperialists teach, is the purpose of all technology.[2] But who would trust a cane wielder who proclaimed the mastery of children by adults to be the purpose of education? Is not education above all the indispensable ordering of the relation between generations and therefore mastery, if we are to use this term, of that relationship and not the children? And likewise technology is not the mastery of nature but of the relation between nature and man.
> WALTER BENJAMIN, 1979

∴

1 Introduction

What is Lenin's place in a work that proposes to discuss the contributions of historical and dialectical materialism to the analysis of International Relations? In general, this question is answered by referring to the theory of imperialism, correctly understood as the theory of the international expansion of capital

---

1 PhD in Geography at the Federal University of Santa Catarina, Brazil, and researcher at the Center for Studies on Historical Materialism and Geography and at the Center for Humanities at the New University of Lisbon. E-mail: ritamcoitinho@gmail.com.
2 Originally published as a chapter of the book "Theory of International Relations: Marxist contributions". Reference: Pautasso D and Prestes A (2021) Teoria das Relações Internacionais: contribuições marxistas. Rio de Janeiro: Contraponto. Translated into English by Jorge Rodolfo Lima. Original title: "A dialética centro-periferia: a contribuição de Lênin para a análise das relações internacionais contemporâneas".

through the bank-industry merger and its consequences in terms of the expansion of central states' power and the rise of conflicts.

In fact, this notion presented by Lenin in the work published in 1917, "Imperialism, the Highest Stage of Capitalism", retains its relevance and heuristic value, as we discuss in this chapter. We will argue that the concept of imperialism works well for the analysis of asymmetrical relations between nations to this day. It is also central to the understanding of political movements that manifest themselves in the imposition of economic and institutional models, whether through economic pressure or war. But it allows us to go further: the live analysis of the world's movements, which involves understanding notions such as classes, class fractions, and blocks of forces, whose articulations or disputes are in line with the formation of monopolies, the search for markets, inputs and infrastructures that make possible the continuous expansion of markets and the realization of capital, as well as the deepening of the countries' financial dependence, which generates a continuous flow of wealth concentration towards the central countries – guaranteed by structural adjustment policies. The goal of this chapter is to analyze the bases and implications of the imperialism category and to highlight what in our understanding is the finish line of Lenin's theory for the study of international relations: the center-periphery dialectic or, in other words, the dispute for hegemony.

2   The Theorist of Praxis

Lenin's theoretical developments were always linked to the theory of revolution. He participated, from a very young age, in revolutionary circles, delving into the philosophical debates of the period at the same time as he became a conspirator against tsarism. A lawyer defending peasants, he quickly became a staunch critic of the tsarist judiciary, while joined the ranks of the Russian Social Democratic Party, dedicating himself entirely to the tasks of a professional revolutionary. Lenin devoted a large part of his effort to the study, dissemination, and theoretical development of Marxism, always organically linked to the revolution in Russia. Without this premise, it is not possible to understand his thought and the reading of his texts would only interest the history of ideas. Like Marx and Engels, Lenin's theoretical effort was entirely oriented towards achieving the hegemony of the workers' party. His developments in the theory of imperialism, mainly from the studies of Hobson (2009), Hilferding (1985), and Bukharin (1986), came to light in this context and were crucial to the development of the theory of revolution, based on conceptions about the State and the tasks of revolutionary parties. This is clear from the polemic with Kautsky in the early years of the Bolshevik revolution.

Shortly after the triumph of the October Revolution, Kautsky, then leader of the German Social Democratic Party, began to criticize the Bolsheviks for imposing a "dictatorship" in Russia, while a revolution through democratic means would be possible and desirable. In response, Lenin argued that without understanding the monopoly stage of capitalism, the questions concerning the 'form' of twentieth century revolutions would not be straightforward. There was no 'form' before concrete reality. The European revolutionary parties of the time faced a state apparatus completely dominated by the bourgeoisie, heavily militarized, which sponsored the counterrevolution and fought violently to maintain class privileges. At the same time, the bourgeoisie supported each other in the different countries against threats to their power by the proletarian parties. Class interests were internationalized, which was clear in the civil war that followed the Russian Revolution, with white armies being openly financed and armed by the European bourgeoisie.

Lenin (1963a) stated:

> Imperialism, i.e., monopoly capitalism, which finally matured only in the twentieth century, is, by virtue of its fundamental economic traits, distinguished by a minimum fondness for peace and freedom, and by a maximum and universal development of militarism. To 'fail to notice' this in discussing the extent to which a peaceful or violent revolution is typical or probable is to stoop to the level of a most ordinary lackey of the bourgeoisie.

With the theory of imperialism, Lenin (1963a) demonstrated that the whole world became the object of distribution among monopolies. He also demonstrated that the colonial policy of finance capital was distinguished from the colonialism of earlier times since it operated through economic subjugation.

> Finance capital is such a great, such a decisive, you might say, force in all economic and in all international relations, that it is capable of subjecting, and actually does subject, to itself even states enjoying the fullest political independence.
> LENIN, 1963a

Thus, for Lenin, in the current stage of capitalist development, national issues are only partially so since international monopolies economically dominate the vast majority of countries. Based on these conceptions, Lenin was a tireless enemy of the imperialist war, while the German Social Democratic Party adhered to patriotic propaganda and voted in favor, in parliament, for the granting of war credits requested by the government. The group led by Rosa Luxemburg rose against this. Lenin, too, was critical of the position of the German socialists. For him, war, as a continuation of politics, should be analyzed and understood by its class character and not by its exclusively national point of view. World War I, against which the Bolsheviks fought in Russia and Rosa Luxemburg's group fought in Germany, was an inter-imperialist war and, as such, should have been denounced and fought relentlessly. For this reason, the Bolsheviks definitively broke with the 2nd International, whose greatest theorist, Karl Kautsky, was aligned with the bellicose policy of the nascent German imperialism.

This passage from the work "The Proletarian Revolution and the Renegade Kautsky" is quite illustrative of the position taken by Lenin:

> (...) the internationalism of Kautsky and the Mensheviks amounts to this: to demand reforms from the imperialist bourgeois government, but to continue to support it, and to continue to support the war that this government is waging until everyone in the war has accepted the formula: no annexations and no indemnities' (...). Theoretically, this shows a complete inability to dissociate oneself from the social-chauvinists and complete confusion on the question of defense of the fatherland. Politically, it means substituting petty-bourgeois nationalism for internationalism, deserting to the reformists' camp and renouncing revolution.
>
> LENIN, 1963b

3   The Theory of Imperialism

As Lukács wrote, Lenin's text "Imperialism, the Highest Stage of Capitalism" is not exactly a detailed study of the economic reasons for the emergence of imperialism and its limits – as are the studies of Rosa Luxemburg and Bukharin -, but a "theory of the concrete class forces that imperialism unleashes and that act within it; *is the theory of the concrete world situation provoked by imperialism*[3]" (Lukács, 2012:63). Even so, the conceptual bases of the definition of imperialism as 'the new phase' of world capitalism are well defined in the

---

3 Our highlight.

text, which is based on the studies of Hobson (2009), Hilferding (1985) and Bukharin (1986), in addition, of course, to the assumptions formulated by Marx and, as is characteristic of Lenin (1963a)'s economic studies, statistics of the time. We now turn to the analysis of Lenin's text.[4]

Lenin's first premise about the characterization of imperialism, which distinguished it from past forms of organization of capitalism, is the absolutization of the phenomenon of monopoly. Of course, this tendency toward the concentration of capital had already been pointed out by Marx in the nineteenth century and came to fruition in the twentieth century. As Lenin notes:

> Marx (...) by a theoretical and historical analysis of capitalism had proved that free competition gives rise to the concentration of production, which, in turn, at a certain stage of development, leads to monopoly. Today, monopoly has become a fact [and] (...) cartels been transformed into imperialism. (...). Concentration has reached the point at which it is possible to make an approximate estimate of all sources of raw materials (for example, the iron ore deposits) of a country and even, as we shall see, of several countries, or of the whole world. Not only are such estimates made, but these sources are captured by gigantic monopolist associations. (...) Skilled labor is monopolized, (...) the means of transport are captured.

Far from understanding monopoly as a 'new' phenomenon, Lenin points to the development of this tendency in an irreversible way, drawing all capitalists, from all areas to the deepening of the social character of production, the result of which is privately appropriated by a decreasing number of individuals. So, Lenin says:

> (...) capitalism, in its imperialist phase, leads to the integral socialization of production in its most varied aspects; drags, so to speak, the capitalists, against their will and without their being aware of it, towards a new social regime, one of transition between absolute freedom of competition and complete socialization. Production becomes social, but appropriation remains private.
> LENIN, 1963a

---

4 In this section, all quotes, except for that of Lukács, in the first paragraph, are from Lenin V (1963a) Imperialism, the Highest Stage of Capitalism. In: *Lenin's Selected Works*. Moscow: Progress Publishers, vol. 1, pp. 667–766.

Free competition, which at least theoretically would have characterized capitalism in its first phase, would be definitively replaced by monopoly. This concept, however, is not sufficiently defined only by the operation of statistically pointing out the concentration of industries, from the most diverse branches. It is essential to reveal the role played by banking institutions. As the importance of bank capital grows, we observe the

> (...) subordination to a single center of an increasing number of formerly relatively "independent", or rather, strictly local economic units. In reality it is centralization, the enhancement of the role, importance and power of monopolist giants. (...).
>
> At all events, banks greatly intensify and accelerate the process of concentration of capital and the formation of monopolies in all capitalist countries, notwithstanding all the differences in their banking laws.
> LENIN, 1963a

As the influence of banking institutions increased, the concentration of capital in these same institutions intensified. Little by little, almost all monopolies began to finance themselves almost exclusively through banks, which led to the phenomenon of a bank-industry merger. Thus, says Lenin, through the concentration of capital and its merger with banks, "dispersed capitalists end up constituting a collective capitalist" (Lenin, 1963a).

> By managing the current accounts of several capitalists, the bank apparently carries out a purely technical, only auxiliary, operation. But when this operation grows to gigantic proportions, the result is that a handful of monopolists subordinate the commercial and industrial operations of the entire capitalist society, putting themselves in conditions – through their banking relationships, current accounts and other financial operations – first, to know exactly the situation of the different capitalists, then to control them, to exert influence over them through the expansion or restriction of credit, facilitating or hindering it, and, finally, to decide entirely on their destiny, determine their profitability, deprive them of capital or allow them to increase it rapidly and in large proportions, etc.
> LENIN, 1963a

Thus, Lenin (1963a) concludes, "the last word in the development of banks is the monopoly", which is developed by the increasing fusion of banking and industrial capital, a fact that occurs concomitantly with the transformation of banks into institutions with a truly universal character. According to Lenin (1963a), "the twentieth century thus marks the turning point from the old to the new capitalism, from the domination of capital in general to the domination of finance capital", whose other face is the increasingly complete dependence of industrial capitalism on banks and, also, the union between industries, banks, and governments, since they start to act in defense of their own financial and industrial conglomerates, as will be seen below.

But the expansion of finance capital is not a phenomenon confined to the sphere of production. Little by little, the 'democratization' of share ownership takes banking institutions to other layers of society, from the small producer to the liberal professional who can 'invest' their small savings in the shares of large companies, financing their worldwide expansion. Keeping an eye on this phenomenon, which began in England, where one could buy a share in a large company for just one pound, the German industrialist Siemens said: "the 1-pound sterling share is the basis of British imperialism".

This is how the imperialist expansion of England obtained vast popular support: all the holders of 1 pound sterling shares were rooting for the good performance of the English companies spread around the world. In parallel with this expansion within the population itself, the financial oligarchies began to enjoy a decisive influence on governments and the press. About this, Lenin (1963a) says: "the omnipresence of the financial oligarchy is absolute, it dominates the press and the government". Step by step, this would cease to be an exclusive characteristic of British imperialism and become a phenomenon of worldwide proportions, even reaching Russia, a country that was just becoming industrialized, as Lenin noted.

Another particularly profitable activity of finance capital "is also speculation with land situated on the outskirts of large, rapidly growing cities" (Lenin, 1963a). The monopoly of the banks merges, in this case, with the monopoly of land rent and with the monopoly of the means of communication. With the expansion of colonial domains, Europeans would also begin to speculate on arable land in their distant domains, whether directly – as in the case of the partition of Africa – or indirectly, as in the case of Latin American countries.

Bank-industry mergers, infrastructure financing in distant countries, export of bank capital, expansion of markets for goods produced in central countries through political and economic dominance across the globe. "The monopoly, once it has been constituted and controls billions, inevitably penetrates *all* aspects of social life, regardless of the political regime and any other particularity" (Lenin, 1963a). The overwhelming expansion of finance capital was recognized, at the time, by bourgeois theorists, such as Hobson himself, quoted by Lenin, and by industrialists and high government officials. Lenin mentions, for example, the German state official, Eschweg, who in 1911 would have predicted in this regard: "not even the widest political freedom can save us from becoming a people of men deprived of their liberty" (Lenin, 1963a).

The official referred to the predominance of finance capital over all other forms of capital, which in fact implies the predominance of the rent-seeking and financial oligarchy, as well as the outstanding situation of a few states with greater financial power in relation to all the others. At the time, Lenin had identified these four countries as pillars of imperialism: England, the United States, France, and Germany (in that order): once great exporters of goods and, in the era of monopolies, the most important exporters of capital.

Having sponsored the 'direct sharing of the world', finance capital created the age of monopolies. And, with these came the monopolistic principles: the use of personal "relationships" for profitable transactions replaces competition in the open market. Thus, the era of imperialism is also that of the rise of plutocracies, in which financial affairs are themselves state affairs. In this text, Lenin analyzes the case of the oil industry, for him the most illuminating example of how, in the era of monopolies, the interests of states, large extraction and refining companies, and banks are intermingled towards the formation of cartels, because just controlling production is no longer enough: it is necessary to control quantities, prices, and distribution policy. Finally, the antithesis of the 'free market'.

> Certain bourgeois writers (now joined by Karl Kautsky) (...) have expressed the opinion that international cartels, being one of the most striking expressions of the internationalization of capital, give the hope of peace among nations under capitalism. Theoretically, this opinion is absolutely absurd, while in practice it is sophistry and a dishonest defense of the worst opportunism. International cartels show to what point capitalist monopolies have developed, and the object of the struggle between the various capitalist associations. (...) the forms of the struggle may and do constantly change in accordance with varying, relatively specific and temporary causes, but the substance of the struggle, its class content, positively cannot change while classes exist.
> LENIN, 1963a

Lenin explains that the class against which to fight is the 'world bourgeoisie'. They start sharing the world among themselves, as the degree of concentration reached makes this sharing mandatory. This world bourgeoisie, however, is not free to compete with each other and does so supported by the power of its states. In this struggle, the strength of each capitalist country varies according to its economic and political development. And this may change in the form: "today peaceful, tomorrow not peaceful, the day after tomorrow again not peaceful." In his words:

> The epoch of the latest stage of capitalism shows us that certain relations between capitalist associations grow up, based on the economic division of the world; while parallel to and in connection with it, certain relations grow up between political alliances, between states, on the basis of the territorial division of the world, of the struggle for colonies, of the 'struggle for spheres of influence'. (...).
> For the first time the world is completely divided up, so that in the future only re-division is possible, i.e., territories can only pass from one 'owner' to another, instead of passing as owner-less territory to an owner.
> LENIN, 1963a

Thus, Lenin (1963a) says, the colonial policy of the epoch of capitalist imperialism is a transitory form. What is permanent, while the phase of imperialism lasts, is the dominant presence of finance capital and the dependence of states on it. Thus, there is an abundance of 'transitory forms of state dependence' and no less transitory forms of relations between the strongest, most determining countries and between these and other countries. In this way, according to Lenin (1963a),

> What is typical for this epoch are not only the two fundamental groups of countries – those with colonies and the colonies – but also the varied forms of dependent countries which, from a formal, political point of view, enjoy independence, but that, in reality, find themselves involved in the meshes of financial and diplomatic dependence.

One of these 'varied' forms mentioned by Lenin is the semi-colony, of which Argentina would be an example, given its financial dependence on London at the time, or even Portugal, which was in a position of financial and diplomatic dependence, despite maintaining political independence from England, being practically a British protectorate.

What is fundamental in this process, from an economic point of view, "is the replacement of free capitalist competition by capitalist monopolies (...) the monopoly is precisely the opposite of free competition" (Lenin, 1963a). The author thus arrives at a definition: "imperialism is the monopoly phase of capitalism". In other words, imperialism is capitalism in the stage of development at which the domination of monopolies and finance capital took shape, the export of capital acquired considerable importance, the division of the world by international trusts began, and the division of all the land between the most prominent capitalist countries ended. [And there are five fundamental traits:]

1) the concentration of production and capital carried to such a high degree of development that it created monopolies, which play a decisive role in economic life; 2) the fusion of banking capital with industrial capital and the creation, based on this 'financial capital', of the financial oligarchy; 3) the export of capital, unlike the export of goods, acquires particularly great importance; 4) the formation of monopolistic international associations of capitalists, who share the world among themselves; and 5) the end of the territorial division of the world among the most prominent capitalist powers.

The trend toward annexation, at least in this phase of expansion of imperialism described by Lenin, is directed at agrarian and industrial regions. This tendency 'is part of the very essence of imperialism', leading to the growth of the 'rivalry of several great powers in their aspirations to hegemony, that is, to seize territories not directly for themselves, but to weaken the adversary and undermine its hegemony'. Thus, one can speak of 'several imperialisms', competing at a given moment, but possibly articulated in specific situations.

In the era of imperialism, the figure of the 'rentier state' appears, defined by Lenin (1963a) as "the state of parasitic and decaying capitalism", whose existence becomes increasingly dependent on the appropriation of externally generated resources. On the other hand, Lenin points out that, to the extent that imperialism leads to annexations, and to the intensification of national oppression, resistance is therefore amplified.

This resistance, as we shall see, characterized a large part of the struggles that followed those years in which Lenin produced his work. The 'peripheries' of the world, oppressed by the expansion of imperialism, especially in the post-World War II period, more than thirty years after Lenin's work, would become the main stage of the struggles of the twentieth century, in many senses impelled by the historical example of that once peripheral country, which made the inter-imperialist war that took place between 1914 and 1918, the disruptive moment necessary for the rise of the first socialist experiment in human history: the USSR. It is for this reason that we begin this text by stating that what follows from the theory of imperialism, the dialectic between center and periphery, is the most fruitful point of arrival of Lenin's theory of imperialism for the analysis of contemporary international relations.

4   Later Developments and Theoretical Debates in the Field of Contemporary International Relations[5]

As discussed in the previous section, in Lenin's sense, how inter-imperialist disputes take place or how monopolies are articulated to continue dominating certain areas of the globe varies in time and space. It is not the way it is presented, but the permanence of the fundamental characteristic that determines whether or not one can still speak of "imperialism", and whether or not this analytical category is still applicable to the social sciences of our time.

We have already seen that Lenin showed that, in the imperialist phase, 'free competition' is replaced by monopolies, which tend to extend to all economic activities. The generalization of the monopoly and the complete financialization of the world economy followed by the deregulation process, exported to most countries of the world through the action of international organizations (such as the IMF and the World Bank nowadays), is the real 'globalization' of capital. In this stage of unprecedented capital expansion, accelerated, especially after World War II, the US control over the economy was consolidated – through its control over the currency – and the policy of forming consensuses, which takes place through the action of multilateral institutions under its direct influence. The economic prescriptions of multilateral institutions were widely applied, especially, but not only, in peripheral countries.

In the late 1960s, Baran and Sweezy (1968) indicated that this prominence of finance capital was being aggravated, rather than changing. The authors identified, at that moment, the rise of a 'neoliberal consensus' that encompassed the vast majority of nations integrated into capitalism. This consensus, instead of extending the validity of the principle of free competition, touted as early as the nineteenth century by mainstream economics as the predominant form that mercantile relations should assume, was at no time the predominant form of relationship among nations. According to Baran and Sweezy,

> there is no free competition in modern capitalism. (...) the typical economic unit in capitalist society is not the small firm that manufactures

---

5   This section resumes and expands some of the reflections originally presented in the book Coitinho R (2019) *Entre Duas Américas – EUA ou América Latina?* Florianópolis: Insular.

> a negligible fraction of a homogeneous production, for an anonymous market, but the large-scale enterprise, which accounts for a significant part of the production of industry., or various industries, able to control their prices, the volume of their production, and the types and volumes of investments. The typical economic unit has the attributes that were once considered exclusive to the monopoly (...). It is impossible [...] to continue treating competition as a general case: [the monopoly must be placed] at the very center of our [analytic] effort (...). We believe that monopoly capitalism is a society of the second type and that any attempt to understand it that limits or seeks to reduce the importance of how the surplus is used is doomed to failure.
> BARAN and SWEEZY, 1968

These authors took up Lenin's definition of imperialism, understood as "the monopoly phase of capitalism" (Baran and Sweezy, 1968).

According to Alain Touraine (1996) and Samir Amin (2006), in the post-World War II period, imperialism emerged from a 'triad': the USA, Western Europe and Japan, with the United States being the only superpower.[6] Western Europe, more precisely Germany, France and England exert influence especially on the European scene, just as Japan still has some strength in Asia (although increasingly overshadowed by the Chinese prominence that constitutes, however, a *sui generis* case, as we will see later). For these authors, Europe works as an auxiliary force of US imperialism, insofar as the 'European project' opted for an Atlanticism hitherto unrestricted.

The strength of each of these states is fundamentally based on the control they exercise over financial flows, although the use of military force is not negligible when it comes to France, and also England, in association with the USA, through NATO. But the ability to unilaterally impose its will through war is an American prerogative, the only 'superpower' in Gramscian terms.[7] The US, in addition to having the largest and best-equipped armed forces in the world, politically controls NATO – and through it compromises any desire for military autonomy on the part of European powers. Perhaps the departure of England (spokesperson for Atlanticism in Europe and seen as a 'Trojan horse' by nationalists such as Charles De Gaulle) from the European Union causes a

---

[6] Here we understand the concept of 'superpower', as formulated by Antonio Gramsci, for whom the term refers to the capacity of a State to "impress state activity with an autonomous direction, which influences and has repercussions on other States" (Gramsci, 1978: 191).

[7] For Gramsci, "the decisive measure to establish what is to be understood by superpower is war." (Gramsci,1978: 192).

change in this alignment and the repositioning of the Old Continent on the world stage, driven by Germany, the main enthusiast of a European military project. However, it is too early to make such statements.

Samir Amin also defended the construction of a 'theory of the world expansion of capitalism', in which the concept of imperialism should be centered. According to him,

> The contemporary world-system will consequently continue to be imperialist (polarizing) for any possible future, as long as the fundamental logic of its achievements remains dominated by capitalist production relations. This theory then associates imperialism with the process of capital accumulation on a world scale, a fact that I consider as a single reality with different inseparable dimensions.
>
> AMIN, 2006[8]

The author criticizes theories that seek to characterize the international system as 'post-imperialist', because they do not address the disparities between what is exhausted in the center of the system and what remains in the periphery, in addition to ignoring that imperialism determines the framework and conditions of class struggle, whether in the center or on the periphery (Amin, 1987: 17). Thus, for Samir Amin, the imperialist system tends to deepen uneven development, which consequently makes the central contradiction of the entire contemporary system the one that opposes monopoly capital to the overexploited masses of the periphery, displacing, thus, the "center of gravity of the struggles against capital to the periphery of the system." (Amin, 1987:105).

With another perspective, Immanuel Wallerstein is confident that US hegemony is in decline. The central question today, according to him, is not "whether or not it is in decline, but whether the United States will manage to fall gracefully, with minimal damage to the world and to itself" (Wallerstein, 2003: 36).In this same line of reasoning, Martins (2016) highlights an 'Atlantic crisis', which began in the 1970s. Faced with the crisis, neoliberalism emerged as the mechanism found to resume the rate of capital gains, by directing public spending to the support of the financial processes of accumulation (Martins, 2016: 45), generating, contrary to what is disseminated by ideological propaganda, the expansion of the state (and not its reduction), but in the sense of maintaining capital gains and not meeting the basic needs of the population.

---

8   This English version was produced from the Brazilian Portuguese translation (Amin, 2006). (Translator's note).

Arrighi and Silver (2001) also argue that the international system is in a period of systemic transition, where the central issue is the balance between the West (led by the US) and the East (especially by the expansion of China).

Petras (2007) diverges from this interpretation that we are witnessing a period of systemic transition, while his interpretation converges with that of Martins regarding neoliberalism. He considers the idea of 'crisis of hegemony' and 'systemic transition' to be a mere exercise in rhetoric. For him, there is no long-term and large-scale change without profound processes of change at the level of class relations at the local, regional and national levels. Thus, what is called 'globalization', which for him is imperialist expansion, is not simply the dissemination of ideologies and their imposition by force or persuasion: "There is a precondition – the existence of political and bureaucratic elites, and important sectors of the ruling class, which have a common political and economic interest and the ability to articulate ideology and implement pro-imperial policies" (Petras, 2007: 26).

For this North American author, imperialism is a real force, whose contemporary movement is the division of the world: "We are in the midst of an important struggle between major and minor, old and new imperialisms, for control of regions, regimes, energy and strategic resources. [through] wars, free trade agreements, military alliances, and economic associations" (Petras, 2007: 48).

The difficulties of the Atlantic 'axis' do not, therefore, imply the end of the era of imperialism, but very likely represent the resurgence of disputes and the increase in the apparatus of domination. For Gandásegui Hijo (2016), the US faces difficulties in maintaining its hegemony, but it will still play a key role for a long time to come. For this author, the world scenario is increasingly tending towards a new polarization between China and the USA.

Other theoretical matrices, further away from the critical spectrum, such as liberalism and neo-institutionalism, in turn, give multilateral institutions and international regimes the role of regulating the world-system and guaranteeing peace, granting institutions objectivity and neutrality that are difficult to be verified. Realism, in turn, views the international order in Hobbesian terms: each state is an autonomous actor, driven by the quest for power. Strong states do not renounce their position of power. They act, in peace or in war, to secure their position of strength. These approaches, despite their profound differences, confer the historic initiative to world powers. However, the rise of China and its current prominence on the international stage shows the opposite.

Neo-institutionalists and realists do not focus on the origins of differences between different nations and grant a degree of autonomy to international relations that seems to override internal struggles within states. They defend the existence of 'national interests' immanent to states, independent of their internal forces. Antonio Gramsci has the formulation that best helps us to lay bare these illusions:

> Do international relations precede or follow (logically) fundamental relations? The former undoubtedly follow the latter. Every organic innovation in the structure organically modifies absolute and relative relations in the international field, through its technical-military expressions. Even the geographical position of a national state does not precede, but follows (logically) structural innovations, even if reacting to them to a certain extent (exactly to the extent that superstructures react on structure, politics on the economy, etc.). Moreover, international relations react passively and actively to political relations (of party hegemony).
> GRAMSCI, 2014[9]

According to Gramsci's formulation, when studying international relations, it is necessary to unravel the interplay of interests within states, but events at the international level have a dialectical structuring effect on national formations. The forces at work on the internal plane, as Lenin already revealed, are social classes. 'National interests' coincide with those of social groups in a dominant position. In other words, the interests of those who control the big monopolies decisively influence the world economy and print the dynamics of international relations. Here, the relevance of the Leninist category of imperialism stands out for the understanding of the relations among the states and, even, the relations internal to them. As Petras (2007) points out, there is no imperialist domination without the collaboration of sectors within the subordinate states themselves. This is what is observed in relations between the US and peripheral countries, especially in Latin America, but, to a certain extent, it is also how the US supremacy over Europe and Japan takes place.

As early as the 1990s, some of the main formulators of US foreign policy highlighted that, after the Cold War, the country should preserve its 'superpower' status. Paul Wolfowitz, for example (who in 1992 was an assistant to the US Secretary of Defense, Dick Cheney), presented a report in which he pointed out the main risks to US hegemony, the main one being the emergence of new poles of regional power that would end up forcing a multipolar

---

9 This English version was produced from the Brazilian Portuguese translation. The original text may be found at Gramsci (2014). (Translator's note).

order. For Wolfowitz, the way to guarantee supremacy would be to strengthen its military presence across the globe, guaranteeing conditions for the US to be able to carry out more than one military conflict at the same time so that no adversary or ally could doubt the US ability to respond militarily to threats to its hegemony.

Joseph Nye (2022), on the other hand, advocates the thesis that the superpower could maintain its status through a mixture of soft and hard power. Political and cultural hegemony could not do without military force, but it would be the most effective way to guarantee US interests. For Zbigniew Brzezinski, "America stands supreme in the four decisive domains of global power: militarily, (...) economically, (...) technologically, (...) and culturally (...). It is the combination of all four that makes America the only comprehensive global superpower" (Brzezinski, 1997).

Gianni Fresu, taking up Rosa Luxemburg's analysis, emphasizes that what

> (...) distinguishes imperialism from the old forms of colonial rule is the fact that imperialism has every interest in the subjugated state continuing to exist as a formally independent institutional entity, keeping the appearances of an intact subject, "freely" subjected to foreign hegemony, because this is the most complete guarantee of maintaining the existing situation.
> FRESU, 2016

It is perfectly possible to extend this conclusion by Rosa Luxemburg to the present day when we analyze the way the US acts in relation to Europe and Latin America, where it seeks to guarantee its hegemony through apparently negotiated actions and by direct influence on the actions of governments through political and ideological pressure. In relation to Asia, the US strategy has evolved from siege to (almost) open confrontation, evidencing its extreme concern with the growth of China's power. In Visentini's view (2006), the period that began with the end of the Cold War actually represented the beginning of a struggle for hegemony and for a new paradigm and not a stable order as wanted by those who rushed to announce the validity of a new paradigm. a unipolar, capitalist and liberal order – which would coincide with the 'end of history'.

In its eight years, the Obama administration maintained the logic of guaranteeing US advantages in international transactions based on asymmetries. It maintained simultaneous conflicts, especially in the Middle East, directly interfering in Iraq and Afghanistan while supporting destabilization actions on the borders of Russia, Syria, Libya, and Iran. These actions, inaugurated during the

US action in Afghanistan during the Cold War, were theoretically conceived by Zbigniew Brzezinski. The idea was to force the creation of a 'Vietnam' for the USSR, which would bankrupt the country's economy and weaken it on the world stage. After the Cold War, the strategy of 'sowing chaos' was maintained. Brzezinski himself presented an analysis of the strategic prospects and political dilemmas of several states in Eurasia and conceived the international scenario as a triangular relationship between China, Japan, and the US, as well as an ambitious strategy aimed at extending the Euro-Atlantic community to the east, comprising Ukraine and all the countries that were once part of the USSR, in order to promote a siege of Russia. Understanding China, at the time, as a 'defensive' actor – while Russia, even weakened, would be an offensive actor – Brzezinski sought to outline a strategy that could guarantee a balance of power in Eurasia, maintaining armed conflicts. In this way, US foreign policy should seek to derail Russia's affirmation as a regional power, sowing and supporting conflicts in surrounding countries. This way of conceiving the international board remains, albeit with nuances.

Under Donald Trump, elected with an apparently isolationist slogan, US foreign policy maintained its characteristic aggressiveness in defending the interests of its conglomerates. The escalation of tensions with China, marked by numerous customs battles, as well as threats to partner countries – especially in Latin America, but also Europe – aimed at interrupting the march of expansion of Chinese business around the world, reminded us of the old days of the nascent European imperialism, the one that led the old continent to the total conflagration in 1914. Although the aggressive rhetoric and systematic attacks on international organizations (such as the UN and the WTO) may sound like a step outside the cadence of what is already traditional in US foreign politics, there was no retreat from the Trump administration regarding the strategic objectives of its main conglomerates and high finance.

For David Harvey, the permanent search for external enemies, which is repeated in every US administration, whether Democrat or Republican, is a response to the problems of internal cohesion typical of "a quite extraordinary multicultural immigrant society driven by a fierce competitive individualism" (Harvey, 2003) that has a chronically unstable democracy (if not impossible to control) and permanently needs an external enemy capable of generating internal solidarity. Furthermore, the maintenance of global asymmetries is necessary for the accumulation of capital, ensuring the drainage of resources from the periphery to the center. According to Harvey,

> imperialistic practices, from the perspective of capitalistic logic, are typically about exploiting the uneven geographical conditions under which

capital accumulation occurs and also taking advantage of what I call the 'asymmetries' that inevitably arise out of spatial exchange relations.

HARVEY, 2013: 35

Concerning this, John Saxe-Fernández (2006) pointed out that, since the 1940s, in the USA, there has been an uninterrupted process of institutionalization of a permanent war economy, which impacts the very structure of power, organized from a conjunction of clientelist relationships and mutual interests between the corporate (military-industrial) apparatus, the Congress and what he calls the 'imperial presidency', endowed with an immense civil-military bureaucracy that carries out industrial, state and private planning operations, internally to the country and in its planetary expansion. According to Saxe-Fernández (with data from the State Department itself), since the late 1960s-70s, the US federal government has spent more than half of its revenue on financing "present, past and future" wars (Saxe-Fernández, 2006: 98).

Currently, the US are losing space to China in most economic sectors and if they are not able to guarantee, to their favor, the maintenance of concerted action with their competitors, and the advantages in the current dispute for the partition of the world, it will lose the hegemonic position. For many analysts, this decline is inevitable and is already underway.

Under capitalism, as Lenin pointed out, development is always uneven. This disparity between 'center and periphery' does not only occur between different nations, but also within capitalist countries. As highlighted by Octavio Ianni,

> imperialism is prolonged internally in the dominant nation itself. The same fundamentals that govern external economic and political relationships also govern internal political and economic relationships. Likewise, within the metropolis, economic, social, and political development is uneven and contradictions persist and worsen (...). The basis of the problem lies, therefore, in the character of the class society that is developing [in the country]. Only from this perspective of interpretation is it possible to explain the internal manifestations of imperialism, that is, of internal colonialism.
>
> IANNI, 1998: 09–10[10]

The concept of imperialism is the theoretical instrument that encompasses the entire problem of relations among states. Only from the understanding

---

10   Our translation from the Brazilian Portuguese original.

that uneven development and resource drainage – which Saxe-Fernández calls 'payment of taxes' – work as the system's organizers, can we see, for example, the logic behind existing trade agreements.

If at the time when Lenin wrote his work the way in which monopolies were expanded was the direct domination of colonial territories, nowadays domination over financial mechanisms and technology are combined. With industrial production spread across the globe and installed primarily in regions where the cost of labor is lower, which guarantees the drainage of resources to the center of the system is the monopoly of the technique. Through the technological difference, dependence on other nations is ensured and, through the patent system, a new method of draining resources is imposed through the payment of royalties on the use of technology (Barbosa, 2018). Producers send huge sums of money to central countries for the payment of intellectual property rights while they are restrained in their possibilities of overcoming technological backwardness, both because of the objective situation of underdevelopment and because of the constraints created by international regimes, which prevent and penalize the reverse engineering.

5 Conclusion

As formulated by Lenin, the concept of imperialism gives dynamism to the analysis of international relations. From there, the focus of studies is no longer directed to the performance of the nation-state, understood as an autonomous unit (eventually provided with a 'nature' as is the case of the realist school), and turns to the movements of the world.

This concept gains explanatory power in combination with another concept, also found in Lenin's works: hegemony, which designates the idea of political leadership: "According to the point of view of the proletariat, hegemony belongs to those who fight with the greatest energy (...) to the ideological head of democracy" (Lenin, *apud* Buonicore, 2015). An enthusiast of Lenin's work, Antonio Gramsci, gave breadth to this concept. The image that best illustrates the Gramscian understanding may be found in his writings on Machiavelli: the idea of the centaur: half human (persuasion), half beast (coercion). Hegemony is, at the same time, political direction and coercion. Gramsci also gives the concept of hegemony a spatial dimension beyond the sphere of political dispute (Cicarelli, 2008: 272–273).

The concepts of imperialism and hegemony both refer to territoriality and the exercise of power. Imperialism refers to capitalist development, its highest stage, where monopolies and finance capital dominate, which control the state apparatus and use it to expand accumulation. The question of hegemony arises in the dimension of power, of the tension between conservation and change.

The concepts of imperialism and hegemony both refer to territoriality and the exercise of power. Imperialism refers to capitalist development, its highest stage, where monopolies and finance capital dominate, which control the state apparatus and use it to expand accumulation. The question of hegemony arises in the dimension of power, of the tension between conservation and change. The control exercised by imperialism can be hegemonic: when the ideological size of imperialism conquers the ruling groups of the other states, preventing the rupture movements. This is done through international institutions (such as the World Bank, the International Trade Organization, or even the UN, OAS, etc.). These institutions influence the economic and political organization of states from the setting of consensus. In this case, even if the imperialist country has the military means to impose its will, they are not always necessary. There may be cases where hegemony weakens. These are the moments when imperialism needs coercion, which can take the most classic form of military interventions or other means, such as economic restrictions (embargoes, difficulty in accessing loans, etc.) aligned – as we have seen in recent years in the 'Arab Springs', or even earlier, in the 'color revolutions' of Eastern Europe or even in the current campaigns of destabilization of leftist governments in Latin America. The weakening of one or more hegemonies and the emergence of others are moments of change, generally conflicting moments, which are, as we find in Gramsci, the conflict between the old and the new 'which cannot yet be born'.

Currently, US policy is guided by the doctrine of full spectrum domination (Ceceña, 2014): economic, political, cultural and military domination. Ceceña shows, based on a study of the main US military documents, that military actions are conceived in articulation with political, economic, and cultural action. With the aim of promoting 'global discipline', US military strategy divides the world into areas of action, just like the old pre-war European imperialism (Ceceña, 2014: 125–126).

It is in this sense that it becomes possible to understand the American economic effort to maintain military bases in the Latin American subcontinent even when there are no wars, while it is dedicated to winning the ideological debate both through the dissemination of its cultural industry and through the permanent expenditure on the financing of scientific and cultural projects in peripheral countries. Building the enemy's image is part of the full spectrum domination strategy.

The doctrine rescues already tested methods. Chiaramonte (1999) demonstrated how USAID operated in Argentina in the 1960s to create a pro-American *intelligentsia*. The same happened in all Latin American countries (in Brazil, we had the MEC-USAID agreements, which greatly influenced the formatting of higher education courses after the Military Dictatorship, as we will see later) and also in Europe, Japan, and South Korea during the Marshall Plan.

However, there may be situations in which a country exercises hegemony without being imperialist: this is the case of Chinese expansion. China currently has great power of attraction over Asian countries and is also beginning to occupy space in regions that are under the control of US (and European) imperialism, such as Africa (more intensely) and Latin America. The expansion of its economic influence is undeniable, which takes place through the establishment of relationships in which the countries involved receive compensation (long-term investments in infrastructure, for example). But China cannot be said to be an imperialist country: control of the Chinese state and most of the economy is in the hands of the Communist Party, not private monopolies. The participation of finance capital in the Chinese economy is not decisive (at least for now). Therefore, the idea of 'imperialism', defined as the fusion of monopoly and finance, cannot be applied to Chinese reality. Nor does the racist component, which opposes 'the nation' to 'the others' seems to be a motivator of Chinese external actions. Its economic importance continues to grow, but it has not yet managed to overcome the military gap that separates it from the great power. Concerning Latin America, it is also noteworthy that China has begun to expand its economic influence without confronting the US in its areas of vital interest. It grabbed market shares in areas where the US was no longer competitive and prioritized investments in infrastructure, which is beyond the scope practiced by the Americans. Now, China is already challenging the US on issues that are dear to them, such as oil and telecommunications.

In social sciences, the concepts of hegemony and imperialism are applied in different ways. Authors like Ianni (1974), Harvey (2013), and Petras (2007) prefer to use 'imperialism' to refer to the relations established between the US and the rest of the world. Wallerstein (2003), Visentini (2006), and Cox (2014) do not use the concept of "imperialism" and prefer to speak of hegemony. Borón (2014), Samir Amin (1987), and Losurdo (2015) use both terms, although they clearly define the US as an imperialist country. The use that the latter authors make of the concepts seems to be the most appropriate, as it shows that the disputes taking place in the state system are not the work of entities that are 'above the classes' but by specific groups that seize and manipulate states according to their interests. C. Wright Mills (1956) defined, in the case of the USA, this triangulation of forces that drives the state:

there is an ever-increasing interlocking of economic, military, and political structures. If there is government intervention in the corporate economy, so is their corporate intervention in the governmental process. In the structural sense, this triangle of power is the source of the interlocking directorate that is most important for the historical structure of the present.

MILLS, 1956

John Saxe-Fernández (2006) named this state system controlled by the US 'imperial presidency'. According to him, the 'military Keynesianism', conducted during the Reagan administration, deepened the prominence of the arms industry in the control of the state bureaucracy, so that currently the US power structure is marked by the presence and continuity of long-term trends that are accentuated extraordinarily from the massive military-industrial mobilization of the World War II and, since then, the consolidation of a permanent war economy.

Part of the literature, however, prefers to characterize the present time as the era of 'globalization'. According to Azzarà (1999), the linguistic and meaning sphere is undoubtedly the first and most elementary dimension of hegemony. He recalls Lenin, who wrote that "capitalism has become a world-system of oppression and financial strangulation of the majority of the world population by a handful of advanced countries" (Azzarà, 1999: 05). The idea of 'globalization' eliminates the subjects who conduct politics in the 'world-system'. while the concept of imperialism highlights the interests of large corporations behind the action of the 'handful of advanced countries'.

This dramatic condition described by Lenin remains and deepens, as demonstrated above. From the persistence of characteristic features and the current reinforcement of the imperialist character of the system, derives the centrality of the national question in this historical phase, from which the tendency towards annexation, that is, the suppression of national independence, stands out. The idea of 'globalization' masks this tension between imperialist expansion and national autonomies. According to Samir Amin (*apud* Azzarà, 1999), the US counter-offensive to reestablish its hegemony, threatened by the strengthening of other imperialisms, and by the struggles for national autonomy, is based on military supremacy. The conflicts spreading around the world are nothing but the new fight for territorial distribution, based essentially on the control of natural resources and technology.

For Atílio Borón (2014), the issue of dominion over resources is vital for imperialism, and the threats to its hegemony make it even more dangerous since the way out when it is no longer possible to exercise control through persuasion is the use of military action. In the Leninist theory of imperialism, the state is not an autonomous entity. It is, rather, an expression of an internal hegemony of one or more classes over others, which translates into external domination over other nations. In this sense, the old formulation of Mao Zedong gains relevance, for whom the national struggle is a dimension of the class struggle.

Domenico Losurdo (2015) puts Zedong's statement in new terms: for the Italian philosopher there are several forms of expression of the class struggle, and one of them is, in times of imperialism, the struggle for national liberation – since it opposes nations subordinate to the class that is in charge of the system (and to its allies within the struggling nation). This also seems to apply to the struggles waged within the 'imperialist metropolis', such as the racial revolts at the center of the system. These can provoke displacements in the central power and thus, play a decisive role in the formation of new hegemonies, since they challenge the control of the small class. This small class, according to Ianni (1998) and Wright Mills (1981), does not comprise more than a tenth of the US population, but their interests and lifestyle definitely separate them from the rest of American society. Within this class, a very small elite controls the structures of companies, the main sector of the economy and, through this control, makes basic decisions about prices and investments that directly affect the entire nation. It is evident, says Ianni, that within the imperialist country itself a kind of 'internal colonialism' operates, disguised as economic, sociocultural imbalances, generational conflicts and racial tensions (Ianni, 1998: 10). Imperialism is thus domination over all classes and class fractions, inside and outside the country that is home to monopoly and financial power. Understanding imperialism and the way it operates is fundamental to understanding the connections between anti-systemic and national liberation struggles.

Due to the political and economic control exercised by the main agents of the large business groups, part of the critical literature seeks to explain the global political and economic setting, characterizing the current moment as controlled by a small club of powerful, no longer ties to the national states. In a different approach, 'realist' theories suggest the permanence of the state as a unit of analysis. But this 'state' of realism is an autonomous, unitary entity, and there is no concern in understanding the internal power play that shapes state action. The 'national interest' is understood as belonging to the nation as a whole, as if domestic political issues did not influence what is done 'outside the borders'.

The effort to define the concepts that we carried out above allows us to demystify these two propositions, which involves facing three problems: the first is the set of theories that weaves an interpretation of the "international system" as something superior or even autonomous in relation to the international system. to the national states. The second notion that we want to remove is the one that reifies the idea of the state and treats it as an autonomous 'entity', leaving hidden the social struggles that develop within it and that are expressed in its insertion in the game of world power, ignoring the fact that national formations presuppose a certain complex state-civil society whose movement decisively interferes with the political positioning of the nation: the imperialist mechanisms for draining resources presuppose ties with the national elites of subordinate states. The third type of problematic approach is the one that ignores that there is a hierarchy in the state system and deals with each one as a full entity and equally capable of fighting for its objectives. To avoid these pitfalls, it is necessary to define this 'hierarchy' among states, an operation that is only possible from an analysis based on the concepts of 'imperialism' and 'hegemony'.

From this point of view, it is necessary to consider an issue that is still central to this day: even though the Chinese economy is undoubtedly thriving, surpassing the US in some sectors, a characteristic deriving from the post-war international system remains, US control over the financial system and the main currency of international exchange: the dollar. According to Coel

> conformation of an international monetary regime with the dollar as the reference currency [which] gave the US government the advantage of covering their foreign liabilities in their own currency of emission. In this way, American monetary policy served as a strategic element in shaping the relative economic power of the superpower.
>
> COELHO, 2011: 773[11]

Based on this conformation of a system of multilateral organizations, the US exported to the world an economic recipe aimed at guaranteeing the permanence of the transfer of resources. Founded on the supremacy of the dollar and on the absolutization of monetary policy as an instrument for managing economic crises, this system, "multilateral" in appearance, has been efficient in maintaining the payment of taxes on a planetary scale, thus restricting the use of national resources for the autonomous development of nations.

As Katz (2016) demonstrates, the US is still capable of exporting internally generated crises due to the control it has over the international financial

---

11   Our translation from the Brazilian Portuguese original.

system and the absence of another monetary power to face it. In this way, the 2008 crisis, which began in the US, was quickly exported, enabling the recovery – albeit incomplete – of the US economy. According to Katz, *"la agenda del FMI se define en Washington. Este poder de Wall Street y de la Reserva Federal explica como pudo la poténcia del Norte exportar una crisis originada en su território"* (Katz, 2016: 130).[12]

Concerning Latin America, US hegemony over financial processes is still undeniable. Attempts such as the creation of a South American Bank or even Brazil's participation in the BRICS Bank have had no practical effect, even though the political developments of the last two decades point to a growth in resistance to this hegemony, led mainly by China. Still, China's immense reserves in dollars and US Treasury bonds play a contradictory role in this process, showing that overcoming the current state of affairs will still take a long time. Dialectically, however, the validity of US hegemony among the ruling classes of peripheral countries – especially in Latin America – is the central factor in restraining resistance movements. In this way, the analysis of the links between national states and US imperialism remains necessary to understand the limits and possibilities of national and international political processes.

References

Amin S (1987) *Imperialismo e Desenvolvimento Desigual*. São Paulo: Edições Vértice.
Amin S (2006) Geopolítica do Imperialismo Contemporâneo. In: *Revista Novos Rumos*, vol. 45. São Paulo. ISSN 0102-5864.
Arrighi G and Silver B (2001) *Caos e governabilidade no moderno sistema mundial*. Rio de Janeiro: Editora da UFRJ/Contraponto.
Azzarà S (1999) *Globalizzazione e Imperialismo*. Napoli: La Città Del Sole.
Baran P and Sweezy P (1968) *Monopoly Capital: an essay on American economic and social order*. New York: Monthly Review Press.
Barbosa B (2018) O new enclosure sobre trajetórias tecnológicas como base geopolítica da biopirataria internacional. In: *Revista tempo do mundo*, v. 4.
Benjamin, W (1979) *To the planetarium*. In: Benjamin W (1979) *One-Way Street and Other Writings*. London: NLB.
Borón A (2014) *América Latina en la Geopolítica Imperial*. La Habana: Instituto Cubano del Libro.

---

12 In our translation: "the IMF agenda is defined in Washington. This power of Wall Street and the Federal Reserve explains how the power of the North was able to export a crisis that originated in its territory".

Brzezinski Z (1997) *The Grand Chessboard: American Primacy and Its Geostrategic Imperatives.* Arizona: Basic Books.

Bukharin N (1986) *A economia mundial e o imperialismo: esboço econômico.* São Paulo: Nova Cultural.

Buonicore A (2015) Gramsci, Lenin e a questão da hegemonia. Available (consulted February 08 2024) at: https://grabois.org.br/2015/06/25/gramsci-lenin-e-a-questao-da-hegemonia/

Ceceña A (2014) La Dominación de Espectro Completo Sobre América. In: *Revista de Estudos e Pesquisas sobre as Américas.* Vol 8, number 2, ISSN: 1984-1639.

Chiaramonte C (1999) *Selling Americanism Abroad: American Cultural Diplomacy toward Argentina, 1953-1963.* Doctoral Thesis – Stony Brook, History Department.

Ciccarelli R (2008) A visão do Centauro: Hegemonia e o Lugar do Oriente em Gramsci. In: Del Roio, M (ed.). *Marxismo e Oriente: quando as periferias tornam-se os centros.* Marília: Ícone. Pages 269–295.

Coelho J (2011) Trajetórias e interesses: os EUA e as finanças globalizadas num contexto de crise e transição. In: *Brazilian Journal of Political Economy*, vol. 31, n. 5 (125) ISSN: 1809-4538: 771–793.

Coitinho R (2019) *Entre Duas Américas – EUA ou América Latina?* Florianópolis: Insular.

Cox R (2014) Fuerzas sociales, estados y órdenes mundiales: Más allá de la Teoria de Relaciones Internacionales. In *Revista Relaciones Internacionales*, n. 24 Universidad Autonoma de Madrid. ISSN 1018-0583: 129–162.

Fresu G (2016) *Lênin Leitor de Marx. Dialética e Determinismo na História do Movimento Operário.* São Paulo: Anita Garibaldi.

Gandásegui M Jr. (2016) Hegemonía, geopolítica y Estados Unidos. In: Gandásegui M Jr (ed.). *Estados Unidos y la nueva correlacion de fuerzas internacional.* Ciudad Autonoma de Buenos Aires: CLACSO: 69–88.

Gramsci A (1978) *Maquiavel a Política e o Estado Moderno.* Rio de Janeiro: Civilização Brasileira.

Gramsci A (2014) *Quaderni del carcere.* Volume secondo. Turim: Einaudi.

Harvey D (2003) *The New Imperialism.* Oxford: Oxford University Press.

Hilferding R (1985) *O Capital Financeiro.* Nova Cultural: São Paulo.

Hobson J(2009) *Estúdio del Imperialismo.* Madrid: Editora Capitán Swing.

Ianni O (1998) *Imperialismo na América Latina.* Rio de Janeiro: Civilização Brasileira.

Katz C (2016) La nueva estrategia imperial de Estados Unidos. In: Gandásegui M (2016) *Estados Unidos y la nueva correlacion de fuerzas internacional.* Ciudad Autónoma de Buenos Aires: CLACSO, 129–144.

Lenin V (1963a [1917]) Imperialism, the Highest Stage of Capitalism. In: *Lenin's Selected Works.* Moscow: Progress Publishers, Vol. 1, 667–766.

Lenin V (1963b [1918]) The Proletarian Revolution and The Renegade Kautsky. In: *Lenin's Collected Works.* Moscow: Progress Publishers, Vol. 28, 227–325.

Losurdo D (2015) *A Luta de Classes: Uma história política e filosófica*. São Paulo: Boitempo.

Lukács G (2012) *Lenin*. São Paulo: Boitempo.

Martins C (2016) El Sistema-Mundo Capitalista y los Nuevos Alineamientos Geopolíticos en el Siglo XXI. Una Visión Prospectiva. In: Gandásegui, M (2016) *Estados Unidos y la nueva correlacion de fuerzas internacional*. Ciudad Autonoma de Buenos Aires: CLACSO, 39–63.

Mills W (1981) *The Power Elite*. Oxford: Oxford University Press.

Nye J (2002) *The Paradox of American Power. Why the World's Only Superpower Can't Go it Alone*. Oxford: Oxford University Press.

Petras J (2007) *Imperialismo e luta de classes no mundo contemporâneo*. Florianópolis: Editora da UFSC.

Saxe-Fernández J (2006) *Terror e Imperio: La hegemonia política y económica de Estados Unidos*. Arena Abierta: México DF.

Touraine A (1996) *Qu'est-ce que la démocratie?* Paris: Fayard.

Visentini P (2006) O sistema mundial entre a uni e a multipolaridade. In: Visentini P and Wiesebron M (2006) *Neohegemonia americana ou multipolaridade? Polos de poder e sistema internacional*. Porto Alegre: Editora da UFRGS.

Wallerstein I (2003) *The Decline of American Power: The U.S. in a Chaotic World*. New York: The New Press.

CHAPTER 5

'War against War'

Rosa Luxemburg as an International Relations Theorist

Miguel Borba de Sá[1]

1 Introduction

The relation between International Relations Theory (IR) and Marxism has been controversial, to say the least.[2] Mainstream IR scholars, whether Realists or Liberals, have jointly ignored, or dismissed, Marxist contributions as unfit to 'their' field of studies.[3] Even proponents of cross fertilization, such as Fred Halliday, concede that "Marxism fits uneasily" (1994: 50) into the discipline's main debates, as if there was a Kuhnian paradigmatic incommensurability between the two epistemic communities. In the worst cases, manuals and handbooks of IR propagate caricatured versions of some Marxist notion about the international realm, often emphasizing the perceived flaws while silencing about possible analytical gains.

On the other hand, Marxists have shown similar disregard towards IR internal debates as they seemed all too biased towards bourgeois standpoints, not to mention mainstream IR's frequent neglect of global capitalism as a central feature of international politics.[4] Attempts to bridge the gap between those two epistemic communities usually took the form of offering a Marxist analysis to some international topic of particular interest, such as financial crises, wars,

---

1 Miguel Borba de Sá is an Assistant Professor at Department of Political Science of the Federal University of Rio de Janeiro (UFRJ), Brazil.
2 This chapter is a development of the article "The hidden presence of Marxism in International Relations Theory: Rosa Luxemburg and the first 'great debate'" (English translation) in the Brazilian journal "Estudos Internacionais", vol. 5, n. 3, 2017. Translated into English by the author.
3 Kenneth Waltz, for instance, dedicated a whole chapter from his classic "Man, the State and War" to prove the inadequacy of 'second image' theories using the collapse of the Second Workers' International as a perfect example of how 'not to' conduct analyzes of international politics (Waltz, 2001:124–158).
4 Robert Keohane, from the other side of the mainstream, also dismisses Marxist standpoints saying that they usually show "less an argument than a statement of faith", while also mentioning that "Marxian analyzes" tend to dismiss IR (especially Liberal-oriented) approaches as a mere "bourgeois error", which is true (1984:55).

or migration issues. Direct intercourse with IR's theoretical debates has been rare, occasionally arising from either neo-Gramscian or world-system theorizing. As a result, few Marxists in IR have attempted to dispute the discipline in its own terms or, at least, to accept some of its canonical self-descriptions as a tactical starting point.

In this chapter, such alternative path is chosen in order to make those epistemic (and political) borders more porous. It is argued that Marxist contributions were already present in what came to be known as IR's 'First Great Debate'. Such presence will remain hidden if we accept mainstream depictions of that debate or, conversely, if we reject the existence of such 'great debate' altogether, like Peter Wilson (1998, 2012) and other 'revisionist' disciplinary historians have attempted to do.

In what follows, a new reading of this alleged foundational debate will be offered with the explicit aim of placing Marxist contributions at its core, revealing how leading Marxist authors have actively participated in the social and intellectual debates out of which IR's foundational discussion emerged from. As it will be shown, Marxists formulated both 'realist' and 'idealist' arguments about the international crises around the two world wars of the twentieth century, combining both perspectives within their own theoretical (and political) standpoint. In order to accomplish this task, the chapter will revisit part of the *oeuvre* left by the socialist revolutionary leader, and prolific author, Rosa Luxemburg, especially her reflections about pacifism, revolution, war, and international crises, as well as those regarding the role of science against utopian analyzes of international issues, i.e., the very themes around which the so-called 'First Great Debate' in IR theory has been discursively structured.

By doing so, it hopes to disturb the foundations of such mode of presenting the discipline and the political consequences it entails. Arguably, this analytical strategy may have greater potential to destabilize mainstream's agenda-setting powers than the unsuccessful attempt to denounce the traditional debates-narrative in IR as a pure myth, a misrepresentation of reality, or a half-truth (Wilson, 1998; Quirk and Vigneswaran, 2005). If, as some revisionists argue, the tale of the First Debate is a retroactive fabrication that serves the purpose of limiting progressive IR scholarship from gaining traction within this field of studies, it seems adequate to propose a more effective way to challenge this disciplinary orthodoxy by providing IR students with radical tools that might be useful to undermine the notorious conservative bias shown by this field of studies.

Also, facing a situation in which even so-called 'critical approaches' that have already established themselves as part of IR's theoretical menu fail to acknowledge the value of Marxist contributions against the discipline's mainstream, it seems worthy to recover some of the hidden, or neglected, formulations made by classical Marxists, such as Luxemburg, that might prove themselves useful to widen the horizons of critical IR theorizing. And, at the same time, hopefully it may offer relevant clues as to the urgent task of analyzing todays' international predicaments regarding war and peace from a radical anticapitalistic, and decidedly anti-imperialist, perspective.

2   The First Great Debate: Myths, Distortions, and Silences

An authoritative voice in the 'debate about the first great debate' is Peter Wilson (1998, 2012:1). While accepting that, as a 'pedagogical device', it may have some 'merit', he nonetheless insists that "the first great debate never actually happened". According to him, not only an "idealist or utopian paradigm never actually existed" but, most importantly, it became a "realist category of abuse" that had a "inhibiting effect on disciplinary development", as a "rich variety of progressivist ideas have been consigned to oblivion" by the "myth" of a debate between Realists and Idealists in the aftermath of the World War I. A debate, moreover, which is "highly misleading" as a "statement of historical fact" (Wilson 1998:1). Later, he conceded that the "idea of a first great debate is not a complete fiction", without altering, however, his basic arguments (Wilson 2012:29–30).

Many have followed such 'revisionist' effort to question the explanatory habit of seeing a chronological sequence of Great Debates in IR theory, with a particular value attached to this foundational one. Brian Schmidt (2012) suggested that a different genealogy of scholarly debates, based on the American instead of the British academic life, would better explain the establishment of IR main tropes, such as the 'political discourse of anarchy'. By the same token, Cameron Thies (2002) concluded that the myth was constructed by Realists 'after' the World War II in order to make a case against their contemporary contenders. By their turn, Quirk and Vigneswaran (2005) apply a contextual analysis in which they argue that "the concept of a 'First Debate' is best regarded as a 'half-truth', or highly distorted and overly simplistic caricature, rather than a complete fiction". Like other revisionists, they question the "usefulness of the realist/idealist dichotomy", as well as the "chronology of the events it purports to explain" (2005:91). According to their research, the notion of a First Debate, as we know it today, was a by-product of the controversies aroused in IR theory around the mid-1970s onwards, when the notion of a 'Third Debate' (Lapid 1988) or 'Interparadigmatic Debate' (Banks 1985) retroactively consolidated the proposition of an original one in order for such numerical sequence to make sense, not so much as a 'conspiratorial' move by Realists but as a 'process' made of "ritually recited (...) perfunctory and superfluous references" that eventually created an "invented tradition", in Eric Hobsbawm's well-known terms (Quirk and Vigneswaran, 2005: 103–105).

However, such condemnations of the notion of a First Great Debate in IR theory fell short of arriving at any meaningful transformation in the 'conventional wisdom' about this field of studies: as Schmidt himself notes, "eighty years after the debate between idealists and realists allegedly occurred, the first great debate continues to occupy a central place in the field's historical consciousness" (2012:2). Even those who acknowledge the dangers of mainstream depictions of Great Debates also concede that "great debates have served to organize the discipline" so that "for IR the infamous great debates actually constitute a form of coherence" for an epistemic community inherently interdisciplinary and diverse (Waever, 2013: 315–317). Hence, for reasons that range from the internal academic struggles to the dominant ideologies on this field, as well as the institutional and the geopolitical backgrounds upon which the discipline constituted itself, the "notion that a disciplinary defining great debate took place in the 1930s and 1940s between idealists and realists continues to persist" (Schmidt, 2012:2). Unsurprisingly, for some contemporary mainstreamers, especially Realists, the First Debate not only did exist but, in fact, never really ended, as the "battle of E.H Carr's" against idealism still "rages on", according to John Mearsheimer (2005).[5]

What neither 'great debaters' nor 'revisionists' have done is to reconstruct the edifice of the First Great Debate taking seriously into account relevant Marxist contributions to it. Such an absence would seem curious in face of the recognition that multiple voices participated in the "lively exchanges on international matters in the 1920s and 1930s" on the questions of "international peace, order, justice, cooperation and conflict"; a conversation in which "Liberal internationalists of various kinds argued against conservatives, some of whom saw themselves as 'realists', *and socialists of various kinds argued against both*" (Wilson 2012:30 – emphasis added)[6]. This tripartite depiction,

---

5 Interestingly, Mearsheimer's vision about the contemporaneous character of the First Debate concludes that there is a bias against realism in course, thus making him, from the point of view of the present chapter, an unexpected bedfellow with those who deny its very existence: both sides agree that the First Debate, whether real or fabricated, produces exclusionary taboos in IR theory. Few of them, if any, bothered to investigate deeply the consequences of silencing Marxist voices about the same topics discussed in the First Debate.

6 To be sure, there were still other voices. There were many diverse groups and individuals who opposed the war, from religious groups, like Quakers, to the many conscience objectors of all kinds: students and women, for instance, organized international encounters against the war

putting Socialists alongside Liberals and Realists, however, remains concealed even by those who call for "greater appreciation of the complexity of the ideational and discursive reality of the time" (Wilson 2012:1).[7] Astonishingly, such negligence remains unaltered even when some of them recognize, *en passant*, such (hidden) presence, as when Peter Wilson, agreeing with David Long, remarks that "Carr's realism was a product of his radicalism: a product of broadly Marxist, certainly dialectical materialist conception of historical process" (Wilson 1998: 12).

A silencing that becomes even more intriguing if we accept Lucien Ashworth's (2002) claim that, instead of an Idealist-Realist debate, the discussions found at IR and Political Science journals back then actually revolved around three main topics, namely: (i) does capitalism cause war?; (ii) appeasement versus collective security; and (iii) intervention versus abstention (from a US perspective). Well, the first of these should automatically draw attention to the wide range of Marxist formulations about this specific issue, from the many collective resolutions adopted by the Workers' International (also called the Second International) regarding this question, to the prolific contributions given by well-known figures like Lenin, Trotsky, Kautsky and, of course, Luxemburg herself, among others.

Yet, in order to claim Luxemburg's participation in IR's foundational debate, two analytical moves are necessary. Firstly, a temporal one. There are many chronological controversies around the First Debate in IR. Revisionists often talk about a "chronological transplant" (Quirk and Vigneswaran 2005: 102), but differ on the question of historical direction: while some try to set the interwar period, and occasionally the early 1940s, as its fixed temporal boundaries (Wilson, 1998, 2012), others argue that what came to be known as IR's First Debate had already started in the final years of the nineteenth century (Schmidt, 2012). And still others make the case for an alleged retroactive projection of late twentieth century discussions into the discipline's historical folklore (Ashworth, 2002; Thies, 2002), not to mention, once more, those

---

even after it started, not to mention official diplomatic initiatives and millionaire individual efforts to promote peace (Hobsbawm, 1989: 302–327). The general Marxist position, held by successive Congresses of the Second International, was, in Luxemburg words, that "peace signifies the world revolution of the proletariat! There is no other way of really establishing and safeguarding peace other than by the victory of the socialist proletariat!" (2004f: 370). For other types of pacifism in that context see: Fellowship of Reconciliation et al. (2013) and Hoschild (2011).

7   Wilson smartly reminds us that a 'realist-realist', as well as a 'utopian-utopian' debate were also part of this complexity (1998:7). His discussion about Carr's motives for abandoning such tropes in his following works is less convincing, though.

mainstream voices who contend that such debate is still ongoing nowadays (Mearsheimer, 2005). A situation, therefore, in which several scholars "clumsily attached an entirely inappropriate chronology to a prior period of disciplinary development" (Quirk and Vigneswaran 2005: 107). Or, at best, a very disputed one, judging by the available literature.

Given such complete lack of agreement on temporal marks, it seems plausible to consider the First Debate to be already in place when rumors of war started spreading widely across advanced capitalist societies during the Age of Empire, i.e., from the 1890s onwards, when the gradual aggravation of great powers' rivalry, imperial disputes and aggressive nationalism were also met with anti-war discourses and peace initiatives until war finally broke out in 1914 (Hobsbawm, 1989)[8]. For instance, according to all accounts, orthodox and revisionists' alike, Norman Angell is undisputedly one of the leading voices in IR's First Debate. However, his masterpiece "The Great Illusion" (2002) was originally published in 1910 (and later reprinted into new editions with added chapters, as the one from 1933, the same year in which he was awarded the Nobel Peace Prize). In his famous book, Angell (1929) dwells against influent militaristic voices of his time such as the geopolitical 'classical' author Halford Mackinder, whose main *oeuvre*, "The Geographical Pivot of History", had been first released in 1904. Hence, if Sir Norman Angell is considered E.H. Carr's main intellectual opponent – Wilson calls him "Carr's *bête noire*" (1998: 2) – it seems mandatory to stretch back the First Debate to the discussions already in place prior to the war. The fact that Rosa Luxemburg was murdered in 1919, therefore, does not prevent us from considering her works and speeches – like the suggestively titled "Peace Utopias", from 1911 – as legitimate discursive artifacts of IR's First Great Debate. In fact, it may even help to alleviate some of the obvious chronological, as well as political, misconceptions found in mainstream depictions of it.

Secondly, another controversy raised by revisionists revolves around the boundaries between strictly speaking academic debates *per se* versus the social and political debates surrounding academic life. According to Wilson, "mixing these things up has certainly led to a lot of confusion" (2012: 12). He criticizes Andreas Osiander's 'alternative narrative' of IR's First Debate precisely on these grounds, accusing him of reconstructing the dichotomy of "idealism/ utopianism vs. realism in this broad sense, whose protagonists include Paine, Kant and Cobden on the one side, and Pufendorf, Burke, von Gentz on the

---

8   As Luxemburg herself says, "as early as the 1880s a strong tendency toward colonial expansion became apparent", so that "[t]he events that bore the present war did not begin in July 1914 but reach back for decades" (1970b: 281, 306).

other" (2012: 7). However, Wilson himself is forced to admit that the frontier between the 'discipline' of IR, narrowly defined, and the broader 'field' of international thought is difficult to sustain, as he himself notes that "if the notion of a great debate between idealism and realism is to make any sense it has to be acknowledged that this was, as mentioned above, a broader public debate". He goes on to stress that those "diverse discourses of inter-war thinking were conducted among a remarkably diverse group of interlocutors – publicists, peace campaigners, journalists, politicians, public servants, and the occasional academic" (2012: 15).

Hence, instead of trying to reify an ontology that separates the domain of disciplinary discussion from the broader societal life to which it is but a part of, it seems more appropriate to perceive the 'historical contingency of contemporary notions of academic purpose' and accept that today's academicist self-isolation from the public sphere was not yet dominant at the beginning of the previous century:

> The authors writing in the pre- and interwar eras adopted a relatively integrated approach to the wider inspirations and implications of their work that differs greatly from the theoretical aspirations that dominate more recent contributions to IR scholarship.
> QUIRK and VIGNESWARAN, 2005: 106

Or, as Wilson himself notes:

> The UK conversation was a broad public one. There were insufficient academic posts, departments, and journals in the field of IR more formally defined (...) In brief, IR was insufficiently institutionalized (...) While journals such as the Round Table and International Affairs existed, from 1910 and 1922 respectively, it is significant that until the 1950s and 1960s the vast majority of contributors to them were not professional students of international relations – not in the sense of personnel who "self-consciously and institutionally thought of themselves" of contributing to the professional study of international relations.
> WILSON, 2012: 10–11

Therefore, one cannot exclude Marxist contributions to those same topics of discussion using the pretexts of: (i) lack of membership to IR academic departments; (ii) speaking to broader audiences than IR students; or (ii) because of too much political involvement – as those criteria would automatically exclude most voices (if not all) traditionally accepted as leading participants in the so-called First Great Debate. Therefore, Rosa Luxemburg writings, either academic or pamphleteering, her passionate speeches against the war, and, above all, her incommensurable body of reflection on the questions of the complexity of international politics in an imperialist era should not, on such grounds, be withdrawn from the 'debate about the first debate'. Much to the contrary, they may serve to illuminate some of the blind spots, or misperceptions, of current accounts, including revisionist ones. And, most importantly, they can underscore the necessity of opening up the intellectual, as well as the political, horizons of thinking about great powers conflicts not only in the past but also nowadays when severe international crises make it a daunting necessity once again.

As it will be shown in the following sections, ignoring Marxist (especially Luxemburg's) alerts about the dangers of militarism, capitalism and imperialism led to catastrophic consequences that were not restricted to the working classes from the belligerent countries (killing themselves at the trenches), or to their political organizations, either national or international (that collapsed after the decision to support the war), but to humanity as such. Breaking the taboo against radical voices in IR is as necessary now as it was a hundred years ago, when the so-called First Debate allegedly occurred. And, just like then, now it is not simply an academic matter. The fact that Luxemburg was assassinated because of her unlawful and insistent participation on such discussions should speak for itself: she not only gave her life to it, but also found her premature death, at the age of 47, precisely because she passionately interfered in what came to be known in IR as the 'First Great Debate'.

3 Rosa Luxemburg as a Realist

The only agreement to be found within the cacophony around the notion of a First Debate is that E.H. Carr's masterpiece "Twenty Years Crisis", published in 1939, is the unquestionable inaugurator of the idealist-realist dichotomy during IR's 'infancy', as he depicted the stage of the discipline back then (2001: 1). To be sure, Carr's point was that the overcoming of this premature phase, marked by excessive utopianism, would be accomplished by the necessary arrival of realist attitudes, even though he dedicates a whole chapter to inform his readers – insisting to the point of exhaustion – that neither "method of approach" alone could satisfy the requirements of a mature 'science of international politics' (2001: 11–22). Whoever reads Carr instead of just mentioning him without due care (which is common in IR, sadly) will immediately notice that his attack on utopianism is meant to correct a specific, momentaneous, and geographically bounded situation in which excessive Liberal-international utopianism was making sensible policymaking impossible. Hence, his self-imposed task was to introduce greater doses of realism in order to restore political, as well as intellectual equilibrium, so that decisionmakers could get it right this time.[9]

Carr (2001) was particularly worried (irritated, one could say) with Liberal projects following the World War I, which revealed a profound lack of understanding about the causes of the last war and, thus, a dangerous incapacity to prevent or, at least, mitigate the extension of the next one. According to him, proposals such as the ones crystalized in Woodrow Wilson's notorious 'Fourteen Points' and other influential channels related to world governance (collective security, a League of Nations, the abolition of secret diplomacy, freedom of navigation and of commerce, arbitration of international conflicts and the right of nations to self-determination, among others) were but misguided attempts to shape the world as one would like it to be, ignoring, nonetheless, the harsh realities of how it actually was. Therein lays the utopianism, or idealism, described in much of his criticisms of Liberal internationalist recipes for ordering international relations peacefully: in its total negligence of the 'factor of power' in either domestic or international politics (Carr, 2001: vii).

Interestingly, a great deal of those same points had already been made years earlier by Rosa Luxemburg, among other Marxists, in the context of the escalation towards the war. Unlike Carr, whose audience was the Anglo-American foreign-policy establishment, Luxemburg's language is overtly Marxist, even though the content of her analysis, as well as good part of her central concepts and discursive tropes, are very similar to IR's foundational realism during the so-called 'First Debate'.[10] In an article called "Peace Utopias" [1911], for instance, those concepts emerge already in the title, but do not stop there. Luxemburg wants to stress the "differences in principle" between "bourgeois peace enthusiasts" and socialist-oriented[11] pacifism, which should be

---

9   It was sent to press in July 1939, shortly before hostilities begun. He dedicates the book 'To the Makers of the Coming Peace'.

10 One should notice that the internal history of Marxism shows the notion that an initial phase marked by 'utopian socialism' (Fourier, Proudhon, Owen, Saint-Simon) occupies a central role in the evolving character of socialist struggles. Just like in IR theory, this infancy had to be supplanted (or corrected) by realist approaches, thus inaugurating 'scientific socialism', so the story goes. It's possible (indeed even likely!) that Carr took this notion from Marxist internal debates, given his profound knowledge and taste for such discussions. He precisely mentions this example right at his first chapter (2001: 7–8). See, also: Engels (1908).

11 It should be noticed that until the collapse of the Second International many socialist, communist and/or Marxist-oriented individuals and organizations called themselves social-democrats, like in Germany, or in Russia.

viewed as "diametrically opposed" and in "mutual opposition" to one another (1970a: 250). She dismisses the good intentions of "[b]ourgeois friends of peace" who "invent all sorts of 'practical' projects for restraining militarism" as some sort of "diplomatic make-believe" (1970a: 251). To her, those are clear demonstrations of the "impracticability" of arriving at a lasting peace in a world divided by "international politics of spheres of influence" and "colonial predatory campaigns" (1970a: 251). In other words (sometimes the same words), the same 'power factor' that Carr would lament the absence a few years later. "A little order and peace is, therefore, just as impossible, just as much a petty bourgeois utopia, with regard to the capitalist world market as to capitalist world politics", she says.

Additionally, she considers, already before the war, that since "[m]ilitarism is closely linked with colonial politics, tariff politics, international politics" (1970a: 251), good doses of realism are always to be welcomed amid those waves of idealist-Liberal projects for peace. And just like Carr, Luxemburg warns against excessive utopianism quite straightforwardly. One should notice that such a stance is of foremost importance to her, not simply an occasional linguistic coincidence. The realist lexicon is part and parcel of her mindset, being one of the cornerstones of her analytical formulations:

> The utopianism of the standpoint which expects an era of peace and retrenchment of militarism in the present social order is plainly revealed in the fact that it is having to recourse to project making. For it is typical of utopian strivings that, in order to demonstrate their practicability, they hatch 'practical' recipes with the greatest possible details.
>
> LUXEMBURG, 1970a: 254

The coincidence with Carr's formulations on the same matter are striking, notably when he discusses the 'visionary schemes' of this 'utopian stage of the political sciences':

> During this stage, the investigators will pay little attention to existing 'facts' or to the analysis of cause and effect, but will devote themselves whole-heartedly to the elaboration of visionary projects for the attainment of the ends which they have in view – projects whose simplicity and perfection give them an easy and universal appeal (...) Schemes elaborated in this spirit would not, of course, work.
>
> CARR, 2001: 5–7

In later interventions, already during the war, she comes back to that same point. The famous "Junius Pamphlet" [1915], written from one of the prisons where she was held captive for anti-war agitation, tackles precisely the same political issues that would constitute the central controversies of IR's First Debate[12]:

> All demands for complete or gradual disarmament, for the abolition of secret diplomacy, for the dissolution of the great powers into smaller entities, and all other similar propositions, are *absolutely utopian* so long as capitalist class-rule remains in power (...) The proletarian movement cannot reconquer the place it deserves by means of *utopian advice* and projects for weakening, taming or quelling imperialism within capitalism by means of partial reforms.
>
> 1970b: 324 – emphasis added[13]

As an appendix to this pamphlet, by the end of the same year Luxemburg formulates her "Theses on the Tasks of International Social Democracy" [1915], where she reiterates that:

> World peace cannot be assured by projects utopian or, at bottom, reactionary, such as tribunals of arbitration by capitalist diplomats, diplomatic 'disarmament' conventions, 'the freedom of the seas', abolition of the right to maritime arrest, 'the United States of Europe', a 'customs union for central Europe', buffer states, and other illusions.
>
> 1970c: 329

The equivalence of utopianism, usually directed at the future, and 'reactionary' projects, which refers to the past, is understandable in face of her Marxist philosophy of history which, again, reveals a strong similarity with Carr's critique of the 'golden age' utopia of those who wanted to resuscitate the Liberal international order from the nineteenth century under twentieth century

---

12   The pamphlet was written in early 1915, but only released a year later due to the difficulties imposed by censorship in war times. The use of the pseudonym "Junius", who signs the document, reflects such hardships. The original intention was to deliver it as a contribution to the Zimmerwald Conference, that brought together socialist cadres from different countries who opposed the war, in September 1915. Lenin immediately considered it "a splendid Marxist work", ignoring the authorship though (Lenin, 1970a: 429).
13   In that same text, she also criticized the "utopian disregard for the class struggle", at both the domestic and international levels, shown by her social-democrat colleagues from the party's leadership (1970b: 296).

conditions (Carr, 2001: 224). In a lesser-known text called "Slavery" [1907], written for the classes she taught at the German Social Democratic Party's (SPD) internal political school, she clearly expresses this conception when referring to a certain "utopian demand to turn back the wheel of history" (Luxemburg, 2004a: 117).[14]

That same motto was to be found also at another well-known work, "The National Question" [1909], part of Marxist internal 'Great Debates' that she had with Lenin and others. While Luxemburg was highly wary about the ideological dangers of nationalism for proletarian class struggles in a broad sense,[15] other eminent Marxists felt it was important to support national liberation movements in Europe (against Russian and Austro-Hungary empires) and elsewhere – to which she agreed as long as such aspirations were kept separated from the bourgeois cry for the 'right of self-determination', a romantic ideal highly deleterious to the political education of the masses, according to her views on the matter.[16] In order to make her point, she appeals to the authority of Karl Marx himself and the "sober realism, alien to all sentimentalism, with which Marx examined the national question" (Luxemburg, 1909: 9). According to her interpretation, "Marx treated the Czech question", for instance, "with no less political realism" (1909: 10).

---

14   Her realist conclusion is almost sarcastic, when she states that "without slavery there wouldn't be socialism", by which she meant a succession of exploitative and oppressive modes of production was, unfortunately, necessary to arrive at a classless society in the coming future (Luxemburg, 2004a: 122 – italics on the original).

15   "The immediate mission of socialism is the spiritual liberation of the proletariat from the tutelage of the bourgeoisie, which expresses itself through the influence of nationalist ideology", she says, also referring to this mission as her "supreme goal" (Luxemburg, 1970c: 331) In several occasions, she would cry against the "chauvinistic intoxication of the masses", amid similar formulations (1970b: 318).

16   "Capitalist politicians, in whose eyes the rulers of the people and the ruling classes are the nation, can honestly speak of the 'right of national self-determination' in connection with such colonial empire. To the socialist, no nation is free whose national existence is based upon the enslavement of another people, for him colonial peoples, too, are human beings, and, as such, part of the national state. International socialism recognizes the right of free independent nations, with equal rights. But socialism alone can create such nations, can bring self-determination of their peoples" (Luxemburg, 1970b: 304–305). Interestingly, both Lenin and Trotsky felt the need to reiterate their divergences with Luxemburg on this matter even when they wrote their respective eulogies of her work and life-example as a true revolutionary. However, such internal Marxist disputes are not the object of the present chapter, not the least because they tend to be exaggerated for short-term political gains, thus distorting a reality in which Marxist arguments are, *grosso modo*, very similar, especially from an outsider's point of view, such as the IR student's one.

Such applause for realist gestures, as well as critiques of utopian standpoints, are to be found in many other texts and passages throughout her reflections concerning international issues. On several occasions she insists that international relations are made of 'world political antagonisms', especially during the epochs of capitalism and imperialism. In those times, she argues that

> a mere reckoning with *facts,* to refuse to realize that these facts give rise to anything rather than a mitigation of the international conflicts, of any sort of disposition toward world peace, is willfully to close one's eyes.
> LUXEMBURG, 1970a:253

> Hence, the bare facts alone show that for fifteen years hardly a year has gone without some war activity (...) Where do they show any tendency toward peace, toward disarmament, toward the settlement of conflicts by arbitration?
> 1970a: 252

Once again, the contraposition of *facts* (emphasized in italics by herself) versus 'self-deceptions' is a longstanding theme in her political interventions that resonates a lot with Carr's applause for realism, because "it places emphasis on the acceptance of facts and on the analysis of their causes and consequences" (Carr, 2001:10). Usually focused more on working-class politics than in world politics alone, that same theme nonetheless occupies Luxemburg's attention since her early days, being already present, for instance, in her intervention at the Hannover Congress of the Second International [1899], when she criticizes those revisionist factions who wanted to arrive at socialism peacefully, avoiding class struggle. A proposition devoid of "historical basis in facts", thus constituting a dangerous "illusion" for the proletariat: "In its struggle, the working class, has no greater enemy than its own illusions" (1971a: 47–49).

Twenty-years later, that same warning is repeated amid the revolutionary upheaval of 1918–1919, when she wrote "Our Program and the Political Situation" [1919] and "What Does the Spartacus League Want?" [1919], two of her last written contributions before she was killed by a right-wing, counter-revolutionary death squad, the *Frëie Korps*.[17] She again warns about 'illusions

---

17 The *Frëie Korps* were illegal paramilitary commandos formed by former soldiers coming back from the war fronts, together with policemen, and other repressive forces personnel that were called upon (by the newly installed SPD government after the proclamation of the republic) to do the dirty work against left-wing leaders and proletarian masses during the revolutionary upheaval of 1918–1919 in Germany.

on all-sides' within the German left, including in her newly formed German Communist Party (KPD). After stating that the question of violence depends on their adversaries, not upon abstract principles, she calls for the "arming of the people and disarming of the ruling classes" in order to bring about the "dictatorship of the proletariat and therefore true democracy" (2004e: 353). If the "fight for socialism is the mightiest civil war in world history", she says, then "the violence of the bourgeois counterrevolution must be confronted with the revolutionary violence of the proletariat" (2004e: 353).[18] Realism is welcomed; utopianism, with regards to the peaceful character of social transformation, is not.[19]

The association of such revolutionary attitudes with what came to be known as IR's realist tradition has indeed deeper connections, as shown by her usage of realism's twin concepts of 'international anarchy' and 'balance of power', both of which are repeatedly mobilized during Luxemburg's reflections. To the former, a particular Marxist redefinition (or substance) is given, locating the roots of international anarchy in capitalism itself, whereas the latter is frequently used in precisely the same manner as IR realists do. Hence the "world political anarchy", in the political and military sense, is "but the reverse side of the anarchic system of production of capitalism" (Luxemburg, 1970a: 252). She goes on to say that

> only those who believe in the mitigation and blunting of class antagonisms, and in the checking of the economic anarchy of capitalism, can believe in the possibility of these international conflicts allowing themselves to be slackened, to be mitigated and wiped out.
> 1970a: 252

Such class of believers can be found in the realm of those 'bourgeois friends of peace' previously mentioned, which include Liberal-idealist critics of imperialism rightfully considered participants of IR's First Debate, such as John Hobson or Norman Angell, both of whom imagined that reforms within capitalism were not only possible, but the necessary step to prevent imperial

---

18   That is, the traditional realist acknowledgement of that which Max Weber would call ethics of responsibility, summarized in the famous reply by Martin Luther to Emperor Charles V, transformed by Rosa in her personal 'watchword' during the war: "Here I stand, I can't do otherwise", as stated more than once in her prison letters (2004h: 387–8).

19   Notably, one of the last chapters from Carr's masterpiece is intitled "Peaceful Change" (2001: 208–223).

expansions.[20] By the same token, Luxemburg also accuses the members of her own party (who voted in favor of the war credits at the infamous Reichstag session of August 4th, 1914) of trying to "save the capitalist state from its own anarchy" by offering a truce in class struggle during the war, the so-called "civil peace" (1970b: 300). Such claims are not occasional ones, as she had been developing this line of thought for many years already. For instance, in her second address to the Stuttgart Congress of the Second International [1898], she says that "no medicinal herbs can grow in the dirt of capitalist society which can help cure capitalist anarchy" (1971a: 42). In a nutshell, in Luxemburg's mind we already lived in what Hedley Bull (1977) would later call an "Anarchical Society"; not only at the international level, but at any level in which the "anarchy of capitalist rule" takes place (Luxemburg, 1971a: 42).

Likewise, when it comes to the realist notion of a 'balance of power', one can find significant similarities between Luxemburg's and IR realist approaches. Not only the concept is employed several times throughout her *oeuvre*, like in the "Junius Pamphlet" [1915] or even in her personal correspondence, with the same meaning as in IR, but she also develops a line of thought that could easily have been defended by the likes of Carr, Morgenthau, Waltz or Mearsheimer, when she states, quoting veteran Marxist Ferdinand Lassalle, that "[t]he true constitution of any country consists not in its written constitution, but in its real balance of power" (1971a: 42). Then she develops the point in a truly realist manner, albeit restricted to the domestic level, even though the connection with militarism turns the international dimension unescapable. To be sure, her formulation is almost neo-realist, if we consider the centrality given to 'material capabilities', in the Waltzian sense, on her statements:

> Constitutional freedoms, if they are to have any permanent worth, must be won through struggle, not through agreements. But what the capitalist state would get by an agreement with us has a firm, brutal reality. The cannon and soldiers to which we would agree will shift the objective material balance of power against us.
>
> 1971a: 42

---

20 While they share a negative view of monopolistic distortions of competition and free-trade, Hobson is much more critical of the role of finance in imperialism, whereas Angell is an ardent apologist of capital markets, being the inventor of the "Money Game", destined to educate young children into the world of finance. See, for instance, his book about "The Story of Money" (1929), ironically released in the same year of Wall Street's infamous crash.

Hence, it is possible to realize the extent to which Realists' insistence on the importance of the 'power factor' in politics, whether national or international, can also be found in Rosa Luxemburg's formulations since the early days of her political and intellectual trajectory in Germany,[21] when she devoted most of her energies to confront Edward Bernstein's reformism (also called 'revisionism' or, simply, 'opportunism').[22] Unlike the revisionist thesis that obliviates the necessity of seizing the state from the ruling classes, thus relying on the expansion of social reforms made by parliamentary decisions, Luxemburg states that "the conquest of political power" away from the bourgeoisie should be the only goal for socialist movements (1971a: 39). Internationally, just like IR realists, she refers to the "game of war" in quite perennial terms, saying that "[t]he game is old" and that it is naïve to believe that its causes rely on the methods used by diplomats, or in the wickedness of particular "captains of nations", who, according to her views, "are, in this war, as at all times, merely chessmen, moved by all-powerful historic events and forces" (Luxemburg, 1970b: 279).

> And if today a number of socialists threaten with horrible destruction the "secret diplomacy" that has brewed this devilry behind the scenes, they are ascribing to these poor wretches a magic power they little deserve, just as the Botokude whips his fetish for the outbreak of a storm.
>
> 1970b: 279

Of course, the content (and style) of such critique echoes Carr's point about the "agitation against secret treaties, which were attacked", according to him, "on insufficient evidence, as one of the causes of the war", and that such

---

21 Before arriving in Germany, Luxemburg already had a political career in the Polish Left, where she enjoyed a revolutionary reputation since her youth (and never ceased to be one of the Polish party's head). Her intellectual career also predates her arrival as she became a PhD in 1897, with a thesis about the "Industrial Development of Poland", at the University of Zurich. For biographical notes about this period, see: Schütrumpf (2008: 11–14).

22 Arguably, this was the central focus of her attention throughout her lifetime within the SDP, warning since the end of the nineteenth century about the dangers of opportunism in German social democracy circles. Dangers that would become obvious to many – like Lenin – only in 1914 (See Trotsky, 1970b). But the phenomenon was not restricted to Germany and Luxemburg also wrote about such tendencies in France in "The Drayfus Affair and the Millerand Case" [1899], where she criticizes French socialists leaders' arguments to accept ministerial posts: "The entry of a socialist into a bourgeois government is not, as it is thought, a partial conquest of the bourgeois state by the socialists, but a partial conquest of the socialist party by the bourgeois state", she says (1899: n.p.).

diplomatic practice, apart from being of little relevance to understand the war, was not to be blamed on "the wickedness of the governments" (Carr, 2001: 2), but on the anarchic structure of international politics itself.[23] Of course, both Luxemburg and Carr were very critical of "disarmament trickeries, whether they are invented in Petersburg, London or Berlin" (Luxemburg 1970a: 254). However, as she says, from a "materialist conception of history" – shared by both – "things have their own objective logic" and, therefore, it becomes a "sterile concoction of the brain" to expect that voluntaristic initiatives alone can either create or avoid wars: to believe that projects like the "United States of Europe" can bring an "era of permanent peace" and "banish the ghost of war forever", as neo-Kantians and many Liberal idealists still propose until our days, are deemed naïve, at best; or cynical, at worst (1970a: 255)[24].

Epistemologically, then, there are many other instances where we can find similarities between Luxemburg's formulations and IR's realist tradition, especially if we accept Carr's association of realism with "determinism", and of utopianism with "free will" (2001: 11–12). In other words, the agent-structure dichotomy, in which, for him, "the realist analyzes a pre-determined course of development which he is powerless to change" (Carr, 2001:11). Here Luxemburg's sides with the realists in countless occasions, usually stressing the "iron laws of development", or that "scientific socialism has taught us to recognize the objective laws of historical development", and that every event or personal attitude has "deep, significant, objective causes" explainable by the "all-powerful law of historical necessity" (1970b: 268–9; 2004f: 366). She frequently talks about social processes as having the "inevitability of a natural law" (1970b: 290) and "objective historic significance" (1970b: 319).

Luxemburg mentions the "vital law" of revolutions with almost positivistic certainty, repeating *ad nauseam* notions like the "fatality of a natural law" with regards to the "internal law of life of the revolution" as an epistemological remedy to the "pseudo-science" of those utopian reformists who ignore the "great historical laws of revolution" (2004g: 376). In other words, she clearly states the opposition between, on the one hand, "the guiding star of scientific

---

[23] Carr sounds almost like Luxemburg when he says that "war lurks in the background of international politics just as revolution lurks in the background of domestic politics" (2001: 109).

[24] She goes on and, quite realistically, concludes with what we would call today a bold decolonial statement: "Every time that bourgeois politicians have championed the idea of Europeanism, of the union of European States, it has been with an open or concealed point directed against the "yellow peril", the "dark continent", against the "inferior races", in short, it has always been an imperialist abortion" (1970a: 256).

knowledge", and, on the other, "utopian undertakings" (1970b: 263). Such an opposition is precisely the same one that Carr would refer to when he calls his first chapter "the beginning of a science" (Carr, 2001: 1). For both of them, thus, science is deemed to be the remedy for the excesses, and dangers, of utopianism.

And just like Carr, Luxemburg is not inclined to theorize in pure abstract terms. Both draw their theoretical formulations from concrete political situations, past or present, virtually all the time. According to Carr, "the utopian believes purely in the application to practice of certain theoretical truths evolved out of their inner consciousness by wise and far-seeing people" (2001: 13). Liberalism is their common adversary, and he accuses the likes of "Sir Normal Angell" of living in some sort of a "dream-world" within which certain "theoretical facts" are far away from "the world of reality where quite contrary facts may be observed" (2011a: 12). By the same token, Luxemburg notes that:

> A 'rights of nations' which is valid for all countries and all times is nothing more than a metaphysical cliché of the type of 'rights of man' and 'rights of the citizen'. Dialectic materialism, which is the basis of scientific socialism, has broken once and for all with this type of 'eternal' formula (...) On this basis, scientific socialism has revised the entire store of democratic clichés and ideological metaphysics inherited from the bourgeoisie.
>
> 1908: np

There would be many other instances in which Luxemburg's writings and speeches can be related to IR's realism, especially of the kind inaugurated by Carr, as well as with regards to the formulations made by other traditional realists. For instance, there are times in which she criticizes the "politics of acquiescence" (1970b: 276) referring to Austria-Hungary's appetite for expansion that anticipate what would later become the question of 'appeasement', which lies at the heart of IR's First Debate[25]

Also, the notion of a 'security dilemma' as developed by John Herz (1950) – full of dialectic reasoning and historical erudition – resembles very much the appraisal Luxemburg makes about the automatic propulsion of the arms race among great powers, which, according to her views on the matter, shows a sort of impersonal (and tragic) mechanism that drives nations to an ever growing

---

25 Carr was, indeed, one of the greatest appeasers, it must be remembered, even though the conventional (American) wisdom later identified appeasement as a weak, coward and, therefore, *idealist* policy line.

spiral of insecurity, in spite of the best efforts to achieve security through military capacity-building[26], She also exhibits a quite skeptical prognosis for the aftermath of the World War I, saying that "every settlement between the military powers unavoidably becomes the starting point of fresh new conflicts" (1970a: 253) and that "imperialism, and its servant militarism, will reappear after every victory and after every defeat in this war", no matter which side wins or loses (1970b: 323).

Yet, the passages recollected here seem already sufficient to demonstrate Luxemburg's realism which, in quite straightforward ways, resembles so much IR's realist position at the 'First Great Debate' to the point of making it possible to conclude that her contributions, like the ones from other contemporary Marxist icons[27], can be rightfully considered as legitimate participants of IR's alleged foundational moment, anticipating in many occasions, *avant la lettre*, many realist theses on international politics. Such contributions constitute, nevertheless, only part of the story, as her works also display important elements of idealist, or utopian, thinking too, to which we now turn our attention.

4 Rosa Luxemburg's Idealism: in Theory and in Action

According to Carr, one important feature of utopianism is the tendency to concentrate attention "almost exclusively on the end to be achieved", in other words, "when whishing prevails over thinking, generalization over observation, and in which little attempt is made at a critical analysis of existing facts or available means" (2001: 8). The example he gives resonates with some of

---

26 For Luxemburg's complex elaborations on the political mechanics of the arms races and security dilemmas, see, among others: "Militia and Militarism", in Luxemburg (1971b) and "The Peace, the Triple Alliance and Us" (2011), originally published in July 1914 (there is a Portuguese translation available, but not an English one for this text). After mentioning "arms races", she says, in the later one, that "the incessant process of military buildup was not a guarantee of peace, but a seed for war", because states, "in their blind drift, provoked the reaction of powers that, in a given moment, will grow bigger than themselves, and will drag them to the whirlwind" by "mechanic means". True, however, is the limit of her realism, in IR terms, to which she spears no critique either: "naïve spirits", she says, believed that "military alliances" should be the "pilar of the European balance of power and peace", but today "even the blind can see that incessant arm races and imperialist bets took us, with inexorable necessity" to the "abyss of a terrible European war" (Luxemburg, 2011a: 497–498).

27 Lenin famously dubbed Luxemburg 'an eagle': "Eagles my at times fly lower than hens, but hens can never rise to height of eagles (...) In spite of her mistakes she was – and remains for us – an eagle" (Lenin 1970b: 440).

the attitudes found on Luxemburg's trajectory, thus revealing, in First Debate terms, her idealist side as well. He says:

> When President Wilson, on his way to the Peace Conference, was asked by some of his advisers whether he thought his plan of a League of Nations would work, he replied briefly: "If it won't work, it must be made to work".
> CARR 2001:8

Quite tellingly, when she writes about the difficulties faced by the German revolution in those same years (1918–1919), Luxemburg assumes the same utopian attitude ('It must!'), just like Wilson in Carr's example. She states that:

> The German revolution has now hit upon the path illuminated by this star. Step by step, through storm and stress, through battle and torment and misery and victory, it will reach its goals. It must!
> p.345

In that same text, "The Beginning" [1918], she literally praises the "unflagging idealism of the masses of the people" as a guarantee of victory in the final struggle, against all the odds and harsh facts they were facing (2004c: 343). By the same token, in a following article she writes about "the action of the great massive millions of people, destined to fulfill an historic mission and to transform historical necessity into reality" (2004d: 352), which is precisely the theme identified at the core of Idealism by Lucien Ashworth's (2002) revisionist history of IR's First Great Debate.[28] Interestingly, also, is the presence, in some of the resolutions adopted by the Second International, not only of political idealism in general, but of a specific type coming from the same breed as IR's utopianism in the First Debate – namely from the likes of David Mitrany and other functionalist apologists of international organizations – when it comes to the formulation of concrete proposals for peace. Some of them, like the ones adopted at the London Congress held in 1896, when Luxemburg probably helped to formulate the draft, ask for: "2nd – The institution of an International Arbitration Tribunal, the decisions of which must have force of law; 3rd – A definitive decision about war or peace directly by the people, in

---

28 In that same passage from "What Does The Spartacus League Want?" Luxemburg criticizes the "attempt of a minority to mold the world forcibly according to its ideal" (p.352), only to reaffirm, nonetheless, her trust in the capacity to precisely perform such task if *minorities* are substituted by *majorities*, thus keeping the voluntaristic assumptions typical of utopianism intact.

the case that governments do not accept the Tribunal's decision" (Luxemburg, 2011a: 489).

Furthermore, notwithstanding her deterministic moments, Luxemburg also reveals voluntaristic attitudes as well,[29] sometimes with a clear tone of sentimentalism and wishful thinking, especially when she blames SPD leaders' inertia and cowardice (or outright opportunism) for the current disaster, as if socialist politicians could have prevented the war or, at least, diminished its duration, or lethality, if only they had decided to do so. "Peace sentiments", she says, "would have spread like wildfire and the popular demand for peace in all countries would have hastened the end of the slaughter, would have decreased the number of its victims" (1970b: 318). The same type of optimism that makes her believe that this could be "the last war", as repeatedly stated in the "Junius Pamphlet" (1970b: 266–268).

Times of war and revolution are indeed prone to euphoria (and despair), and this may be reflected in the way historical time is conceived as being shortened, as if 'great leap forwards' in collective mentalities became suddenly possible, or inevitable. In a text called "The Socialization of Society" [1918], Luxemburg succumbs precisely to such utopian temptations and, in doing so, places idealism as a central lesson to be learned by revolutionaries:

> We do not need, however, to wait perhaps a century or a decade until such a species of human beings develop. Right now, in the struggle, in the revolution, the mass of the proletarians learns the necessary idealism and soon acquire the intellectual maturity.
> 2004d: 348

Another central feature of the so-called Idealism from IR's First Debate is what John Herz's (1950) famously called 'chiliastic' attitudes, i.e., the belief that a drastic transformation in humanity's fate will inaugurate an era of indefinite peace, prosperity, and happiness, leaving all the troubles behind. He dedicates a whole section, for instance, to show the reversal of the 'chiliastic hopes' held by the Second and Third Workers' Internationals, and another one to the 'general idealism' of what "may be broadly described as pacifism" (1950: 172). In its religious versions, chiliasm brings the notion of 'millenarism' to the forefront,

---

29 To be sure, much of her writings on the matter tried to sustain a balanced account of the agent-structure debate, even if sometimes she pended towards either deterministic or voluntaristic extremes. In general, though, she followed Marx's account as developed in the opening line of the "Eighteen Brumaire", for instance, when she says: "Mas does not make history of his volition, but he makes history nevertheless" (Luxemburg, 1970b: 269).

whereas in its socialist versions the 'entire new world' will not be the work of a Christ returned, but the result of the qualities of the next generation of socialist workers themselves.

> In enlisting capable fighters for the current revolution, we are also creating the future socialist workers which a new order requires as its fundament. The working class youth is particularly well-qualified for these great tasks. As the future generation they will, indeed, quite certainly, already constitute the real foundation of the socialist economy. It is already now its job to demonstrate that it is equal to the great task of being the bearer of the humanity's future. An entire old world still needs overthrowing and an entirely new one needs constructing. But we will do it young friends, won't we? We will do it!
> 2004d: 348

In fact, the notorious slogan by which Luxemburg continues to be reminded until today – "Socialism or Barbarism" – is in itself a great example of chiliasm: "Today matters have reached a point at which mankind is faced with the dilemma: either collapse into anarchy, or *salvation through socialism*" (2004f: 364 – emphasis added). The same is valid for some romanticized formulations present in texts like "What Does the Spartacus League Want?", where she also points to the need of the "highest idealism" in order to build the road to socialism (2004e: 351). In those occasions, she shows a remarkable capacity for idealizing a future socialist society for someone who, at the same time, liked to praise Marx's sober realism so much. Nevertheless, her idyllic vision of 'socialist civic virtues' renders her analysis quite utopic because, as we know today, especially after the experience of Stalinism, "stupidity, egotism, and corruption" can be found in socialist societies as well:

> The highest idealism in the interests of the collectivity, the strictest self-discipline, the truest public spirit of the masses are the moral foundations of socialist society, just as stupidity, egotism, and corruption are the moral foundations of capitalist society.
> LUXEMBURG 2004e: 351[30]

---

30   The same logic is also valid for her best hopes of "[r]eplacement of the military cadaver discipline by voluntary discipline of the soldiers" under socialism (2004e: 354). In "Slavery" [1907], for example, she concludes the text in a quite chiliastic manner as well: "In the socialist society", she says, "knowledge will be the common property of everyone. All working people will have knowledge" (2004a: 122).

As Herz (1950) argues, the exaggeration of a given situation is also a chiliastic feature of idealist thinking, especially when it comes in the form of the projection of one's own conditions to different, distant realities, in time and in space. Luxemburg is full of such hyperboles, especially when she considers the universal importance of the immediate struggles that she was involved in. In other words, one can detect a sort of parochialism, typical of idealism according to Herz (1950), and often found in universalist discourses. "There is a world to win and a world to defeat", she claims regarding the German revolution, "in this final class struggle in world history for the highest aims of humanity" (2004e: 357). Again, as we know today, it was not the last struggle. "It is the realization of the ultimate goal of socialism which is on today's agenda of world history", she said (2004c: 345). In fact, world history showed it was not. And she felt the consequences to the fullest when political defeat came together with the abrupt end of her own life, a few weeks after publishing these words.

Luxemburg's last written work, "Order Reigns in Berlin" [1919], also reiterates the wishful thinking mode behind the idealist self-denial of harsh realities, even when presented in dialectical fashion, "in which the final victory can be prepared only by a series of 'defeats'" (2004g: 376). Such line of reasoning, which reveals the tension between despair and hope in the most difficult of the situations, must aggregate a certainty in historical necessities with the praise of, not surprisingly, 'idealism' itself, once again. After saying that "history leads step by step, to the ultimate victory!", she concludes with a mixture of tragedy and optimism typical of utopianism, as identified by Carr (2001) and others: "Where would we be today without those "defeats" from which we have drawn historical experience, knowledge, power, idealism!" (2004g: 376). Days after writing those words, she would meet her ultimate defeat.

There would be many other examples of Luxemburg's idealist side, either in her political writings or in her personal letters. Like the one she sent to her partner and comrade, Polish socialist leader Leo Jogiches, in 1902, where she vows not to lose her 'idealism' during the struggles within the SPD, promising him that she would not "employ methods other than the use of [her] own talent" (2004h: 384). In such private moments, she would explicitly reveal her utopian belief in changing the course of history by means of "the power of ideas" (2004h: 382), as if it was just a matter of "correcting a defect in understanding" among the masses, in the words of Carr when referring to Norman Angell's utopianism. Such educational hopes – for example, that "war was simply a 'failure of understanding'" and that "with increasing knowledge, enough people would be rationally convinced of its absurdity to put an end to it" (Carr, 2001: 25–26) – resonate with Luxemburg's hope to end capitalism (and war) by pedagogical means: "I want to affect people like a clap of a thunder, to inflame their minds not by speechifying but with the breadth of my vision, the strength of my conviction, and the power of my expression" (2004h: 382), she declares[31].

Things, however, proved to be more difficult, and Luxemburg's hopes for putting the "socialist revolution on an international footing", or "to shape and secure the peace by means of [a] international brotherhood" of the "world proletariat" (2004e: 355–356) never became an enduring reality, even after workers' strikes (and soldiers' mutinies) destroyed the monarchic regime and sealed Germany's final defeat in the imperialist war. The failure of this faith, which is not only hers, must not, therefore, reinforce certain images, or myths, about 'Red Rosa', as Hanna Arendt (1968) wisely adverts us against in an inspiring political biography of Luxemburg: to avoid both the "glamorous image" of the "legend" who became a "nostalgic symbol" for the New Lefts, on the one hand, and "the old clichés regarding the quarrelsome woman who was neither realist nor scientific", on the other (Arendt, 1968: 36–38).

In this chapter, this avoidance was sought via recourse to firsthand contact with Luxemburg's own writings (as opposed to 'Luxemburguists' or 'anti-Luxemburguists' disputes about her legacy[32]) in order to keep interpreting her provocative ideas and experiences of struggle from innovative standpoints, such as seeing Luxemburg as an IR theorist who took part in the discipline's First Debate. Ideas and political activity that usually came together and intertwined in Luxemburg's life: one that she lived "between love and anger", i.e., between revolution and war (Schütrumpf, 2008: 9). Her addresses to political events, such as the Second International Congresses, or speeches to large crowds (of 9 thousand people in Hippodromes, for instance), were full of theoretical elaboration and pedagogical gestures.

Moreover, in occasions like her "Self-Defense Speech" [1914] at the Frankfurt Criminal Court, during a trial against her, Luxemburg takes the opportunity

---

31   Luxemburg would later change this position when war and revolution became the real clap of the thunder: "Fortunately, we have gone beyond the days when it was proposed to 'educate' the proletariat socialistically (...) To educate the proletarian masses socialistically meant to deliver lectures to them, to circulate leaflets and pamphlets among them. No, the school of the socialist proletariat doesn't need all this. The workers will learn in the school of action" (2004f: 372). Herein lies the alleged 'spontaneity' theses attributed to her, usually by detractors.

32   On the issues involving the (mis)appropriations of her legacy within the Left, which is not our focus here, see Arendt (1968), and the volume edited by Waters (1970), which contains excellent introductions to the intellectual and political contexts of the uses and abuses of Luxemburg's legacy. On this volume, there are, for instance, two insightful articles by Leon Trotsky, one of them intitled "Hands Off Rosa Luxemburg" [1932] in which he fiercely replies to Stalin's defamation campaign against Luxemburg.

to lecture not only the prosecutor and the judge, but also to teach the audience some basic notions of socialist international politics. Just a few months ahead of the war, she must reply to charges of inciting German soldiers, during a speech, to shoot their own superiors if the conflict started, as it eventually did in August. She denies the accusation, using an idealistic formula, saying that:

> When the majority of the people get convinced that wars are a barbaric phenomenon, profoundly immoral, reactionary and enemy of the people, then wars become impossible – even if soldiers, in a first moment, keep obeying the command of their superiors!
> 2011b: 485[33]

It is nonetheless in her final, heroic confrontation with the prosecutor, during the trial, where she shows her best idealism in action. After saying that he "dared to raise suspicions about [her] personal honor" when he hinted at the possibility of an escape attempt if convicted, she shouts back to him and say: "Mister prosecutor, I believe that *you* would flee. A social democrat does not flee. He recognizes his actions and laugh at his prison sentences. Now, gentlemen, condemn me!" (Luxemburg, 2011b: 492). Brave idealist words that were immediately printed, becoming a pamphlet on the very next day, being widely distributed in the streets of Berlin and other major industrial centers across Germany.

5 Concluding

Rosa Luxemburg's mixture of idealism and realism is not necessarily evenly balanced, and the relative weight of each is not our primary concern here. But it might as well constitute a topic for further research, just like the pejorative connotation that she gives to 'utopianism', as opposed to the highly valued tone she dispenses for 'idealism'. Other fruitful path is to inquire if she tends to be more realist when it comes to international politics, while retaining idealism for the domestic realm.[34] Our main purpose here was to show that Luxemburg's

---

[33] There is no full English translation (as far as we know) of this speech. There is a Portuguese translation (Loureiro 2011), taken from the German original, which we use here, retranslated by the author of this chapter into English.

[34] This, of course, is in tune with the line of reasoning developed by R.B.J. Walker (1993) and Richard Ashley (1988) about the 'inside/outside' dichotomy in IR and the political effects of the 'anarchy theses'. If true, this would make her closer to the mainstream, being one more reason to include her into IR 'great debates'.

Marxist approach to world politics can be considered part of IR's theoretical toolkit and to encourage a serious engagement of IR students with her original texts. Hence, this chapter is far from an exhaustive work, being rather a modest contribution to the growing collaborative effort to take Marxism seriously in IR, of which this book certainly constitutes an important part.

Idealism and realism are not IR creatures. They are part of a longstanding tradition of political thinking and action. If they find themselves separated as opposed beings in IR debates, this is because of the peculiar composition of this field of studies. And even there, in mainstream IR, such opposition is to be questioned: the person who allegedly imported such dichotomic tropes to IR – E.H. Carr – unlike the caricatural images of political realism that try to make us believe otherwise, never took side in this eternal debate precisely because he advocated for a dialectical synthesis of both. Something that should be the result of the amalgamation of idealism 'and' realism, which is also the position of figures such as John Herz, even though he was not at all sympathetic to Marxism like Carr was.

In fields other than IR, then, this fabricated separation of idealism and realism – this fictitious, antagonistic debate, or 'myth', in the words of IR revisionist historians – is not even rehearsed. The Marxist tradition, for instance, has always welcomed (one might say it was constituted by) both realism and idealism simultaneously (Halliday, 1994: 50). If that is a good thing or not; if it leads to good politics or sound policymaking, that is a different matter (our answer would be yes, to both). What is certain, at this point, is that such structuring division of IR's so-called First Great Debate also finds itself present, but in the form of a dialectical totality, in the works of major Marxist thinkers at the historical contexts around the two world wars of the twentieth century.

The example of Rosa Luxemburg demonstrates it clearly. Hence, the attempt to erase Marxism from the official history of IR since its beginnings must be confronted: either to correct this important theoretical negligence, thus helping the revisionist effort of bringing more rigor to the story of the First Debate; or even to improve the quality and impact that IR theorizing can have on policymaking, especially in our understanding of war and peace, through the incorporation of certain dimensions that only Marxists seem to give priority in their appraisals of international politics, such as the logics of capitalism as system, the clashes of imperialisms, and class struggles at the global level. A task which is not easy, even if so necessary in times when nuclear confrontation among great powers again haunts the world, "when the security dilemma", as Herz says, becomes "more clear-cut than it ever was before": fears of atomic annihilation inspired him to search for a 'Realist Idealism', which is, unfortunately, "the most difficult of arts" and "the most difficult of sciences" (1950: 179–180).

In a situation like this, all help is necessary. Marxism must be truly invited into the conversations happening in IR theory, since the start, i.e., since the First Great Debate. Firstly, because it was there already, not only embodied in one major participant (Carr), but also through the voices of Marxist leaders and theoreticians, like Rosa Luxemburg, that were debating world politics in much the same terms, at the same epoch: voices usually unheard in IR textbooks but echoed in every place of their societies back then. Secondly, and most importantly, because the epistemic community dedicated to the study of war and peace urgently needs to draw renewed inspiration from the complex formulations of great minds who devoted their lives to the elaboration of a political praxis composed by the highest idealism 'together' with a profound sense of realism. Figures like Luxemburg, who must, more than ever, guide our path, in theory and in practice, into the directions open by another well-known aphorism from her: 'war against war!'. A conclusion that she arrives at from both idealist and realist reasonings, and that should remain the "guiding line of practical policy" (1970c: 330) until imperialism prevails in world politics, as it still does today.

References

Angell N (1929) *The story of Money*. New York: Garden City Publishing Co.

Arendt H (1968) *Men in Dark Times*. New York: Harvest Books/Harcourt, Brace & World Inc.

Ashley R (1988) Untying the Sovereign State: A Double Reading of the Anarchy Problematique. *Millennium – Journal of International Studies*, 17(2), 227–262.

Ashworth L (2002) Did the Realist-Idealist Great Debate Really Happen? a Revisionist History of International Relations. *International Relations*, 16(1): 33–51.

Banks M (1985). The Inter-Paradigm Debate. In: Light M and Groom A (eds.) *International Relations: A Handbook of Current Theory*. London: Bloomsbury Academic, 7–26.

Bull H (1977) *The Anarchical Society: A Study of Order in World Politics*. London: Palgrave.

Carr EH (2001) *Twenty Years' Crisis (1919–1939): An Introduction to the Study of International Relations*. New York: Perennial Books.

Engels F (1908) *Socialism: Utopian and Scientific*. Chicago: Charles Kerr & Co.

Fellowship of Reconciliation, Pax Christi, Peace Pledge Union, Quaker Peace and Social Witness and Women's International League for Peace and Freedom (2013) *Opposing World War I: Courage and Conscience – an information briefing about conscientious objection and peace activism in the World War I* .Available (consulted in September

10, 2023) at: https://wilpf.org.uk/wp-content/uploads/2014/11/Opposing-World-War-One-21.pdf.

Halliday F (1994) *Rethinking International Relations*. London: MacMillan.

Herz J (1950) Idealist Internationalism and the Security Dilemma. *World Politics*, 2(2): 157–180.

Hobsbawm E (1989) *The Age of Empire (1875–1914)*. New York: Vintage Books.

Hoschild A (2011) *To End All Wars: A Story of Loyalty and Rebellion (1914–1918)*. Boston and New York: Hougton Mifflin Harcourt.

Keohane R (1984) *After Hegemony: Cooperation and Discord in the World Political Economy*. New Jersey: Princeton University Press.

Lapid Y (1988) The Third Debate: On the Prospects of International Theory in a Post-Positivist Era. *International Studies Quarterly*, 33(3): 235–254.

Lenin V (1970a) On the Junius Pamphlet. In: Waters MA (ed) *Rosa Luxemburg Speaks*. New York: Pathfinder.

Lenin V (1970b) Notes from a publicist. In: Waters MA (ed) *Rosa Luxemburg Speaks*. New York: Pathfinder.

Loureiro I (2011) *Rosa Luxemburgo: textos escolhidos – volume 1 (1899–1914)*. São Paulo: Editora Unesp.

Luxemburg R (1899) *The Dreyfus Affair and the Millerand Case*. Available (consulted in July 2023) at: https://www.marxists.org/archive/luxemburg/1899/11/dreyfus-affair.htm.

Luxemburg R (1909) *The National Question*. Available (consulted in July 2023) at: https://www.marxists.org/archive/luxemburg/1909/national-question/index.htm.

Luxemburg R (1970a) Peace Utopias. In: Waters MA (ed.) *Rosa Luxemburg Speaks*. New York: Pathfinder.

Luxemburg R (1970b) The Junius Pamphlet: The Crisis in the German Social Democracy. In: Waters MA (ed.) *Rosa Luxemburg Speaks*. New York: Pathfinder.

Luxemburg R (1970c) Theses on the Tasks of International Social Democracy. In: Waters MA (ed) *Rosa Luxemburg Speaks*. New York: Pathfinder.

Luxemburg R (1971a) Speech to the Hannover Congress (1899). In: Howard D (ed.) *Selected Political Writings of Rosa Luxemburg*. New York/London: Monthly Review Press.

Luxemburg R (1971b) Militia and Militarism. In: Howard D (ed.) *Selected Political Writings of Rosa Luxemburg*. New York/London: Monthly Review Press.

Luxemburg R (2011a) A Paz, a Tríplice Aliança e nós. In: Loureiro I (ed.) *Rosa Luxemburgo: textos escolhidos – volume 1 (1899–1914)*. São Paulo: Editora Unesp.

Luxemburg R (2011b) Discurso de defesa em 20 de fevereiro de 1914. In: Loureiro I (ed.) *Rosa Luxemburgo: textos escolhidos – volume 1 (1899–1914)*. São Paulo: Editora Unesp.

Luxemburg R (2004a) Slavery. In: Hudes P and Anderson K. (eds.) *The Rosa Luxemburg Reader*. New York: Monthly Review Press.

Luxemburg R (2004b) Martinique. In: Hudes P and Anderson K (eds.) *The Rosa Luxemburg Reader*. New York: Monthly Review Press.
Luxemburg R (2004c) The Beginning. In: Hudes P and Anderson K (eds.) *The Rosa Luxemburg Reader*. New York: Monthly Review Press.
Luxemburg R (2004d) The Socialization of Society. In: Hudes P and Anderson K (eds.) *The Rosa Luxemburg Reader*. New York: Monthly Review Press.
Luxemburg R (2004e) What Does the Spartacus League Want? In: Hudes P and Anderson K (eds.) *The Rosa Luxemburg Reader*. New York: Monthly Review Press.
Luxemburg R (2004f) Our Program and the Political Situation. In: Hudes P and Anderson K (eds.) *The Rosa Luxemburg Reader*. New York: Monthly Review Press.
Luxemburg R (2004g) Order Reigns in Berlin. In: Hudes P and Anderson K (eds.) *The Rosa Luxemburg Reader*. New York: Monthly Review Press.
Luxemburg R (2004h) Selected Correspondence, 1899–1917. In: Hudes P and Anderson K (eds) *The Rosa Luxemburg Reader*. New York: Monthly Review Press.
Mearsheimer J (2005) E.H. Carr vs. Idealism: The Battle Rages On. *International Relations*, 19 (2).
Quirk J and Vigneswaran D (2005) The construction of an edifice: the story of a First Great Debate. *Review of International Studies*, 31(1), 89–107.
Schmidt B (2012) The First Great Debate. *E-International Relations*. Available (consulted in July 2023) at: https://www.e-ir.info/2012/09/28/the-first-great-debate/.
Schütrumpf J (2008) *Rosa Luxemburg or the price of freedom*. Berlin: Klaus Dietz Verlag/ Rosa Luxemburg Foundation.
Thies C (2002) Progress, history and identity in international relations theory: the case of the idealist-realist debate. *European Journal of International Relations*, 8(2), 147–185.
Waever O (2013) Still a discipline after all these debates? In: Dune T, Kurkis M and Smith S (eds.) *International Relations Theory: discipline and diversity*, 3rd Edition. Oxford University Press.
Walker R (1993) *Inside/Outside: International Relations as Political Theory*. Cambridge: Cambridge University Press.
Waltz K (2001) *Man, the State and War: A Theoretical Analysis*. New York: Columbia University Press.
Waters MA (1970) *Rosa Luxemburg Speaks*. New York: Pathfinder.
Wilson P (1998) The Myth of the First Great Debate. *Review of International Studies*, 24(5),1–15.
Wilson P (2012) Where Are We Now In The Debate About The First Great Debate? *LSE Research Online*. Available (consulted in July 2023) at: http://eprints.lse.ac.uk/41819 /1/Where%20are%20we%20now%20%28LSERO%29.pdf.

CHAPTER 6

The Imperialist Chain of the Interstate Relations

Nicos Poulantzas' Theory on Imperialism

Caio Martins Bugiato[1]

1   Introduction

The following text is an explanation of the theory on imperialism contained in the studies of Nicos Poulantzas.[2] The author published his main works over a period of ten years, reinvigorating and strengthening Marxist political theory: "Political power and social classes" in 1968, "Fascism and dictatorship" in 1970, "Classes in contemporary capitalism" in 1974, "The crisis of dictatorships: Greece, Spain, and Portugal" in 1975 and "State, power, socialism" in 1978. In this text, we first present significant concepts that he elaborated before his studies on imperialism, such as social formation, social classes and class struggle, bourgeois state, and power bloc, Second, we extract the theory on imperialism from his works that address the theme, "Classes in contemporary capitalism", in which the author elaborates his theory of imperialism, and "The Crisis of dictatorships: Greece, Spain, and Portugal", in which he operationalizes it, analyzing the overthrow of dictatorial regimes in those countries[3]

The construction of Poulantzas's theory on imperialism (1978) begins with the resumption of other theories on international relations between states and bourgeoisie in the twentieth-century capitalism, to which he defers a series of criticisms. First, Poulantzas criticizes a group of authors, like Paul Sweezy

---

[1] Professor of Political Science and International Relations at the Federal Rural University of Rio de Janeiro and at the postgraduate program on International Relations of the Federal University of ABC, Brazil. Coordinator of the research group Marxist Studies on International. Researcher for the Network of Studies in International Relations and Marxism.

[2] Originally published in the Brazilian journal "Questio Juris", vol. 2, n.2, 2014. Original title: A cadeia imperialista das relações interestatais: a teoria do imperialismo de Nicos Poulantzas. Translated by Alberto Resende Jr.

[3] Some authors maintain that there is a periodization in Poulantzas' thought, as he would have passed from his affiliation with the thought of the Marxist philosopher Louis Althusser, a thought present in "Political Power and Social Classes", to the field of democratic socialism, rectifying some theoretical assumptions throughout his intellectual trajectory, concentrated in "State, power, socialism". For such periodization, see Codato (2008).

and Harry Magdoff, named as participants in Karl Kautsky's updated version of the ultra-imperialism. For Poulantzas they underestimate the inter-imperialist contradictions based on uneven development: they only see in the imperialist chain (the group of imperialist states) the delimitation that separates on one side the imperialist metropolises and on the other the dominated countries (periphery). This means that there are no conflicts and contradictions in the central countries of capitalism; they identify the relations of the metropolises among themselves based on pacification and integration under the domination of US capital.

The second criticism is directed at two theses that have a common basis, which states and bourgeoisies are autonomous and independent of each other at the international level, and the process of internationalization of capital only reaches the economic level. On the one hand, authors such as Ernest Mandel, in addition to adopting the same and unique delimitation of the previous thesis, analyze the inter-imperialist contradictions as they were in the past: autonomous and independent states and bourgeoisie in the struggle for hegemony, disregarding the complex interdependence among them, as if they were related only on the external plane, considering at best market connections. However, in a contradictory way, in those international relations, hegemony takes place as in the past, with the construction of hegemonic centers (empires) over dominated and dependent countries. On the other hand, the analysis of the Western communist parties, particularly the French one, in which the internationalization of capital affects only the productive forces, which creates a kind of 'cosmopolitan capital' or 'cosmopolitan capitals'. Thus, autonomous and independent states and bourgeoisies have an agreement at the economic level, under the domination of US capital, in which the (cosmopolitan) monopolies are assigned to pursuit of high rates of profit. For Poulantzas, those theorists were unable to apprehend the changes in the imperialist chain, especially the relations among the imperialist metropolises. Let's look at the author's theory then.

2 Conceptual Explanations

Before approaching Poulantzas' theory of imperialism, it is necessary to explain the concepts of social formation, social classes and class struggle, bourgeois state, and power bloc, which are present in this theory. For now, we need to understand that social formation means the concrete and simultaneous existence of several modes of production in a given location with a predominance of one of them. Social formations "are the effective places of existence and reproduction of modes and forms of production", "they comprise several modes of production, in a specific articulation", and "these modes of production only exist and reproduce in historically determined social formations" (Poulantzas, 1978: 23–24). Thus, every social formation, in its predominant base, has an ultimate determination in the economic sphere. In the case of a capitalist social formation, in general, what prevails are the production relations in which the workers, deprived of the means of production and 'free' to negotiate their labor power in the market, become wage earners of the bourgeoisie, which, on the other hand, derives its profits from the extortion of surplus labor.

In a social formation where the capitalist mode of production is dominant, the functions of the state are related to the levels of economy, ideology, and politics. At the economic level, the function of the legal system is, in general, to organize the production process, regulate contracts for the purchase and sale of labor power, and regulate capitalist exchanges. At the ideological level, the state establishes norms for education, communication, and information systems at the national level. Moreover, in politics, the role of the state consists in maintaining political order in the conflict among classes. Those functions cannot be seized if they are not inserted in the global political role of the state: the maintenance of the unity of a social formation within which the domination of some class(es) over another(s) takes place. In this way, the functions of the state in the economy and the ideological plane are not technical and/or neutral but constitute political functions insofar as they aim at maintaining the unity of the social formation.

Class struggle is present in every social formation, a struggle that fundamentally opposes the bourgeoisie and the proletariat. For Poulantzas, "social classes are a set of social agents determined mainly, but not exclusively, by their place in the production process, that is, in the economic sphere" (Poulantzas, 1978: 13–14). Social classes mean conflict, as each pursues its specific interests, contrary (but not always) to the interests of other classes. A social class is defined by its set of social practices, that is, by its place in the production process, the political actions it takes, and its ideological position. That means that a set of social agents establishes themselves as a social class to the extent that its unity crosses the economic, political, and ideological spheres.

Such concepts are necessary for us to understand the state in general. The state is a cohesion factor of a social formation traversed by class struggle. The state is the factor of order and regulator of the overall balance of the system, whose purpose is to maintain the unity of a social formation, its function, and its reproduction. It reflects the contradictions of social formation, which is the antagonism among social classes. Ultimately, the state prevents the annihilation of social classes, which means that it prevents the destruction of a social formation (Poulantzas, 1977). Therefore, the definition of a bourgeois (or capitalist) state is based on a type of state that organizes a particular mode of class domination and on a state that corresponds[4] to capitalist production relations (Saes, 1985). Let us see.

The bourgeois state, the core of the juridical-political structure of the capitalist mode of production, is conceptually an articulated system of four elements: bourgeois (or capitalist) law, bureaucratism, the isolation effect, and the representation of unity effect. Bourgeois law,[5] legal values that regulate and frame the economic practices and social relations conditioned by it, consists of attributing to all production agents, regardless of the place they occupy in the production process, the condition of 'equal' and 'free' individual subjects, capable of lawfully performing acts of will. Bureaucratism[6] (bureaucratic values) determines that a) all production agents, regardless of their place in the production process, have formal access to the practices that regulate and frame the economic practices and social relations conditioned by them (universal access to the state bureaucracy) and that b) the agents of such practices

---

4 The term correspondence is in opposition to the economicist and mechanistic way that considers the formation and organization of the capitalist state as a reflection of the dominance of capitalist production relations in a social formation. Correspondence does not consist of a one-to-one causal relationship. A particular type of state corresponds to a particular type of production relations "to the extent that only a specific legal-political structure makes the reproduction of production relations possible" (Saes, 1985: 26). Only the bourgeois state makes possible the reproduction of capitalist production relations (Saes, 1985).

5 We may consider the law as a "set of rules (written or not) that discipline and regularize the relations between production agents [...] in order to enable their reiteration" (Saes, 1985: 36) and that "it also establishes predictability in the relationships between agents and, therefore, also creates the possibility of repetition" (Saes, 1985: 36). Saes (1985) lists the components of bourgeois law: the law, a system of norms imposed on production agents – constitution, codes, etc., and the law enforcement process, the implementation of its imposing character. Both are part of a material and human organization, the judiciary, which creates the conditions for the reproduction of capitalist production relations.

6 Bourgeois bureaucratism is the particular way of organizing the set of material and human resources of the bourgeois type of state. The elements of this set are the armed forces and the collecting forces (agents that collect various taxes destined for the maintenance and functioning of the state). In this way, bourgeois bureaucratism is the particular way in which the bourgeois state organizes the armed forces and the collecting forces. It is not restricted to the armed forces and collectors; it encompasses other branches of the state apparatus such as administration and the judiciary. According to Saes (1985), bureaucratism derives from two fundamental norms: a) "the non-monopolization of State tasks – armed forces and collecting forces – by the exploiting class or the non-prohibition of access to these tasks by members of the exploited class" (Saes, 1985: 39) and b) "hierarchization of the state's tasks according to the criterion of competence, that is, the level of knowledge required of those willing to perform them" (Saes, 1985: 39).

are hierarchical, so that this scaling does not appear as subordination, but formally as a gradation of individual competences required by the different tasks of this social activity (Saes, 1998).

Capitalist bureaucratic values constitute the expression and deployment, on a more restricted level, of capitalist legal values; one is the condition of existence of the other, forming a unit. If, on the one hand, law defines production agents as 'free' and 'equal' individuals, they all have the right to claim the performance of bureaucratic practices. On the other hand, the hierarchization of agents in charge of carrying out bureaucratic practices (non-prohibition of access to these tasks to members of the exploited class) is formalized through the criterion of individual competence for the performance of tasks. These elements conceptually allow for the unity of the capitalist political-legal structure (Saes, 1998).

According to Poulantzas (1977), this political-legal structure produces political-ideological effects on production agents: the isolation effect and the representation of unity effect. Capitalist legal values combine with the economic structure (which atomizes the collective of direct producers) and produce the isolation or individualization effect. That consists in the regular reproduction of capitalist production relations by a) encouraging the economic practice of seeking by its own will (and not by extra-economic coercion) the individualized sale of labor force to an individual owner of the means of production and b) preventing the emergence of political practice through which workers take a collective stand against the owner of the means of production. Bureaucratic values, by converting the agents in charge of regulating and framing economic practices and social relations conditioned by them into a 'universalist', and 'competent' bureaucracy, allow such a group to ideologically unify all agents. They, already individualized by the isolation effect, then constitute a symbolic community: the 'nation people' composed of all production agents inserted in a given territory. This process, linked to the isolation effect, is qualified as the representation of unit effect. That contributes to the reproduction of capitalist production relations insofar as it frustrates the constitution of antagonistic social groups (social classes) by bringing them together in the 'nation-people' represented in a state of supposed universal access, the nation-state.

The Marxist tradition follows the statement by Marx and Engles, in the "Communist Manifesto", according to which the modern state is the executive committee of the common business of the entire bourgeois class, to conceive the bourgeois State as the representation of the domination of class. A question arises here: if the state tends to isolate people as individuals and reunite them as a 'nation people', how does the bourgeoisie (that also suffer the effects of isolation and unity) manage to take over the state to fulfill their interests and become the ruling class? According to Poulantzas, the function of the state as a maintainer of the unity of a capitalist social formation is the fundamental objective of the bourgeoisie: maintenance of existing social relations. Moreover, in order to achieve this, the conservation of the State is essential. This practice of the bourgeoisie of conservation of social relations is what gives unity to the class. In addition, its ideological operation, which "consists in the fact of trying to impose, on society as a whole, a 'way of life' through which the state will be lived as representative of the 'general interest' of society, as holder of the keys to the universal in the face of 'private individuals'" (Poulantzas, 1977: 209), constitutes it as a social force. The bourgeois state "does not directly represent the economic interests of the dominant classes, but their political interests: it is the center of the political power of the ruling classes insofar as it is the organizing factor of their political struggle" (Poulantzas, 1977: 185). Ensuring class domination is part of the role of the state, as the state as an institution does not have its power. It is worth noting that power, for Poulantzas, is the ability of a social class or fraction to carry out its specific interests.

The author elucidates the complex relationship between the ruling class, its fractions, and the bourgeois State by the concept of the power bloc. The power bloc is the contradictory unit of the fractions of the bourgeois class around general objectives – referring to the maintenance of capitalist production relations – a unit that does not eliminate the particular objectives of each fraction. The power bloc is not an explicit political agreement but a community of interests of the owners of the social means of production. Its unity is guaranteed by the common interest of the fractions to directly or indirectly govern the State, making it meet their general interests (the maintenance of private ownership of the means of production and the reproduction of the labor force as a commodity) and specific to each fraction. The state is, therefore, a factor in the political unity of the power bloc (Poulantzas, 1977).

In the power bloc articulation, there is a tendency towards the formation of a hegemonic core composed of one (or more) fractions, the hegemonic fraction. Hegemony is conquered through the ability of a fraction to make its particular interests prevail within the power bloc, as the fraction can obtain priority benefits, mainly from the state's economic policy (that is, other state policies, such as social and foreign policy, are also relevant)[7]. State policies (especially

---

7 Two illuminating observations. First, the economic preponderance of one fraction over the others is not an indicator of hegemony. That is, it does not mean that a greater share in the profits of global surplus value that determines hegemony. Economic policy must be a privileged criterion for detecting hegemony within the power bloc. The process of formulating

economic policy) provoke the constitution of fractions and, at the same time, indicate their position within the bloc. The relationship between the bourgeois state and the fractions take place in the sense of its political unity under the aegis of one (or more) hegemonic fraction.[8] As we have already said, the class or fraction that holds power, as the State does not have its own power.

3   The Theory on Imperialism

Once those concepts are known, we already have enough elements to understand how Poulantzas deals with relations among (bourgeois) States. For Poulantzas (1978), the capitalist mode of production (CMP) is characterized by the concomitant double tendency of reproduction in a social formation, where other modes of production are consolidated and dominated, and of extension to abroad. The second, caused by the tendency of the rate of profit to fall, is marked predominantly by the export of capital concerning the export of goods. Poulantzas – agreeing with Vladimir Lenin (1991) – calls imperialism this tendency of capital towards abroad, in which the export of capital predominates and its destination is the exploitation of other social formations. The capitalist state system, the set of social formations in which the capitalist mode of production prevails, suffers from an unequal development of the productive forces and production relations. That means that different countries have different 'degrees' of development of the capitalist mode of production in their territory, resulting in a delimitation of the current between imperialist metropolises – autochthonous centers of capital accumulation/ 'advanced capitalism' – and dominated and dependent social formations (DDSF) – externally dependent accumulation process / 'backward capitalism'.

---

an economic policy means that the particular interests of a fraction are satisfied to the detriment of others. Thus, such a process is a field of struggle where issues of class interests are decided, and its result reflects the power relations between the ruling fractions (Perissinoto, 1994). Second, a class fraction that is not preponderant in the economic sphere can conquer political hegemony, which serves to leverage its new economic preponderance. However, in the medium and long term, the trend is the correspondence between political hegemony and economic preponderance. "It is when a policy anticipating economic preponderance becomes a policy of adaptation to this prevalence" (Farias, 2010: 31).

8   For Poulantzas, hegemony has two fields of action: within the power bloc among the fractions of the bourgeoisie and from the power bloc to the dominated classes, a process analyzed by Antonio Gramsci in which the way of life and the interests of the ruling class are rooted in the thinking of the dominated classes.

Imperialism, according to the author, can be distinguished in phases. First, the transition from competitive capitalism to monopoly capitalism, that goes from the end of the nineteenth century to the interwar period, in which monopolies were formed in the metropolises and there was a balance between the form of export of goods and the form of export of capital. Second, the consolidation phase of the imperialist stage (after the 1929 crisis), in which the metropolises monopoly capitalism dominates competitive capitalism. In those two phases, the DDSF went from simple conditions of a colonial and commercial capitalist type (export of agricultural products) to conditions in which the CMP prevails, in unequal 'degrees' and obviously lagging behind the metropolises. The dominance of the CMP did not extinguish the other modes and forms of production but progressively eliminated the old dichotomy of metropolis/city/industry versus dominated formations/countryside/agriculture, giving rise to the so-called underdevelopment or peripheral industrialization.

> It is no longer about social constructions of relatively external relations. The process of imperialist domination and dependence now appears as the reproduction, within the dominated social formations and in specific forms for each of them, of the relationship of domination that links it to the imperialist metropolises.
> POULANTZAS, 1978: 46[9]

During these two phases, regarding the relationship between the imperialist metropolises, the inter-imperialist contradictions provoked the alternating predominance of one metropolis over the other (Great Britain, the United States, Germany), a predominance based on the domination and exploitation that each one imposes on its DDSF 'empire'[10] and on the pace of capitalist

---

[9] Poulantzas continues: "A social formation is dominated and dependent when the articulation of its own economic, political and ideological structure expresses constitutive and asymmetrical relations, with one or several social formations that occupy, concerning the first, a situation of power" (Poulantzas, 1978: 47). One issue only mentioned by the author is that such asymmetrical relations have repercussions on class relations and the state apparatus of the dominated formation, reproducing the forms of domination of the class(es) in power in the dominant social formation. That is, those forms of domination correspond to forms of exploitation of the popular masses in an indirect way (when the foreign bourgeoisie exploits through the local bourgeoisie) or directly (when the foreign bourgeoisie directly exploits local workers). A similar question was raised by Ruy Mauro Marini when he dealt in his studies, among them "Dialectic of dependency" (1973), with the overexploitation of labor in dependent countries in Latin America.

[10] Gerson Moura, in his book "Autonomy in dependency" (1980), refers to such empires as systems of power.

development within the metropolis itself. Third, after the end of World War II, what Poulantzas calls the current phase, which retains the characteristics of the consolidation phase, emphasizing the dominance of the CMP in the DDSF not simply from the outside, but rather through its dominance within the latter, where the mode of production in the metropolises is reproduced in a specific way. Reproduction that provokes in those formations the accommodation of capital in forms of light industry and inferior technology, the exploitation of the labor force mainly through low wages – maintaining its low qualification – reserving qualified work for the central countries, the existence of sectors isolated with high concentrations of capital and labor productivity and a high degree of expatriation of profits (Poulantzas, 1976). That process the author calls internalized and induced reproduction, which affects economic, political (including State apparatuses), and ideological relations.

This uneven development does not constitute for Poulantzas a remnant of impurity in the CMP due to its combination with other modes of production: it is the constitutive form of the reproduction of capitalism on a world scale in the imperialist stage, in its relations with other social formations that contain other modes of production. This internationalization of the CMP, or its current phase for the author, tending to cover all corners of the world, is not an integration of social formations but the internalized and induced reproduction of the CMP of the metropolises in the DDSF.

The current phase (for Poulantzas) of the international division of labor – imperialist metropolises versus DDSF – introduces another new line of demarcation. A demarcation in the inter-imperialist field: on one side, the hegemonic metropolis, the United States, and on the other, the imperialist metropolises of Europe. The relationship between both is marked by the predominance of US monopoly capital and its internalized and induced reproduction within other metropolises, equally reproducing US imperialism's political and ideological conditions. This dependency relationship, however, is not identical to that between metropolises and DDSF, as metropolises continue to constitute autochthonous centers of capital accumulation.

Poulantzas (1978) identifies elements of this new demarcation under the hegemony of US capital, modified by the tendency of the rate of profit to fall. 1) The growth of the global volume of US investments in the post-war period created a gap between this country and the other metropolises. 2) The privileged destination of the US capital is no longer the peripheral formations but the European metropolises. 3) These investments are mostly direct (in fixed capital and/or that tend to take control of companies) to the detriment of portfolio investment (purchase of short-term financial/stock exchange operations) and, in comparison with the formations' peripheral regions, the reinvestment of profits in the region is significantly greater. 4) Most US investment in Europe is in the manufacturing industry (productive capital) to the detriment of the extractive industry (raw materials) and the service and trade sectors, while European direct investment in the US is mostly in the service sector. 5) US investments in Europe come from branches of high concentration and centralization of capital (monopoly) and go towards branches of strong concentration. US productive capital imposes the concentration of the European productive capital; the branches invested are those with more advanced technology and rapid expansion, that is, with high productivity and intensive exploitation of labor due to the high organic composition of capital[11]. 6) The export of US capital to Europe also includes the concentration of money capital, large banks, and financial holdings, which does not mean that the accumulation of capital and its rate of profit is determined by the valuation D – D', but this goes along with investments in the cycle of productive capital.[12] All those elements converge towards one objective: a high exploitation rate to counterbalance the tendency of the rate of profit to fall. Therein lies the motive for the induced and internalized reproduction of monopoly capital in external social formations.

In short, the current phase of imperialism for Poulantzas is composed of the internationalization of the capital process described above (in which the US is not the only exporter of capital) and the international socialization of labor processes. This in general means, the constitution, under single ownership, of effective complex production units closely articulated and integrated with labor processes, whose various establishments are distributed in several countries. The empirical synthesis of these elements is the transnational industrial companies, which, in addition to dominating production, dominate

---

11   Poulantzas explain the shift of US investments to Europe as a process of dislocation of exploration. "This shift is itself a function of the main character of monopoly concentration: the rise in the organic composition of capital, that is, the increase in constant capital concerning variable capital (wage costs), and the decrease in living labor about 'dead labor' (embodied in the means of labor). This high organic capital composition, inversely proportional to the rate of profit, is where the current trend toward technological innovations is inscribed. But labor always remains the basis of surplus value: this is what explains the current tendency towards an increase in the rate of exploitation due to the main deviation from intensive exploitation of labor, directly linked to the productivity of the worker (relative surplus value)" (Poulantzas, 1978: 68).

12   Poulantzas differentiates banking capital, capital in the form of money, which corresponds to a stage of the production process in which banks operate mainly and can become a class fraction, from finance capital, which is not a fraction of capital like the others, but a joint process and the mode of functioning of several capitals gathered in search of valorization.

international exchanges since trade among units (especially located in metropolises) accounts for a high percentage of world trade.

Before entering into the political relations of imperialism (because so far, we have addressed economic relations), it is necessary to reaffirm, then, that the international division of labor in the state system has two dynamics (intertwined): on the one hand, imperialist metropolis-DDSF relations and on the other the metropolis-metropolis relations. Each one presents a distinct form of exploitation. The exploitation of the popular masses in the DDSF by the ruling class of the metropolis takes place primarily indirectly (through the local ruling class) and secondarily directly (foreign capital invested in its interior). In the metropolis-metropolis relationship, the direct form is the main one and the indirect one secondary[13] (Poulantzas, 1978). Therefore, we can say that for Poulantzas, there is an international system of bourgeois states divided into metropolises and DDSF, in which imperialism is the relationship (capital is, above all, a social relationship, as Marx demonstrates in "The Capital") that takes place many times (but not always) among them, through the internalized and induced reproduction of the MPC. Imperialism is nothing friendly, to use the author's words, it is a power relationship in which the state plays a decisive role. Let us go to them.

Once defined the concepts of the bourgeois state, social classes, and power bloc, let us deal with the bourgeoisie. The bourgeoisie is a class endowed with complex heterogeneity. Its economic cleavages are given by the cycle of capital reproduction (commercial, industrial, banking capital, etc.), by the concentration and centralization of capital (large and medium and monopolist and non-monopolist), by relations with imperialism (national, inner and comprador bourgeoisie), among other aspects, as well as the political and ideological dimensions that can generate the formation of a certain class fraction. These cleavages can combine in varied and dynamic ways and as a basis for the agglutination or political division of fractions. Whether or not such cleavages favor the formation of bourgeois fractions depends on the circumstances and the reaction of these sectors of the bourgeoisie, mainly in the face of the state's economic policy.

---

13 An example that clarifies such relationships can be found in dependent industrialization. In this process, the peripheral bourgeoisie acquires machinery and equipment (outdated for the central countries) from abroad, needing, in addition to the high-profit rate, to pay interest and amortization. Hence, the high intensity of labor exploitation related to the exploitation of the local bourgeoisie and the condition of dependence on the central bourgeoisie. In the case of the metropolis-metropolis relationship, foreign capital is present within the social formation, directly exploiting workers.

In this text, we are particularly interested in the relations between the bourgeoisie and imperialism. According to Poulantzas (1976 and 1978), the fractions of this class are distinguished into the comprador bourgeoisie, the national bourgeoisie, and the inner bourgeoisie. The comprador bourgeoisie is the fraction whose interests are directly subordinated to those of foreign capital, which serves as a direct intermediary for the implantation and reproduction of foreign capital within a social formation. The interference of foreign capital "can only, in general, play a decisive role in the various dependent countries [...] by articulating, in those countries, with internal power relations" (Poulantzas, 1976: 20). This fraction does not have its accumulation base and generally has its activity linked to land ownership (DDSF) and speculation, concentrated in financial, banking, and commercial sectors, but equally able to operate in industrial branches, in those wholly subordinated and dependent on foreign capital. From the political-ideological point of view, it is the support and agent of imperialist capital. The national bourgeoisie is an autochthonous fraction, which has its own accumulation base within the social formation and political-ideological autonomy vis-à-vis imperialist capital. At certain junctures, in alliance with the dominated classes, this faction can adopt an anti-imperialist stance and/or get involved in a national liberation struggle. The inner bourgeoisie occupies an intermediate position between the comprador bourgeoisie and the national bourgeoisie, presenting contradictions with foreign capital. It has its own accumulation base, thus trying to limit the presence of foreign capital in the domestic market, but at the same time, it is dependent on this capital in areas such as investment and technology.[14]

> The inner bourgeoisie, on the contrary, despite being dependent on foreign capital, presents contradictions concerning it. Firstly, because it feels frustrated at sharing the pie of exploitation of the masses: the leonine transfer of surplus value is carried out to its detriment and in favor of foreign capital and its agents, the comprador bourgeoisie. Secondly, because concentrated, mainly in the industrial sector, it is interested in industrial development (...) and in state intervention that guarantees some domains within the country and that would make it more competitive in the face of foreign capital. It wants the expansion and development of the internal market through a small increase in the purchasing power and consumption of the masses, which would offer

---

14   Poulantzas formulates the concept of the inner bourgeoisie because, according to him, the old dichotomy between the national bourgeoisie and the comprador bourgeoisie does not explain the movement of bourgeois fractions in the current phase of imperialism.

it more outlets. Finally, it seeks help from the State, which would allow
them to develop exports.

POULANTZAS, 1976: 36–37

The emergence of this fraction is linked to the induced and interiorized reproduction of the capitalist relations in the various social formations – both peripheral and central – being dependent on the internationalization processes of capital under the aegis of foreign capital. Such dependence, among other factors, explains its political-ideological weakness and its consequent impossibility of exercising long-term hegemony over the power bloc.

Rejecting the theses about the process of suppression that the national States would be suffering,[15] Poulantzas (1978) affirm that the states, central and peripheral, that are in charge of the interests of capital (through public subsidies, tax exemptions, industrial policy favorable to certain interests, etc.) either in the metropolis-metropolis relationship or in the metropolis-DDSF relationship. The national state intervenes in the struggle between classes and class fractions, organizing hegemony and hierarchy in the power bloc. Thus, the power bloc cannot be apprehended on a purely national level but rather in a complex international system of bourgeois states in which each state is in charge of the interests of 'national' and foreign capital in a social formation, organizing the intra-bourgeois correlation of forces and constituting a certain configuration in the power bloc. In this configuration, the hegemonic fraction has its interests primarily served by state policies to the detriment of other fractions. The State is both an arena and an actor and not an instrument that can be manipulated at the will of the ruling class. It is an arena of struggle among fractions of the bourgeoisie, in which one (or a group) of them assumes the condition of hegemonic power. Thus, in its foreign relations, the State is an actor in international politics and in the universal reproduction of capital, that represents primarily the interests of the hegemonic fraction of its power bloc.[16]

---

15 On this debate, see Bugiato (2011).
16 Poulantzas briefly comments on the ideological conditions (ideas, practices, habits, modes, rituals) of the induced and interiorized reproduction of imperialism, saying that the extension of metropolitan ideological forms in the DDSF has as its main characteristic a profound disarticulation of 'original ideological sectors' provoking a false image of a dualistic society (advanced versus backward). While in non-hegemonic metropolises, such an extension affects practices and modes related to production (knowledge), creating an image of only economic backwardness (Poulantzas, 1978). The author also makes quick comments on the problem that the unequal development of the countries of the

4 Conclusion

From the historical point of view, Poulantzas' theory of imperialism has a high explanatory power on the development of capitalism in the post-war period. As for the relations between the metropolises, the author identifies the consolidation of the United States as the hegemonic State in the capitalist world and clarifies that their relations with the European States were not at all friendly concerning the ruling classes and class fractions. The role that the US capital played in the reconstruction of Europe fulfilled essential functions for the states and bourgeoisie of the old continent, such as the development and dynamization of capital accumulation, building the dynamic axis of world capitalist accumulation in the post-war period (USA-Europe). In addition, the preservation of Europeans in the capitalist world, given the polarization of the Cold War, however generating friction among the class fractions more and less likely to accept the interference of foreign capital interests. Regarding the relations between metropolises and the DDSF, peripheral countries such as Latin America bargained their industrialization processes with imperialist capital, preserving the dependency relations (not in the same format) established since the colony. In the case of Brazil, after 1930, governments negotiated national industrialization mainly with US capital, which in the post-war period was interested in its economic and strategic-military objectives in Europe. In the so-called developmental period (1930–1985), the Brazilian big bourgeoisie was divided into 'deliverers', those who claimed ample participation of imperialist capital in national industrialization, and 'nationalists', those who defended a more autonomous development of Brazilian capitalism. The Brazilian big bourgeoisie was never national (in Poulantzas' terms), given that the Brazilian economy was born subordinate to the external market and its modernization process was always associated with imperialism in its different phases. What was at stake in Brazil was the degree of that association, a game played on the front line between the comprador bourgeoisie and the inner bourgeoisie.

In the imperialism theory, Poulantzas anticipates a debate that emerged in the 1990s. The so-called globalization led intellectuals of different theoretical shades to decree the decline or end of the national state since its sovereignty and authority would be victims of the irreversible triumph of the global market; people, goods, investments, services, knowledge, technology, information would circulate freely in a world economy without borders, destroying the

---

imperialist chain entails, such as rural exodus, urban concentration, unemployment and marginality, and social tensions intensified by immigration (Poulantzas, 1976).

traditional forms and functions of the state. Poulantzas (1976 and 1978), analyzing the internationalization of capital in the 1970s, finds that this process does not suppress and does not undermine national States, either in terms of the triumph of the global market or in terms of the formation of a supranational state on the rubble of old institutions. On the contrary, the States are the nodes of the internationalization process and privileged targets of the struggles among the fractions of the bourgeoisie, for they are responsible for incorporating or rejecting the interests of imperialist capital within the social formation, just as they are responsible for representing the interests of the power bloc at the international level. The state's legal-political structure, which celebrates international agreements and treaties, allows the export of capital and goods, defines exchange rates, interest, customs taxes, and the protectionist policy in general, and resolves commercial disputes in international organizations, among other prerogatives.

Lastly, Poulantzas' contribution to the study of International Relations is expressive. Fred Halliday, in "Rethinking International Relations" (2002), wrote that those who do not want to talk about capitalism should not debate international relations; and that (Marxist) imperialism rarely had a foothold in this area. Poulantzas places capitalism as a central structure in the analysis of the international system and imperialism as a fundamental concept for understanding international relations. Furthermore, his theoretical instruments contribute to alternatives in the study of international relations, given that it differs from the dominant theories in the field (which rarely touch on the issue of capitalism and imperialism), providing a more complex theory related to the interaction between social classes, state and international politics and remains relevant to the current reality and its transformation. "It is evident that a country's dependence on imperialism can only be broken by a national liberation process [...] that includes a process of transition to socialism" (Poulantzas, 1976: 18).

References

Bugiato C (2011) Declinio do Estado-nação? Unpublished dissertation of masters. University of Campinas, Campinas.

Codato A (2008) Poulantzas, o Estado e a revolução. *Revista Crítica Marxista*. São Paulo: Editora Unesp, v. 27, p. 65–85.

Farias F (2010) Estado e classes dominantes no Brasil (1930–1964). Unpublished doctoral thesis. University of Campinas. Campinas.

Halliday F (2002) *Rethinking International Relations*. Vancouver: Univ of British Columbia Pr.

Lenin V (1991) *O imperialismo: fase superior do capitalismo*. São Paulo: Global.

Marini R (1973) *Dialectica de la dependencia*. México, DF: Era.

Moura G (1980) Autonomia na dependência. Rio de Janeiro: Nova Fronteira.

Perissinotto R (1994) *Classes dominantes e hegemonia na República Velha*. Campinas: Editora da Unicamp.

Poulantzas N (1976), Nicos. *A crise das ditaduras*. Rio de Janeiro: Paz e Terra, 1976.

Poulantzas N (1978) *As classes sociais no capitalismo de hoje*. Rio de Janeiro: Zahar.

Poulantzas N (1977) *Poder político e classes sociais*. São Paulo: Martins Fontes, 1977.

Saes D (1985) A *formação do Estado burguês no Brasil*. Rio de Janeiro: Paz e terra.

Saes D (1998) A questão da autonomia relativa do Estado em Poulantzas. *Crítica Marxista*, n. 7.

CHAPTER 7

Hegemonic Struggle and Populism

Agonistic Solutions to the Identity Challenge

Mayra Goulart da Silva[1]

1 Introduction

The object of this chapter is the concepts of Hegemonic Struggle and Populism presented in the works of Chantal Mouffe and Ernesto Laclau, which will be analyzed from the hypothesis that both formulations mark a turning point in theory and praxis that goes beyond the limits of traditional Marxism.[2] Thus, after substantiating this argument through a brief genealogy of the concepts, three axiological developments of this movement will be pointed out.

The first development concerns the conceptual framework established in "Hegemony and Socialist Strategy" (HSS) which, although written twenty years before the publication of "On Populist Reason" (PR), offers us an interesting theoretical instrument for understanding the political goals of the Laclaunian recovery of the concept of populism. These purposes result in the creation of a category capable of positively framing the new leaderships that were ascending electorally in Latin America at the beginning of the 21st century. With this, Laclau uses his own reflection as a tool of the hegemonic struggle waged in the region, reconciling theory and praxis in one movement.

The second development, in turn, aims to frame this new meaning of the concept of 'hegemonic struggle', as a synthesis of antipodal theoretical formulations that aim to deal with the question of the general will and, consequently, the emergence of political identities, overcoming the gap created by the implosion of metaphysical foundations that supported the belief of the proletariat as a universal subject.

The third development, finally, concerns this new way of conceiving the process of identity formation in which subjects are presented without any allusion to transcendent contents, identities or essences, being understood, therefore, as a product of a particular historical and linguistic context, ephemeral

---

[1] Professor of Political Science at Federal University of Rio de Janeiro (UFRJ).
[2] Article originally published in the Brazilian journal "Revista Sul-Americana de Ciência Política", vol. 4, n. 1, 2018. Translated into English by the author.

and unstable by definition. In this dynamic of production of immanent identities, populism emerges as a particularly efficient operator for questioning the 'status quo', which would allow us to view it as a 'counter-hegemonic' tool understood as an effort to break with the political structures committed to a global economic system defined by the oppression of the lower classes. In view of this, my goal will be to outline the risks of such association, since the possible (but not necessary) connections between populism and Caesarism can drain the emancipatory potential of the movements engaged in the hegemonic struggle.

2 Populism and Hegemonic Struggle in Latin America: Theory and Praxis in the Work of Chantal Mouffe and Ernesto Laclau

Polysemic, controversial and cliché, the concept of populism can be used as a marker of the turns that Latin American political thought and praxis have taken. This compass function, which is able to lead the interested observer through the labyrinthine paths of political history of this subcontinent, results from the sensitivity of the concept to mood swings in the region, but also from the recurrence of some of its themes such as personalism, multiclass and the weakness of liberal institutions. In particular, such recurrence is associated with a structure in which civil society has little room for the exercise of autonomy, given the excessive concentration of economic resources and, consequently, political power, in the hands of local leaders lacking national projects subsequent to the maintenance of their power.

Given this, political elites who aim to implement a programmatic agenda at the national level depend on the regimentation capacity of these two elements, whose interests are mostly antagonistic. Throughout history, however, the combination between the two has often occurred in inversely proportional terms, that is, the more support from the elites, the less the need to dispute the support of the people, and vice versa. In this way, when they take the second option, seeking political support in popularity among ordinary citizens to the detriment of traditional elites, these political actors are typified as 'populists'.

Nevertheless, if we look at one of the axiological origins of the concept in this subcontinent, it is clear that the term was used as a kind of negative film in which Marxists and liberals[3] developed their impressions of nationalist

---

3 Among the countless possible references, I highlight as an example of Marxist criticism of populism the contributions of Weffort (1968) and Cardoso and Faletto (1969). Among the liberals, in turn, I highlight O'Donnell (1972) and Pereira (1991).

governments. Stimulated by the opportunities created in times of war, this type of national-developmentalism is disseminated trough Latin America, assuming several facets, such as the Argentine Juan Domingo Perón (1946–1955 and 1973–1974); the Chilean Carlos Ibañez del Campo (1927–1931 and 1952–1958); the Brazilian Getúlio Vargas (1930–1945 and 1951–1954) the Mexican Lázaro Cárdenas (1934–1940); the Peruvian Fernando Bealúnde Terry (1963–1968 and 1980–1985); and the Ecuadorian José María Velasco Ibarra (1934–1935, 1944–1947, 1952–1956, 1960–1961 and 1968–1972)[4]

In this negative film, the picture of this period is revealed by its absences. In the case of Marxists, the multiclass character of these movements is highlighted and denounced as a lack of class consciousness. In the case of liberals, the complaint revolves around the absence of an autonomous and enterprising civil society.

Until the beginning of the twenty-first century, 'populism' spread in Latin American political vocabulary as a negative category used to denounce governments that manipulated workers and co-opted economic actors, blocking the understanding of their interests and the achievement of their 'true' purposes. Ultimately, Marxists and liberals united in an understanding of the state and its operators as obstacles to the free action of those who would be responsible for progress.

The interpretations that in some way attribute or see in the State the role of operator of the transition between this traditional arrangement and modern industrial societies do not present themselves as a middle ground or as a third way between the two currents presented above, but as an essentially distinct perspective. This is the case of the reformist interpretation, presented by authors such as Gino Germani, Octavio Ianni and Torcuato Di Tella (1973) who see an intermediate strategy between fascism and the bourgeois revolution in the class alliances articulated by 'populist' discourses.

With this, these leaders would have been able to overcome the limits determined by the landowner and agro-exporter mentalities of traditional oligarchies, achieving, to a greater or lesser extent, the strengthening of the domestic market and the promotion of a protectionist trade and exchange policy, aimed at stimulating industrialization through the substitution of imports (Dorbussch and Edwards, 1991; Sachs, 1989).

However, even if they are closer in economic terms and more distant from Marxist and liberal readings, this sociology of modernization assumes different positions in the face of the political developments of the nationalist

---

4 For a more complete historiography I suggest: Ianni (1975) and Vilas (2004).

regimes in question, which are identified either as decidedly authoritarian, as in Germani's interpretation, or as Di Tella (1965) considered, as the 'possible democracy' under those circumstances (Mitre, 2008).

Advancing in time, it can be observed that, in the 1980s and 1990s, the controversy about the political developments of populism loses space for a set of considerations that focus on its economic effects, characterized as a 'cursed legacy' bequeathed by national-developmentalist governments (Dornbush and Edwards, 1991; Faucher, Ducatenzeiler and Rea, 1993; Kaufman and Stallings, 1991). As expressions of the neoliberal ideology hegemony, understood as the Washington Consensus, these approaches criticize exactly what was considered the main legacy of populism: the national-developmentalist modernizing strategies. From this perspective, these options would have resulted only in a precarious industrialization, the indebtedness of the State and the creation of a parasitic bourgeoisie.

Economic populism becomes, then, an expression used to typify expansive monetary and fiscal policies, supported by the cyclical availability of international reserves and exchange rates overvaluation. The result of these policies, in the short term, would be associated with a hyperbolic rise in inflation and, in the long term, debt crisis. In addition, when attempting to mitigate the inflationary process, these governments sometimes resorted to import subsidies, accentuating the dynamics of indebtedness and capital flight (Weyland, 2001).

The debt crisis – which erupts in different Latin American countries during the 1980s and 1990s – is, therefore, the result of a vicious cycle of currency devaluations, decrease of worker's purchase power, and government and investment revenues on the one hand, and, on the other, the reduction of economic production and the increase in unemployment (Pereira, 1991).

Faced with the imminence of a collapse of their economic systems, a consensus was formed among national elites, creditors and international actors around the implementation of stabilization measures based on the containment of fiscal spending and the freezing of wages. In this context, a group of leaders committed – in more or less explicitly way – to this agenda, that was developed through readjustment programs implemented with the assistance of the International Monetary Fund appears on the Latin American political horizon. The main examples of the period are Carlos Menem, in Argentina (1989–1999), Fernando Collor de Mello, in Brazil (1990–92) and Alberto Fujimori, in Peru (1990–2000).

However, observing their political trajectory, it is possible to notice that, although critical of national-developmentalism, these characters gather a series of political attributes that bring them closer to classical populism, such as personalism, criticism of instances of traditional representation and the concentration of powers in the Executive. In common with the past populism, these new leaders present rhetoric aimed at the common citizen, as opposed to the 'elites'. This category, however, is resignified to encompass other actors, in particular those who represented the basis of national-developmentalist populism, that is, the formal workers and the national bourgeoisie, organized, respectively, in trade unions and employers' entities (Schneider, 1991)

In its neoliberal phase, populist discourses are directed to a social base that is enlarged by orthodox reforms: the unemployed, informal workers, the excluded, the oppressed and the poor in general. In their speech acts, however, these subjects are presented in an antagonistic relationship that ignores the impact of neoliberalism, emphasizing the privileges granted by national-developmentalism to the elites associated with it. Still, due to their scope, these categories find adherence in a panorama that is marked by profound changes in the labor market, in addition to being able to aggregate a multitude of individuals who have gone through poverty and unemployment, whose hopes are placed on the economic recovery to be achieved through these adjustments (Weyland, 1996).

It is from the frustration of these expectations that the most recent turn in the concept of populism, propitiated by the dissatisfaction with the results achieved through the neoliberal agenda and with the leaders committed to it (Vilas, 2004). This feeling translates, at the dawn of the 21st century, into a situation of serious economic and political crisis which culminates in the electoral victory of actors who represented a change of direction.[5] It is in this context that the object of this work arises: the Laclaunian concept of populism.

3   Hegemonic Struggle and Populism in the 21st Century: Theory and Praxis

Shared by portions of the middle class and the popular classes, which were particularly affected by the deleterious consequences of neoliberal onslaughts, the rejection of austerity discourses manifested itself in different degrees. In

---

5 In 2000, two years after Hugo Chávez's victory in Venezuela, Ricardo Lagos, of the Socialist Party of Chile, was elected. In 2002, it was Lula's turn, followed by Néstor Kirchner who was elected president of Argentina in 2003. A year later, Tabaré Vázquez, of the Broad Front, wins in Uruguay. In 2005, it was the turn of Evo Morales, from the Movement to Socialism. The following year, the Ecuadorian Rafael Correa of the PAIS Alliance, was elected president, also defeating traditional political leaders. Finally, in 2008, Fernando Lugo, in Paraguay, won an unprecedented victory over the Colorado Party, which was in power for more than 60 years.

some countries such as Venezuela, Bolivia and Ecuador, it assumed a spectrum of singular radicalism (La Torre, 2013), in others, however, such dissatisfaction did not acquire similar features, with the idea of change being supported by commitments to the traditional elites, especially those identified with financial capital. In these cases, notably Brazil and Chile, the reversal of some austerity policies and the adoption of income transfer programs were the result of bargaining dynamics established at the level of civil society and in its representative bodies (Lanzaro, 2007).

Inserted in the logic described in the previous section, the greater the distance from the interests of the elites, the greater the dependence on popular support and, therefore, the more strongly these leaders are identified with the concept of populism. However, although it has maintained its main elements – such as the popular base, personalism and the concentration of powers of the Executive – it is in this context that the category undergoes its most radical transformation, operated by the reformulation carried out by Ernesto Laclau, in PR.

As we wish to argue through this brief historiography about the changes of the concept in Latin America, for the first time, the term loses its pejorative feature, assuming a perspective that presents itself as descriptive, although it assumes a cryptonormative function. This second characteristic is associated with the author's political purposes in the context of the hegemonic struggle waged in the region by a new political elite, which came to power in the 21st century. With this goal, the category was redefined to typify these new actors, highlighting their main common elements: the recovery of a national-developmentalist ideal, discursively constructed by the rejection of the neoliberal agenda, and, above all, by the polarization of society between the oppressed and the oppressors.

However, although it is possible to detect in the populism of the past the configuration of antagonistic borders, in their new phase they are distinguished by an identity dimension, which is revealed in the intention to recognize[6] actors who have remained in a position of invisibility and subalternity throughout history. In this new sense, the populist leader does not guide or lead the people, he represents them because he is part of them, since he shares their identity (Arditi, 2005).

According to the argument elaborated here, the Gramscian concept of hegemony, recovered in HSS, may be indicative of Laclau's purpose of reformulating

---

6 The concept of recognition and its relation to the 'counter-hegemonic' proposal analyzed here is briefly addressed in the next section. However, I hope to look more closely at the issue in a forthcoming text.

the concept of populism, stripping it of its negative features in order to allow it to act as an instrument in the political struggle waged by the leaders typified therein. Thus, it is possible to imagine a connection between the two works, seeking in the first (HSS) the key to the understanding of the second (PR), in order to shed light on the reasons that lead the author to reformulate the concept of populism, draining it of its negativity.

In "On Populist Reason" (2005), Ernesto Laclau takes on the difficult task of explaining how some social agents can 'totalize' the set of experiences that surround them, being able to represent these experiences before the subjects who share them. From this perspective, the unity of the group does not admit to being reduced to a simple aggregation of social demands, which can, of course, be crystallized in sedimented social practices. Aggregation at the political level presupposes, on the contrary, an essential asymmetry between the community as a whole (the 'populus') and its constitutive parts, the governed or the oppressed ('plebs') depending on the characterization. The unity, therefore, depends on a process of catachresis, in which one of the parts identifies itself with the whole (Laclau, 2005). Because it is incapable of being apprehended *per si*, given its abstract and amorphous nature, this dynamic is essential to the whole ('populus') becoming, firstly, understandable and, then, a political subject capable of acting.

Thus, Laclau clarifies that the aggregation of demands in a chain of equivalence presupposes an essential asymmetry between the community as a whole and its constituent parts, and this unity depends on a process of catachresis, in which one of the parts identifies itself with the whole (Laclau, 2005). The logic of this operation is what the author calls 'populist reason'[7].

Populism is defined as a form of identification that considers the concept of popular sovereignty its inevitable corollary. From this perspective, the 'populist reason' would be the mechanism of constitution of a popular identity, through the affirmation of a group that sees itself as a fragile link in a relationship of antagonism with the established order. In pragmatic terms, this makes the category particularly useful to account for movements that invoke the name of the people in an opposition to the 'status quo'. Hence its affinity with 'counter-hegemony', which, as will be argued in the last section of this article, is mitigated by a 'Caesarist drift', inherent in the theory of representation that structures this category and reduces its emancipatory potential.

---

7 In the author's words: "it is in this contamination of the unity of the *populus* by the partiality of the '*plebs*' that the peculiarity of the people as a political subject and historical actor lies. the logic of its construction is what I have called 'populist reason'" (Laclau, 2005: 224).

This argument, consequently, will not be built from elements exogenous to the author's theorization, finding support in one of his most important works, "Hegemony and Socialist Strategy" (HSS), published in 1985, in partnership with Chantal Mouffe. In the book, we can notice the configuration of a post-foundationalist horizon characterized by the implosion of the metaphysical foundations that supported the idea of a universal subject. In this context, the 'counter-hegemonic' struggle, outlined by the authors as a project of radical democracy, depends on an artificial and contingent articulation between the different collective subjects, each one bearing a demand not met by the current order (Silva, 2013).

Twenty years later, Laclau presents the populist leader as the preferred catalyst for this dynamic. In the words of the authors in a passage in which they address the problem of the articulation of 'counter-hegemonic' political subjects in a context marked by the plurality of demands and social identities:

> One of its central principles is the need to create a chain of equivalence between the various democratic struggles against different forms of subordination. We argue that the struggles against sexism, racism, sexual discrimination and environmental protection need to be articulated with those of workers in a new hegemonic left-wing project. To put it into the terminology that has recently become fashionable, we insist that the left needs to address issues of "redistribution" and "recognition". This is what we mean by "radical and plural democracy".
> LACLAU and MOUFFE, 1985: 17

Seeing the leaderships that emerged at the end of the twentieth century as an alternative to the formation of a 'counter-hegemonic' political subject, Laclau makes a risky choice, whose risks will be explored in the last section of this work. Instead of focusing their approach on 'absences', as Marxists and liberals have done in the past – denouncing in populism the lack of class consciousness or the removal of the canons of liberal democracy – the author focuses on their qualities, which relate to the inclusive character of these governments, to the implementation of a distributive economic agenda and to a greater openness to popular participation.

In this effort, Laclau addresses those who see a threat of authoritarian upsurge in these leaders, paying attention to the contribution of legitimacy that is conferred by the broad support of the majority of the population. With this, it would be possible to obtain democratic advances (in particular in its material dynamics) in a context of weakness of liberal institutions. This is the main legacy of populism in the region.

Although it is possible to detect the configuration of antagonistic borders in the populism of the past, in its new phase, it is are distinguished by an identity dimension, which reveals itself in the intention of 'recognizing' actors who have remained in a position of invisibility and subalternity throughout history. In this new sense, the populist leader does not guide or lead the people, he 'represents' them because he is part of them, since he shares their identity (Arditi, 2005). It is on this 'post-foundational' way of understanding identity formation and political subjects that I will discuss in the next section.

4 Populism and Hegemonic Struggle: Agonistic Solutions to the Identity Challenge

The concept of hegemony originates in the Marxist tradition, marking an inflection in the theoretical debate about the relationship between economic structure and political superstructure, emphasizing the importance of the latter in the configuration of the web of social relations that forms the different communities distributed in time and space. With this, civil society and ideology emerge, respectively, as space and tool of power struggles. However, although it was first formulated by Vladimir Lenin, it is with Antonio Gramsci that the notion of hegemony assumes a central role within Marxism. The formulations of the two authors follow a continuity relationship, but are addressed to different historical contexts.

Lenin addresses a unique political situation, marked by social upheavals (the February Revolution of 1917, which in turn succeeded the Russian Revolution of 1905) characterized by organizational difficulties on the part of the political forces involved and by the engagement of a large number of militarized citizens (especially after Russia's involvement in the World War I). Faced with this panorama, the author composes an ode to the party as a structure of collective action organization, aimed at conquering the State apparatus through weapons.

Gramsci, however, addresses a country where State institutions and political parties were better organized, while the common population remained relatively low in mobilization when compared to the Russian case. In this context, it is the intellectuals who gain prominence as instruments of ideological irradiation in a dispute for hearts and minds, whose priority locus is the civil society.

Leaving aside a series of debates and reformulations of the concept of hegemony, this text will stick to the appropriation made by Chantal Mouffe and Ernesto Laclau. Addressing the distinct historical and intellectual panorama marked, in the political field, by the failure of real socialism and, in the theoretical sphere, by the critique of the rational and normative assumptions that structured it, the authors operate a significant conceptual engineering. In HSS it is noticeable the attempt to base dialectics on a post-foundational horizon through the incorporation of a philosophical framework unrelated to the Marxist tradition, in which the reference to the work of Jürgen Habermas and Carl Schmitt stands out. In this approach, structured from a deepening of the idea of antagonism originally present in the notion of hegemonic struggle, the subjects are presented without any allusion to transcendent contents, identities or essences, being understood as products of a particular historical and linguistic context – ephemeral and unstable by definition.

Thus, when assuming the category of 'post-foundationalism' to define its epistemological horizon, Laclau and Mouffe assume the possibility of resuming the modern ideal of 'self-assertion' by separating it from the notion of 'self-foundation'. This is because the idea of 'self-foundation' presupposes the capacity of human reason to find ultimate fundamentals for existence and is consequently incompatible with the rejection of its metaphysical, essentialist and universalizing bases. In this effort, the authors present a theory about the formation of political subjects stripped of any essentialism, in which every identity is configured from a relational perspective, that is, through a relationship of antagonism. The identity of a subject ceases to be conceived as something intrinsic or aprioristic, becoming a contingent result of the relationship established with other terms in a historically constructed and unstable system of differences, since it consists of antagonistic discursive structures (and subjects) that prevent its complete closure in a single totality (Alves, 2010).

Hegemony is then understood as an attribute inherent to the formation and transformation of political communities, emerging as a precarious and provisional solution to a crisis in which a part that was supposed to fill the void of the totality, ceases to be able to do so, being replaced by another. Or, in other words,

> The concept of hegemony does not emerge to define a new type of relationship in its specific identity, but to fill an open gap in the chain of historical necessity. Hegemony will allude to an absent totality and the various attempts to recompose and rearticulate it that, by overcoming this original absence, makes it possible to give the struggles a meaning and the historical forces to be endowed with full positivity. The contexts in which the concept appears will be those of a failure (in the geological sense) of a fissure that needs to be filled, of a contingency that needs to

be overcome. Hegemony will not be the majestic unfolding of an identity, but the response to a crisis.

LACLAU and MOUFFE, 1985: 07

This understanding recovers, therefore, the Heideggerian philosophy that conceives existence as being marked by the 'polemos'. This, in turn, appears as a transhistorical instance that allows us to understand the 'being' as a product of struggles, that is, antitheses or unfriendly frictions through which new terms are created. Despite its originality, Heidegger is not, however, the fundamental reference for the authors studied here, – Mouffe and Laclau – who focus their attention mainly on the contributions of Carl Schmitt.

Incorporating the Schmittian lexicon, the authors see themselves before a political universe ineluctably constituted by antagonistic boundaries, in which only the phenomena of equivalence and differentiation can engender the formation of political subjects, which are constituted in an unstable, precarious and ephemeral way, through a 'hegemonic relation'. According to this approach, the idea of equivalence corresponds to a simplification of political space in two antagonistic fields, whose internal differences are subsumed before the centrality of what is identical (Laclau and Mouffe, 1985). The idea of difference, on the contrary, would tend to complexify this same space, paving the way for the diversification of meanings and for the pluralism of identities.

Thus, according to the hypothesis that structures this work, by emphasizing the antagonism component that is originally present in the formulation of the concept of 'hegemonic struggle', abandoning the metaphysical claim to base it on an undeniable foundation of legitimacy, this proposition surpasses the limits of traditional Marxism. According to Mouffe and Laclau, only this overcoming would allow us to glimpse a truly radical model of democracy, whose objective is to transform the relations of power within societies.

In the name of this ideal, the authors claim a renunciation of anthropological optimism, understood as the mainstay of the proposal presented by Jürgen Habermas, which, despite rejecting the metaphysical components of the 'philosophical discourse of modernity', rests on a concept of communicative reason, defined as an 'universal pragmatic' that is capable of basing the legitimacy of the democratic ideal on universal bases (Habermas, 2002). According to the argument defended by Mouffe in "The Democratic Paradox" (2000), this reason, besides being unavailable, is not a desirable foundation for a radical project of democracy. On the contrary, by removing the negativity inherent in an 'agonistic' understanding of human sociability, it blocks the recognition of violence and exclusion as unavoidable components of the process of forming the general will. Thus, the Habermasian proposal makes contemporary democratic theory unable to deal with the nature of 'the political' in its dimension of hostility and antagonism (Mouffe, 2000).

To acquiesce in the ineluctability of the conflict, according to the author, does not presuppose an acceptance of the status quo or the dictates of power, but, on the contrary, enables a notion of democracy that stimulates its contestation, since "no consensus can be established as a result of a pure exercise of reason" (Mouffe, 1994: 11). From this perspective, any rationalist approach (even those of a communicative nature) is denounced as an obstacle to the legitimization of polytheism of values as a constitutive element and a value of a democratic order[8]

The opposition to the Habermasian model emphasizes the empirical impediments to the implementation of this order without a radical transformation in power relations in society, which is another element that reinforces the hypothesis presented here about the affinity between this conceptual framework and 'counter-hegemonic' political movements. However, even in a more just society, it is necessary to recognize the ineluctability of the borders of exclusion. As pointed out by Chantal Mouffe in "Democratic Paradox" "consensus, in a liberal-democratic society is, and always will be, the expression of a hegemony and the crystallization of relations of power" (Mouffe, 2000: 49).

'Agonism', therefore, presents itself as a model of democracy that is structured according to the recognition of these limits, since inclusion becomes a horizon of expectations whose intangibility does not imply abandonment and lack of commitment to the marginalized. From this normative perspective, a project of radical democracy whose precondition is the 'recognition' of multiple identities is unfolded. But also, the legitimacy of divergences and disputes of the boundaries that separate included and excluded that begin to be understood as the product of contingent, changeable and criticizable power relations.

A second consequence of this 'post-foundationalist' approach to the identity issue, which also concerns the modes of articulation between different actors, highlights the constitutive role of 'the political' in this equation. This is because, in this interpretative key, the dimension in which radical changes ('radical institutions') are located is the political dimension ('the political')[9] as

---

8 Moreover, the belief in a rational formation of the general will would prevent the recognition of the limits of pluralism within a legal-political order, with regard to the fact that certain ways of life and certain values are, by definition, incompatible with others; being properly the differentiation that constitutes them (Mouffe, 1994: 11).

9 I refer here to the distinction incorporated in Mouffe's work between politics – as an institutional dimension – and 'the political' – as an identity dimension (Mouffe, 2000).

a condition of understanding and transforming the social. Under this prism that demarcates the detachment from the fundamentals of the Marxist tradition, political movements are considered self-founding, insofar as no social or economic dynamics have priority in the process of signification of phenomena. Social interactions do not bring within themselves either their conditions of intelligibility or the solutions to their own problems, and it is therefore up to 'the political' to structure them from the boundaries of antagonism.

Resuming Hannah Pitkin's inquiry (1972) – seminal with regard to the recovery of a concern with the idea of representation, that is, with the founding character of the political dimension on the social – the political life is defined by the problem of the continuous creation of unity on an amorphous social plane, full of diversities, conflicting interests and multiple demands. Political discourses and movements thus have the role of constituting particular forms of unity between distinct interests, linking them to a common project or way of life through the establishment of borders that define opposing forces to this project. It is this communality that will transform a multitude of individuals, which are dispersed in their identity particularities, into a unified political subject capable of acting in favor of overcoming their unmet demands, united in a chain of equivalence (Mouffe, 1995). This is the authors' commitment to the emergence of a 'counter-hegemonic' subject capable of articulating the different groups that see themselves as oppressed and demand the 'recognition'[10] of their identities.

To recognize that this project always arises from a relationship of otherness, does not mean that its terms are always the same. In fact, in the concept of 'political', engendered by Carl Schmitt (1999, 2001, 2004) and incorporated in the work of Laclau and Mouffe, there is a 'transhistorical' dimension that fixates it as an instance of necessary and constitutive transcendence of the social. However, it is essential to emphasize that this 'transhistorical' element is void of content. At this point, it appears as one of the most fruitful aspects of Laclau's and, above all, Mouffe's argumentation, which aims to amortize the risks of the Schmittian inheritance by reconciling it with Wittgenstein's discursive fallibilism – emphatic about the incomplete and questionable character of any identity. Thus, it results in an understanding of 'the political' that is focused on the contestation and transformation of societies and of the identities crystallized in them.

---

10 For a better understanding of the issue of recognition and its relations with redistributive demands, I suggest the classic: Taylor and Gutmann (1994).

In this sense, no relationship of oppression takes precedence over the others. Consequently, the concept of hegemony that derives from it breaks with the traditional Marxist interpretation, present not only in Gramsci, but in most of his heirs, who see in the class struggle a prioritary and constitutive dissociation. From this conceptual engineering, which superimposes different traditions of thought, a normative and 'counter-hegemonic' claim originally alien to the Schmittian (and realistic) understanding of the 'political' is introduced (Scheuerman, 1999, 2006). Nevertheless, despite the normative commitment of Mouffe and Laclau, the Schmittian inheritance entails risks that permeate this way of understanding the formation of subjects and political identities. This is the theme of the next section.

5   The Limits of Populism as a Counter-Hegemonic Operator: the Caesarist Drift and the Schmittian Legacy

Since the publication of PR in 2005, Laclau has become a theorist that is requested by politicians and academics to explain the changes that have occurred at the present time, marked by the emergence of actors in Latin America and in the world who, despite their idiosyncrasies, are characterized by discourses that contest the *status quo*. However, despite its analytical and normative virtues, populism, as well as the Weberian 'charism,'[11] incorporates an element of instability, since it is not located in the plane of rationality (instrumental or deontological), but in the sphere of will (subjective and immanent).

This characteristic allows it to update the links between the factual/institutional dimension and the ethical/evaluative plane, renewing its pretensions of legitimacy. Therefore, as a charismatic movement, the 'populist reason' would fulfill the role of reversing – albeit for a short time – the routinizing tendency that affects every legal-political order, bringing it closer to its ethical-moral bases. Thus, as I argued throughout the previous sections, due to its theoretical attributes, but also the practical direction given by the author, populism emerges as a 'counter-hegemonic' operator. That is, as a useful instrument in

---

11   On 'charism' and its relation to the other forms of domination (traditional and rational-legal) I suggest Weber M (1991) *Os três tipos puros de dominação legítima*. In: Cohn G. (ed) *Weber: Sociologia,* Coleção Grandes Cientistas Sociais. São Paulo: Ática, 79–127; and, Mommsen WJ (1989) *The political and social theory of Max Weber*. Chicago: University of Chicago Press.

the struggle for transformation in the structures of power that perpetuate the oppression of the lower classes.

However, despite the recognition of such attributes, the purpose of this section is to highlight its drawbacks, given other characteristics of the concept that give it what I call Caesarist drift.[12] These elements, in turn, come from the theoretical framework that structures this way of conceiving the political. More precisely, this 'drift' is brought about by the incorporation of an elitist theory of representation, outlined by Thomas Hobbes and updated in Max Weber (Mommsen, 1989). Finally, this theory finds its most radical understanding in the work of Carl Schmitt, whose considerations are the object of particular attention throughout this work, not only because of its influence on Laclau and Mouffe, but mainly because of the risks inherent to its formulation.

The Schmittian conceptualization highlights the dimension of homogeneity, presenting it as a normative unfolding of a realistic corollary, that is, of the Weberian assumption that, in modernity, representation, as a moment of identification between rulers and ruled, is an inextricable component to political systems, which can no longer resort to transcendent foundations of legitimacy (Schmitt, 2006).

Schmitt solves this problem through the concept of 'acclamation', which would indicate a democratic dynamic through which the people express their approval to the leader. Their actions, when acclaimed, could be seen as an expression of popular sovereignty (Schmitt, 1990). Weber, however, points out that this ideal is not enough to structure 'rational-legal' systems that are necessary for the organization of politics and economics in modern societies (Weber, 1991). In light of this, the author emphasizes the importance of respect for individual freedom and pluralism of values, pointed out as the only legitimacy criteria compatible with a secular world.

Laclau, however, criticizes this necessary association between individualism and pluralism, although he believes that the mere manifestation of popular sovereignty is also not a sufficient criterion, as it disregards the historical articulation between democratic and liberal traditions, sedimented over the seventeenth, eighteenth, nineteenth and twentieth centuries (Laclau and Mouffe, 1985). According to this hypothesis – which finds points of contact with the theory presented by Rosanvallon in "Le peuple introuvable: histoire de la représentation démocratique en France" (1998) – of the modernization process, a fundamental transformation of the structure of societies takes place,

---

12   Caesarism, or Bonapartism, is understood as the process through which, in the face of a crisis of hegemony, "power is embodied in a 'heroic personality' of a military or charismatic character, preventing the 'normal' functioning of democracy (SILVA, 2015: 9).

which, in addition to being demographically superior, would have become more complex and plural. In this new context, it has become impossible to think of the people as a unitary agent capable of expressing themselves sovereignly unequivocally, since they are composed of countless groups with contradictory interests, identities and wills.

Homogeneity, however, is an intrinsic element to the idea of representation presented by Laclau, although it is mitigated by the consideration of its precariousness and the gap between representatives and represented, which attributes to every act of identification a character of incompleteness. For the author, the process of complexification does not occur only within society, but also in individuals themselves, who, because they are composed of numerous evaluative dimensions, are no longer able to identify completely with anything or any person. Every form of identification becomes partial and temporary, so it is necessary to link the legitimacy of the representatives to something more than their ability to identify with those represented (Laclau, 1994).

It is necessary to recognize, therefore, Laclau's effort in affirm that, from a normative perspective, the acclamation of the majority is not sufficient to grant legitimacy to a political order, which is a central point for the argument undertaken here, insofar as it avoids a precipitous association between populism and Caesarism. According to the argument outlined in this commentary, populism is not the best tool for the hegemonic struggle, but not because it necessarily gives rise to authoritarian regimes. Its incompatibility stems from the elitist character of the conception of politics and representation that structures it, which, because it is too centered on the function of the leader, becomes insufficiently emancipatory from the perspective of the demos.

Moreover, post-fundamentalism itself, as an epistemology that is impermeable to transcendent principles, brings with it some drawbacks. For, if the act of representation constitutes both representatives and represented, without a collective essence or general will that transcends it, it becomes more difficult to subordinate it to any idea of responsibility unrelated to its dictates, since it is not clear to which wills or interests the representatives should be responsive to and what kind of control the people should exercise over them (Rodrigues and Silva, 2015).

In other words, unlike the notions of reason and emancipation, which serve as the normative horizon of the Marxist tradition in general and, in particular, of the idea of hegemonic struggle presented by Antonio Gramsci, populist reason does not operate based on evaluative criteria, whose legitimacy refers to a later foundation to the act of representation established between representatives and represented. In the absence of such criteria, the risk that, by presupposing a substantive identity with the people, the leader disengages himself, acting on his behalf as he sees fit, including counteracting any 'counter-hegemonic' commitments that have forged his identification with the popular classes, is aggravated.

On the other hand, in contrast to the principles that guide the liberal understanding of the representative mechanisms, which emphasize the plurality of opinions and the protection of minorities, the Laclaunian understanding tends to highlight majority dynamics. In light of this, two central problems stand out: (1) what to do with portions of the population that do not share the same identity as the majority groups?; (2) what are the limits of this majority identification, in view of the multifaceted character of individuals and social groups?

In the tension between the rule of majority – as a principle that feeds the pretensions of democratic legitimacy – and pluralism – as an inherent element of any decision-making process in modern societies – lies the main obstacle to the survival of the democratic ideal in a context that is very different from that which originated it. For, as pointed out by Chantal Mouffe in "Deliberative Democracy or Agonistic Pluralism" (2000), if we take into account the expectations and values shared by its citizens, democracy cannot be achieved at the expense of liberalism, nor vice versa.

Faced with this dilemma, 'agonism', as a model of radical democracy, serves as an indispensable counterpoint to dynamics that value the majority dimension, inherent to populism. According to this understanding, despite any conceptual antinomy, liberalism and democracy cannot be considered as functional substitutes, or as elements in a bargaining process. The demands for equality and freedom, disseminated by the Enlightenment tradition and incorporated by most contemporary societies, can only be properly achieved by regimes that give rise to an articulation between these two components. If there is any freedom of moderns this refers to theoretical and political struggles that articulate the demands for popular sovereignty and individual rights.

Nevertheless, recognizing a tendency to the encapsulation of individuals in their private lives, 'agonism' incorporates the banner of deliberative and participatory models of democracy, considering that the institution of political and social spaces of deliberation and participation can help stimulate interest in the *res publica*. For this reason, from the emphasis on deliberation and participation as social practices to be associated with liberal institutions and values – such as Parliament, the division between State and Church, State and Civil Society, the guarantee of individual freedoms, etc. – 'agonism' becomes an alternative to compensate for the harms of leadership and the risk of populism, since it removes from leaders the possibility of presenting themselves as representatives of the totality (Rodrigues and Silva, 2015).

Thus, responding to the question raised throughout the text, by incorporating institutional proposals aimed at avoiding the degeneration of populist phenomena in Bonapartism regimes, plebiscite democracies or caesarean dictatorships, the agonist model is presented as a more appropriate paradigm to 'counter-hegemonic' movements that contemplate an emancipatory ideal, in which the sovereignty of the people is not obtained at the expense of their individual freedoms or the oppression of minorities.

6   Conclusion

This chapter presented a proposal for a theoretical-political framework for the Neo Gramscian approach of Chantal Mouffe and Ernesto Laclau. Focused on the concepts of Hegemonic Struggle and Populism, this analysis undertook a historical-conceptual genealogy that sought to correlate theory and praxis. After this first effort, which sought to situate the work of both authors as an inflection point in the Marxist tradition, three axiological developments of this movement were developed. The first, concerning the relationship between the concept of populism and the conceptual framework established in "Hegemony and Socialist Strategy". The second, presented such a formulation as a synthesis between two theoretical antipodal constellations that go beyond the limits of traditional Marxism: Habermasian proceduralism and Schmittian substantialism. The third one highlighted the limits of this synthesis that, despite its affinities with 'counter-hegemony', incorporates some risks inherent to a theory of representation centered on the figure of the leader.

The objective of this work, in turn, was to demonstrate that the recovery operated by Ernesto Laclau and Chantal Mouffe in the Gramscian concept of hegemony allows the overcoming of the paradigm of the universal subject, in which the proletariat was configured as a monolithic essence incapable of encompassing the plurality of identities that constitute contemporary societies. Thus, according to the post-foundationalist assumptions, incorporated into the Marxist legacy by the conceptual effort of the authors, an 'agonistic' conception of a political subject emerges. Fragmented in numerous conflicting and divergent collective identities, this subject is understood as an empty signifier, whose identity can only be filled by ephemeral, incomplete and precarious meanings.

However, the recognition of such precariousness by Mouffe and Laclau does not imply the rejection of the emancipatory horizon present in the Marxist tradition. On the contrary, it gives rise to a project of radical democracy, in which the understanding of the political as a universe structured by antagonism is counterbalanced by the emphasis on deliberative processes of understanding and the critique of hegemonically established identities. From an 'agonistic' perspective, representation – as a link between rulers and ruled – and popular sovereignty- as an expression of the will of the people – should be understood as fictions that, together with the idea of individual freedom, make up the evaluative horizon of Western societies.

To this extent, by emphasizing the artificial and precarious character of identities and consensus combining them with the defense of a radical project of democracy, this model offers the basis for an 'immanent' critique of the existing institutional regimes. For this reason, 'agonism', in addition to compensating for the risks inherent to populist phenomena, presents a structural affinity with 'counter-hegemonic' movements that, in addition to contesting the 'status quo', envision an emancipatory ideal incompatible with the philosophy of the subject that once fed it.

References

Alves A (2010) O conceito de hegemonia: de Gramsci a Laclau e Mouffe. *Lua nova*, São Paulo, 80, 71–96.

Arditi B (2005) Populism as an Internal Periphery of Democratic Politics. In: Panizza F (ed.) *Populism and the Mirror of Democracy*. London/New York, Verso, 73–104.

Cardodo FH and Falleto E (1969) *Dependencia y desarrollo en América Latina: ensayo de interpretación sociológica*. México: Siglo veintiuno.

Conniff M (1982) Introduction. In: Conniff M (ed.) *Latin American populism in comparative perspective*. Albuquerque: University of New Mexico Press, 3–30.

Di Tella T (1965) Populismo y reforma en América Latina. *Desarrollo Económico*, vol. 4, n. 16, 391–425.

Dornbusch R and Sebastian E (1991) The macroeconomics of populism. In: Dornbusch R and Sebastian E (eds) *The macroeconomics of populism in Latin America*. Chicago: University of Chicago Press, 7–13.

Ducatenzeiler G, Faucher P and Rea J (1993) Amérique latine: les échecs du libéral-populisme. *Canadian Journal of Development Studies/Revue canadienne d'études du développement*, v. 14, n. 2, 173–195.

Germani G, Ianni O and Di Tella T (1973) *Populismo y contradicciones de clase en Latinoamerica*. México, Ediciones Era.

Habermas J (2002) *Inclusão do outro*. São Paulo: Edições Loyola.

Ianni O (1975) *La formación del Estado populista en América Latina*. México: Ediciones Era.

Kaufman R and Stallings B (1991) The political economy of Latin American populism. In: Dornbusch R and Sebastian E (eds) *The macroeconomics of populism in Latin America*. Chicago: University of Chicago Press, 15–43.

La Torre C (2013) In the Name of the People: Democratization, Popular Organizations, and Populism in Venezuela, Bolivia, and Ecuador. *European Review of Latin American and Caribbean Studies*. No. 95, October, 27–48.

Laclau E (2005) *On Populist Reason*. London-New York: Verso.

Laclau E (1994) Minding the Gap: The Subject of Politics. In: Laclau E (ed.) *The Making of the Political Identities*. London, Verso, 1–40.

Laclau E and Mouffe C (1985) *Hegemony and Socialist Strategy: Towards a Radical Democratic Politics*. Londres: Verso.

Lanzaro J (2007) Gobiernos de izquierda en América Latina: entre el populismo y la social democracia – Una tipología para avanzar en el análisis comparado. *Análise de Conjuntura Observatório Político Sul-Americano* OPSA, IUPERJ/UCAM, Rio de Janeiro, n.12, dez, 1–20.

Mitre A (2008) As peregrinações de um conceito: populismo na América Latina. *Cadernos de História* PUC-Minas, v. 10, n. 13, 1–15.

Mommsen W (1989) *The political and social theory of Max Weber*. Chicago: University of Chicago Press.

Mouffe C (1995) Post-Marxism: democracy and identity. *Environment and Planning D: Society and Space*, 13.3, 259–265.

Mouffe C (200) *The Democratic Paradox*. London – New York: Verso.

Mouffe C (2000) *Deliberative Democracy or Agonistic Pluralism*. Vienna: Institute for Advanced Studies.

Mouffe C (1994) Pensando a democracia moderna com, e contra, Carl Schmitt. *Cadernos da Escola do Legislativo*. Belo Horizonte.

Pereira L (1991) Populism and economic policy in Brazil. *Journal of Interamerican Studies and World Affairs*, v. 33, n. 2, 1–22.

Pitkin H (1972) *The Concept of Representation*. Berkeley and Los Angeles: University of California Press.

Rodrigues T and Silva M (2015) A razão populista de Ernesto Laclau: uma crítica agonística. *Teoria e Cultura*, UFJF, Juiz de Fora v. 10, 173–195.

Rosanvallon P (1998) *Le Peuple introuvable : Histoire de la représentation démocratique en France*. Paris : Éditions Gallimard.

Sachs J (1989) *Social conflict and populist policies in Latin America*. Cambridge MA: National Bureau of Economic Research.

Scheuerman W (1999) *The End of Law*. Lanham: Rowman & Littlefield Publishers Inc.

Scheuerman W (2006) Carl Schmitt and Hans Morgenthau: Realism and Beyond. *Institute of German Studies*, v. 09, n 2.

Schmitt C (1990) Légalité et légitimité. In: Benoist A (ed.) *Du Politique, 'Légalité et légitimité' et autres essais*. Puiseaux: Pardès.

Schmitt C (1996) *A Crise da Democracia Parlamentar*. São Paulo: Scritta.

Schmitt C (1999) *Ethic of State and Pluralistic State, in The Challenge of Carl Schmitt*. New York: Verso.

Schmitt C (2001) El Concepto de lo Político. In: Aquilar H (ed.) *Carl Schmitt, Teólogo de la Política*. México: Fondo de Cultura Econômica.

Schmitt C (2004) *El Leviatã en la teoría del Estado de Tomás Hobbes*. Buenos Aires: Editorial Struhart & Cia.

Schmitt C (2006) *Teologia Política*. Belo Horizonte: Del Rey.

Schneider B (1991) Brazil under Collor: anatomy of a crisis. *World Policy Journal*, v. 8, n. 2, 321–347.

Silva M (2013) Entre César e o Demos: Notas agonísticas sobre a democracia na Venezuela. Unpublished doctoral thesis. University of the state of Rio de Janeiro, Rio de Janeiro.

Silva M (2015) Populismo, rentismo e Estado mágico: Notas agonísticas sobre a democracia na Venezuela. *Oikos*, v. 13, 91–114.

Taylor C and Gutmann A (1994) *Multiculturalism: Examining the Politics of Recognition*. Princeton, NJ: Princeton Univ. Press.

Vilas C (2004) ¿Populismos reciclados o neoliberalismo a secas? El mito del "neopopulismo" latinoamericano *Revista de Sociologia e Política*, n. 22, 135–151.

Weber M (1991) Os três tipos puros de dominação legítima. In: Cohn G (ed.) *Weber: Sociologia – Coleção Grandes Cientistas Sociais, 13*. São Paulo: Ática, 79–127.

Weffort F (1968) *Classes populares e desenvolvimento social: contribuição ao estudo do populismo*. Santiago: ILPES.

Weyland K (1996) *Democracy without equity: failures of reform in Brazil*. Pittsburgh: University of Pittsburgh Press.

Weyland K (2001) Clarifying a contested concept: Populism in the study of Latin American politics. *Comparative politics*, 1–22.

CHAPTER 8

Imperialism as a Complex System of Domination
An Approach from Domenico Losurdo

Diego Pautasso[1]

1   Introduction

It is undeniable that the field of International Relations (IR) was born within the Anglo-Saxon countries, and, consequently, intertwined with their geopolitical interests.[2] This contributes both to the enhancement of ethnocentric biases as much as those averse to systemic criticism. Indeed, the tributary perspectives of Marxism had a late contribution due to, among other factors, the collapse of the Soviet camp and the predominance of the Realist and Liberal (sub)currents. It was only from the 1970s onwards that Marxism began to make a more significant contribution to the area, escaping the first 'great debates' (utopian vs. realists, and traditionalists vs. positivists) that took place after the World War I, when this field of knowledge was formed (Halliday, 1999). From the end of the Cold War on, however, the collapse of real socialism shook Marxism deeply, as globalization and the 'end of history' narratives became dominant.

In Brazil, the field of International Relations had a late development and Marxist approaches even more so. Its various sub-areas, such as International Political Economy and International Security Studies, paid little (or no) attention to the problem of imperialism, whether under geopolitical and/or geoeconomic aspects. The same neglect has occurred with the various theories of globalization (Ianni, 1996) or with the many theories of the contemporary world (Kumar, 1997). The paradox is that this has occurred precisely in the Post-Cold War period, when the use of force by the superpower – in a condition of provisional unipolarity – deepened. In this sense, it is crucial to rescue Domenico Losurdo – and the classics of Marxism – to understand the interlacing of the global reproduction of wealth and power, the uneven and combined

---
1   Professor of the Military College of Porto Alegre, Brazil.
2   Originally published as a chapter of the book "Theory of International Relations: Marxist contributions". Reference: Pautasso D and Prestes A (2021) *Teoria das Relações Internacionais: contribuições marxistas*. Rio de Janeiro: Contraponto. Translated into English by the author.

development of the world market, the reconfigurations of the international division of labor and the interstate asymmetries and contradictions. In this chapter, we try to demonstrate that the Italian author treated imperialism as a complex system of domination, dealing with its multifaceted character, even without debating the genealogy of the concept, as he did with other concepts, such as Liberalism.

This chapter adds to the efforts to promote the Marxist debate within the scope of IR, in this specific case, highlighting the contributions of Domenico Losurdo. This effort unites with others aimed at i) carrying out a balance of his work as a critical approach to international studies (Pautasso, 2014); ii) discussing the genealogy of Liberalism and the way in which the US intertwines neoliberal globalization with the various neocolonial interventionist mechanisms of today (Pautasso, 2020); and iii) approaching the national matter from the national-international dialectic (Pautasso, Fernandes and Doria, 2020).

Losurdo, it is worth noting, began his academic career by focusing his studies on classical philosophers, especially the Germans Kant, Fichte, Schelling, Hegel, Notrecht, Heidegger and Nietzsche, in addition to other themes that went through issues related to the French and American revolutions, to liberalism and to thinkers like Constant, for example. But with the collapse of the Soviet camp, in a context of deep ideological disbandment, the author made a progressive approach to themes of his time, such as a balance of real socialism and the contemporary and western left; a deep genealogy of liberalism; and a comprehensive critique of imperialism in its many forms.[3] All this effort took place without ever abandoning scientific rigor, the ability to relate classical authors to contemporary issues, and the mobilization of remarkable erudition in historical comparisons. And the "rigor of objectivity is absolutely primal", dealing with the "most possible coherent development of the determinations inscribed in the object" (Azzara, 2020: 11).

That being said, we've organized the chapter as follows. In the first part, we discuss the origins and debates about the concept of imperialism, as well as the way in which it has been neglected, especially in the area of International Relations and/or in topics related to contemporaneity. In the second part, we approach the lexicon and language of the Empire, as well as its various technologies of warfare and multimedia firepower. Last but not least, we deal with the mechanisms of imperial economic expropriation, as well as the corresponding struggles against the de-emancipation processes and their paths.

---

3 See the author's production of articles and books on his official page, available at: http://domenicolosurdobibliografia.blogspot.com/.

2   Imperialism: Genealogy and Its Paths

The violent expansion of empires and/or territorial units throughout history is not a recent phenomenon. However, the debate and theories about imperialism only date back to the end of the nineteenth century. On the one hand, this was the context of major productive transformations, with the passage from the First to the Second Industrial Revolution and from competitive to oligopolistic/monopolistic capitalism, giving rise to large global corporations. On the other hand, the great powers carried out expansion and sharing of vast territories, especially in Africa and Asia. Critical theoretical reflections and political movements unsubmissive to imperialism, in this sense, resulted from the hostility of its violence and looting, from the maturing of the understanding about the systemic dynamics of capitalism and from the strengthening of concepts like sovereignty and self-determination of peoples in the context of the modern state system conformation.

In this sense, it is worth summarizing a panoramic view of the Marxist debate on the political economy of imperialism, based on the balance of Fernandes (1992). Rudolf Hilferding, in 1909, demonstrated the relationship between imperialism and the process of monopolization and the increasingly intertwined link between industrial and banking capital. Hilferding did not equate imperialism with colonialism, as domination prescinded from territorial control – and could even be a factor in the rapid development of productive forces in the periphery. Rosa Luxemburg, in turn, in a work from 1913, understood that capitalism would experience a permanent 'crisis of realization', providing imperialist impulses to non-capitalist regions, in order to make accumulation viable. Kautsky, in an article from 1915, developed the idea of ultra-imperialism, given that monopolization could even lead to the elimination of wars. Bukharin, in a 1915 writing, defined imperialism as the policy of finance capital, whose monopolistic organization would reduce inter-imperialist competition and even systemic crises.

But it was Lenin's work, from 1916, that gave more projection and systematization to the concept. According to the Russian leader, imperialism was the monopoly phase of capitalism, with traits such as 1) concentration of capital, 2) fusion of industrial and banking capital, 3) predominance of capital exports, 4) formation of associations of global corporations and 5) territorial division. To him, monopoly was intensifying, instead of eliminating competition; and the export of capital itself would play a role in promoting development (albeit distorted). Later, Dobb, Sweezy, Baran, Frank, Emmanuel, Amin, Wallerstein, among others, emphasized exploitation taking the sphere of circulation as its starting point, rather than the dynamics of production, reiterating that imperialism would play a blocking role in the development of peripheral countries. (Fernandes, 1992: 15–62).

Some authors in the Marxist field supported the debate about imperialism after the collapse of real socialism, as highlighted by Leite's (2014) balance sheet when citing authors such as Chesnais, Went, Harvey, Boron, Sakellaropoulos, among others. The eclectic and polysemic use of the concept implied analyzes such as those of Hardt and Negri (2001), according to which we would be experiencing a time when the empire occurs without imperialism, in which transnational companies would supplant the power of States. Basically, these authors dematerialize, deterritorialize and, at the limit, depoliticize the power of capital, ignoring that, in fact, such companies are national companies with global operations, as defined by Chang (2009). Arrighi (2012) himself consistently historicized the relationship between capital and territorial state in the conformation of the modern world-system.

Progressive or critical sectors have abandoned the concept of imperialism. Kumar (1997), in fact, takes stock of the new theories about the contemporary world, discussing the information society, post-industrial and post-Fordist economies or the post-modern world. The idea of globalization, depending on the approaches, was identified as those about the global village and/or variations of narratives linked to the new world without borders, without States or even without ideologies.

In general, the narratives of globalization have contributed to camouflaging contradictions and the uneven and combined character of the accumulation of wealth and power, as well as inter-imperialist rivalries, center-periphery dynamics and policies of resort to force. Let's see how Batista Jr. (1998) demonstrates the false premises that underlie the economic dimension of globalization. According to him, this 1) did not produce an unprecedented integration, because in several aspects, the degree of international integration at the turn of the nineteenth-twentieth century was even higher; 2) it did not generate a phenomenon of a supranational character, but something inter-state, asymmetric and unequal in terms of States and sovereignties; 3) it did not result in the inexorable predominance of neoliberal policies, as it did not even stop the trend of increasing government weight, measured by indicators such as the ratio between public expenditure and revenue and GDP; 4) it did not imply the formation of global corporations free of national identification and loyalties; 5) and it did not mean the creation of a 'global' capital market, either due to the territorial ties of capital, or because of the preponderance of national markets for any development experience.

In the IR area, we can take some manuals as an example, because, although the intrinsic limits of these works are known, it is evident that they serve both as a reference in many courses, as they express the theoretical frameworks and the predominant themes. In the book International Political Economy, by Reinaldo Gonçalves (2005), there is only one mention of the concept of 'imperialism' and a few paragraphs discussing the subject. In the important work International Security Studies, by Buzan and Hansen (2012), the concept is simply disregarded. Even approaches with a neorealist matrix, in which the subject of power and the use of force are at the epicenter of the analyzes, the fundamental question is the security of States in an anarchic international system. It is a Hobbesian approach incapable of understanding the intertwining between national and global, State and market, power and capital, as a Marxist approach proposes. And the analytical shift to the issue of 'human security', which considers food, environmental and community security, etc. continues disregarding those dialectical pairs mentioned above.

In the field of IR in Brazil, perhaps the exception is the book Imperialism, State and International Relations, by Luiz Felipe Osório (2018), whose concept of imperialism assumes analytical centrality. Furthermore, only in the theoretical field itself, such as the jounal "Crítica Marxista", the debate remained alive, as illustrated by some texts by Ianni (1996); Moraes (1996); Visentini (1996); Del Roio (1996); Dumenil and Levy (2004); Ruccio (2005); Fontes (2008), among others. Let us see, therefore, how Losurdo's work can not only animate Marxist debates on the subject, but also the critical thinking in the field of International Relations.

3   Lexis of Imperialism and Its War Technologies

The Italian author did not deal with a genealogy of imperialism, a method so common in his writings, as the study on liberalism illustrates (LOSURDO, XXX). However, it did not give in to theories and approaches that considered concepts such as imperialism and class struggle – so dear to sectors of the left averse to the experiences of real socialism – to be obsolete.

In fact, Losurdo characterized three stages of the struggle between colonialism and neocolonialism: 1) from the October Revolution (1917) and its appeal to the resistance of slaves in the colonies to Stalingrad and the defeat of Nazi imperialism; 2) from Stalingrad to the US triumph in the Cold War, marked by the defeat of classical colonialism and the emergence of the cunning neocolonialism led by Washington; and 3) from the defeat of the socialist camp to the present day, expressed by the triumph of the US empire (Losurdo, 2016: 249–250). In other words, the author brings imperialist practices to the center of his analysis, periodizing and seeking the lines of continuity and discontinuity between colonialism and neocolonialism and their mechanisms of resistance. And always approaching the problem in a complex and multifaceted way, by articulating the theoretical and philosophical dimensions to the historical and political developments.

In this sense, his first major contribution was to demonstrate the liberalism-imperialism symbiosis. Its two epicenters, Great Britain and the USA, combined liberal universalism based on the defense of international institutions, the opening of markets and the defense of human rights alongside imperial and ethnocentric policies aimed at the destabilization of governments, the forced opening of markets and military interventions. More than that: the expansion of the West mobilized liberal rhetoric to carry out a practice with a clear colonial-racial component, of racializing the enemy, seeking to legitimize domination and segregation. It is enough to turn to the genealogy of liberalism to perceive its 'unique twin birth' not only with the slave trade from Great Britain, but with the systematic dispossession and/or annihilation of Irish and Indians, exploitation of coolies and looting of colonized peoples. There is no contradiction between what American thinkers called herrenvolk democracy ('democracy for the people of the lords'), white supremacy and/or the far west against the redskins (Losurdo, 2006a: 47 and 119, 2006b: 148).

The Napoleonic pax shielded itself in the 'perpetual peace' of the French Revolution, the British pax, in the 'age of commerce' defended by Constant, and the American pax in the 'definitive peace' of Wilson, respectively, those are an expression of their military triumphs (Losurdo, 2018a: 402). This liberal narrative takes place through the defense of the 'sacred space' of the free and proprietors against the 'profane space' of subaltern social groups, using political and economic means, law and force to sustain their social position. The merit of liberalism is to place itself as a 'religion of freedom', while simultaneously perpetuating and fostering the relations of enslavement of blacks, decimation of indigenous people and oppression of colonial peoples, in systematic imperialist policies (Losurdo, 2017: 327).

The second aspect highlighted by Losurdo concerns the language of the empire. One of the most interesting approaches refers to what he calls the 'lexicon of American ideology'. Therefore, the unilateral and distorted use of categories, disseminated by the control of the media, makes up the basis of the US imperialist discourse, complementing its gigantic military apparatus. They are Manichaean, polysemic and ideological discourses that present themselves as universal to legitimize the supremacy of certain power structures. In this sense, the concept of terrorism has become an instrument to unleash the Global War on Terror. In the name of this crusade, all kinds of dehumanization, massacres against civilian populations, use of arbitrary violence promoted by secret services (CIA) and death squads, transformation of societies into hostages through embargoes, among others, are valid (Losurdo, 2010b: 43). The same goes for the concept of fundamentalism, as it became a key category to legitimize a holy war of the West against 'barbarians' and "pre-moderns" (Losurdo, 2010b: 63–96). In other words, a Manichaeism that divides the world between, on the one hand, barbarians, terrorists, fundamentalists, Negroids/browns, authoritarians and/or Islamists and, on the other hand, the West, formed by those who are civilized, modern, democratic, Judeo-Christian, etc.

The West (such concept itself is vague and polysemic) celebrates 'universalism' and therefore proclaims itself as the moral conscience of humanity. The result is that West feels entitled to the role of world police, promoter of democracy, human rights and free market. It is neither difficult to understand the links between imperialism and liberalism, nor how exalted 'universalism' easily converts into ethnocentrism. Through the control of the narrative, a war syllogism expressed in exceptionalism is molded – as an 'international sheriff' interpreter of universal values -, sanctioning the law of the strongest in the international field and making war eternal (Losurdo, 2016: 125, 154 and 218, 2018a: 384).

The third point that the Italian author calls attention to refers to the terrible multimedia firepower. The new means of the society of the spectacle, hegemonized by the West, make it possible to vilify enemies, exerting a certain control over the production of emotions and historical memory. The artificial production of indignation through images and the fabrication of the dichotomy 'civilized' versus 'barbarians' becomes an expedient of international politics. New technical means – in addition to television, cell phones, computers and social networks – ignite the hatred of public opinion and coerce the undecided to act or support actions against the new enemy. It is a true psychological war (Psywar), based on a quasi-monopoly over global communications, capable of promoting a dehumanization and demonization of the victim to the point of legitimizing and spectacularizing any destabilization and/or 'humanitarian war' (Losurdo, 2016: 113–114). Democratic and humanitarian interventionism, its versions of responsibility to protect, is the opposite of democracy and peace (Losurdo, 2012: 301).

The media dimension is linked to the fourth aspect, that is, the mobilization of new war technologies and the second wave of coups. The current wave of coups, different from the one that prevailed between the Truman Doctrine (1947) until the coup in Allende (1973) based on military dictatorships immune to public opinion, tends to occur through the establishment of 'protected democracies'. In those cases, the isolation and criminalization of the country and the bloody disinformation campaigns are part of the legitimation of public opinion to stimulate violence from below (and in fact with external support) and provoke regime change. Such 'protected democracies' deepen economic dependence and weaken sovereignty, generally submitting the country to the designs of power structures under Washington's management, from the IMF to NATO (Losurdo, 2016: 88–89 and 191).

It should be noted that the new technological means have increased international asymmetries and governance on a global scale. The multiplication of intervention capabilities of imperialist countries is remarkable, which includes kill list practices and extra-judicial executions; unilateral sanctions and embargoes; right to war (jus ad bellum) via NATO outside the UN Security Council; interference through NGOs acting as missionaries; bombing via new means provided by the Revolution in Military Affairs-RAM, etc. As summarized by Losurdo: white supremacy originating in the USA became a western supremacy, in this case ignoring any symmetry between nations, as well as the effectiveness of democracy and the rule of law on an international scale (Losurdo, 2016: 90, 93 and 104).

The intertwining between communication technologies mobilized for psywar (psychological warfare) and new technical means for war (Revolution in Military Affairs-RAM) alters the power relations at the international level. RAM takes place through the command of space and artificial intelligence, with automation of various operations, such as guided munitions, drones, cyberwar, etc. These new means have allowed recurrent direct interventions in Afghanistan (2001), Iraq (1991–2003) and Libya (2011); the sophistication of coups and regime change policies, such as color revolutions (Georgia, Roses in 2003; Ukraine, Orange in 2004–14; Kyrgyz, Tulips in 2005); the constitutional coups in Honduras (2009), Paraguay (2012) and Brazil (2016); in addition to the Arab Spring, whose external action has become very evident (Bandeira, 2016). Parallel to this, the expansion of NATO and military bases in the support of the Global War on Terror unleashed from 2001 on and the attempt to build anti-missile shields in Europe (Romania, Poland) against Russia, and in Asia, the High Altitude Air Defense Terminal (Thaad) in South Korea against China and North Korea.

There is no denying, as Losurdo well summarizes, that there is an economic-technological-judicial neocolonialism. It became possible to subjugate by imposing embargoes and economic siege, leading to military impotence given the superiority of means of force, villainizing through multimedia firepower and guaranteeing impunity to the aggressor thanks to dual jurisdiction (Losurdo, 2016: 257–8). After the Cold War, the unilateral use of force was enhanced, since the US reached a status of a superpower without rivals, including conventional bombing or drone strikes, outside organizations and international law. In other words, the US and its allies assume such a broad sovereignty (wide and imperial) that it allows them to nullify the sovereignty of the rest of the world through the exceptionalism of the 'indispensable nation' and 'chosen by God', so that international institutionality itself has become a burden to the hegemon (Losurdo, 2018b: 406).

An illustrative note for the US case. Domestically, there is a 'competitive one-party system', in which two parties represent interest groups (Wall Street, military-industrial complex, oil sector) that control the country's wealth and political life – while polarization and mass incarceration grow in a nation whose history is based on a racial state (Losurdo, 2016: 83). It is those governments that, internationally, invest themselves in the 'imperial mission', with moral and religious contours, to carry out wars (War Clause) without institutional restraints (Damin, 2013). A Bonapartism with popular investiture of a plebiscitary type capable of extending its powers to the state of exception if it is to carry forward the ideologies of war and the empire of freedom (Losurdo, 2004: 300). In other words, the theoretical currents presented as antagonistic in the scope of International Relations, Liberalism and Realism, compose different and complementary strategies of projection and maintenance of the power structures of the great powers, combining discourses in favor of international institutions and the use of force.

4   Imperialism, Expropriation and Resistance

Hasty and anachronistic readings tend to attribute an ethnocentric bias to Marx himself. First, if we disregard the context of the nineteenth century and the evolution of the author's work, as the mature Marx approached colonialism, oppression and national liberation struggles with concern. His analyzes of India, Algeria, Indonesia and China became more complex, as elements (ethnicity and nationality) were added to the dynamics of capital to form a totality (Anderson, 2019: 355). Second, such analyzes are counterfactual, given that communist parties formed a field that, at its peak in the 1980s, reached 32 nations and a third of the world's population, transforming a backward country into a superpower, promoting processes of modernization and paving the way for unprecedented experiences of government – and some, such as China, Cuba, People's Korea, continue to resist and reinvent themselves today (Visentini, 2017).

In addition to the various mechanisms of regime change, imperialism is expressed through several socio-economic instruments of dismantling and expropriation. At present, neoliberalism is undoubtedly an imperial mechanism for increasing the polarization of intra and interstate wealth. As well as the construction, the annihilation of Social Welfare States is the very expression of class struggles. There is no doubt that social struggles and union action, as well as the existence of the socialist camp, shaped the extension of rights, just as the counter-revolution after the fall of the Berlin wall has driven the suppression of conquests. In addition to emptying rights, neoliberal policies erode political representation and institute a 'plutocracy'. At the international level, neoliberalism intertwines with neocolonialism, as the imposition of liberalizing agendas (via Washington Consensus, IMF, World Bank) on peripheral countries strengthens the projection of the great powers and their corporations (Losurdo, 2016: 39 and 68).

In a context of profound asymmetries, inequalities and violence on a global scale, the fight against imperialism is the supreme stage of the class struggle. Therefore, in his general theory of social conflicts, Losurdo emphasizes the need to overcome the binary reading of social conflicts – without being restricted to directly antagonistic subjects. According to him, class struggles take different forms, intertwining the dimensions of redistribution (via overcoming the social division of labor) and recognition (via overcoming dehumanization processes). In this way, social conflicts assume different priorities in each concrete situation in space and time, and, therefore, hierarchies, contradictions and conflicts between divergent liberties. Thus, social, gender, family, ethnic-racial matters and between states and nations are part of a broad system of social conflicts.

To shed light on the complex system of domination that encompasses imperialism, Losurdo placed great emphasis on the national question and anti-colonial struggle. For this reason, he even begins by reconstructing the trajectory of important authors to support his point of view. He highlights Lenin's emphasis on national liberation struggles and self-determination, as well as Mao's statement that "patriotism is an application of internationalism" (Losurdo, 2015: 153–185). Gramsci himself, in a critique of Trotsky, stated that 'internationalism', to be authentic', must be 'profoundly national', given that universalism is only justified to the extent that it is able to include particularity (Losurdo, 2018a: 249).

While drawing attention to the national issue, Domenico Losurdo (2010a) highlights its nuances and contradictions.[4] On the one hand, nationalism can assume reactionary and xenophobic forms, aimed at legitimizing

---

4 In another article, we discuss, based on the work of Losurdo, the complex dialectic between national and global (Pautasso, Fernandes and Doria, 2020).

expansionism, war and racial supremacy. On the other hand, it can be a driving force for the emancipation of nations, anti-imperialist struggles, the promotion of development, sovereignty and self-determination. Likewise, at the opposite pole, internationalism and cosmopolitanism can also be the defense of the global moral and legal foundations of capitalism; or they could be the movements that fight for a society that overcomes the logic of capital. That is, simplifying expressions at national and international level leads to false antagonisms, dysfunctional Manichaeism and misunderstandings (Domingos and Martins, 2007: 2–4 and 20).

But if the national question is crucial for peripheral countries to resist imperialism, this often produces misunderstandings about hierarchies and dilemmas about international insertion. Losurdo, as a tributary of the Leninist tradition, knew that imperialism entails a contradiction between the expropriation of surpluses and the export of surpluses and, therefore, the dialectic between plunder and the development of productive forces in peripheral regions. Although he did not address concepts such as sub-imperialism and/ or neo-imperialism, the Italian author was enthusiastic about China's trajectory. Obviously, in addition to development and sovereignty linked to the national question, emerging countries can play a key role in the multipolarization movement and strengthening of international institutions – as opposed to interventionist unilateralism and the liberalizing agenda radiated by the US and its allies (economic-technological-judicial neocolonialism).

From Losurdo's work, it would not be exaggerated to say that the national question is the link between sovereignty and development and, in turn, the possible amalgam for the various emancipatory struggles. Thus, any possibility of both anti-imperialist actions and emancipatory policies on the margins of national development projects and state capacities seems narrow. In this sense, beyond the specificities of each emancipatory struggle, there is a growing difficulty in overcoming legitimate identity demands for justice and equality and/or articulating such agendas to comprehensive collective projects. Or, as Haider says, identity has become a trap when it becomes identitarism, leading to the hyper fragmentation of the political struggle (Haider, 2019). What happens now is an incessant search for individual recognition, true rituals of self-affirmation and imprisonment of people in a unidimensional characteristic. Transposed to the digital arena, this policy has amplified irrationality and militantism, eroding the public sphere with authoritarian practices (cancellations and lynchings) and emptying any principle of universality. The result is that the segmented emancipatory struggles themselves subsume in the misunderstanding of the complexity of the system of domination, turning legitimate attempts into movements that breed antagonistic forces to the development of peripheral countries and to anti-imperialist struggles.

Here we can highlight another important issue that runs through imperialism and forms of resistance. Important sectors of the left neglected the imperative of force, the dialectic of war and peace, the dynamics of violence throughout history. On the one hand, non-violence was associated with maintaining the status quo and its various processes of oppression, including condemning the violence of the weakest (non-state movements) and legitimizing the violence of the strongest. Often, the ideal of non-violence went hand in hand with the celebration of the West as the guardian of humanity's moral conscience and therefore legitimized the right to intervene in favor of 'civilization' and against 'barbarians'. On the other hand, in opposition to the ideological capture of non-violence and perpetual peace, there is neither an aesthetic celebration of violence and war, nor an appeal to resentment and revenge. Violence and war, as well as peace, must respond to the anti-imperialist political struggle, according to the rational analysis of the forces involved and the social objectives in dispute (Losurdo, 2012: 89).

In short, imperialism intertwines several dimensions in its process of expropriation and dismantling. And it is a central element of the multifaceted character of class struggles. Despite this, the absent left, as Losurdo calls it, succumbs to the indignation promoted by Western multimedia power and is silent in the face of interventions (Yugoslavia, Iraq, Libya); criticizes socialist experiences (China, Vietnam, People's Korea) or non-aligned countries (Iran, Venezuela, Syria); delegitimizes the conquests of the Welfare States, etc. (Losurdo, 2016: 319–370).

5 Conclusion

The International Relations field of study has an Anglo-Saxon lineage, originally linked to the decision-making circle of the powers, above all Great Britain and the USA. Associated with this, studies on the contemporary world were riddled with enthusiastic narratives of the so-called globalization. And even perspectives that were intended to be critical, ended up moving away from issues such as the interweaving between the accumulation of wealth and power. The triumphalism that followed the collapse of real socialism made concepts such as imperialism and class struggle underestimated if not considered obsolete – by sectors of the left, inclusive.

Ironically, the concept of imperialism fell into disuse precisely when the Post-Cold War world intensified both the polarization of wealth by means of various mechanisms of expropriation, and the escalation of open or covert interventionism in the form of regime change policies with an unprecedented combination of war technologies and multimedia power. More than ever, it is necessary to understand imperialism as a complex system of domination and central to class struggles, taking into account the various dimensions brought by Losurdo.

References

Anderson K (2019) *Marx nas margens*. São Paulo: Boitempo.
Arrigui G (2012) *O longo século XX*. Rio de Janeiro: Contraponto.
Azzarà S (2020) Domenico Losurdo 2014–2018. In: Moraes J (ed.) *Losurdo: Presença e Permanência*. São Paulo: Anita Garibaldi, 11–30.
Bandeira L (2016) *A desordem mundial*. Rio de Janeiro: Civilização Brasileira.
Batista P Jr (1998) Mitos da "globalização". *Estudos Avançados*. 12 (32), 125–186.
Buzan B and Hansen L (2012) *A Evolução dos Estudos de Segurança Internacional*. São Paulo: Editora Unesp.
Chang HJ (2009) *Maus Samaritanos – o mito do livre-comércio e a história secreta do capitalismo*. Rio de Janeiro: Elsevier.
Damin C (2013) Poder de Guerra nos Estados Unidos: a Cláusula de Guerra, o precedente coreano de 1950 e a autonomia do Comandante-em-Chefe. Unpublished doctoral thesis. Federal University of Rio Grando do Sul, Porto Alegre.
Del Roio M (1996) Globalização e imperialismo: a globalização é uma fase do Capitalismo em processo. *Crítica Marxista*, v. 1, n. 3, 53–155.
Domingos M and Martins M (2006) Significados do nacionalismo e do internacionalismo. *Tensões Mundiais*, v. 2, n. 1, jan./jul., 80–111.
Dumenil G and Lèvy D (2004) O imperialismo na era neoliberal. *Crítica Marxista*, v.1, n.18, 11–36.
Fernandes L (1992) URSS – ascensão e queda. São Paulo: Anita Garibaldi.
Fontes V (2008) *Marx, expropriações e capital monetário – notas para o estudo do imperialismo tardio. Crítica Marxista*, v.1, n.26, 9–31.
Gonçalves R (2005) *Economia Política Internacional*. Elsevier: São Paulo.
Haider A (2019) *Armadilha da identidade – raça e classe nos dias de hoje*. São Paulo: Veneta.
Halliday F (1999) *Repensando as relações internacionais*. Porto Alegre: UFRGS.
Hardt M and Negri A (2001) *Império*. Rio de Janeiro: Record.
Ianni O (1996) Globalização e imperialismo. *Crítica Marxista*, v.1, n.3, 130–131.
Kumar K (1997) *Da sociedade pós-industrial à pós-moderna*. Rio de Janeiro: Zahar.

Leite L (2014) Sobre as teorias do imperialismo contemporâneo: uma leitura crítica. *Economia e Sociedade*, v. 23, n. 2 (51), 507–534.

Losurdo D (2018a) Um mundo sem guerras. São Paulo: UNESP.

Losurdo D (2018b) *O Marxismo ocidental*. São Paulo: Boitempo.

Losurdo D (2017) *Guerra e Revolução*. São Paulo: Boitempo.

Losurdo D (2016) *Esquerda ausente: crise, sociedade do espetáculo, guerra*. São Paulo: Anita Garibaldi.

Losurdo D (2015) *Marx e o balanço histórico do século XX*. São Paulo: Anita Garibaldi.

Losurdo D (2012) *A não violência: uma história fora do mito*. Rio de Janeiro: Revan.

Losurdo D (2010a) *Stalin. História crítica de uma lenda negra*. Rio de Janeiro: Revan.

Losurdo D (2010b) *Linguagem do Império*. São Paulo: Contraponto.

Losurdo D (2006a) *Contra-história do Liberalismo*. Aparecida-SP: Ideias & Letras.

Losurdo D (2006b) *Liberalismo. Entre civilização e barbárie*. São Paulo: Anita Garibaldi.

Losurdo D (2004) *Democracia ou bonapartismo*. Rio de Janeiro: UFRJ/UNESP.

Moraes J (1996) A miragem global e a rearticulação imperialista. *Crítica Marxista*, v.1, n.3, 143–145.

Osório LF (2018) *Imperialismo, Estado e Relações Internacionais*. São Paulo: Editora Ideias & Letras.

Pautasso D (2014) Elementos para uma teoria marxista das relações internacionais na obra de Domenico Losurdo. *Crítica Marxista*, n° 39, 57–76.

Pautasso D (2020) Estados Unidos, liberalismo e imperialismo: uma leitura a partir de Domenico Losurdo. *Tensões Mundiais*. v. 16, n. 31,143–164.

Pautasso D, Fernandes M and Doria G (2020) Marxismo e a questão nacional: Losurdo e a dialética nacional-internacional. In: Moraes J (ed.) *Losurdo - presença e permanência*. São Paulo: Anita Garibaldi, 57–84.

Ruccio D (2005) Globalização e imperialismo. *Crítica Marxista*, v.1, n.20, 49–69.

Visentini P (1996) Imperialismo e globalização. *Crítica Marxista*, v.1, n.3,149–152.

Visentini P (2017) *Os paradoxos da Revolução Russa*. Rio de Janeiro: Alta Books, 2017.

CHAPTER 9

David Harvey and the International Relations
Some Appointments

Leonardo César Souza Ramos[1], Rodrigo Corrêa Teixeira[2], and Marina Scotelaro de Castro[3]

1 Introduction

David Harvey certainly occupies a prominent position in contemporary Marxist studies.[4] For some, Harvey would be one of the great references of Marxism in recent decades, both in terms of certain analytical innovations brought about and in terms of the debates in which he has constantly engaged (Castree, 2007; Callinicos, 2006).

This chapter therefore seeks to present some of the central elements of the Marxism of David Harvey, highlighting aspects that can contribute to a critical understanding of International Relations. In this process, attention will be given to his understanding of the geography of capitalist accumulation, of the processes of accumulation by dispossession and their implications for the configuration of a new type of imperialism under way in the neoliberal phase of capitalism. Finally, some brief considerations about possible points of dialog of Harvey's approach with critical aspects of International Relations will be presented.

Such reflection in itself is already relevant insofar as it contributes to the understanding of the dynamics of expropriation in course in the contemporary world economic order; but in addition, it is important to bear in mind that such a perspective helps in a unique way to highlight the relevance of David Harvey's analytical contributions to the understanding of International Relations. In other words, ultimately, the present discussion intends to

---

1 Professor of International Relations at Pontifical Catholic University of Minas Gerais.
2 Professor of International Relations and Geography at Pontifical Catholic University of Minas Gerais.
3 Professor of International Relations at Centro Universitário de Belo Horizonte.
4 This chapter is a revised and expanded version of the following article: Scotelaro, Teixeira and Ramos (2018). Translated into English by the authors.

contribute to a new vision of David Harvey, this time also as a theorist of the international.

2 Towards a 'Geography of Capitalist Accumulation'

In general terms, it is possible to say that, based on a revisitation of the Marxist theory of accumulation, Harvey contemporizes the Marxian concept of primitive accumulation, replacing it with the term accumulation by dispossession. Thus, the author seeks to expand the scope of the category, which would, therefore, also deal with the current practices of intense spoliation in periods of crisis of overaccumulation. The reiteration of such practices would be recurrent strategies present in the accumulation processes that, in addition, also depend on a geographic expansion that, in turn, would result in interregional and international rivalries. This would explain the recurrence of imperialist moments in the history of world capitalism, which would be better understood once they are situated in a historical geography of capitalism. Such a perspective would reveal the uneven development of the processes of accumulation and externalization of the internal contradictions of capitalism to vulnerable spaces in neoliberalism. Ultimately, the understanding of contemporary international processes would be conditioned to the historical understanding of the uneven geographical development of capitalism, which would bring in itself explanatory elements of the dynamics of power between and through states.

In order to get a better understanding of this historical geography of capitalism, it is crucial to understand Harvey's attention to the geography of capitalist accumulation. According to the author, Marx's theory of accumulation presents a clear perspective on the spatial structure. In this sense, such discussion is central as a way of identifying what would be "the crucial link between Marx's theory of accumulation and the Marxian theory of imperialism" (Harvey, 2001: 237). According to Harvey, spatial organization and geographic expansion are fundamental aspects in the processes of capital circulation and accumulation, since these only occur in specific spatiotemporal configurations (Harvey, 2011, 2018). Overall, the need for accumulation generates, at the same time, the concentration of production and capital on the one hand and, on the other, an expansion of the market. In this process of market expansion, a new spatial structure was created. In other words, in the quest to overcome spatial barriers to accumulation, new spatial structures are created that, in the end, become barriers to further accumulation. In concrete terms,

> these spatial structures are expressed, of course, in the fixed and immovable form of transport facilities, plant, and other means of production and consumption which cannot be moved without being destroyed. (...) the geographical landscape which fixed and immobile capital comprises is both a crowning glory of past capital development and a prison which inhibits the further progress of accumulation because the very building of this landscape is antithetical to the 'tearing down of spatial barriers' and ultimately even to the 'annihilation of space by time'.
>
> HARVEY, 2001: 247

In fact, "the imperative to accumulate consequently implies the imperative to overcome spatial barriers" (Harvey, 2001: 243). In this sense, according to Harvey, a constant feature in the process of capitalist development is the construction of a physical landscape suitable for accumulation only to, at a later stage, have to destroy it. This usually occurs at a time of crisis, which leads the author to state that "temporal crises in fixed capital investment, often expressed as 'long-waves' in economic development (...) are therefore usually expressed as periodical reshaping of the geographic environment to adapt it to the needs of further accumulation" (Harvey, 2001: 247–248).

In short, understanding the geography of capitalist accumulation is one of David Harvey's great contributions to a more complex understanding of the processes of capitalist accumulation. It is from this discussion that other aspects of his argument become clearer, such as his theory of imperialism. But before going into this question, it is essential to discuss the processes of dispossession present in the history of capitalism.

3 Accumulation by Dispossession

The modern state is linked both to the structure of the historical geography of capitalism and to the accumulation practices set in motion at each historical moment by the ruling classes (Harvey, 2003). Given the fact that the modern state concentrates both political power and the legitimate monopoly on the use of force, it has the capacity to maintain the institutional and constitutional arrangements necessary for capitalist activities to develop in the sphere of production as well as in the sphere of circulation. On the one hand, the state is able to reallocate investments around spatially specific organizations, thus making spaces of accumulation more dynamic. Furthermore, the state is equally capable of creating physical spaces aimed at absorbing these surpluses from investments in infrastructure. In addition, this role of the state was originally fundamental for the accumulation itself, enabling the creation of private property and the regulations between the nascent capitalist class and the workers – which leads us to the Marxian idea of primitive accumulation (Marx, 2013).

On this basis, David Harvey argues that the process of accumulation depends on the idea of primitive accumulation in a double way: that is, it depends on primitive accumulation as its moment of origin, but also – and in an extremely significant way – as a continuous process that is fundamental in the expanded reproduction of capital. According to the Marxian perspective, the specific configuration of the capitalist mode of production was based on changes in previous productive structures. The historical origins of capitalism would thus reside in an initial process of breaking with these past social formations, something fundamental for the creation of the means of production that could be accumulated. In this process, the modern state is the institution that formalizes the expropriation of communal lands and, at the same time, provides the basis for the circulation of money that starts to mediate the social relations between the holders of the means of production and the suppliers of labor power.

This double dispossession of capacities for autonomous work, land and means of subsistence was carried out from the emergence of the modern bourgeois state, which is structured to provide the necessary dimensions for the establishment of the capitalist model. This strategy of expelling individuals from the countryside – as well as other strategies implemented – depended on an association between the nascent bourgeois class and the state apparatus. The latter deals with the negative externalities of the non-absorption of this entire layer of workforce created by extensive processes of dispossession, and thus starts to exercise a disciplinary function on the working class, constraining it to accept the laws of the liberal regime in consolidation. The commodification and monetization of the countryside as a tradable good, allied to the workforce also treated as a good, were intensively explored, developing in increasingly broader markets and strengthening land, commercial, banking and financial capital. The possibility of emergence of these modalities of capital was only possible to be achieved once the state actively acquired new sources of accumulation essential for the transformation and complexification of capitalist production processes and relations (Harvey, 2003, 2013b).

The violent appropriation of pre-existing non-capitalist modes of production was not something limited to Europe, but extended worldwide through the violent domination of different peoples beyond the original borders of capitalism. In this sense, colonialism was a crucial moment for the establishment of capitalist relations on a world scale, since it inaugurated a large-scale flow of goods from the metropolis and colonies – be they goods or the labor force itself. The same processes of dispossession of land are carried out elsewhere, and the growing working class is used as a fundamental element in the management of crises of accumulation. From the beginning, the way in which states act in the geographic space beyond their national borders has already been evident, acting actively in the solution of their internal problems of capital realization. These forms of external relief from the contradictions of domestic accumulation have existed since the beginning of the system, anchored in state support, given the very expansionist nature of accumulation (Harvey, 2001, 2003, 2013b).[5]

The fact that the process took place violently and demanded control of foreign spaces captures the importance of understanding the conquests and domains of the state in relation to other regions to guarantee the power of the alliance of national classes. It is at this point that Harvey advances his thesis on the Marxian concept of primitive accumulation: this would not only be a founding element of capitalism that allows the consolidation of the power of modern states, but also a fundamental element for the continuous and expanded reproduction of capitalist accumulation processes on a world scale.

In this sense, the theoretical-conceptual inflection proposed by Harvey considers the nature of primitive accumulation practices as recurrent strategies to deal with overaccumulation problems. In order to differentiate them, Harvey moves away from the 'primitive' or 'original' content of the concept and calls the continuity of the process as 'accumulation by dispossession'. The aspects of primitive accumulation that refer to the use of geographic expansion to realize value remain, but the main strategy involves the devaluation of overproduction assets at minimal costs to be recycled more profitably in other spaces. In this sense, accumulation through dispossession occurs contingently according to the needs of realizing value within different moments of the historical geography of capitalism. This difference between primitive accumulation and dispossession is fundamental, since the latter not only contains the practices established during the "original process" of accumulation, but also brings

---

5 At this point, Harvey calls attention to the fact that, before Marx, it was Hegel who presented, in "The Philosophy of Right", "imperialism and colonialism as potential solutions to the serious and stressful internal contradictions of what he considered to be a 'mature' civil society" (Harvey, 2004b: 43). In other words, it would be possible to see in Hegel the seeds of the Marxian understanding of the necessity of spatial fixes due to the internal contradictions of capitalism.

with it other forms of concentration and centralization of power over capital (Harvey, 2003: 144, 164).[6]

This means that, once the traditional possibilities of accumulation in a specific space-time configuration are over, the state undertakes new expansionist stages based on processes of commodification and privatization of productive spaces already occupied by the capitalist production model (Harvey, 2013b, 2018). This does not mean a dismantling of the productive structures already in place, but a revolution in the existing productive space, a true spatial adjustment as a way of dealing with the contradictions inherent in the very development of capitalism.[7] And it is from this process of spatiotemporal fix that the theme of imperialism, in conjunction with the concept of accumulation by dispossession, gains importance for the understanding of the historical geography of capitalism according to David Harvey.

4   The New Imperialism in This Context

David Harvey thus seeks to expand the scope of the phenomenon of primitive accumulation by demonstrating that the theorists of imperialism who use primitive accumulation as a framework for such actions circumscribe it to a specific historical period. Thus, although he agrees with such perspectives regarding the foundation and development of capitalism until the first half of the twentieth century, his objective from this point on is to expand the concept of accumulation by dispossession as a recurrent strategy and applied it to other moments of crisis of overproduction made possible by the actions of the states.

---

6 It is in this sense that Jim Glassman's statement about the novelty of David Harvey's discussion of accumulation through dispossession can be understood. According to Glassman, although the idea of primitive accumulation has been constantly mobilized in development studies, Harvey's novelty is the use of this category – now rethought as accumulation by dispossession – "to describe processes that are taking place in the capitalist countries of the Global North" (Glassman, 2006: 608).

7 Harvey bases on the "Grundrisse" to think about this destructive/reconstructive tendency of the capital: "capital drives beyond national barriers and prejudices as much as beyond nature worship, as well as all traditional, confined, complacent, encrusted satisfactions of present needs, and reproductions of old ways of life. It is destructive towards all of this, and constantly revolutionizes it, tearing down all the barriers which hem in the development of the forces of production, the expansion of needs, the all-sided development of production, and the exploitation and exchange of natural and mental forces" (Marx, 2011: 334).

Ultimately, unlike readings that consider primitive accumulation as a 'primitive' and 'external' moment of the accumulation process that gives rise to the imperialist phase – which would be the case of Lenin and Rosa Luxemburg, for example (Harvey, 2013a: 554) –, for Harvey these processes are perpetuated in time from various forms of accumulation by dispossession that lead to new processes of intense exploitation and control of capital accumulated from new phases of geographic re-expansion.[8] These strategies depend on a renewed role of the state and justify the existence of other imperialist moments corresponding to class alliances – national and transnational, of capitalists and workers – in each historical period (Harvey, 2001, 2003, 2004a). In this case, the result is a dialectical interconnection between the territorial logic of political power and the spatiality of capitalist accumulation from the intervention of the state, both in the process of reproletarianization of previously winning sectors – associated with the dismantling of the existing working class, and of 'reconquest' of new spaces aimed at revaluation of devalued assets.

> It is at this point that the territorialized politics of state and empire re-enter to claim a leading role in the continuing drama of endless capital accumulation and over accumulation. It is the state that is the political entity, the body politic, that is best able to orchestrate institutional arrangements and manipulate the molecular forces of capital accumulation to preserve that pattern of asymmetries in exchange that are most advantageous to the dominant capitalist interests working within its frame.
>
> HARVEY, 2003: 132–133

The implication of these dialectically connected logics is the continuous appropriation, transformation and domination of capitalist spaces through accumulation through dispossession as a recurrent practice of capitalism that shapes new imperialist moments (Harvey, 2003, 2013a, 2013b).

---

8 Even if this is not a central point in our argument, it is important to note that, although he disagrees with classical Marxist approaches to imperialism, David Harvey is significantly close to Rosa Luxemburg's (1988) theory: in fact, her argument about capital's necessity to expand into pre-capitalist zones in order to be able to continue accumulating ("colonialism and imperialism were, in her view, necessary and central to capital's survival") (Harvey, 2018: 135) – an issue intimately linked to her view about the meaning of the primitive accumulation process – is a fundamental point of Harvey's theorizing about the new imperialism and accumulation by dispossession (Harvey, 2003, 2007).

In a context of creation of "spaces of neoliberalization" (Harvey, 2005a, 2005b), the state, insofar as it directs in these terms the process of rationalization of contemporary capitalist accumulation, ends up undertaking a new phase of accumulation by dispossession that, in turn, inaugurates a new phase of imperialism in global capitalism (Harvey, 2007). Such imperialist moments arise when class relations within a state do not result in local solutions to the problem of overaccumulation – that is, when there is not, in a satisfactory way for the reproduction of the dynamics of capital circulation, the reinvestment of valued capital in domestic structures.

In this case, the internal capitalist production processes can be understood as regions where their own logics of accumulation are developed. As seen, capital as a social relationship creates particular geographies, specific spatio-temporal configurations that are unstable in view of the very contradictions generated by capitalism. In this sense, such dynamism is driven by the dialectical relationship between possibilities and limits of accumulation in existing productive structures and the hierarchical arrangements between social fractions located on the borders of the state (Harvey, 2013a).

If imperialist behaviors involve "the sense that the contradictions of capitalism can be cured through world domination by some omnipotent power" (Harvey, 2013a: 552) it is through the export of capital that it takes place beyond the use of force – capital export which also has the state as a support point. Surplus capital can be exported through loans to other states to stimulate international purchases or function as foreign direct investment; however, it is essential to understand at this point that, regardless of the destination given to the over accumulated capital, the fundamental motivation will be to obtain an average rate of profit higher than the national possibilities. Now, once new productive forces are created outside the capital's region of origin, the state not only exports the internal contradictions of accumulation but also new moments of devaluation from the emergence of rivalries and competition between national and foreign capital put in shock.

Capital is "value in motion" (Harvey, 2018: 129), and in this movement in search of the realization of value abroad, state actions should not, therefore, be understood as a simple territorial expansion, but understood in the light of imperialist movements that translate into different interregional hierarchies. The idea of "new imperialism" (Harvey, 2003, 2013a) thus stems from a new dialectical relationship between the exercise of state power internally through actions associated with privatization and flexibilization of productive relations, and inter-regional competition in spaces open to the movements of over accumulated surplus capital. This, in turn, implies different movements of 'export' of devaluation, spatially and socially determined by the internationalization of capitalist rivalries that informs the uneven historical-geographical development in capitalism. Thus, some specific regions – such as the most economically vulnerable states, for example – undergo intense processes of devaluation, generating localized crises, which, in turn, have the function of mitigating the possible systemic crises of capitalism (Harvey, 2001, 2004a, 2013a).

Harvey affirms that, if in recent decades it is possible to perceive a growing volume of surpluses being accumulated in East Asia, one can also perceive the emergence of certain imperialist practices in such regions. In this sense, the corollary of the argument is that, ultimately, the new imperialism is not characterized by being an imperialism in the singular, but imperialist practices dispersed through an unequal geography of the distribution of the capital surplus intimately connected to the transformations that have been taking place since the 1970s (Harvey, 2007).

5 New Imperialism and Neoliberalism

Therefore, the intimate relations between the new imperialism and neoliberalism can be seen: in fact, this contemporary phenomenon is historically inserted in the neoliberal moment, and in this sense, it is constituted by a space-time dimension distinct from the previous imperialist forms when situated in the historical geography of capitalism. Thus, it is possible to understand the processes of neoliberalization

> either as a utopian project to realize a theoretical design for the reorganization of international capitalism or as a political project to re-establish the conditions for capital accumulation and to restore the power of economic elites.
>
> HARVEY, 2005a: 19

Once seen in these terms, neoliberalism, as an effort to restore the power of dominant capitalist elites, restores the power of certain class fractions through the reconfiguration of certain hierarchical arrangements – whether monetary systems, political structures or organizational forms that have an impact in the processes of reproduction and accumulation of capital in its local or global aspects (Harvey, 2005a, 2005b, 2013a). In this process of retaking the power of the capitalist class, the restructuring of institutional arrangements and class relations involves financialization processes related to the power to control capital movements, and also to the concentration of the volume of capital.

In addition, in a context of neoliberal globalization (Harvey, 2004b) the establishment and consolidation of new market relations supported by a privileged relationship of access to the institutional support offered by the neoliberal state and by international arrangements is fundamental. In this sense, the state promotes a series of privatizations – a fundamental step both for accumulation by dispossession and for the restoration of the power of the capitalist class – and at the same time it builds a structure aimed at guaranteeing both the functioning of capital markets and the free circulation of capital goods. In turn, international organizations manage and institutionalize the introduction of neoliberal practices of deregulation of the movements of production inputs and control over the conditions of capital remuneration. Ultimately, the connection between these state-led actions and neoliberal practices is evident: "The umbilical cord that ties together accumulation by dispossession and expanded reproduction is that given by finance capital and the institutions of credit, backed, as ever, by state powers" (Harvey, 2003: 152).

Now, to maintain and sustain this reconfiguration of power on a global spatial scale, "the Wall Street-Treasury-IMF complex" (Harvey, 2003: 185) manages crises located in more vulnerable territories, preventing that the devaluation arising from such crises return to the center of accumulation, a phenomenon that have occurred recurrently since the oil shocks that started in the 1970s. This becomes explicit when attention is turned to the crises that the world economy has been going through since the 1970s and the real impacts of these at the center of accumulation – until the 2008 crisis, of course. In this case, the outbreak of a crisis of significant proportions in central countries ends up having consequences not only for the reproduction capacity of the neoliberal model but also for the historical geography of capitalism in force until then (Menezes and Ramos, 2018). In this context, the role of China and its actions to guarantee the export of capital accumulated until then (a globalization with Chinese characteristics, with particular institutional aspects associated with both the new multilateral banks – BAII and NDB – and the Belt Road Initiative), and the US responses to such actions (such as the recent creation of the Development Finance Corporation, as well as the clashes around the geopolitics of 5G technology, for example) stand out (Borquez and Shoaib, 2019; Vadell, Secches and Burger, 2019). All these issues draw attention to the fact that, through certain structural adjustments, "(...) state interventions and of international institutions (...) orchestrate devaluations in ways that permit accumulation by dispossession to occur without sparking a general collapse" (Harvey, 2003: 151).

6   Dialogs and Limits with International Relations

The innovations brought by David Harvey are certainly not unanimous. Starting from a Marxist perspective, Raju J. Das, for example, criticizes Harvey's theory of uneven geographical development, highlighting what, in his opinion, would be the author's major problems: a limited view of class relations in capitalism that, in turn, would be intimately connected to a certain fetishization of the power of spatial relationships (Das, 2017). From another perspective, closer to poststructuralism, Andrew Jones presents a critique of ontological and epistemological aspects of Harvey's approach, which would be expressed particularly in his defense of Marxist dialectics (Jones, 1999).

With regard to issues close to International Relations, the same occurs – see, for example, the important debate made possible by his work "The New Imperialism", which ended up involving prominent authors in the Marxist field, such as Ellen Wood, Robert Brenner and Alex Callinicos, among others.[9]

Even so, there is a perpetuation of a certain "mutual negligence": neither Harvey engages with the literature and authors of International Relations itself (nor even the critical theorists and authors critical from IR field), nor do they customarily engage with the questions raised by David Harvey. One point that could contribute to build a bridge for dialog concerns the issue of subjectivity and culture – an important issue to the critical perspectives of International Relations.

In this case, it should be noted that David Harvey mentions the cultural dynamics associated with the postmodern condition (Harvey, 2008). In particular, from such discussions Harvey highlights, at various times, what would be constitutive aspects of the subjectivity of the neoliberal individual – a possessive, short-sighted individualism and in contradiction with what would be the interests of humanity and nature – and the need to its overcoming in the search for the construction of qualitatively distinct and superior social (international) relationships.

Furthermore, when he talks about the "seven distinctive 'activity spheres' within the evolutionary trajectory of capitalism", attention is paid to the seventh sphere – "mental conceptions of the world" (Harvey, 2011: 104)[10] –, which is closely linked to the constructions of subjectivities. However, this is little

---

9   This debate was published in the journal "Historical Materialism", 14 (4), 2006.
10 The seven activity spheres would be as follows: "technologies and organizational forms; social relations; institutional and administrative arrangements; production and labor processes; relations to nature; the reproduction of daily life and of the species; and 'mental conceptions of the world'" (Harvey, 2011, p. 104).

explored, and seems to occupy a secondary place in the author's argument. In this case, there is a potential dialog with the Marxist-inspired perspectives that emerged in International Relations from the late 1990s with the processes of construction of hegemony at the global level and how, in these processes, ideological issues are a fundamental aspect of the process.[11] Even without engaging so openly in the ideological issues of this process, Jonathan Pass, for example, presents a possibility of such a dialog between David Harvey and the neo-Gramscians in his neo-Gramscian proposal, engaging with the works of Giovanni Arrighi, David Harvey and Robert W. Cox in order to deal with the spatial aspects of world hegemony, using systemic cycles of accumulation as an analytical reference (Pass, 2019).

Even so, other routes can also be explored; in particular, the Coxian, Amsterdam and cultural perspectives (Ramos, 2020), each from its own particularities, can contribute in a distinct and rich way to the debate, pointing out fundamental ideological aspects on which world hegemony is sustained, and how the processes of implementation of neoliberal logic in the world are intimately related to such processes of hegemonic struggle on a world scale. The concept of new constitutionalism explored by Stephen Gill is an example.

According to Stephen Gill and A. Claire Cutler, the new constitutionalism concerns to "the legal and political frameworks that are equally significant in facilitating neo-liberal forms of global economic integration and the extension of the world market" (Gill and Cutler, 2014: 6). Closely related to the emergence of a market civilization, the new constitutionalism expresses the political-legal counterpart of disciplinary neoliberalism[12], incorporating a series of regulatory and political-legal mechanisms aimed at guaranteeing neoliberal patterns of accumulation. In this process, a central element of the new constitutionalism is the construction and extension of market logic – which "includes rewriting laws and statutes to facilitate primitive accumulation" (Gill, 2014: 39). That is, in this sense, the potential for dialog between theorizing about the new constitutionalism and Harvey's idea about accumulation by dispossession and their respective analytical derivations is clear.

---

11   Just by mentioning Gramsci, especially in his discussions about Fordism (Harvey, 2008), David Harvey, however, does not advance a more substantive discussion about the processes of struggle for hegemony and its potential implications – and relationships – with the processes of spatial adjustment of capitalist production and accumulation.

12   Disciplinary neoliberalism concerns "primarily to the processes of intensifying and deepening the scope of market disciplines associated with the increasing power of capital in organizing social and world orders, and in so doing shaping the limits of the possible in people's everyday lives" (Gill and Cutler, 2014: 6).

In addition, the theoretical-conceptual advances of David Harvey can also contribute in a unique way to such perspectives – authors such as John Agnew (2005) and Jonathan Pass (2019) highlight in this case the importance of paying attention to the spatial dimensions of world hegemony, particularly of US hegemony. However, important aspects of this process still require further studies, such as issues related to investments in infrastructure and US and Chinese actions at this point. In short, dialog in this case can contribute to a next step in the processes of developing a critical understanding of International Relations and International Political Economy.

7   Conclusion

As seen, David Harvey presents an original and significantly relevant contribution to the understanding of the processes of capitalist production and accumulation in space. On the other hand, a dialog with certain critical perspectives of International Relations could also be fruitful, enriching Harvey's analytical framework dealing with cultural aspects of capitalism, in addition to the insights he had already developed. In particular, this would dialectically contribute to a better understanding of the processes of hegemony on a world scale, and how these relate to the geography of capitalist accumulation.

More than seen only from an exclusively absolute perspective, space, for David Harvey, is a significantly active aspect in the process of capitalist production, being a fundamental element in the internal dialectical relations (Ollman, 1992) concerning the processes of spatio-temporal adjustment of historical geography. of capitalism (Harvey, 2006, 2008). In this process, regional distinctions are a fundamental element that is closely linked to the processes of restructuring the expanded reproduction of capital on a domestic scale as well as internationally. In this case, this question is fundamental, because despite the criticisms raised against Harvey's theoretical-analytical construct, there is a unique potential for contribution to the field of International Relations: his creative inter-scalar dialogs between Marx's theory of accumulation with Marxist theories of imperialism (and neoliberalism, via the concept of accumulation by dispossession) from their spatial theory of capitalism can help not only to strengthen critical approaches to International Political Economy but also to question the limits of the separation between Political Economy International and International Relations – or, in the author's own terms, the separation between the territorial logic and the logic of capital. But these are points for future development, to which the present chapter intends to have made a brief contribution.

References

Agnew J (2005) *Hegemony: The Shape of Global Power*. Philadelphia: Temple University Press.

Borquez A and Shoaib F (2019) El Banco Asiático de Inversión en Infraestructura Apuntando al Camino del Medio: Uniéndose a las Filas de los Bancos Multilaterales de Desarrollo, pero con Características Chinas. *Estudos Internacionais*, 7(3): 103–20.

Callinicos A (2006) David Harvey and Marxism. In: Castree N and Gregory D (eds.). *David Harvey. A Critical Reader*. Malden: Blackwell.

Castree N (2007) David Harvey: Marxism, Capitalism and the Geographical Imagination. *New Political Economy*, 12(1): 97–115.

Das RJ (2017) David Harvey's Theory of Uneven Geographical Development: A Marxist Critique. *Capital & Class*, 41(3): 511–36.

Gill S (2014) Market Civilization, New Constitutionalism and World Order. In: Gill, S. and Cutler, A. C. (eds). *New Constitutionalism and World Order*. Cambridge: Cambridge University Press.

Gill S and Cutler A (2014) New Constitutionalism and World Order: General Introduction. In: Gill, S. and Cutler, A. C. (eds). *New Constitutionalism and World Order*. Cambridge: Cambridge University Press.

Glassman J.(2006) Primitive Accumulation, Accumulation by Dispossession, Accumulation by 'Extra-Economic' Means. *Progress in Human Geography* 30(5): 608–25.

Harvey D (2001) *Spaces of Capital: Towards a Critical Geography*. Edinburgh: Edinburgh University Press.

Harvey D (2003) *The New Imperialism*. New York: The Oxford University Press.

Harvey D (2004a) The New Imperialism: Accumulation by Dispossession. In: *Socialist Register* 40: 63–87.

Harvey D (2004b) *Espaços De Esperança*. São Paulo: Loyola.

Harvey D (2005a) *A Brief History of Neoliberalism*. New York: Oxford University Press.

Harvey D (2005b) *Spaces of Neoliberalization: Towards a Theory of Uneven Geographical Development*. München: Franz Steiner Verlag.

Harvey D (2006) Space as a Keyword. In: Castree, N. and Gregory, D. (eds). *David Harvey: A Critical Reader*. Malden: Blackwell.

Harvey D (2007) In What Ways Is 'The New Imperialism' Really New? *Historical Materialism* 15(3): 57–70.

Harvey D (2008) The Dialectics of Spacetime. In: Ollman, B. and Smith, T. (orgs). *Dialectics for the New Century*. Basigkstoke: Palgrave.

Harvey D (2011) *O Enigma do Capital e as Crises do Capitalismo*. São Paulo: Boitempo.

Harvey D (2013a) *Os Limites do Capital*. São Paulo: Boitempo.

Harvey D (2013b) *Para Entender o Capital*. São Paulo: Boitempo.

Harvey D (2018) *A Loucura da Razão Econômica: Marx e o Capital no Século XXI*. São Paulo: Boitempo.

Jones A (1999) Dialectics and Difference: Against Harvey's Dialectical 'Post-Marxism'. *Progress in Human Geography* 23(4): 529–555.

Luxemburg R (1988) *A Acumulação do Capital.* 3. ed., São Paulo: Nova Cultural.

Marx K (2011). *Grundisse*. São Paulo: Boitempo.

Marx K (2013) *O Capital*. Livro 1. São Paulo: Boitempo.

Menezes R and Ramos L (2018) Apresentação – 10 Anos da Crise Financeira (2008–2018): Leituras e Interpretações. *Conjuntura Internacional*, 15(2): 1–2.

Ollman B (1992) *Dialectical Investigations*. New York: Routledge.

Pass J (2019) *American Hegemony in the 21st Century: A Neo Neo-Gramscian Perspective*. New York: Routledge.

Ramos L (2020) Gramscian IPE. In: Vivares E (ed) *The Routledge Handbook to Global Political Economy: Conversations and Inquiries*. London: Routledge.

Scotelaro M, Teixeira R and Ramos L (2018) Acumulação por Despossessão, Novo Imperialismo e Neoliberalismo: Notas sobre David Harvey e o Internacional. *Crítica Marxista,* 46: 163–172.

Vadell J, Secches D and Burger M (2019) De la Globalización a la Interconectividad: Reconfiguración Espacial en la Iniciativa Belt & Road e Implicaciones para el Sur. *Global Revista Transporte y Territorio*, 21: 44–68.

PART 3

Marxist Theories on Imperialism

∴

CHAPTER 10

Notes on Imperialism, State and International Relations

Luiz Felipe Brandão Osório[1]

1   Introduction

In the midst of the centenary jubilee of the first debates, imperialism comes back to the spotlight.[2] Given as exhausted and overcome, it was resurrected as current and unavoidable in international discussions. After a short interregnum of illusory prosperity on the threshold of the transition between centuries, the much-vaunted term returns to the mouths and ears of analysts and scholars of international relations. Today's leading role is largely due to the practical and theoretical directions that impacted the study of the international system. It has become an indispensable tool for understanding a world that boasts unprecedented levels of productivity and technological development and, at the same time, suffers from the exponential deterioration of social conditions across continents. The events recorded in the first decades of the twenty-first century (which, despite being brief, already show interesting contrasts) impose new tasks on theoretical perspectives and political struggles.

On a practical level, the scene of degradation illustrates the disastrous scenario: rising rates of violence; intensification of social upheavals, with the respective concentration of income; patent economic and social exploitation, marked by racism, intolerance and xenophobia; and exacerbation of interstate rivalries, accompanied by military movements and specific conflicts, present in all corners of the globe. In theory, after the brief period of mists at the end of the twentieth century, the international reality brought up again the indispensability of the critical debate on the role of the State in capitalism, fostered

---

1   He is the author of the book "Imperialism, State and International Relations", by Editora Ideias e Letras. Post-doctorate in Political and Economic Law and PhD in International Political Economy. Professor of International Relations at Federal Rural University of Rio de Janeiro (UFRRJ).
2   Originally published as chapter of the book "Marxism and International Relations": Bugiato C (2021) Marxismo e Relações Internacionais. Goiânia: Editora Phillos Academy. Translated into English by the author.

by the harmful reverberations of the phenomenon of the intensification of the internationalization of production relations, reflected in the different areas of knowledge.

The misery and horror that inhabit the concreteness of international relations prompt the urgent consideration of imperialism, both in practice and in theory, as an undisguised and structural element. Reflecting on this word is not a simple exercise. He has translated the directions of the development of capitalism since the nineteenth century, having fluctuated like no other in the systemic trajectory. From a critical concept it became criticized, from virtuous to distorted. From a glittering theme, it was relegated to the shadows, considered outdated and exhausted, until its resurgence. Focused on its uncomfortable present day, the critical view of international relations turns to the source of imperialism. This phenomenon is of such magnitude that it does not fit in itself, or in artificial borders, its developments occur and/or affect the international scope by essence. Imperialism and international relations mix as if they were Siamese twins, and one cannot be treated without aiming at the other. The inherent interface is not, however, the work of chance or a given and unfinished construction. Yes, it was built over the years, with the historicity of this figure having a nodal aspect, gaining distinct features. In this vein, it is essential to point out its necessary specificity, so that theoretical precision is not lost in abstract, a-historical and transcendental approaches.

The concept of imperialism carries with it for centuries contents and stereotypes that can regress to the level of theoretical imprecision. From the rescue of the empires of antiquity, such as the Roman, through the great feudal powers, through the modern absolute monarchies, until reaching the contemporary era of empires, this entire historical arch was and can be painted randomly under the ink of imperialism. Although the existence of violence, oppressions and exploitations is verified as conditioning at all times, the linkage to the quantitative aspect confines the scientist to the appearance of phenomenal investigation, losing the precision of the analytical lens in a diffuse and distinct space in its bases. The decisive scientific step to unravel the real essence of imperialism takes the direction of understanding the mechanisms and structure that give it specificity, that is, its qualitative aspect,[3] which allows to identify imperialism, from a certain historical point, with content and particular ways, which contrast irrevocably with previous experiences.

---

3 It is possible to perform an analogy to the reasoning exposed by Mascaro (2013), to explain the law in contemporary times, didactically using the quantity/quality pair to reveal the legal essence.

Despite punctual coincidences or exceptionally similar traits, there is no way to delineate links that bring together interims as disparate as the Roman Empire of antiquity and the contemporary empires of the post-nineteenth century. Although the ancestral meaning of the Latin lexicon[4] brings with it the use of force and domination, the historical phenomena are not coincident or even comparable. This is because violence to impose the will of the strongest is a phenomenon that transcends historical systematizations. It can be verified from antiquity to contemporary times. Which does not mean to say that the concept of imperialism is reduced to coercion, nor that it must be taken up and traced back to the beginnings of civilizations. In this sense, it is crucial to outline guidelines that guide the scientific narrative.

2   Imperialism, Marxism and International Relations

It is from the emergence of the capitalist mode of production, inaugurating the historical contemporaneity, that certain social and economic relations carved the specific structural bases of imperialism, outlining international relations. In past modes of production, what is tried to be associated with imperialism is imprecise, happening in completely different dynamics, given that the central gears are not similar at all. In other words, imperialism is founded and unfolds in a very specific political-economic context, one shaped by concrete capitalist social relations. At the heart of this construct is the mercantile form, from which the mechanisms of operationalization of this sociability derive, such as the state political form (in which the bourgeois state, the nation-state or the national state is inserted), which is the actor that characterizes namely the interaction of agents. Thus, imperialism is based on the fullest manifestation of capitalism, the international system, through the economic pillar, capitalist accumulation permeated by the contradiction between nationalization and internationalization of capital in the world market, and the political vector, by the political organization given in a multiplicity, a collectivity of States, grouped in a dynamic network of permanent competition between materially unequal forces.

Thus, before further conceptual deepening, it is essential to point out that the understanding of imperialism necessarily passes through the understanding

---

4 For Anderson (2016) and Kurz (2003), the Latin word *imperium* already has the inherent connotation of the power to order. The power of domination and its repressive character can be verified in the most remote civilizations, which, in no way, allows them to be compared to the capitalist specificity that shaped the contours of the phenomenon today.

of capitalism, and consequently of the national state. Therefore, to speak of imperialism is to speak of capitalism; to approach international relations is to touch capitalism. This first demarcation leads to an escape from the traps that it encounters along the way to unraveling the meaning of imperialism. Abandoning the vulgar totalizing visions, it is necessary to overcome the contemporary trends that seek to connect with critical conceptions and, thus, confuse them. There are a lot of books or studies that aimed to map imperialism, whether to understand it, to bury it or even to resurrect it. From compartmentalized analyzes (conceptualizing it by separate biases, as just a political or strictly economic term), to positive and negative perspectives, as well as theoretical and empirical approaches, it is possible to identify readings of the most disparate political nuances. More than an academic concept, it has become a watchword and a political banner.[5] Therefore, attempts at appropriation abound. The myriad of approaches is very disruptive, as it leads to confusion and, consequently, to theoretical and conceptual inaccuracies. The multiplicity of writings on the issue does not exhaust it, however; needs to be elucidated.

The full and broad explanation of imperialism as a specific manifestation of capitalism is given by the theoretical horizon of International Relations. The current scenario demands an organic and systematic study of international relations, which inexorably permeates the establishment of methodological guidelines that enable a coherent and rigorous look at its trajectory. Focusing on this endeavor, it is pertinent to delve into International Relations, as a scientific field. In this exercise, it is up to the reader to pay attention to the fallacies posed by the abstractions that co-opt this scientific field for a verve proudly and manifestly flaunted as conservative.[6] It is interesting to point out how the scientific narrative of International Relations deals with its promiscuous relations with governmental apparatus, bragging that it is a science that limits itself to repeating and, eventually, to sophisticating the official discourses and positions of national States. When, in fact, they ratify domination strategies, universalizing concepts in abstractions that disguise the interests of singular social classes. There is a whole literature that is claimed to be the dominant one in the study of International Relations that underpins the beginning of the academic and scientific verve of the matter in the throes of the World War I.[7] In the emergence of a new scenario, of British decadence and American

---

5 See Hirsch (2010).
6 See Teschke (2016).
7 International Relations would have been thought, as a science, from the creation of the 'Woodrow Wilson Chair' at the University of Wales, in 1919, held by bureaucrat and diplomat

ascendancy in a fraternal condominium of power that imposed itself on the then threatened capitalist world, post-1917. As if, for example, the previous discussions, notably those of the Second International, the pioneering debates and the polemic between Lenin and Kautsky had not even existed.[8]

From the expansion of capitalism through the quadrants of the globe, scientific research opened new levels, but maintained its biased character. Theoretical aridity predominates on its horizon. There is a flagrant limitation between the theoretical paradigms, based on the innocuous discussion between idealism/liberalism and realism, and its consequences.[9] By exclusion, what does not fit this axis is placed in the basket of (carelessly called) critical theories. The imprecision and incorrectness of this grouping make the alternative study even more difficult. In order for criticism not to be compromised, it is essential to extrapolate the Anglo-Saxon monopoly, without which it is impossible to see beyond the surface. The unique and technical thinking seeks to detach itself from criticism by presenting itself as pure, appearing to be scientific rigor. International Relations suffers from the same evil of specialization that contaminates the social sciences as a whole. The lack of a broad approach that focuses on the object of study, but is not limited to it, adding other areas, is the rule and not the exception. The inter or multidisciplinarity of International Relations is not its stain, as purists think, on the contrary, it is its immanence, which is not in line with the dogmatism of departmentalization and consequent segregation of areas of knowledge.

Therefore, Marxism reveals itself to be the science capable of deciphering the sphinx-like enigmas of international relations. Marxism is essentially internationalist science, one capable of capturing the fullness of capitalism, a mode of production that is only completed internationally. In the midst of the historical and structural context of heterogeneity between countries that predominates in the international system, there is nothing better than evoking the concreteness of the social totality of social phenomena to grasp its essence. The insertion of Marxism in international debates, in addition to being essential, is unavoidable to overcome the appearance of sophistication and penetrate

---

Edward Carr (1892–1982), one of the main negotiators of the Treaty of Versailles. His outstanding performance at the post-war conference qualified him to occupy the academic post. This symbol of the biased construction that was sold to other countries as the inaugural milestone of a scientific nature of International Relations belongs to the monopoly of Anglo-Saxon theories in the dispute also for knowledge worldwide (Monteiro and Gonçalves, 2015).

8 The debate between Lenin and Kautsky, which revolves around the growing competition for territories between capitalist countries, associated with the intense concentration of capital, has historically been overcome (Arrighi, 1983).

9 See Fernandes (1998).

to the heart of reality. It is the Marxist tradition that will provide the methodological and theoretical frameworks so that a sophisticated, complete and reliable scientific interpretation of international relations can be drawn. It is the Marxist authors who focus on the role of the State and capitalism in international dynamics. Therefore, they have imperialism as their central category, giving this political-economic phenomenon its highlights.

3   Marx and International Relations

In this endeavor, it is perfectly plausible to resize the beacons of the study of international relations. In this vein, the second introductory demarcation follows the reasoning: if imperialism is shaped by capitalism and manifests itself, in essence, at an international level; it is Marxism in international relations that will enable its central reading. It is the aspect that will open the theoretical horizon necessary to develop the directions of scientific knowledge. In short, as Marx's vision is focused on the anatomy of capitalist society,[10] the time frame can only be contemporaneity, the consolidation and spread of the capitalist mode of production throughout the world. It is only in capitalism that imperialism acquires specificity, becoming a structural element, without which the essence of international relations cannot be fully understood. Historically, it was verified the existence of forms around exploitation, violence and dependence, which acquired a determined face with capitalism, from the reproduction of production relations by the quadrants of the globe. The

---

10   In the mid-nineteenth century, with bourgeois sociability already established in England and in full expansion across continental Europe, Karl Marx (1818–1883) and Friedrich Engels (1820–1895) completely transformed social thought by elaborating a critical theory about the way of capitalist production in its permanent movement of evolution, tracing the anatomy of bourgeois society, with the fulcrum of interpreting reality, but not only. The ultimate goal was to understand it in order to radically transform it (from the root), revolutionize it. Thus, they lay the foundations of the most complete critical thinking of contemporaneity, based on the historical-dialectical materialist method. The study of capitalism with a focus on its historical origin as a socioeconomic system and its place in the history of humanity inaugurates the rupture with previous trends and structures new foundations of social thought. According to this conception, what can be seen as a result of the modes of production over time is the inherent conflict between material forces, in a necessarily dual and conflicting relationship, and one class cannot exist without the other, and never unitary. The accommodation of struggles leads to concrete social forms that structure capitalist sociability. Reflections that propose criticisms about the current reality inexorably depart from the Marxian premises. See Marx, 2013; Rosdolsky, 2001; Naves, 2008.

globalizing dynamic was already announced by the German from Trier, in the joint work with Engels, in the midst of the industrial reality in the meantime.

> Driven by the need for ever new markets, the bourgeoisie invades the entire globe. It needs to establish itself everywhere, explore everywhere, create bonds everywhere. By exploiting the world market, the bourgeoisie gives a cosmopolitan character to production and consumption in all countries.
> MARX and ENGELS, 2010: 43

This has been proven since the first research sketches on capitalist sociability. Throughout the various lines of his works,[11] as well as in the study plan he outlined, Marxian reflections on the State and the world market were present. The world market is developed as a final concluding part of your research.[12] From the outlines of the critique of political economy, it is already possible to discover elements that provide the theoretical substrate necessary for the analyzes. In his time, Marx had already outlined the features that would circumvent debates that permeated the history of capitalism and international relations.

> Here appears the universal tendency of capital which differentiates it from all preceding stages of production. Although limited by its very nature, capital strives for [the] universal development of the productive

---

11 It is possible to identify sparse excerpts from his works that deal with the world market, monopolies and competition, as well as the expansion of capitalism around the world, with greater emphasis, from the "Communist Manifesto" (1848), which he wrote with Engels, through the "Grundrisse" (1857–1858) and, more clearly, in Volumes I and III of "The Capital" (1867 and 1894), without completely relegating other works.

12 What emerged with the publication of the "Grundrisse", from 1857–1858, was the relevance of the international scope for a full understanding of capitalism. The original structural plan for Capital covered the entire path in 6 volumes, namely: 1) on capital (with a section for capital in general, with an emphasis on the production process, circulation and profits and interest; a second section on competition, a third on the credit system, a last on share capital); 2) on land ownership; 3) on salaried work; 4) on the state; 5) on international trade; 6) on the international market and crises. Almost ten years later, in 1865, Marx opted for a leaner scheme and closer to the one actually published, divided into four books. Book I would deal with the capital production process. Book II concerning the capital circulation process. Book III concerning the global process of capitalist production. Finally, Book IV on the history of theory. Despite all the polemics about 'post-mortem editions and compilation', what is denoted, for now, is the concern in Marxian reflections with the expansion of capitalism in the international space. See Marx, 2011; Rosdolsky, 2001.

forces and, in this way, the presupposition of a new mode of production arises, based not on the development of the productive forces to reproduce and, at most, expand a determined state, but where the very development of the productive forces – free, unobstructed, progressive and universal – constitutes the presupposition of society and, therefore, of its reproduction; where the only presupposition is the overcoming of the starting point. Such a tendency – which capital possesses, but which at the same time contradicts it as a model of limited production and, therefore, impels it to its own dissolution – differentiates capital from all the preceding modes and, at the same time, contains within itself the fact that capital is posited as a simple point of transition.

MARX, 2011: 445–446

The immanent tendency towards the expansion of capital is detected by Marx, without having made direct reference to the term imperialism and without having carried out a systematic study of international relations. Even so, the premature death of the German intellectual, in 1883, did not prevent the fertilization of his ideas in a century of boiling and consolidation of the working class.[13] At his time, he made brilliant analyzes of British colonialism in different places, denouncing the essence of this practice, which had repercussions worldwide (Carnoy, 1994). Despite Marx's relevant writings on international politics, in which he imposed his view on British overseas experiences in conjuncture articles published in periodicals, the German thinker did not bequeath systematic and finished works on the subject. Even so, the expansive tendency of capital was highlighted throughout his writings. "The tendency to create the world market is immediately given in the very concept of capital". (Marx, 2011: 332).

In addition to sketches and sketches, also in his magnum opus, Marx (2013), when dealing with the production relations, emphasized the dynamics between anarchy and despotism that surrounded capital, which within itself are arbitrary, but among themselves are rivals in frank uncoordinated dispute and without spatial limits. In this sense, capital only exists in multiplicity,

---

13   With the nodal support of Engels, the continuation of his writings could constitute other volumes of his most significant and impactful work that could still be published. The following volumes of Capital were published post-mortem by Engels. Volume II in 1885 and Volume III in 1894. From 1904 to 1910, Karl Kautsky published other texts by Marx, whose compilation was called Volume IV, whose original title was Theories of Surplus-Value, in Portuguese. Kautsky's editing work was heavily criticized, not being accepted by many as a continuation of Marx's work (Rosdolsky, 2001).

collectivity; through the interaction between the many capitals the general laws of capitalism are concretized. A single universal capital is a contradiction in terms. It is characteristic of capitalism, which develops through competition, which is the source and expression of the anarchy of production. Therefore, for Marx (2013), capitalist social relations take the dual form of anarchy and despotism. Among many capitals there is anarchy; within each capital, despotism. Each relationship, anarchy and despotism, is the condition of each other. So it is also between States, within their borders before their nationals (subject to their law), sovereign, despotic; and outside, in the interrelationship with their peers, anarchy reigns, the lack of a central and hierarchically superior command.

Despite the absence of an explicit section on the subject, a closer look leads the reader to the keys of Marxian reflection, which necessarily pass through the most developed capitalist form, the world market. Also, in section 1 of book I, the tendency towards internationalization and the relevance of the scope of the world market are evident, when it comes to world money, which, when leaving the internal sphere of circulation, strips itself of national clothes, entering the world market.

> On leaving the sphere of internal circulation, money strips itself of its formal local standards of price measurement, currency, symbolic currency and value symbol, and returns to its original form as a bar of precious metal. In world trade, commodities unfold their value universally. Therefore, their autonomous figure of value confronts them, here, as world money. Only in the world market does money function fully as a commodity whose natural form is, at the same time, the immediate social form of the realization of human labor *in abstracto*. Its form of existence becomes adequate to its concept.
>
> MARX, 2013: 15

It is only in book III of Capital, in the unfinished meeting edited by Engels, that the most assertive observations appear. Entitled The Global Process of Capitalist Production, this final volume of the critique of political economy basically argues that the world market generally constitutes the basis and vital atmosphere of the capitalist mode of production, being the presupposition and result of the reproduction of capitalist social relations (Marx, 2017). This perception suggests that the world market is not the product of the sum of several States or their national economies, but rather is the condition through which relations between States exist. The world market presents itself as the universal form of capitalist existence. In other words, it is through the world market that the commodity changes from being national to being irreproachable capitalist. With this theoretical legacy, it was not essential, therefore, for Marx, to write a specific book on the subject for it to gain consistency and a further remarkable development. Far beyond his time, the philosopher from Trier was already shrewdly interpreting the consequences of the intensification of capitalist production relations.

The transformations in industrial production, with the strengthening of monopolies, the concentration and centralization of production, the emergence of the financial sector and the growing export of capital, as well as the intensification of rivalries and the intensification of the use of violence and domination around the world, boosted capitalist production relations to other levels. Marx did not experience this moment of exponential transmutation and internationalization of capitalism, but his premises were nevertheless ratified over time. The authors who survived him, and from him extracted the theoretical matrix, sought to interpret his ideas about international relations and capitalism, in view of the unprecedented expansion of production relations around the world. In this field, the debates of imperialism are imposed, which not only inaugurate, but fundamentally carry the study of contemporary international relations.

Therefore, the imperialist phenomenon demands to be debated, according to Marxist trends, in terms of the development of capitalism. It is crucial to go beyond shallow analyzes that are limited to the immediate identification between imperialism and capital exports or invasive policies and military interventions. Thus, the Marxist theoretical edifice of imperialism is erected, even though different interpretations can be found on its various floors amid important moments of inflection in its trajectory. From this construct, the interface between imperialism and international relations is verified, stimulating the joint and intertwined vision of both. Marx himself had already tested clues that would cement the foundations of investigations into the expansive and universalizing tendency of capital, a trail that was followed, with greater or lesser linearity, by those who departed and depart from Marxian premises. In the myriad of vectors that present themselves and in the oscillations suffered by the concept, the task of systematization and organization of considerably different interpretations emerges, which are impossible to be homogeneously grouped. Therefore, the third introductory demarcation touches on the observation that, even within the Marxist spectrum, it is necessary to emphasize the plethora of asymmetrical approaches. This study focuses on this pressing task.

4   Three Debates on Imperialism

Based on the premises espoused in this introduction, this text is guided, from its theoretical link, through the journey between the most varied Marxist conceptions of imperialism, bringing and reinforcing elements of materialist criticism for the understanding of the phenomenon in the midst of the interface between capitalism and international relations. Therefore, the construction of an argument in theoretical and historical cycles that will end up at the top of the Marxist building, coined here as full criticism, without failing to suggest possibilities for the deepening and consequent development of the fruitful and necessary, but still atrophied, dialog between Marxism and International Relations. Therefore, the book is structured by the intertwining of two beacons of systematization of thought on imperialism, which are not necessarily corresponding: a) the chronological one that encompasses the historical periodization in three phases, since its genesis in the transition between the nineteenth and twenty centuries until its present-day form in the twenty-first century, with a view to the transformation of capitalism amidst the concreteness of international relations, from 1870 to 1945, from 1945 to 1970 and from 1970 to the present day; and b) the theory that organizes the different perspectives on imperialism by the emphasis that the concept gives to the economic aspects (law of value, its movements and its manifestations), to the political ones (struggle and correlation of classes and groups) and to the interrelation of these within the Marxist spectrum. Armed with these criteria, the work will be sewn into three major debates.

Regarding the temporal demarcation, there is an approximation regarding most of the literature. What can be deduced from the bibliographic survey is that the authors, for the most part, trace the stages of imperialism, taking into account the great world transformations[14]. By different denominations and similar characterizations, most of the renowned authors point to three moments. Thus, Anderson (2016), Callinicos (2009), Harvey (2005); Hirsch (2010); Kurz (2003), Martins (2011), Miguez (2013); Panitch and Gindin (2004; 2006); have Brink (2008); Valencia (2009); Wood (2014) divide the transmutations of imperialism into a first period, classical or polycentric, which would go from 1870 to 1945; a second that spanned the Cold War, until 1991,

---

14   One cannot ignore in this context the authors who, for various reasons, see only two periods of imperialism, either because of the chronological limitation of their work or because of the view that the unfolding of the world is still grounded in the post-1945 configuration. Within this spectrum fit, for example: Arrighi (1983); Barone (1985); Brewer (1990); Leite (2017); Rowthorn (1982).

called superpower imperialism, bipolar, neo-Marxist; and a third that would range from the collapse of the Soviet Union and the consolidation of globalization to modern times, coined as post- Cold War, monocentric, or globalization era imperialism. In this vein, the research axis revolves around three cycles, whose conformation approaches the capitalist historicity (based on structural crises) taken by the French regulationist school[15], incorporated and adapted by Hirsch 's materialist theory of the State (2010) and, partially, by Callinicos (2009) and, essentially, by Mascaro (2013).

Therefore, there is no logical and linear assumption in history or mechanical theoretical effects deduced from the law of value that guide capitalist development, but the complex and contradictory historical interaction between social actors and concrete material practices, rooted in the social conditions of production. The shining merit of this theoretical framework touches on the interrelation of the different phases of capitalist development with the strategies

---

15   In this sense, the theories of regulation come to aggregate in a mutually conditioning relationship to the materialist theory of the state. Within the theoretical spectrum that ended up being formed on regulation, the vector that needs to be highlighted is the one that dialogs with Marxist political economy, starting from the premises of Louis Althusser, whose pioneering emphasis turns to Michel Agliettà . This current emerged in France in the context of the crisis of the 1970s, and can be considered as an economic interface of the derivationist theories of West Germany, due to the Althusserian matrix. The driving question of the research was to know how capitalism managed to survive, given the conflictive character and inherent bearer of crises in the capitalist relationship, which would make continued accumulation unlikely. There would be some specific social forms that would try to regulate and couple tensions and antagonisms. The context of the 1970s and the crossroads that were approaching the state and capitalism were propitious for theoretical reflections of this magnitude. Initially developed in universities (in Paris and Grenoble) and in the circle of CEPREMAP (Center d' Études Economic Outlook/Mathématique Appliqués à la Planning), its craftsmen, armed with these concerns, sought answers to the crisis of the social welfare model by criticizing political economy that could, at the same time, reject the dominant economic theories, of a highly abstract nature. Economic structures and processes should not be analyzed using criteria of pure rationality, but influenced by social and power relations. The illusion of broad political leadership driving relatively crisis-free capitalist development has been dispelled. From the exhaustion of the social welfare model (and consequently of Keynesianism), analyzes were built over the following decades on the continuity, crises and historical changes of capitalist societies. Thus, an alternative to the dominant (Keynesian) political economy emerges, without ceasing to fulminate the abstraction typical of neoclassical economic theory and monetarism, and even to point out the vices of Marxist cycles (reviewing the Marxist critique of political economy, rearticulating social structure objective and social action). Supported by institutionalist economic theory and Marxist theory by Althusserian verve, the initially French theory of regulation proved to be fruitful and was not restricted to academic ghettos, it soon gained worldwide repercussion. For more see: Hirsch and Roth (1986), Boyer (1990), Lipietz (1988), Hirsch (2010) and Jessop (1991).

of valorization presented, with the corresponding political-institutional forms and with social relations of forces. From this perspective, the intermediate categories of political economy proposed to conduct the discussion about the phases of rupture and stability of capitalism are the regime of accumulation and the mode of regulation (Boyer, 1990). The regime of accumulation is primarily economic, but not limited to it, involving a particular combination of production and consumption that can be reproduced despite capitalism's tendency to crisis. The appropriation of the result of the work of others happens legitimized by an institutional nucleus (formal and informal), constituted by social forms and practices, sufficient and aimed at accumulation, the mode of regulation. This institutional set, together with a vast complex of norms, ensures the reproduction of capitalism. Duality (accumulation regime and regulation mode) is not the joining of indifferent elements or the superposition of two equal ones, but the structural coexistence, which reveals a certain degree of articulation between its terms (Jessop, 1991). Based on these two vectors, they establish the trajectory of capitalism in three moments: liberal capitalism (here called the pioneer debate), Fordism and post-Fordism. Crises are not exceptional interregnums, but structuring and driving elements of the three phases.

With regard to the guiding thread of ideas, the distance is more noticeable. The emphasis here attributed to the core of the interpretations is distinct. The conceptual course of imperialism is guided (immersed in the broad spectrum of the general tradition of Marxist thought, but it does not necessarily coincide with it, with approximations and distances) and permeated by the emphasis, in its definition, attributed to economic and political aspects. In this sense, an attempt is made to escape the foundation on which most of the specialized literature is based, the one that long before had been identified as outdated, centered on the characterizations of imperialism, whether ultra-imperialism, super-imperialism or collective imperialism, in an attempt to build controversies over the inaugural polemics. from the clash between Lenin and Kautsky . Regardless of temporal characterizations, the aspects that insist on these pillars are equipped with the necessary adaptations.[16] In addition to this dynamic, very original systematizations stand out, such as those by Callinicos (2009); Corrêa (2012); Kurz (2003); Leite (2017); Martins (2011); Miguez (2013); and Brink (2008). This research, however, does not adopt any of them specifically, but seeks to extract their positive points from valid contributions. In fact, the

---

16 To a greater or lesser extent, classifications that, for various reasons, do not overcome past paradigms nor, for obvious reasons of time, reach a broad view of today's imperialism, we can list: Arrighi (1983); Barone (1985); Brewer (1990); Rowthorn (1982).

driving force behind imperialism's inflections should not be held separately from the theoretical trajectory of Marxist thought in general, but inserted in the transformations and directions taken by capitalism and its critical reflection. Therefore, the theoretical guide that will guide the organizational link is the emphasis given to the economy, politics or the interaction of both by the unfolding of Marxist visions, as they do, each in its own way, Elbe (2010); Hirsch (2010); Mascaro (2013); Boucher (2015). Therefore, the interface of the historical-theoretical axes occurs in three moments: in the first, the economistic conception is inaugurated, which would be linked to the period of expansion of capitalism until the World War II; in the second, there is a rupture of Eurocentrist limits and an expansion of the focus of imperialism, through a comprehensive, systemic vision, which is situated in a paradigm transition, but with an economistic bias still glistening, in a short interregnum that will approximately go from 1945 to 1970; and in the third, an arc that goes from the crisis of Fordism in the 1970s, through the consolidation of post-Fordism in the 1990s, to the current two, there is an explosion of horizons, creating a wide universe (beyond de, but without discarding economism), which can be systematized from the rise of politicism, its variables (partial politicism) and its contestations (full criticism), which opens the way to reach the materialist critique of imperialism.

The inaugural debate is called the pioneer.[17] From the last quarter of the nineteenth century to the World War II, it is possible to trace a common thread between the ideas that investigated in depth the transformations of capitalism. Exhaustively discussed, in view of the genius and centrality of his conceptions for the unfolding of future conceptions, the list of authors approached is almost consensual. Taking the intellectuals who are avowedly inspired by the Marxian matrix of thought, and at that moment saw themselves as direct continuators or successors, pair up Hilferding, Luxembourg, Kautsky, Bukharin and Lenin. The peculiarity of each one is reserved, there are elements that allow them to be combined in the same interregnum. The concerns that the authors of that time were concerned with are linked to the reasons for the expansion of capitalist relations around the world and its consequences, such as interstate rivalries, competition and resulting wars. Gravitating around

---

17 Due care is taken not to repeat the name 'classic', because, despite being more widespread, it carries a certain methodological imprecision, since classics in thought would only be the Greek philosophers of antiquity. Nor is it intended to equate to Warren's (1980) conception of imperialism as a pioneer or midwife of capitalism. The term is intended only to illustrate the vanguard of the authors who took Marxism to the inaugural reflections on the subject.

these premises, each one assumes a particular posture, exposing its singularities within this range. To a large extent, they noted the evident transformations in the mode of production and their effects throughout the world. The increase in the concentration of production, the growing export of capital, the emergence of monopolies, state intervention and organization in economies, mergers between capitals and the emergence of finance capital, colonial incursions and the outbreak of wars around the world were inevitable traits of living reality. These signs evidenced the expansion of capitalism across the globe, which, in turn, illustrated a crisis and the consequent intensification of the contradictions in the mode of production, opening cracks that could lead to its socialist transition or its revolutionary overcoming. After the phase of competitive capitalism, the conditions detected presented the last era of monopoly capitalism. The readings of this scenario were guided by the economicist bias, attributing to the economic material base the determining force of social relations, including the state political entity, observing the State as a result of the financial dynamics, inevitably attending to the bourgeois interests.

The second debate is the Fordist one.[18] In a very different context from the predecessor, the pioneering visions are revised and adapted to the new concrete reality, which will run from 1945 to the 1970s. In this list, reflections on imperialism are expanded, tearing the limits of the European continent and covering other regions around the world. In effect, a duality of central conceptions is established, which deny and reaffirm imperialism, adapting it to the new conditions; and visions focused on the periphery, which substantially contribute and innovate to the debate, thus being the object of a more detailed investigation. In this tuning fork, the current of monopoly capital, the Marxist dependency theorists and the Third Worldists are present. The emergence of the United States, as a hegemonic power, and the rise of the Soviet Union, which symbolized the arrival of the left to power, as well as the spread of capitalist relations across the quadrants of the world map, gave capitalism a new face. The reconfiguration took place along Fordist lines, in a composition of political forces around social well-being that made it possible to achieve, in the central portions, growth rates without parameters in the history of the mode of production. In peripheral regions, the reason for blocking modernization and selective industrialization was questioned. Revised, the concept of imperialism, having the pioneers as a beacon (the emphasis on accumulation

---

18   Name given in function of the influence that the theory of regulation and the materialist theory of the state exert on the perspective expressed in this work. The term itself refers to the mode of organization of capitalism, which will be better delineated in the specific topic.

crises, interstate competition and wars), is diluted in other aspects, such as the domination from the center to the periphery and the dependence of the latter on central capitalism. In spite of the substantial changes in the way capitalism is organized, it is noteworthy that this Fordist debate, in theoretical terms, is closer to what distances it from the pioneers. The economistic veneer remains perceptible in the analyzes, which does not allow them to break completely with their predecessors, but place them as nothing more than a remarkable complement to the inaugural ideas of imperialism. For this characterization and for its chronological brevity, the Fordist debate can be pointed out as a fertile interregnum of transition until the inflection in the interim successor.

The third and current debate is the post-Fordist one.[19] Created in the midst of the crisis of Fordism in the 1970s, and consolidated with the spread of financial globalization in the 1990s, this time lapse persists to the present day. In the wide range of authors who are inscribed, in the midst of chronologically irregular and theoretically varied and innovative dynamics, it is crucial to divide them into three strands, politicism, partial politicism and full criticism. In a context of deconstruction of the social welfare model and the introduction of neoliberal dictates, the transformation of the face of capitalism has a strong impact on political, economic and social relations. Merging the eclipse and the resumption of the concept of imperialism, it is reconstructed on new theoretical bases. From this cycle onwards, the economistic matrix starts to share spaces with political approaches and those that interrelate both. At this stage, the internationalization of production relations takes on other levels, since production ceases to reside on the national-state basis and starts to spread throughout the world, in a diffuse and deconcentrated organization. From Fordism, we move to Toyotism, in the sense of further rationalizing the organization of work. The State changes the guidelines in the intervention in favor of public policies and social rights, reconfiguring itself even more open to the flavors and unpleasantness of the international market. Thus, the collapse of social indices and the fall in the general standard of living are inevitable. An

---

19 It is noteworthy that the term post-Fordism is and can be used by non-Marxist currents as well. What underlies the use of the concept in this research is the meaning given by the Marxist strand of the French theory of economic regulation. Following the logic of previous cycles (pioneer and Fordist), the post-Fordist is based on the conception of a mode of organization of capitalism that breaks with the previous one, in reaction, offering new levels from the rupture of the past. More often it is coined as contemporary, because it is of the current moment. If we consider the historical conception of the philosophy of ideas, contemporaneity is inaugurated with the bourgeois revolutions at the end of the eighteenth century. Therefore, the entire period since then will be contemporary. Therefore, this nomenclature cannot be adhered to.

income-concentrating model emerges, oriented towards the service of specific financial interests, undermining the post-war social democratic agreements. A direct consequence of the new correlation is the even more intense and now more porous spread of conflicts and tensions around the world, in diffuse and unusual violent actions, significantly altering the global panorama. Countless attempts to reread this inflection emerge, in an amorphous dynamic, due to the vastness of different perspectives. In the midst of the impacts suffered in the academy by the changes, the political bias, its consequences and its criticisms stand out. From this systematization of imperialist thought, the path to the top of the Marxist edifice, the materialist critique of imperialism, will become clearer.

Cycles are not hermetic. Which means to say that the intertwining of theoretical matrices at different moments is inescapable. For example, in the Fordist debate it is possible to find positions that merely adapt the pioneering conceptions to the reality of the new temporal interregnum without innovating substantively, as it can be seen that, even in the post-Fordist debate, economistic views are still present and of great relevance., including. Therefore, it is not intended here to delimit the porosity of ideas, but to mark the inflection periods in the trajectory of development of theorization on imperialism. Therefore, the demarcation in three phases, the pioneer (from Europe to the world), the Fordist, the one that broadens the scope, focusing on the world-system as a whole, and the post-Fordist, fraught with the explosion of reflections on imperialism. Naturally, one does not have the scope to exhaust the subject (which would not even be possible); the aim is to provide the specialized literature with a stimulus for future discussions.

What is important to emphasize to readers in this essay is that the focus of the study is imperialism and Marxist theories of the State, in their articulation with international relations, naturally. Based on the theoretical framework developed in this work, the relevance of this phenomenon to a full understanding of the subject will be evident. There are other concepts that interrelate with it and flirt with a tenuous threshold within the reflection of authors that will be addressed here. For example, hegemony. This word demands a lot of care in your discussion. As much as it appears mixed with imperialism in some perspectives, due to the obvious and necessary respect for approaches that are based on hegemony to explain international relations, it is emphasized that the concept of hegemony will not be addressed in this research (despite all its appeal among the authors of political verve), when evoked laterally, due to the inevitability of its presence and the consideration of the primacy of imperialism, which places the reflection of hegemony as an auxiliary, much more tangent to conjunctural than structural issues.

Through the exposition of the introductory notes of the study that will flow in a broader format, as a book,[20] in this short space the goals that guided further deepening are outlined. Due to specific limitations, the objective of the essay is precisely to stimulate discussions and ferment reflections on the centrality of the theme for International Relations, as a scientific field.

5 Conclusions

In view of the theoretical epic traced in this study, which starts from the threshold between the twilight of the nineteenth century and the dawn of the twentieth century and which currently completes its centenary jubilee, it was sought, in the midst of a terrain populated by various approaches and fruitful debates, to pave a path, within the Marxist spectrum, that could lead the reader to a full understanding of the capitalist phenomenon, structuring international relations: imperialism. In the tune of the permanent distrust of labels,[21] within the capitalist mode of production, it is always current and necessary to unveil the real character of a concept as disputed, multifaceted and treacherous as imperialism. The tool is the umbilical relationship between Marxism and International Relations.

If the task was to trace a route that explained the different theoretical emphases allied to the great world changes, the result of this endeavor was to overcome the strictly economistic look (emphasis on the law of value, its movements and its manifestations) and politicist (emphasis on political issues, struggle and correlation of classes and groups) towards the rescue of the new reading of Marx initiated in the 1970s to explain the theory of the state.

Capitalism is constituted in its most developed form in the international system. The world market is the widest range of manifestations of capitalism. It is the arena that fully captures capitalist phenomena. It is the basis and atmosphere of life of the capitalist mode of production. Therefore, studying the state and capitalism without delving into international issues is like playing the violin with just one hand.[22] The capitalist state does not emerge in isolation, but collectively, as a state system, this multiplicity being a structural feature of capitalism. The geographic space of capital is not that of state

---

20 It should be noted that this chapter is part of the larger study, condensed in the book "Imperialism, State and International Relations", by Editora Ideias & Letras, published in 2018.
21 See Lipietz (1988).
22 See Barker (1991).

borders, but the international one. Therefore, imperialism can only be debated from a perspective that is attentive to the structure and dynamics of global capitalism and the state system.

In short, in today's scene, in the midst of the intensification of contradictions via the dissolution of the modernizing mirages of post-Fordist capitalism, it is urgent to revisit the concept of imperialism, recovering its relevance, which is not a simple task, but demands the assumption of a theoretical and practical posture, which encourages the reader to escape the comfort of certainties. Faced with the misty scenario, the inclination towards Marxism is relevant for two reasons. The first is related to the search for escape valves in the current context of struggles. The second touches on the need for a theoretical horizon to lead political militancy to transformation. Understanding today's directions is a task that inexorably permeates the discussion between imperialism, the state and international relations.

At a time of crisis of world accumulation, the return to previous teachings opens up alternatives for thinking and for the struggle for new horizons. The overcoming of capitalism involves the deconstruction of its gears. Imperialism is undoubtedly one of its cardinal pieces.

References

Anderson J O (2016) Imperialismus. Text written for *Historischkritisches Wörterbuch des Marxismus*. Seconf Version, July 2001. Available (consulted in August 12, 2023) at: http://www.marx-seura.kaapeli.fi/archive/imperialism.htm.

Arrigui G (1983) *The Geometry of Imperialism. The limits of Hobson's paradigm*. London: Verso.

Barker C (1991) A note on the theory of capitalist states. In: Clarke S (ed.) *The State debate*. London: Palgrave Macmillan, 182–191.

Barone C (1985) *Marxist Thought on Imperialism. Survey and Critique*. New York: ME Sharpe Inc.

Boucher G (2015) *Marxismo*. Petrópolis-RJ: Editora Vozes.

Boyer R (1990) *A Teoria da Regulação. Uma análise crítica*. São Paulo: Nobel.

Brewer A(1990) *Marxist theories of imperialism: a critical survey*. 2nd. ed. London: Routledge.

Brink T (2008). *Staatenkonflikte. Zur Analyze von Geopolitik und Imperialismus -ein Überblick*. Stuttgart: Lucius & Lucius.

Callinicos A (2009) *Imperialism and Global Political Economy*. Cambridge; Malden: Polity.

Carnoy M(1994) *Estado e teoria política*. Campinas-SP: Editora Papirus.

Corrêa H (2012) Teorias do imperialismo no século XXI: (in) adequações do debate no Marxismo. Unpublished doctoral thesis. Fluminense Federal University, Niterói.

Elbe I (2010) *Marx im Westen: Die neue Marx-Lektüre in der Bundesrepublik seit 1965*. Berlin: Akademie.

Fernandes L (1998) O Manifesto Comunista e a dialética da globalização. In: Filho D (ed.) *O Manifesto Comunista 150 anos depois*. São Paulo: Contraponto/Editora Perseu Abramo,109–120.

Gonçalves W and Monteiro L (2015). O monopólio das teorias anglo-saxãs no estudo das Relações Internacionais. *Revista Século XXI/ESPM* vol. 6 n° 1. Porto Alegre, January/July.

Harvey D (2005) *O Novo Imperialismo*. São Paulo: Loyola.

Hirsch J (2010) *Teoria Materialista do Estado*: processos de transformação do sistema capitalista de Estados. Rio de Janeiro: Editora Revan.

Hirsch J and Roth R (1986). *Das neue Gesicht des Kapitalismus: vom Fordismus zum Post-Fordismus*. Hamburg: VSA.

Jessop B (1991). Regulation theory, post Fordism and the State. More than a reply to Werner Bonefeld In: Bonefeld W and Holoway J (ed.) *Post-Fordism & social form. A Marxist debate on the Post -Fordist State*. London: Macmillan Academic and Professional LTD, 69–91.

Kurz R (2003). *Das Ende der Souveränität und die Wandlungen des Imperialismus im Zeitalter der Globalisierung*. Berlin: Horlemann Verlag.

Leite L (2017) O Capital no mundo e o mundo do Capital: uma reinterpretação do imperialismo a partir da teoria do valor de Marx. Doctoral Thesis. Federal Fluminense University, Niterói.

Lipietz A (1988) Miragens e Milagres. Problemas da industrialização no Terceiro Mundo. São Paulo: Nobel.

Martins C (2011) *Globalização, dependência e neoliberalismo na América Latina*. São Paulo: Boitempo.

Marx K and Engels F (2010 [1848]). *Manifesto Comunista*. São Paulo: Boitempo.

Marx K (2011 [1858]) *Grundrisse. Manuscritos econômicos de 1857–1858. Esboços da crítica da economia política*. São Paulo: Boitempo.

Marx KARX, Karl (2013 [1867]). *O Capital*. Crítica da Economia Política. Livro I: o processo de produção do capital. São Paulo: Boitempo.

Marx K (2017 [1894]) O Capital. Crítica da Economia Política. Livro III: o processo global da produção capitalista. São Paulo: Boitempo.

Mascaro A (2013) *Estado e Forma Política*. São Paulo: Boitempo.

Miguez P (2013) El estado capitalista, la crisis financiera y el debate império-imperialismo. In: Kan J and Pascual R (eds.) *Integrados (?) Debates sobre las relaciones internacionales y la integración regional lationoamericana y europea*. Buenos Aires: Imago Mundi, 89–122.

Navez M (2008) *Marx: Ciência e Revolução*. São Paulo: Editora Quartier Latin.

Panitch L and Gindin S (2004) Capitalismo global e império norte-americano. In: Panitch L and Leys C (eds) *O novo desafio imperial*. Buenos Aires: CLACSO, 11–53.

Panitch L and Gindin S (2006) As Finanças e o Império estadunidense. In: Panitch L and Leys C (eds) *O Império Reloaded*. Buenos Aires: CLACSO, 65–104.

Rosdolsky R (2001) *Gênese e Estrutura de O Capital*. Rio de Janeiro: Editora Contraponto/ Editora UERJ.

Rowthorn R (1982) O imperialismo na década de 1970: unidade ou rivalidade? In: Rowthorn R (ed.) *Capitalismo, Conflito e Inflação*. Rio de Janeiro: Zahar Editores, 46–73.

Teschke B (2016). Repensando as relações internacionais: uma entrevista com Benno Teschke. *Outubro Revista*, n. 27, November.

Valencia A (2009) Neo-imperialismo, dependência e novas periferias na economia mundial. In: Martins C and Valencia A (eds.) *A América Latina e os Desafios da Globalização. Ensaios em Homenagem a Ruy Mauro Marini*. Rio de Janeiro: Editora PUC, 111–134.

Warren B (1980) *Imperialism: Pioneer of Capitalism*. London: Verso, 1980.

Wood E (2014). *O Império do Capital*. São Paulo: Boitempo.

CHAPTER 11

The Marxist Debate on Post-World War II Imperialism

Caio Martins Bugiato[1] and Tatiana Berringer[2]

1   Introduction

The Marxist theory of imperialism has been debated and developed for at least one century.[3] Its inaugural debate[4] took place with Vladimir Lenin (1982), Nicolai Bukharin (1986), Karl Kautsky (2008), and Rosa Luxemburg (1985), in the heat of the explosion of World War I and since then there have been numerous advances and resumptions of those theses. The main disagreement occurred between Lenin and Kautsky, which for this chapter, needs to be briefly explained here. For Lenin (1982), the export of capital takes on great proportions in a world context in which the ruling classes are divided into national social formations, whose power is represented by the strength of their respective state. The process generates unequal developments between imperialist states, colonies, and dependent states, as well as rivalry among them. Thus, the thesis is that imperialism tends to intercapitalist wars. In this sense, Lenin maintains the inevitability of wars as long as capitalism lasts, especially because there would be a dispute over control of markets and access to raw materials, in addition to maintaining the rate of profit and the need to export capital. On the other hand, Kautsky (2008) understands that the drama of war allows capitalists to see greater possibilities of obtaining surplus value from a stage that avoids warlike confrontation. It would then be possible to transform the policy of imperialism into a policy of alliance between imperialist

---

1 Professor of International Relations at the Federal Rural University of Rio de Janeiro. E-mail: bugiato@gmail.com.
2 Professor of International Relations at the Federal University of ABC. E-mail: berringer.tatiana@gmail.com.
3 Originally published as an article in the Brazilian journal "Princípios", volume 42, number 166, 2023. Translated into English by Alberto Resende Jr.
4 About the inaugural theories and debates, the authors mentioned as follows, as systematizers, they present good explanations in their books. Specifically on the debate between Kautsky and Lenin, see Bugiato 2017.

states, conforming to ultra-imperialism.[5] That is a capitalist phase in which the major world powers renounce the arms race (as there is no longer any meaning in those conflicts for the export and accumulation of capital) and come together in a federation. This federation would be a cartelization of foreign policy derived from an alliance of imperialist states and their ruling classes to stabilize the international system and guarantee the domination of the bourgeoisie in its national states and over the periphery.

Lenin's perspective had a greater impact on Marxist debate both in theory and in political practice during the first half of the twentieth century – and in some cases, it extends beyond that period. However, after World War II, with the emergence of a single great power in the capitalist world, Leninist theory ended up being questioned and revised by important Marxist theorists. Such a debate took place among Harry Magdoff, Ernest Mandel, Nicos Poulantzas, and others. Those three Marxist authors wrote articles and books on imperialist theory in the 1960s and 1970s, against the backdrop of changes in production and on the relations between metropolis states and dependent states under U.S. domain. However, to bring out the most important points for this chapter from his vast works, we are guided by the following question: Do the conflicts between them remain or not? In the debate among those authors, relevant issues arise for understanding international politics.

Therefore, the objective of this chapter is to systematize this debate, mainly because it does not appear in important works in the Marxist field that seek to deal with the issue in question, such as Barone (1985), Brewer (1990), Noonan (2017), Osório (2018), and Kiely (2020). Those, when dealing with the history of the Marxist theory of imperialism, curiously refer and/or highlight the contributions of the world-system Theory or the Dependency Theory to interpret international relations after World War II, ignoring or just mentioning in passing the debate. In addition to locating this discussion vis-à-vis the inaugural debate of the Marxist theory of imperialism, we seek to demonstrate the points of convergence and divergence they had between them. To this end, each of the following three sections is dedicated to one of the selected neo-Marxist authors, and later we present final considerations with comparisons. In addition, from a more general point of view, this text demonstrates the richness and pertinence of Marxism for International Relations, despite being obscured.

---

5 In order not to confuse the denominations throughout the chapter, it should be noted that what Kautsky calls ultra-imperialism is what Mandel calls super-imperialism, which is also Magdoff's conception. What Mandel calls ultra-imperialism is something still different from those, which comes close to Hardt and Negri's (2001) definition of empire.

2 Harry Magdoff[6] and the US Super Imperialism

According to Magdoff (1972, 1979) US imperialism resulted from the structure of the colonial system before World War I that gave rise to the structure of dependence and domination of the centers over the peripheries. The main difference is that an imperialist network or system was formed, which adapted the economic structure of the former colonies to the role of appendages of the metropolises: 'Price formation, income distribution, and resource allocation evolved, with the help of military power and blind market forces to continually reproduce dependency' (Magdoff, 1979: 120). Capitalism is, therefore, a world power system. But the author argues that dependence is an economic, political, and social relationship, which is not only carried out through the relationship between dominant states and dominated states but is linked to the practices of the dominant classes in dependent countries, whose interests are connected to foreign forces. In such a way that they sustain and reproduce asymmetrical relationships, constituting a real obstacle to the development of peripheral social formations.

Capitalism as a world-system is inherently expansionist in nature, that is, the dominant bourgeoisie of central states tends to operate on a world scale since, within social formations, there are competitive pressures and technical progress and recurring imbalances between production and demand create tensions for market expansion. In the period of imperialism without colonies (after World War II), the export of capital is operated by the monopoly company; much higher than in the previous period, as more companies operate in a greater number of countries. In addition, the US is the main exporter of capital.

Magdoff argues that the advent of the monopoly company (monopoly capitalism, unlike the phase that preceded it, nineteenth-century competitive capitalism) does not mean the end of the competition, but its elevation to a new level: operating on a global scale to ensure existence and profit growth, the arrangements to divide the market and/or the competitive struggle between gigantic companies, supported by their national states – from protectionism to militarization –, extended to a large part of the planet. It is worth noting then that monopolies are not at odds with the state system and the imperialist

---

6 The American Harry Magdoff was co-editor of the Marxist journal "Monthly Review", and his ideas have an affinity with the theories of Paul Baran and Paul Sweezy. His analysis of postwar US foreign policy, more empirical than theoretical, brings very important data about the conquests of foreign markets and their importance to the US economy.

network but rather represent the symbiosis of monopoly capital with the state of its country of origin.

After the World War II, through military bases and direct military support, the local ruling classes maintain dependence on imperialism despite (formal) political independence. In some cases, the armed forces of the dependent social formations fulfill this function. Furthermore: the supposed cooling of inter-imperialist rivalries would have been a factor of unification of the central states given the threats of national liberation struggles and socialist revolutions inaugurated with the Russian Revolution. Thus, the rise of the US as the greatest economic, political and military force implied the ability, at an opportune moment, to organize and direct the imperialist network. According to the author:

> Fundamental to the period of imperialism without colonies is the new role of the United States. The shattering of other imperialist centers following World War II and the concomitant emergence of strong revolutionary movements generated the urgent need for the United States to restore the stability of the imperialist system and to seize the opportunity to advance in self-interest.
> MAGDOFF, 1979: 123

The expansion of the US imperialist system was supported by the state in financing advanced technology, driven by the military sector, such as atomic energy and satellite communication, as well as new forms of transport and cultural production, based on Hollywood cinema. The foreign policy of the United States, expansionist and aggressive, would aim, directly or indirectly, to control the greatest possible extension of the planet to maintain openness to trade and investment by large US companies. Opening and keeping the 'open door' requires constant vigilance, strength, and persistence to control and influence the politics and economy of dependent states to ensure the reproduction of capital. The imperialist network is, therefore, operated by a group of giant US companies, which dominate a vast part of world markets – despite having their activities mostly destined to Europe and Canada. In addition to the dominant position of commerce and its industrial monopolies, they rely on the imposition of the dollar as an international means of payment, credit, and reserves and a largely internationalized banking network associated with the expansion of commerce and industry.

Once colonialism became difficult to practice, the US state and its ruling class put in place other practices – traditional, new, and not so new – of exploitation and domination, which can range from military occupation to subtle techniques of influence, depending on circumstances and actions of political and military leaders. Referring to Rosa Luxemburg, according to which imperialism necessarily implies the use of military force for the reproduction of capital, Magdoff (1979) notes that the general development of military technologies, logistics, and tactics – installation of military bases abroad, military interventions and occupations, and so on – in the foreign policy of the United States are the pillar of the control and influence of this state in the world-system. In the economic and political-ideological sphere, the author cites the constitution of preferential trade agreements, economic blocs, and international organizations (United Nations, Organization of American States, International Monetary Fund, World Bank) in which the diplomacy of the USA plays a leading role in the direction of economy and politics in world capitalism. In addition, the United States began to use widely in foreign policy what Magdoff (1972) calls foreign aid, a procedure of international cooperation that consists of granting donations, loans, consultancy, training, and so on, to countries with the general purpose of keeping the 'door open' and pro-US governments and preventing revolts, revolutions, and Soviet aid. In cases where there were threats or blocks to indirect control, the US promoted counter-revolutions. That means putting political and military programs into practice, through the financing of electoral campaigns, *coups d'état*, military assistance and training of cadres of the local armed forces. Besides, free access to the internal market; legal conditions for foreign capital to act, such as avoiding its expropriation, discrimination and interference in ownership and management; and making the beneficiaries dependent on the US market, with loans and debts that perpetuate the subjection to the aid. Sometimes such 'cooperation' is carried out under the auspices of international organizations, so US impositions seem more subtle. Behind those practices hover the operations of the Central Intelligence Agency (CIA).

For the author, US dominance is indisputable. Although he indicates in passing (1972) when discussing the configuration of world capitalism, that US capitalism admits (economic) competition of capital from other centers (Europe), he asserts that it exerts political and military supremacy. For him in the imperialist system there is a centripetal force that ties the core countries to the USA. As with new and old practices, the United States exerts economic, political, and military supremacy in international relations, configuring the American empire, which indicates affiliation to Kautsky's thesis on ultra-imperialism.

3   Ernest Mandel[7] and the Permanence of Inter-imperialist Rivalries

According to Mandel (1967, 1982, 2009) US imperialism takes shape in a period he calls late capitalism, which is a stage of the monopoly phase that began at the turn of the nineteenth to the twentieth century. That is different from competitive capitalism and divided into two phases: the classic and the current. The current moment corresponds to late capitalism and begins with the third technological revolution in 1940/45, based on monopolies and productive internationalization. The concentration/centralization and export of capital, according to the Belgian author, are determined by the hunt for technological super-profit, which is the search for extraordinary profit in the context of technological innovations that increase demand. Furthermore, late capitalism also consists of a permanent war economy: political, diplomatic, and military measures of the imperialist states serve as a stimulus to the development of productive forces and contribute to the removal of obstacles to the export of capital. Such expansionism is the expression of the inherent character of the capitalist mode of production, the so-called uneven and combined development: capital and the socioeconomic and political relations that it carries tend to take over and shape the regions of the planet, bringing all countries together in a hierarchical organic unit. This unit brings together centers and peripheries, in which those centers – advanced capitalists – dominate and exploit those – dependent capitalists – and hinder their development.

In the 1960s and 1970s, US superiority were challenged by socialist experiences and national liberation struggles (Cuba is a great example). So, fearing that they would abandon the capitalist camp, the US strategy was to restore and strengthen the economic power of Europe and Japan in the 1960s. This process was also the result of an economic necessity inherent in US capitalism. Its economy, already dominated by capital-exporting monopolies, follows the logic by which, in general, the export of capital occurs as a function of competition, to first compete with a national competitor, then to achieve on an international scale, and, finally, to fight against foreign competitors. Mandel (2009) reports the superiority of US monopoly companies, which hold great technological advances due to the subsidies they receive from the state.

Rigorous with the explanation and differentiation of processes, Mandel (1982) presents his concept of centralization of capital.

---

[7] Belgian economist Ernest Mandel was a scholar of political economy, one of the main references of the Trotskyist movement and leader of the Fourth International.

Centralization of capital implies central directing power, or *centralization of control over the means of production* – in other words, centralized private ownership. In this context, it is not important to know whether the shares are distributed internationally among small or large shareholders, since one of the notorious traits of capitalist companies in a joint-stock company, and in monopoly capital as a whole, is that the possession of a large amount of capital within of a large corporation allows control over even greater amounts of capital. The international centralization of capital, therefore, means central control of the capital from different origins and national controls.

    MANDEL, 1982: 227 Author's emphasis

In turn, the international centralization of capital can take two forms: first, large companies of different national owners become controlled by a single class, from a single country; or the second, large companies of different national owners merge into an international company without control held by just one class of a particular country.

The author goes on (Mandel, 1982: 228–9) to distinguish four processes of internationalization of capital:

1) internationalization of the realization of surplus-value, which is the sale of goods (international trade, exports);
2) internationalization of the production of surplus-value (branches under the direct control of the parent company; associations, companies founded by foreign companies in countries abroad; large monopolies with which foreign companies join);
3) internationalization of the purchase of labor force merchandise (international mobility of labor force);
4) internationalization of capital control, the true internationalization of capital, which consists of the transfer of ownership, either from one country to another, or from one national group of capital owners to another; in other words, international alteration of capital ownership (which is not necessarily congruent with 1, 2, and 3).

In different ways, in the classical phase the formation of monopolies (capitalization centralization) was a phenomenon restricted to the national space and dissolved over time due to crises, recessions, wars, and new correlations of forces among imperialist states. In the late capitalism such formation takes place internationally, is concentrated among the imperialist metropolises – the

United States and Europe[8] – and takes place in sectors with greater technological content. International centralization, therefore, corresponds to a central ruling power that controls the means of production.

According to Mandel (1982) there are three types of relationship between the (late) capitalist state and the international centralization of capital. They are:

A)   Centralization accompanied by the international expansion of the power of a single state, which corresponds to the first form of internationalization of capital mentioned above: when a national class of capitalists exercises decisive control over the international production apparatus, and foreign capitalists participate as minority partners. In this case, the international power of a single imperialist state corresponds to the international supremacy of a national group of capital owners on a global scale.

B)   Centralization comes together with reduction of the power of a set of national capitalist states and the emergence of new federal-state power, a supranational capitalist state. This type corresponds to the second form of internationalization of capital mentioned above, in which the international merger of capital takes place without the domination of a specific national capitalist group (the multinational company).

C)   Relative indifference of capital towards the state, which tends to be a transitional process between the two previous types. Here, companies internationalize their activities to such an extent and in so many countries that they become indifferent to the political and economic situation in their country.

Thus, three models of the imperialist political system among the metropolises stem from those three types of relationship between the international centralization of capital and the late capitalist state: super-imperialism, ultra-imperialism, and continuous inter-imperialist rivalries. In super-imperialism – Magdoff's model, according to Mandel (1982: 223) – a single imperialist power exercises hegemony, and the other imperialist states lose their real independence, becoming small semi-colonial powers. In the long term, that process rests on both the military supremacy and the ownership and control of production and capital concentrations. In ultra-imperialism, the international fusion of capital is such that all differences among the economic interests of capital owners of different nationalities disappear. The processes of capital accumulation spread evenly throughout the world, ignoring the political juncture and

---

8   It is important to point out that the formation of European multinational companies and a European supranational state appear in Mandel's theory as a sketch, as a process in an embryonic stage.

institutions to create a large world market, whose dynamics would be free competition between large companies, freed from their national states. The tendency is for a supranational world state to emerge, defending the interests of all capital owners against threats of economic crisis, revolts, revolutions, and so on. In continuous inter-imperialist competition, the fusion of capital takes place on a continental level, forming a small set of imperialist superpowers competing. The intercontinental competition then intensifies, and imperialist rivalries continue, but no longer among national units, but among such superpowers: US imperialism (which controls Canada and Australia), the less powerful Japanese imperialism (which controls part of Asia), and Western European imperialism. In this model, the probability of world wars like those of the first half of the twentieth century is low, with economic rivalries prevailing, which does not exclude imperialist wars by proxy, colonial wars of pillage, anti-revolutionary wars and wars against national liberation struggles, and nuclear war against the socialist bloc.

Therefore, the central point of international political economy for Mandel is the advance of US imperialism over other central social formations and the European reaction in a way that rivals the USA. This process trends towards the formation of European multinational companies and a European supranational state (European Economic Community/EEC, which will give rise to the European Union later). In other words, the trend in the Old Continent would be towards what he classified as the second type or type B of relationship, between the capitalist state and the international centralization of capital, as described above. Regarding the models of the imperialist political system between the metropolises, for the author, the continuity of imperialist rivalries predominates as a dynamic of international relations (revamped, since the European imperialist agent in the post-World War II period would be a conglomerate of states, not a single state). The interference of US capital within the borders of the EEC represents a means by which part of the European market is taken away from a European capital. It is a process of intensifying international capitalist competition, which leads to the dominance of US companies in Europe, resulting in the subordination of European capital. Given this, the emergence of the supranational state will be decisive and a real gain for the groups and leaders of the Western European bourgeoisie, even becoming the most efficient anti-recession instrument. Thus, for Mandel (1982), both employers' organizations and EEC authorities recognize and desire the interpenetration of capital and the formation of European monopoly companies, as they understand that only a unified European bourgeoisie can stand up to the USA (not the individual nationalism, such as that of De Gaulle). The contradiction among the interests of large national capitals finds resolution in the state factor, given that the tendency of capital interpenetration makes the national state an ineffective instrument, and it is necessary to find a new form of state that corresponds to the new socioeconomic reality: supranational European institutions.

A European capital would demand a European bourgeois state as a more capable instrument to promote and guarantee its profits, as well as to defend it against all its adversaries (Mandel, 1967: 29). Large European companies are pushing for the consolidation of the EEC: to leave the free trade zone towards economic integration and successfully compete against the US, otherwise, they have witnessed the divestiture of their companies (the first form of international centralization described above) and/or a throwback to economic nationalism/customs protectionism. The future of supranational institutions ultimately depends on the level at which the process of the international interpenetration of capital has reached. A European capitalist federation could only be born out of the phenomena of international monopolies. However, Mandel believes that this European process is still a sketch of the stage of the huge national capital, and the national state has not been overcome yet. Regardless of the stage, rivalries between the metropolises still take place. It is, therefore, in Europe and North America that the decisive struggle takes place between the big monopolies and the imperialist powers.

4   Nicos Poulantzas,[9] Imperialism and Bourgeois Factions

According to Poulantzas (1974, 1976, 1978) the rise of the Third World movement affected theories of imperialism, which ended up focusing on analyzes of center-periphery relations, on issues related to unequal development and dominance between those countries. Therefore, he thought it was important to reflect on inter-imperialist conflicts, that is, the relations among imperialist metropolises in the current phase of imperialism and the implications for revolutionary strategy. Specifically, in his Marxist theory of the state (Poulantzas, 1978), he asks how relations among imperialist states affected the capitalist state apparatus.

---

9   The Greek Nicos Poulantzas settled in France in the 1960s, where he encountered the intellectual group of the philosopher Louis Althusser. Under this influence, in part of his political and academic career, he sophisticatedly reinterpreted the classics of Marxism -Marx, Engels, Lenin, and Gramsci – and thus promoted advances in the Marxist theory of politics, especially in the theory of the capitalist state.

The author (Poulantzas, 1978) recalls that there are three positions on this. 1) Positions as Kautsky, such as Magdoff's, in which all capitalist states and their respective bourgeoisies are subordinated to US super-imperialism. 2) Positions like Mandel's on imperialist rivalries between autonomous and independent units. 3) And his position according to which there was a change in the imperialist chain that affected the relations among the metropolises and, in particular, on the states and the bourgeoisie. The critique to Mandel and others is that for them, the current phase of imperialism is not marked by a change in the structure of relations among the imperialist metropolises. For the Belgian economist the inter-imperialist conflicts between the center have the same meaning at present as in the past (in the classic of imperialism, about which Lenin wrote) and, are placed, in a context of autonomous and independent states, guided by their national bourgeoisie, fighting for supremacy. In particular, in this vision (Mandel), the expansion of the EEC is considered cooperation and internationalization of European capital from different countries that lead to a European supranational state for the elimination of the supremacy of US capital.

Poulantzas (1978) differs from the positions of Magdoff and Mandel and explains the change in the structure of relations among the imperialist metropolises. He considers that the capitalist mode of production has a double tendency, which is: it becomes dominant within the national social formation and expands abroad. Under the domination of monopoly capital, and because of the fall in the profit rate, this expansion is accentuated through the export of capital. That is the imperialism phenomenon that occurs in the core countries of capitalism, which tend to dominate and exploit the rest of the world. In addition to this consideration, he indicates that imperialism is marked by phases that correspond to different forms of domination and dependence. They are 1) end of the nineteenth century until the interwar – transition from competitive capitalism to monopoly imperialism; 2) consolidation phase; 3) the current phase that was established after the end of World War II, which is the object of his reflection. The highlight here is that imperialist domination is no longer 'from the outside' but in an induced and internalized way. Imperialist foreign capital is reproduced within national social formations, projecting itself and acting economically, politically, and ideologically.

In this phase, then, there is a new line of demarcation among the imperialist metropolises. The USA on one side and other metropolises, in particular Europe, establish a relationship in which the US monopoly capital exercises domination within those metropolises. It is this induced and internalized reproduction of foreign capital, originating in the US, within European countries that characterizes the current phase (post-World War II) and which also implies the extended reproduction within them of the development of US imperialism.

The interference of capital from abroad to a national social formation has the objective of increasing the rate of exploitation to neutralize the tendency to fall in the profit rate. Furthermore, such interference does not mean some form of association but rather a relationship of strength. A power relationship between the different fractions of the ruling class of the central capitalist states. This is the structural change for Poulantzas: the emergence of a new fractionation of the bourgeoisie in the face of international relations that no longer consists of the old dichotomy between foreign bourgeoisie versus national bourgeoisie.

Thus, Poulantzas identifies (1976, 1978) that in the relations among the central states a new type of fractionation of the dominant class is constituted, with emphasis on what he calls the internal bourgeoisie, which cannot be confused with the fraction of the comprador (or associated) bourgeoisie nor with the fraction of the national bourgeoisie. The comprador bourgeoisie is the fraction whose interests are directly subordinated to those of foreign capital and which serves as a direct intermediary for the implantation and reproduction of foreign capital within a social formation. The interference of foreign capital 'can only, in general, play a decisive role in the various dependent countries [...] *by articulating, in those countries, internal power relations*' (Poulantzas, 1976: 20. Emphasis by the author). This fraction does not have its accumulation base and, in general, has its activity linked to large estates and speculation, concentrated in financial, banking, and commercial sectors, but also able to act in industrial branches, in those entirely subordinated and dependent on foreign capital. From a political-ideological point of view, it is the support and agent of the imperialist capital. The national bourgeoisie is an autochthonous fraction, which has its accumulation base within the social formation and has political-ideological autonomy in the face of imperialist capital. In certain circumstances, in alliance with the dominated classes, this fraction may adopt an anti-imperialist stance and/or engage in a national liberation struggle. The internal bourgeoisie occupies an intermediate position between the comprador bourgeoisie and the national bourgeoisie, presenting contradictions with foreign capital. It has its accumulation base, thus trying to limit the presence of foreign capital in the domestic market, but at the same time, it is dependent on this capital in areas such as investment and technology.

> The internal bourgeoisie, on the contrary, even being dependent on foreign capital, presents contradictions concerning it. First of all, because it feels frustrated in sharing the pie of exploitation of the masses: the

leonine transfer of surplus-value is carried out to its detriment and in favor of foreign capital and its agents, the comprador bourgeoisie [...] the development of the internal market through a small increase in the purchasing power and consumption of the masses, which would offer them more outlets; finally, it seeks help from the State, which would allow it to develop exports.

POULANTZAS, 1976: 36–7

It is precisely by taking into account the existing forms of alliance, and the contradictions, among the bourgeois factions in the central countries, that it is possible to pose the question of national states. For Poulantzas (1978), writing in the 1970s, the internationalization of capital does not suppress or abbreviate national states, nor in the sense of peaceful integration of capital over states, with all internationalization processes working under a particular country, nor in the sense of its extinction under the U.S. superstate, as if the US capital simply swallowed the other imperialist bourgeoisie. The states themselves assume responsibility for the interests of the dominant imperialist capital in its extended development within the national formation in its complex interiorization. The currently dominant form of inter-imperialist contradiction is not between international capital and national capital, nor among the imperialist bourgeoisies understood as juxtaposed entities. In other words, the contradictions of autochthonous capital are, through complex mediations, extrapolated by US capital that establishes conflicts or alliances with fractions of the ruling class. In its role as a promoter of hegemony in the power bloc, therefore, the national state intervenes in an interior field already crossed by inter-imperialist contradictions and where the contradictions among the dominant fractions within its social formation are already internationalized. Thus, state interventions in favor of certain large foreign monopolies and against others, in favor of large national monopolies or even middle sectors of capital and against others, are expressions of the class struggle within the bourgeoisie of the central states of capitalism. If the European bourgeoisie does not cooperate or do not isolate themselves in the face of US capital, it is due to the bias effects on them of the new structure of dependence on that capital. This new relationship works through the internalization of US capital and the struggle around it to fight it or ally with it. It is not the emergence of a new state over European countries that those nations are witnessing, but rather splintering in the ruling class underlying existing national states. In other words, the imperialism phenomenon, the conflicts, and alliances between the capitalist powers and the US political and economic world supremacy are linked to such fragmentation and the struggles of the bourgeois factions at the national and international level.

5 Conclusion

We know that the debate on US imperialism is even more profound, diverse, and controversial. Nevertheless, the authors in question brought a rich polemic and contribution to these studies, especially when it comes to the international politics of the second half of the twentieth century under US domains. It is important to mention that the Marxist literature dealing with the history of the theory of imperialism has significant publications on the inaugural debate and what might be called the current debate (see the footnote 10 below). However, we see an absence of the systematization of this debate at stake. In this sense, it is not our aim here, but it is worth thinking about how these contributions have repercussions for analyzing international relations today.

What we can say is, first, that the theories presented approach, distance or rectify the so-called inaugural debate, resuming most of the differences between Lenin and Kautsky[10] to think about imperialism after World War II. In summary, we can say that Mandel and Poulantzas, in their way, corrected the

---

10   The ideas and disagreements between Kautsky and Lenin go beyond the debate presented here between Magdoff, Mandel and Poulantzas. To cite one example, the debate between Leo Panitch/Sam Gindin and Alex Callinicos on the dynamics of imperialism in the 21st century carries the divergences of the inaugural debate. Panitch and Gindin (2004), who contradict Lenin's perspective on the perennial inter-imperialist rivalry in the international relations of capitalism, argue that pioneering theorists would have elevated the moment of World War I to an immutable dynamic of the global capitalist order. The authors attribute to the capitalist state the role of paving the way for the expansion of its capital abroad, monitoring and managing this expansion and ensuring the conditions for capital accumulation. The US state began to build relations among the major capitalist countries, especially in Europe after World War II to form what they call the informal American empire, which is generally characterized by the ability of the US state to penetrate and coordinate the other leading capitalist states so that they make an unforced adherence to US capitalist dynamics. Callinicos (2009), for his part, claims that the conceptions of Panitch and Gindin are the theory of ultra-imperialism renewed for the 21st century and follows the Leninist thesis according to which imperialism corresponds to conflicts in the current phase of development of contemporary capitalism. For him, the supremacy of the United States does not mean that there are no internal contradictions between these states. Following Lenin's idea that in capitalism, just as the companies of the same branch are always in competition, the big corporations also compete among themselves, and so the states run by the interests of their bourgeoisies are in constant conflict. For the author this means that when conflicts escalate and the possibilities of understanding or persuasion are exhausted, the use of force becomes an imperative. On

Leninist thesis of defending the permanence of conflicts between imperialist states, while Magdoff, in a similar perspective to that of Kautsky, defended the constitution of an ultra-imperialist alliance, which eliminates the possibilities of conflicts between imperialist states.

Second, we can say that the questions those three authors asked themselves were: would the United States have the capacity to exercise a super empire, eliminating the capacity for conflicts with other imperialist states, especially with Europe and Japan? Despite the establishment of an alliance between the United States and Europe, would this alliance led by the United States still be permeated by conflicts among the states? What is the role of European integration? The background of this debate is not only productive internationalization, that is, the increase in foreign direct investment, whose concentration takes place in the flow between the United States and Europe, but also in the conflicts and interests of nation-states. Those questions remain current and central to analyzing contemporary international politics.

Third, Marxist theories of imperialism maintain that there is a tendency towards the concentration and centralization of capital and the export of capital, and a permanent domination and dependence relationship among states in the international power structure, the former being the juridical-political units of the way of capitalist production. The three authors that were presented agree that there is superiority or dominance of the United States in the current phase. They find that there is a concentration of investment flows between the United States and Europe and argue that the process of productive internationalization is linked to the monopolization/centralization of capital, but they ended up differing on the relationship between the United States and the European Economic Community. Magdoff, similarly to the thesis of ultra-imperialism, ends up approaching a conception of hegemony since there is a world-system of power that consists of an amalgamation between the dominant classes of dependent countries with foreign forces, shaping the political, economic structure, and social dependence. He also argues that US imperialism is uncontested militarily and politically, which implies the end of the idea about inter-imperialist conflicts. That is: there is no rivalry between the United States and the European States or the European Economic Community. In this sense, he also draws attention to the dollar's role in guaranteeing US supremacy. In addition, it incorporates important elements to think about political-ideological and cultural domination as the role of cinema and international

---

the three debates in the Marxist theory of imperialism, the foundational moment, the post-WWII moment and the early 21st century moment, see Bugiato and Berringer, 2021.

cooperation. For him, the imperialist network presupposes not only the unity among the imperialist bourgeoisies on behalf of the reproduction of capital, but it is a counterrevolutionary political alliance that aimed to contain the processes of national liberation struggles and oppose the USSR.

Mandel argued that the trend towards the internationalization of capital control (formation of transnational monopolies) would have altered the relationship between the national states and internationalized capital. Especially in Europe, a formation process of supranational states would have been opened that would have regulated and given support to the merger of national capitals in the face of competition with US monopolies. It was about the tendency to form a supranational federal state, or supranational bourgeois state, in which the EEC (European Economic Community) would be a great example. At this point, productive internationalization and the internationalization of the State are related, in the sense that the state adapts and assumes different forms/typologies based on the demand of capital. This position seems to be influenced by an instrumentalist and/or derivationist[11] conception of the state.

Poulantzas, in turn, brought a theoretical innovation by supporting the idea of an imperialist chain and the relationship of dependence and conflict among imperialist states. In that sense, revolutionary struggles could take place around the anti-imperialist strategy in Europe and other peripheral social formations. The idea of an imperialist chain allows us to think that the relationship between the United States and Europe takes place under the domination of the former, without a permanent alliance among the states. They are links of dependence that are created from the internationalization of production, but that do not eliminate conflicts among classes and class fractions, especially among states. What happens is the formation of a new fraction of the class, the internal bourgeoisie, which maintains specific relationships to foreign capital and the national social formation. However, Poulantzas ends up not reflecting on the expansionist policy and military power of the United States, highlighted in Magdoff and Mandel.

---

11   The German Derivationist School, of which Joachim Hirsch is one of the main exponents, seeks to extract from the categories of political economy presented by Marx, especially in The Capital, the understanding of the political institutions of the capitalist production mode, particularly the state. For the derivationist authors, the capitalist state is intimately integrated into capitalist production and distribution relations in a way that palaces itself as a fundamental defender and reproducer of those. Therefore, the state is derived from the production mode in an indissoluble relationship in which the state form corresponds to its economic function. Although not explicitly, Mandel (1982) seems to agree with this theory when dealing with the state in late capitalism.

Fourth and in sum, the relationship between the United States and Europe, in the light of the internationalization of production and the international dominance of the first, were treated as undisputed dominance of the USA for Magdoff, the possibility of competition from the formation of European conglomerates and the future formation of a supranational state for Mandel, and an imperialist chain creating new ties of dependence and conflict for Poulantzas. Those divergences within the Marxist theory of imperialism show the existing plurality not only among the classics but also among the authors who proposed to discuss and update the imperialism theory. The unity between them is Historical Materialism, the idea of class struggle, dispute or alliance between states and revolution, a problem that still seeks place in International Relations.

References

Barone C (1985) *Marxist thought on imperialism: survey and critique*, Hampshire: M. E. Sharpe.

Brewer A (1990) *Marxists theories of imperialism: a critical survey*, 2nd ed, London: Routlege.

Bugiato C (2017), Kautsky e Lenin: imperialismo, paz e guerra nas relações internacionais. *Novos Rumos*, 54, 2: 24–44.

Bugiato C and Berringer T (2021) Cooperação e conflito interimperialista: um debate teórico secular. *Revista do Sul Global*, 1,1: 63–74.

Bukharin N (1986 [1915]) *A economia mundial e o imperialismo: esboço econômico*. São Paulo: Nova Cultural (Os economistas).

Callinicos A (2009) *Imperialism and global political economy*, Cambridge: Polity Press.

Hardt M and Antonio N (2001) *Império*. Rio Janeiro: Record.

Kautsky K (2008 [1914]) O imperialismo e a guerra. *Revista História e luta de classes*, 4, 5: 211–220.

Kiely R (2020) Globalização e imperialismo. In: Saad-Filho A and Fine B (eds.) *Dicionário de Economia Política Marxista*. São Paulo: Expressão Popular.

Lenin V (1982 [1916]) Imperialismo: fase superior do capitalismo. In: *Obras escolhidas em três tomos*, Volume 2. São Paulo: Alfa Omega.

Luxemburgo R (1985 [1913]) *A acumulação do capital: contribuição ao estudo econômico do imperialismo*. São Paulo: Nova Cultural (Os economistas).

Magdoff H (1972 [1969]) *A era do imperialismo*. Porto: Portucalense.

Magdoff H (1979 [1978]) *Imperialismo: da era colonial ao presente*. Rio de Janeiro: Zahar.

Mandel E (1967) International Capitalism and "Supra-Nationality". *Socialist Register*, 4: 27–41.

Mandel E (1982 [1972]) *O capitalismo tardio*. São Paulo: Abril Cultural (Os economistas).
Mandel E (2009 [1970]) *Europe vs. America*. New York: Monthly Review Press.
Noonan M (2017) *Marxist theories of imperialism: a history*. London: I. B. Tauris.
Osório, LF (2018) *Estado, imperialismo e Relações Internacionais*. São Paulo: Ideias e Letras.
Panitch L and Gindin S (2004) Global capitalism and American Empire. *Socialist Register*, 40: 1–42.
Poulantzas N (1974) Internationalization of capitalist relations and the nation-state. *Economy and Society*, 3, 2: 145–79.
Poulantzas N (1976 [1975]) *A crise das ditaduras: Portugal, Grécia e Espanha,* Rio de Janeiro: Paz e Terra.
Poulantzas N (1978 [1974]) *As classes sociais no capitalismo hoje*. Rio de Janeiro: Zahar.

CHAPTER 12

Imperialism
The Question of System Stability

Marcelo Pereira Fernandes[1]

> The bourgeois system has become too narrow to contain the wealth created within it.[2]
>
> MARX and ENGELS, "Communist Manifesto"

∴

1   Introduction

One of the main controversies within the Marxist theory of imperialism is the ability of the system to organize itself economically and politically, creating a stable environment for large businesses. The famous polemics between Lenin and Kautsky in the early twentieth century, about the possibility that capitalism would be peacefully managed by the great powers and corporations that compete for world wealth, persists in much of the current debate.

Currently, since imperialism is a hot topic, much of the discussion is precisely about the problem of system stability. Some authors emphasise relative economic or political stability, but the central idea is of a more structured capitalism with a greater capacity to resolve conflicts that could hinder the global process of capital accumulation. Therefore, the idea of interstate competition would be outdated.

This chapter intends to examine the Marxist literature on imperialism that somehow understands that capitalism is more organized nowadays, to the point of overcoming the rivalries between great powers.[3] Such literature has

---

1 Professor at Federal Rural University of Rio de Janeiro. E-mail: mapefern@gmail.com.
2 Originally published, in English, as article in the journal "Contexto Internacional", volume 40(1) jan/apr, 2018.
3 There is also a wider discussion on the perspectives of order in the international system in the twenty-first century, in particular on the possibilities for stability of the system, developed by several authors in the area of International Political Economy, beyond the frontiers

its roots mainly in the analyzes of Eduard Bernstein and Karl Kautsky in the early twentieth century, but we can also find its germs in Rudolf Hilferding and even in Nikolai Bukharin. Using terms such as globalization, transnational capital and empire, authors such as Robinson (2007, 2008), Robinson and Harris (2000), Hardt and Negri (2001), Panitch and Gindin (2005), albeit with differences, also share the notion that the world has reached such an economic and political organization that in practice there are no longer national borders, which would make the activity of large private corporations relatively safer and beyond the reach of nation-states.

The critique of the notion of an organized capitalism can be found in Harvey (2004), Callinicos (2009), Gowan (2004), Harman (2003), Marshall (2014), Sakellaropoulos and Sotiris (2015), Sakellaropoulos (2009). However, for the purpose of this work, the analyzes of Sakellaropoulos, Sotiris and Marshall will be highlighted. By seeking in Lenin concepts such as uneven development and imperialist chain, these authors present a more radical critique, demonstrating the relevance of the concept of Imperialism as a stage of capitalism capable of responding to the challenges posed at this unique moment the world goes through.

In addition to this introduction, this chapter is divided into four sections. In the second section, Stability is analyzed in the classical theory of imperialism. The third section examines some contemporary authors who are close to the views of the authors mentioned in the first section. In fact, all of them believe that Imperialism is no longer an indispensable concept to explain the present moment of capitalism. In the fourth section, I perform a critique of the notion of system stability, based on the Leninist theory of imperialism. Thus, we show that the perception that capitalism has reached a degree of organization that can deny the validity of the concept of imperialism is questionable, and is not in accordance with the structure that drives the system. Lastly, our final considerations.

---

of Marxist thought on imperialism. However, for the scope of this chapter we seek to situate the debate only in Marxist circles, since we understand that these are already sufficiently broad and controversial, as we can observe throughout the text. Moreover, from our point of view, the Marxist analysis of imperialism provides more promising elements on the current international order.

2 Stability in Classical Imperialism

Rudolf Hilferding was the first Marxist author to call attention to the emergence of finance capital as the dominant capital in the era of monopolies, considered as a new stage of capitalism. At this stage, the separation between industrial capital and financing capital, characteristic of the period of competitive capitalism, disappears. In the classic "Finance Capital" of 1910, considered as the greatest contribution to Marxist economics of its time (Bottomore, 1985: 1), Hilferding would, to some extent, consider the possibility that capitalism might attain a degree of organization in which it was no longer subject to production anarchy, eliminating economic crises.

According to Hilferding, capitalism tended to create cartels all over the economy. At the limit, there would be a world cartel where the entire capitalist production would be rigorously planned by a responsible superior body that would perfectly dictate the total amount of goods to be produced and distributed in all fields. The amplitude of economic planning would reach the point in which even money[4] would no longer be necessary[5] (Hilferding, 1985: 226–227). By restricting production, cartels would be able to eliminate commodity overproduction crises, but not the crisis derived from the overproduction of capital (Hilferding, 1985: 278). Hence, even if cartelization could change the character of crises, it would not be able to completely suppress them.

In this sense, by comparing the struggle of industrial capital for more freedom in the mercantilist period, Hilferding (1985: 314) concluded that finance capital in the imperialist stage hated the anarchy of competition. With interconnected interests, it preferred organization, but only to resume competition at a higher level.[6]

Like Hilferding, Nikolai Bukharin also concluded that the economy tends to become highly organized at the stage of monopoly capitalism. In the work

---

4 Brunhoff (1992: 55) states, "Hilferding seems to indicate that the organization of capitalist production would indeed be possible, thanks to a single central bank that would have the monopoly of public funding, which, according to him, would allow it to attenuate or even eliminate crises".
5 However, Hilferding did not expect planning to reach this limit, or that international cartel competition could be eliminated.
6 Later on, in the article "Organized Economy" of 1927, Hilferding believed that the birth of an organized economy would make the transition to socialism easier, among other reasons because "Capitalism, therefore, abdicates from the main objection it could raise against socialism and, at the same time, the last psychological objection to socialism falls down" (Hilferding, 2002: 526). According to Kuhn (2000: 71), many have identified in this view a progressive and conceivably peaceful side of imperialism.

"Imperialism and World Economy", Bukharin stated, "Imperialism is the policy of finance capitalism, that is, of highly developed capitalism, which presupposes a certain maturity – very important in this case – of the productive organization" (Bukharin, 1986: 128).

According to Bukharin, competition and conflict between capitalists would be eliminated at the national economy level and transferred to the international arena. Therefore, there is a double movement in Bukharin's analysis: on the one hand, the tendency towards the internationalization of capital, on the other, the tendency towards its penetration into the state (state capitalism). This double movement would be the main contradiction of modern capitalism, and the cause of hostilities among the great powers: the central problem for Bukharin is not economy, but war (Callinicos, 2009: 57; Brewer, 1990: 111).

Hence, the capitalist system would tend to overcome production anarchy and achieve economic planning. And it did not reach its full organizational potential only because the world is divided into national units (Howard and King, 1989: 247).

> Competition reaches its maximum development: *the competition of national capitalist trusts in the world market.* Within the limits of national economies, competition is minimized, to outgrow, beyond these limits, to fantastic proportions, unknown in previous historical epochs.
> BUKHARIN, 1986: 112

However, Callinicos (2009: 62) noticed that taking into account that capitalism really became highly organized as Hilferding and Bukharin expected, why believe that such organization would cease inside national borders? According to Bukharin himself (1986: 129), if national trusts could reach an agreement, imperialism would indeed cease to exist. But that would not be possible due to political and social reasons. The necessary condition for such agreement would be related to the equality of conditions among trusts in the world market. Since equality does not occur, the trust that holds a more advantageous position – both strictly at the economic level and at the economic-political level (association of capital with the state) – would have no interest in establishing agreements (Bukharin, 1986: 130–131).

Within the Marxist tradition, the notion that capitalism could organize itself to the point of eliminating even inter-imperialist wars was proposed by Karl Kautsky. Kautsky (1914, 2002) considered that the fundamental thrust of imperialism would be the distortion between industry and agriculture in capitalist economies. The reason for that is that the impetus towards capital accumulation and production increase is much stronger in the industry than in agriculture. This greater investment capacity of the industry would cause a tension in both sectors, since for the industry to continue growing it would be necessary that the agricultural sector continued supplying raw materials and food.

Imperialism would be the consequence of highly developed industrial capitalism. But it is not a new stage of capitalist development as Hilferding argued, but the preferred policy of finance capital.[7] States would be forced to build a large national industry in order to maintain their independence, while those remaining agricultural would decay (Kautsky 2002: 457). In this perspective, there is a trend towards occupation and subordination of agrarian countries, which causes a strong rivalry between industrial countries and consequently an arms race. Kautsky (2002: 459) also considers that there would be a tendency of advanced capitalist states to block the industrialization of agrarian countries in order to prevent the emergence of competition.[8]

However, according to Kautsky, the conflicts between the great powers for the exploitation of agricultural regions could not continue. The arms race and the costs of colonial expansion would reach a level that hinders the very process of accumulation and becomes an obstacle for the development of capitalism. Therefore, there is no need to remain in a state of war, since it contributes only with a single sector of the bourgeoisie: the arms industry. The domination of the large monopolies over the economies of the imperialist nations leads to the renunciation of the arms race in favor of the alliance for peace. That is why "Every far-sighted capitalist must call out to his associates: capitalists of all lands unite" (Kautsky, 2002: 460).[9]

This implies that capitalism reaches a certain point of development and organization that attenuates its contradictions until war becomes unnecessary. This level of development in which there is a transfer of the cartelization of the economy of the developed countries to the international arena was called by Kautsky 'ultra-imperialism'.[10]

---

7   Kautsky described Hilferding's "Finance Capital" as a conclusion of Marx's Capital. See Howard and King (1989: 100).
8   Kautsky's idea is similar to the so-called dependency theory, of Marxist inspiration, that emerged in the mid-1960s.
9   Hilferding also saw a similar possibility when he explained why economic rivalries among states do not lead to a violent solution. According to Hilferding (1985: 312): "The very export of capital creates tendencies that resist such a violent solution. (...). Thus, tendencies towards solidarity of international capitalist interests arise".
10 As Milios and Sotiropoulos (2009: 60) pointed out, the idea of ultra-imperialism was already present in a text written by Kautsky in 1892 ("The Class Struggle" [Erfurt Program]). John Hobson, who influenced the main theorists of imperialism, also raised a similar argument using the term 'inter-imperialist': "Christendom thus laid out in a few

Thus, in relation to Hilferding and Bukharin, Kautsky maximizes the organizational capacity of the system by concluding that capitalist powers would reach an agreement so that the reproduction of capital would occur in a peaceful manner all over the world.

> From the purely economic standpoint, however, there is nothing further to prevent this violent explosion from finally replacing imperialism by a holy alliance of the imperialists. The longer the War lasts, the more it exhausts all tile participants and makes them recoil from an early repetition of armed conflict, the nearer we come to this last solution, however unlikely it may seem at the moment.
> KAUTSKY, 1914

The post-World War II Golden Age of capitalism under the United States hegemony revived the Kautskyan idea of an Ultra-imperialism (Callinicos, 2009: 63). However, in Kautsky's terms, the reasons that would prevent a new conflagration between the powers were not met. There was never a reduction in military expenses, and armed conflicts did occur in several parts of the world, even after the end of the Cold War, when the idea of the organization of capitalism has reached its peak under the sign of "globalization", as we will see in the next section.

3 Stability in the Post-cold Aar

After the collapse of real socialism in Eastern Europe and the end of the USSR in the early 1990s, new questions were raised about the role of the nation-state, based on the neoliberal concept of market supremacy. The opinion that nations are interdependent and that financial and commercial openness would be beneficial to all nations was widely spread. In the context of Marxism, some authors began to argue that capitalism came to be dominated by large companies that have no ties to their home states. Capitalism would have reached a degree of organization that would prevent conflicts between states.

This was the analysis of Hardt and Negri (2001), in a much-commented study that came to be curiously nicknamed anti-globalization manifesto. According to the authors, imperialism would no longer exist, and no country

---

great federal empires, each with a retinue of uncivilised dependencies, seems to many the most legitimate development of present tendencies, and one which would offer the best hope of permanent peace on an assured basis of inter-Imperialism" (Hobson, 2005: 332).

would be able to fulfill the leading role that European nations held in the past (Hardt and Negri, 2001: 14). Power would now be decentralized and without a particular territory. Instead of imperialism, the 'empire' would emerge, defined as a global power, without borders and above nations.[11] A new form of sovereignty composed of national and supranational bodies united by a single logic in which national states would no longer be able to regulate economic and cultural exchanges. With decaying sovereignty, no state would be able to act as an imperialist nation (Hardt and Negri, 2001:12).

This way, the empire would be born after a transitional period after the end of World War II, in a world defined and organized around three mechanisms: i) decolonization, that would gradually recover the world market hierarchically under the leadership of the United States; ii) gradual decentralization of production; iii) the construction of a structure of international relations that would spread the disciplinary productive regime and the disciplinary society in its successive evolutions worldwide. According to the authors, these are the three mechanisms that contribute to the evolution from imperialism to the empire (Hardt and Negri, 2001: 266).

In the empire, there would not be a definite place for the new productive forces because they would be everywhere, producing not only commodities "but also rich and powerful social relationships,"[12] in a world where national borders would tend to simply disappear (Hardt and Negri, 2001: 230). Now, transnational corporations would be responsible for the economic and political transformations of postcolonial countries and subordinate regions (Hardt and Negri, 2001: 268). They would be the ones to dictate the pace of production at each moment. "The state has been defeated and corporations now rule the earth!" (Hardt and Negri, 2001: 328).

Still according to Hardt and Negri (2001), imperialist wars would be replaced by 'just wars', which are in fact a form of police action, because if borders practically no longer exist, then there would be no reason for wars. Rivalries between countries would be eliminated. Therefore:

> The history of imperialist, inter-imperialist and anti-imperialist wars is over. The end of such history has introduced a kingdom of peace. Or

---

11 The concept of empire would arise from a long tradition that refers to the old Roman Empire (Hardt and Negri, 2001: 28).

12 In an attempt to summarize Marx's analysis of the capitalist mode of production, the authors do so based on the controversial underconsumption thesis, largely based on Luxemburg (1970), in which the central problem of capitalism lies in the lack of purchasing power of workers to absorb the goods produced. See Hardt and Negri (2001: 243–244).

> more exactly, we have entered the era of minor and internal conflicts. Every imperial war is a civil war, a police action – from Los Angeles and Granada to Mogadishu and Sarajevo.
> HARDT and NEGRI, 2001: 209

Hence, for the authors, there would also be no armies anymore. The United States would have a world police force that would not act for imperialist interests, but for imperial interest in the name of peace and order (Hardt and Negri, 2001: 209). The stability of capitalism would reach its climax.

Like Hardt and Negri (2001), William Robinson (2002, 2007, 2008) and Harris (2012) believed that capitalism would currently be very organized by transnational institutions at the service of transnational capital, in a world where borders would be dissolving. In several works, Robinson emphasized that capitalism has undergone great changes since the classical period of imperialism analyzed by Hilferding, Lenin etc.,[13] and would find itself in a new stage known as globalization, which would be a product of transnational capital.

Nowadays, the dynamics of the capitalist system could not be understood considering the nation-state as the center. Therefore, the term globalization ('the latest stage of capitalism') would be very consistent with the current moment (Robinson, 2002; Harris, 2012). Harris (2012: 2) asserts that the fundamental logic of capitalism would not change in terms of its power to accumulate and exploit labor. However, the method by which they would take place would be new.

In turn, Robinson (2007, 2008) presupposes at least four changes that would characterize the capitalist system today: i) the rise of a truly transnational capital and the integration of all countries into a new global productive and financial system. National or regional capital would still exist, but transnational capital, strongly divorced from any country, would be dominant; ii) the emergence of a new transnational capitalist class; iii) the rise of transnational state apparatuses ('transnational state') and; iv) the emergence of new relations of power and inequality in the global society.

However, Robinson (2007) argues that his theory shares little or nothing with Kautsky's thesis on ultra-imperialism, since the latter assumed that capital would remain national and unite itself internationally. In his view, the conflict between capitals is endemic to the system, but it would present itself in new forms in globalization, not as wars between states. For that reason,

---

13   Robinson prefers to call it the 'national corporate stage of capitalism' rather than monopoly capitalism, in order to highlight the important role of the state in the circuit of accumulation during the twentieth century. See Robinson (2008: 3).

competition among nation-states would no longer exist in the globalization era, only among companies. "As national states are captured by transnational capitalist forces they tend to serve the interests of global over local accumulation processes." (Robinson 2007: 17).

In an analysis very close to Hardt and Negri, Robinson (2007) concludes that we are facing an 'empire of global capital', based in Washington only for historical reasons. This empire would no longer serve the interests of a national bourgeoisie, but of a transnational capitalist class.

> We are witness to new forms of global capitalist domination, whereby intervention is intended to create conditions favorable to the penetration of transnational capital and the renewed integration of the intervened region into the global system. US intervention facilitates a shift in power from locally and regionally oriented elites to new groups more favorable to the transnational project. The result of US military conquest is not the creation of exclusive zones for 'US' exploitation, as was the result of the Spanish conquest of Latin America, the British of South Africa and India, the Dutch of Indonesia, and so forth, in earlier moments of the world capitalist system. The enhanced class power of capital brought about by these changes is felt around the world (...). In sum, the US state has attempted to play a leadership role *on behalf of* transnational capitalist interests.
>
> ROBINSON 2007: 19–20

According to Robinson (2008: 9), the US state would be a key instrument for the reproduction of the global capitalist system, since it would act as a defender of the interests of big capital, repressing the sectors that opposed it. Therefore, the increase in US militarization after 11/09 would be related neither to a quest for hegemony, nor to the resurgence of the inter-imperialist rivalries seen at the end of the nineteenth century, but to a contradictory response to the deep crisis of global capitalism that began in the late 1990s. In Robinson's view, worldwide social polarization brought about by globalization has restricted the ability of the world market to absorb production, reducing the system's expansion capacity.[14] The invasion of Iraq, for example, would create favorable conditions for the penetration of transactional capital and help integrate the region into global capitalism. And although it has directly benefited some US companies (US capital), these firms are in fact transnational conglomerates

---

14   As in Hardt and Negri, the association with underconsumption theses is clear.

with interests that are not tied to 'US capital', but to global capital (Robinson 2007: 22).

Thus, the analyzes by Hardt and Negri (2001), Robinson (2007, 2008), Robinson and Harris (2000) and Harris (2012) emphasized that capitalism was sufficiently organized to the point where wars would no longer be necessary. However, Hardt and Negri are more emphatic as regards the state, when they say that in practice there would be no armies, but rather a type of transnational police called from time to time to maintain order anywhere in the world.

Panitch and Gindin (2005, 2012) also consider that globalization would not stimulate inter-imperialist rivalries, but would instead encourage a form of cooperation that would allow the system to have a period of stability. According to the authors, to understand this new stage of imperialism, one would have to understand the role of US imperialism in the post-World War II. At that moment, the creation of stable conditions for global accumulation of capital would be carried out by an 'informal empire', the American Empire, which would be able to integrate the other capitalist powers into a system under its rule.

Thus, to understand imperialism and current globalization, it would be necessary to begin by theorizing about the capitalist state along three dimensions: economic, political and territorial. In the economic dimension, the state would no longer be part of the organization of production, investment and appropriation of surplus; but it would still be indispensable to maintain legal regulation, administration of macroeconomic policy and as a 'lender of last resort' whenever necessary. Without these prerogatives of the state, capitalism would not be able to survive (Panitch and Gindin, 2005: 102). In the political dimension, the authors say that with the end of the Cold War, liberal democracy would become a model for all capitalist states. The territorial dimension would be implicit in the first two dimensions. Capitalism has evolved by deepening economic ties, especially within territorial spaces. Within these spaces, national borders and identities would be built (Panitch and Gindin, 2005: 103). States would continue to be subordinated to capital accumulation and capitalist logic, but ultimately that would not eliminate the importance of the state.

However, the end of the Cold War would reveal a new hierarchy among the advanced nations. The process of separation of economics and politics in the international sphere would facilitate global integration, and competition would no longer have to be expressed by imperialist rivalry, as understood by part of the Marxist theory of the early twentieth century. In that regard, Panitch argues that the term imperialism itself could be obsolete, since interimperialist rivalries would no longer exist (Gowan, Panitch and Shaw, 2001: 17). That is, the informal American Empire would replace geopolitical conflicts.

That said, according to Panitch and Gindin (2005: 104), it would be necessary to investigate how the separation of economics and politics has happened at the international level in the last two centuries.

> This involves not only an understanding of the progressive marketization and commodification of social life, but also of the processes by which the national-territorial capitalist state, in its modal liberal-democratic form, was universalized and inscribed into the constitution of international institutions and international law by the mid-twentieth century.
> PANITCH and GINDIN, 2005: 104

It is the separation between economics and politics in the international sphere that would make the existence of informal empires possible. This separation would have been incomplete in the globalization between 1870 and 1920 (Panitch and Gindin, 2012: 13). That is why the expansion of colonialism, the resistance in adopting liberal democracy, and the particularism of each state in relation to capital accumulation would generate severe contradictions in the three dimensions of the capitalist state, which would in turn lead to interimperialist rivalries. At that moment, Marxist theory understood that the contradictions generated by this situation would be impossible to solve.

Panitch and Gindin (2005: 106) consider that the definition of imperialism as a stage of capitalism would avoid the pitfalls of an ahistorical general theory of imperialism. However, the authors criticize what they understand as theoretical fundamentalism, since if imperialism is considered as the last stage of capitalism, it would mean that there could be no changes.[15] According to the authors, that would be wrong: after World War II, the agreement conducted by the United States made rivalries between the capitalist powers subordinate to collaborationism. US democracy would bring the credibility of the US state to the world, even when its militarism was explicit.

However, the other powers would not become passive actors of American imperialism; they would continue to operate with relative autonomy in relation to the internationalization of the state, and their actions would reflect the balance of social forces and internal political initiatives in each state. This would allow them to pressure the United States to carry out their responsibilities in

---

15 Criticism is aimed at Lenin with reference to the title of his work, "Imperialism, the Highest Stage of Capitalism". In fact, as the editors of "Monthly Review" (2004) have shown, there is a great deal of confusion as to the title, for it did not actually talk about the final stage of capitalism, but rather about the 'most recent stage'. See also Lorimer (1999).

the management of global capitalism in a more autonomous way of pressures emanating from within the American social formation itself. But in doing so, the capitalist powers would recognize that the United States has the capacity to play the leading role in the expansion, protection and reproduction of capitalism (Panitch and Gindin, 2012: 18). Thus, the country would be more than a mere agent of the particular interests of American capital, as it also assumed the responsibilities for the making and management of global capitalism (Panitch and Gindin, 2005: 112). Hence, the European bourgeoisie and states would not have any interest in defying US imperialism, for it would ultimately serve the interests of a global capitalist class.

Even with such accumulated power, Panitch and Gindin (2012) recognize that the United States failed to bring the capitalist economy to a new level of stability. However, global financial volatility and the ensuing crises would make the peripheral countries of Asia, Africa and Latin America more dependent on interventions from the American empire. Thus, the success of the United States would be in its ability to create a sphere of influence that would make the use of military force unnecessary. So, for the authors, there would be no more inter-imperialist rivalries.

The analyzes by Panitch and Gindin present some relevant 'insights' regarding the international system and the conduct of the United States as an imperialist power. However, the authors overestimate the capacity of the American state as the organizer of the system and the driving force of global development, while neglecting the role of class struggle in capitalist development inside each nation-state (Milios and Sotiropoulos 2009: 82). And when class struggle is mentioned, it is subordinated to the will of the dominant state. Consequently, Panitch and Gindin's observations are closer to a super-imperialism,[16] in which one nation has a relative control over the other powers.

4   End of Rivalries?

There is a reasonable list of authors within the Marxist camp who deny the idea that capitalism could reach a level of stability capable of putting an end to inter-imperialist rivalries. Among others, we can mention Harvey (2004), Callinicos (2009) and Gowan (2003). But we believe that the analyzes of authors such as Sakellaropoulos (2009), Sakellaropoulos and Sotiris (2015) and Marshall (2014) have a more consistent understanding of the phenomenon,

---

16   Regarding the concept of super-imperialism, see Rowthorn (1975).

since they develop an explanation based on Lenin's theory of imperialism. Therefore, they manage to establish some opposition to the idea of system stability analyzed in the previous sections.

First, on the notion of imperialism. For Lenin (1979), imperialism was a specific stage of the capitalist mode of production, which was the result of a substantial change in its organizational structure, the stage of monopoly capitalism, and not merely a 'preferred' policy of finance capital for territorial expansion and economic-political control. Initiated not before the last quarter of the nineteenth century, imperialism would be the result of the inherent tendencies of the process of capital accumulation – in which concentration and centralization prevail – and of the contradictions arising from class struggle in capitalism analyzed by Marx.

At this stage, in which monopolies prevail, crises would not be suppressed, nor would competition among different capitals be eliminated. Far from it, monopolies would amplify the anarchy and contradictions of the economic world, bringing competition to a level in which conflicts would escalate.

> The statement that cartels can abolish crises is a fable spread by bourgeois economists who at all costs desire to place capitalism in a favorable light. On the contrary, monopoly which is created in *certain* branches of industry increases and intensifies the anarchy inherent in the system of capitalist production *as a whole*.
> LENIN 1979: 701

Lenin (1979) also identified finance capital as the central force of imperialism. In the financial sphere, there would be a qualitative change in the system: unlike the earlier stage in which industrial capitalism prevailed, the economic impulse of imperialism was now in the 'haute finance'.

Thus, the particularity of imperialism would be in the intrinsic need to export capital, not in the exportation of commodities. It would be precisely through the export of capital that the international character of capitalism with all its economic and social contradictions would assert itself in an aggressive and irreversible way. And not through formal incorporation of territories, as Lenin (1979: 735) highlighted when he mentioned the informal British domination over Brazil, Argentina, and Uruguay (Mazzucchelli, 1985: 99, Sakellaropoulos and Sotiris 2015: 91).[17]

---

17 As Hobsbawn (2001: 92) noted, only in the sixth of its ten chapters ("Imperialism, the highest stage of capitalism") Lenin addressed 'the division of the world among the great powers'.

Even so, the state plays an essential role in the functioning of capitalism. Given that there is no global government, capital cannot reproduce itself without nation-states. In order to ensure the interests of the bourgeoisie, the state develops strategies to manage labor force, intervenes to maintain the profit of national capitals and promote their expansion in the international economy (Sakellaropoulos, 2009: 63). However, the export of capital also leads to competition among states, since they also play the role of mediating the interests of different ruling classes. Monopolies can join in several parts of the world, yet they need to be closely linked to their home states where they receive legal protection, even outside legal rules when it is convenient (Harman, 2003).

Therefore, international conflicts (economic, political and/or military) are intrinsic to the system, although moments of cooperation may prevail (Lenin 1979). Capital expansion does not necessarily require war conflagrations, but they cannot be ruled out. For that reason, activities linked to arms acquire a privileged position in national economies. That causes a permanent warmongering atmosphere, since it is interesting for monopolies linked to the war industry to have external enemies, whether real or illusory, to justify military purchases.

Therefore, the term 'globalization', which describes a capitalist world without borders, available and docile to a supposedly stateless capital of a unified bourgeoisie, hides or denies crucial aspects regarding the functioning of the international system[18] (Halliday, 2002; Petras and Veltmeyer, 2007; Ruccio, 2003). In reality, the concepts of imperialism and globalization are not compatible. Although several authors of the Marxist camp started to use them as a way to explain the current situation of capitalism, it is not appropriate to adopt both concepts at the same time, since the idea of globalization suppresses a series of questions related to the historical development of the relations of exploitation within the capitalist system, and the role of imperialism as a theoretical and historical reference (Sakellaropoulos, 2009).

The view advocated by different Marxist authors that the international system is characterized by stability seems to find support in certain passages of the "Communist Manifesto" by Marx and Engels (2010). According to this understanding, the source of conflicts in the system would be almost exclusively the division between bourgeois and proletarians at the international

---

18   In fact, "The term 'globalization' not only serves as description and explanation of what is going on. It refers even more to a prescription – those certain developments, particularly 'the liberalisation of national and global markets', will produce 'the best outcome for growth and human welfare' and that they are in everybody's interest" (Petras and Veltmeyer, 2007: 39).

level. Since international capital would have attained unprecedented power, there would be little room for protest movements that could undermine the structure of the system. This view underestimates the importance of the state and other forms of struggle, such as the struggle of the nations oppressed by imperialism. However, even in the "Communist Manifesto" the nation-state problem, is already mentioned when the authors call for the national liberation of Poland (Marx and Engels, 2010: 68). Similarly, another example is the struggle for women's liberation in countries like the United Arab Emirates and Saudi Arabia that may be taken into account. These are countries where the oppression of women is a structural problem – although not necessarily connected to the multinationals – and any deeper gender-related change-favoring women can cause great instability, since the region plays an important role in the geopolitical interests of imperialist countries.

The notion that multinational companies have an extraordinary capacity of coordination that facilitates international exploitation is also more or less explicit in the writings of the authors mentioned in the previous sections. However, this is a questionable theoretical assumption in the context of Marxism. The tendency toward centralization and concentration of capitals inherent in the movement of capital does not eliminate competition, but rather brings it to another level, as Lenin pointed out following in the footsteps of Marx. The reason is that it is precisely competition that forces the capitalist to accumulate uncontrollably. Capital produces without considering its limits, because it has an intrinsic expansionist force; hence the crises that occur from time to time when such limits are exceeded. For the capitalist, there is no other way but to continue seeking a continuous expansion: in the logic of capital there is no room for sentimentality, "he who does not rise, descends". Therefore, there can be no unified bourgeoisie exploiting markets around the world in an organized way, capable of suppressing economic crises and their economic-social effects.

In fact, the upsurge of capital internationalization in the post-Cold War and the image of companies producing simultaneously in several countries – although it is not something new, of course – create the perception that these companies are no longer related to their states, as Robinson (2007) mistakenly suggests, for instance.[19] But we need to understand what is appearance and what is reality. We can mention at least two recent events that demonstrate what actually occurs. When the automakers General Motors and Chrysler filed for bankruptcy in 2009, the billionaire financial bailout came exactly from the

---

19 It is important to remember that this is not a new discussion. See Michalet (1984).

United States government, country of origin of both companies, and cost US$ 80 billion for the American Treasury until 2013 (Beech, 2014). Another example concerns the French bank Paribas. It was fined unbelievable $ 8.9 billion by the New York court of justice in 2014 because it broke a law inside the United States, the International Emergency Economic Powers Act, a Federal Law of 1977, by facilitating financial transactions with Cuba, Iran and Sudan, countries that were under US embargo (Lauer, 2014). The French government directly intervened in the case, even by its president François Hollande. The Paribas case also runs counter to Panitch and Gindin's idea that the United States is a country that, first and foremost, serves the interests of a world capitalist class.

Thus, in contrast to 'globalization', the concept of 'imperialist chain' formulated by Lenin, is still an accurate description of the hierarchical, uneven and complex relations arising from the reproduction of capital in the international system.[20] It brings together the existing capitalist powers, each of them with a different level of development. According to Milios and Sotiropoulos (2009: 19), the notion of imperialist chain would lead to the formulation of two questions. Firstly, the law of uneven development. According to Lenin, the stability of the system is impossible because uneven development would cause changes in the correlation of forces of the more advanced nations, tending to erode the center's power in relation to new poles of power with greater economic dynamism. Consequently, the contradictions among the powers that comprise the imperialist chain would escalate (Lenin, 1979: 760). The law of uneven development is critical to explain the relations among the countries of the imperialist chain, providing an economic basis for military conflicts.

Secondly, the question of the weakest link in the imperialist chain. The uneven development would create the possibility of revolutions in the relatively weaker links of the imperialist chain, and not in those states in which the productive forces are more advanced, as Marx had initially predicted. However, it is important to emphasize that this is a relative position: the countries that are part of the imperialist chain are weaker or stronger compared to the other links in the chain (Poulantzas, 1979: 23).

Indeed, the international scenario that emerged at the beginning of the twenty-first century does not seem to confirm the idea that the system tends to stability. On the economic front, crises have become more frequent in the 'globalization' era. They began with the Mexican crisis (1994–1995), the first of this period, which had serious repercussions since Mexico used to be

---

20 Lenin's goal was precisely to combat the idea of 'global capitalism', which was predominant among the left (Milios and Sotiropoulos, 2009: 196).

considered as a model to be followed, due to the neoliberal reforms implemented in the country since the late 1980s. Later on, the crises in East Asia (1997–1998), Russia (1998) and Brazil (1998–1999) exposed the fragility of the international financial architecture that emerged in the 1970s. The turn of the century was the stage for new economic turmoil, as in Turkey and Argentina in 2001. Afterwards, the international economy went through a period of relative calm that lasted around five years, but soon the world witnessed the United States subprime crisis in 2007 and in mid-2008 the most severe economic crisis since the Great Depression of the 1930s.

The crisis of 2008 began at the center of capitalism, affecting a great part of Europe. This fact exposed the fragile international financial architecture and caused unrest about the economic order in several governments and within the American society itself, as evidenced by the protest movement 'Occupy Wall Street'. Despite the intense debate that followed on the reforms needed to prevent a crisis of such magnitude from happening again, few proposals have been implemented, mainly because of the contradictory interests inside the imperialist chain. In turn, low economic growth tends to make the environment even less conducive to understanding, stirring up contradictions. Given that, it seems impossible to conclude that the system is more stable economically, despite the enormous capacity of intervention of central banks, the Fed in particular, as it became evident during the worst moments of the crisis of 2008.

Likewise, it is not admissible to presume that competition between states no longer exists, and that the problem remains only in the economic sphere. Countries continue to use uneven structures of power to maintain and conquer new spaces of accumulation according to the interests of their capitalists. During the 1990s, when the United States sustained an unprecedented economic expansion, it managed to maintain its hegemony over other powers, preventing autonomous regional strategies with relative success. This fact did not make the US state more friendly, as Fiori (2008), Gowan (2004) and Sakellaropoulos and Sotiris (2015) demonstrate. In fact, shortly after the end of the Cold War, some means of intervention came to be considered legitimate by the central powers, justified by arguments related to violations of human rights,[21] the war on drug cartels in Latin America, the fight against corruption, the preservation of international security, and more recently the preventive

---

21 There are several examples of human rights violations without any military intervention from the central powers, simply because imperialist interests were not at risk (Sakellaropoulos and Sotiris, 2008: 221).

war against terror (Bandeira, 2014; Sakellaropoulos and Sotiris, 2008: 220; Johnson, 2004: 31).

However, as the law of uneven development prevails, new poles of power are emerging. Cooperation becomes more problematic due to the growing multipolarization of the international system – as it can be seen in the formation of the BRICS and the Union of South American Nations (USAN), for example – and consequently with the relative decrease of US power that is currently observed (Fernandes, 2016).

This situation helps explain the growing reaction against US foreign policy, which after '11 September' began to use a clearly warmongering and interventionist language. Since then, the United States has fomented conflicts in several parts of the world, ignoring the sovereignty of countries like Afghanistan (2001) and Iraq (2003). Libya and Syria were also targets of US interventions in conjunction with France, Britain and a group of Middle Eastern countries with diverse interests in the region (Bandeira, 2014: 382–384). Following the bombing of Libya in 2011, the regime of Muammar al-Gaddafi was overthrown. The same modus operandi was used in Syria[22] However, Russia's reaction to the conflict has been decisive to preserve the Bashar al-Assad regime to this date. More recently, the intervention in Ukraine has created strong instability in the region, leading to the holding of a referendum on the reincorporation of Crimea to Russia.[23] This is evidence that rivalries between the great powers continue to the present day, and that Russia has been playing an increasingly active role.

Finally, it should be noted that arm expenses remain high in several countries, especially in Europe, despite the economic crisis the world has been experiencing in recent years (Marshall, 2014: 328). According to the Stockholm International Peace Research Institute (SIPRI), in 2015, military spending in the world reached US$ 1.68 trillion, representing a real increase of 1.0% over 2014. This is the first increase since 2011. But before that, expenditures grew steadily for 13 years between 1998 and 2011 (Perlo-Freeman et al., 2016). The

---

22 According to Bandeira (2014: 372), in relation to Syria, "the goal of the United States and other Western powers (...) was to take control of the Mediterranean and politically isolate Iran, Syria's ally, as well as contain and eliminate the influence of Russia and China in the Middle East and the Maghreb".

23 Bringing chaos to certain states seems to be a tactic of imperialism today (Losurdo, 2015: 278). Vianna (2015) appropriately called these states 'zombie states'. This goes against the idea of 'failed states', published by the magazine "Foreing Policy", that says it is an internal problem, serving as an argument for intervention by capitalist powers. In the case of zombie states, it would be precisely external interventions that make them ungovernable territories.

United States is by far the country that spends more in armaments – 36% of the total in 2015 – but Europe deserves to be mentioned. As shown in detail by Slijper (2013), it is impressive to realize the continued high military spending of countries such as Spain, Greece and Italy that were at the epicenter of the crisis in the euro area and immersed in economic austerity programs that were difficult to attain due to the high social costs. This is clearly in direct confrontation with the Kautskyan perspective, which predicted a reduction in military spending as a primary commitment of ultra-imperialism.

5   Conclusion

In this work, we sought to show that the notion of the possibility of capitalism to organize itself comes from the classic authors of imperialism. Hilferding had already predicted the feasibility of a world cartel to control production efficiently, maintaining the system stable. In Bukharin, we can also find a tendency toward stabilization inside national economies under the control of a cartel, while competition would remain in the international sphere. In Kautsky, stability would be achieved by an agreement between the great powers to a point where wars would no longer be necessary.

There are currently several authors who analyze the system from the point of view of stability. Hard and Negri, Robinson and Harris, and Panich and Gindin no longer consider the term imperialism adequate. For these authors, the term empire is more in line with the current structure of the international system. Hard and Negri go even further, by suggesting that the world has entered into a global paradigm in which there would no longer be room for national sovereignty, and that now wars would actually be only police actions.

Authors such as Sakellaropoulos, Sotiris, and Marshall are able to understand the international system more satisfactorily, based on the Leninist theory of imperialism. As noted, Lenin's analysis of imperialism is not limited to a strictly economic or political view. Nor does it seek to approach the phenomenon as if it were a mere expansionism of some more powerful states. Imperialism is a system of economic and political relations that grants unparalleled dynamism to capital while aggravating the economic contradictions of capitalism and the antagonisms among states.

This way, we sought to demonstrate that the current international situation suggests a scenario closer to Lenin's perspective than to the ones proposed by the authors presented in the third section. There is increasing political and economic instability in several parts of the world. The effects of the crisis of 2008 still have repercussions in Europe and the reforms proposed as important for a new world economic governance do not move forward. This situation is very different from the notion of globalization.

In this sense, the leadership of the United States is questioned, as there is in fact a strong discomfort with the unilateral form that its policies are conducted both in the military and in the macroeconomic areas. On the other hand, movements of great relevance such as the BRICS and the USAN emerge, which added to the economic condition that China has achieved in recent years and the repositioning of Russia in the international scenario, may intensify inter-capitalist antagonisms and competition, not the opposite. Therefore, war remains a concrete possibility, as it has in fact been happening.

Finally, the concept of imperialism not only remains valid but is still the one that best expresses relations of exploitation, property, class struggle and revolutionary transition, which are very far from any possibility of stability of the international system.

References

Bandeira L (2014) *A segunda guerra fria: geopolítica e dimensão estratégica dos Estados Unidos – Das rebeliões na Eurásia à África do Norte ao Oriente Médio*. 2nd edition. Rio de Janeiro: Civilização Brasileira.

Beech E (2014) *U.S. government says it lost $11.2 billion on GM bailout*. Available (consulted in September 3, 2023) at Reuters (on line): http://www.reuters.com/article/us-autos-gm-treasury-idUSBREA3T0MR20140430.

Bottomore T (1985) Introdução à edição inglesa. In: Hilferding R(1985[1910]) *O Capital Financeiro*. São Paulo: Nova Cultural.

Brewer A (1990) *Marxist Theories of Imperialism: A Critical Survey*. 2nd edition. London and New York: Routledge.

Brunhoff S (1992) *Moeda e produção: teorias comparadas*. Brasília: Editora Universidade de Brasília.

Bukharin N (1986[1915]) *A economia mundial e o imperialismo: esboço econômico*. Os Economistas. 2nd edition. São Paulo: Nova Cultural.

Callinicos A (2009) *Imperialism and global political economy*. Cambridge: Polity Press.

Fernandes L (2016) Transição global e ruptura institucional: a geopolítica do neologismo no Brasil e na América Latina. *Princípios*, 143, 30–40.

Fiori L (2008) *O mito do colapso do poder americano*. Rio de Janeiro: Record.

Gowan P (2004) Triumphing toward International Disaster. The Impasse in American Grand Strategy. *Critical Asian Studies* 36 (1), 3–36.

Gowan P, Panitch L and Shaw M (2001) The state, globalization and the new imperialism: a roundtable discussion. *Historical Materialism*, 9, 3–38.

Halliday F (2002) The Pertinence of Imperialism. In: Rupert M and Smith H (eds). *Historical Materialism and Globalization*. London: Routledge.

Hardt M and Negri A (2001). *Império*. Rio de Janeiro: Record.

Harman C (2003) Analyzing imperialism *International Socialism* (online) Available (consulted in March 03, 2023) at https://www.marxists.org/archive/harman/2003/xx/imperialism.htm.

Harris J (2012) Global monopolies and the transnational capitalist class. *International Critical Thought* 2 (1),1–6.

Harvey D (2004) *O novo imperialismo*. São Paulo: edições Loyola.

Hilferding T (1985[1910]) *O Capital Financeiro*. São Paulo: Nova Cultural.

Hilferding R (2002[1927]) A economia organizada. In: Teixeira A (ed.) *Utópicos, Heréticos e Malditos: os precursores do pensamento social de nossa época*. Rio de Janeiro: Record.

Hobsbawn E (2001) *A era dos impérios*. Rio de Janeiro: Paz e Terra.

Hobson J (2005) *Imperialism: a study*. New York: Cosimo Classics.

Howard, MC and King, JE (1989) *A History of Marxian Economics*. Volume I: 1883–1929. Princeton, New Jersey: Princeton University Press.

Johnson C (2004) *As Aflições do Império*. Rio de Janeiro: Record.

Kautsky K (1914). *Ultra-imperialism*. Available (consulted in August 22, 2023) at http://www.marxists.org/archive/kautsky/1914/09/ultra-imp.htm.

Kautsky K (2002[1913–1914]) O imperialismo. In: Teixeita A (ed). *Utópicos, Heréticos e Malditos: os precursores do pensamento social de nossa época*. Rio de Janeiro: Record.

Kuhn R (2000) Capitalist breakdown debate. In: O'Hara P (ed.) *Encyclopedia of Political Economy*.London: Routledge.

Lauer S (2014) *La BNP paiera une amende de près de 9 milliards de dollars aux Etats-Unis*. Available (consulted in June 23, 2023) at Le Monde Diplomatique (on line): http://www.lemonde.fr/ameriques/article/2014/06/30/la-bnp-devra-regler-8-834-milliards-de-dollars-d-amende-aux-etats-unis_4448280_3222.html.

Lenin V (1979[1916]) El imperialismo, fase superior del capitalismo In: *Obras Escogidas*, tomo: 1. Moscou: Editorial Progreso.

Lenin V (1974[1915]) On the Slogan for a United States of Europe. In: *Collected Works*, Volume 21, 339–343. Moscow: Progress Publishers.

Lorimer D (1999) Introduction. In: Lenin V (1999) *Imperialism, the Highest Stage of Capitalism*. Resistance Books.

Losurdo D (2015) *Marx e o balanço histórico do século 20*. São Paulo: Anita Garibaldi.

Luxemburg R (1970[1913]) *A acumulação de capital: estudo sobre a interpretação econômica do imperialismo*. Rio de Janeiro: Zahar.

Marshall A (2014) Lenin's Imperialism Nearly 100 Years on: An Outdated Paradigm? *Critique: Journal of Socialist Theory* 42:3.

Marx K and Engels F (2010[1848]). *Manifesto do partido comunista.* São Paulo: Boitempo.

Mazzucchelli F (1885) *A contradição em processo: o capitalismo e suas crises.* São Paulo: Brasiliense.

Michalet CA (1984) *O capitalismo mundial.* Rio de Janeiro: Paz e Terra.

Milios J and Sotiropoulos D (2009) *Rethinking Imperialism: a study of capitalist rule.* Houndmills: Palgrave Macmillan.

Monthly Review (2004) Note from the Editors. Available (consulted in march 02, 2023) at Monthly Review, 2004, 55 (8): http://monthlyreview.org/2004/01/01/mr-055-08-2004-01_0/.

Panitch L and Gindin S (2005) Superintending global capital. *New Left Review,* 35, 101–23.

Panitch L and Gindin S (2012) *The making of global capitalism: the political economy of american empire.* London: Verso.

Perlo-Freeman, S, Fleurant P and Wezeman Siemon (2016) Trends in world military expenditure, 2015. Available (consulted in April 12, 2023) at SIPRI Fact Sheet (on line): https://www.sipri.org/publications/2016/sipri-fact-sheets/trends-world-military-expenditure-2015.

Petras J and Veltmeyer H (2007) Globalization or Imperialism? *Cambridge Review of International Affairs,* 14:1.

Poulantzas N (1979) *Fascism and dictatorship: the third international and the problem of fascism.* London: Verso.

Poulantzas N (1977) *O Estado em Crise.* Rio de Janeiro: Edições Graal.

Robinson W (2002) Capitalist globalization and the transnationalization of the state. In: Rupert M and Smith H (eds). *Historical Materialism and globalization.* London: Routledge.

Robinson W (2007) Beyond the Theory of Imperialism: Global Capitalism and the Transnational State. *Societies Without Borders.*

Robinson W (2008) *Understanding global capitalism.* Available (consulted in May 12, 2023) at: http://www.soc.ucsb.edu/faculty/robinson/Assets/pdf/understandingglobalcapitalism.pdf.

Robinson W and Harris J (2000) Towards A Global Ruling Class? Globalization and the Transnational Capitalist Class. *Science & Society,* Vol. 64.

Rowthorn B (1975) Imperialism in the 1970s – Unity or Rivalry In: Radice H (ed). *International firms and modern imperialism.* London: Penguin Books.

Ruccio D (2003) Globalization and imperialism. *Rethinking Marxism,* 15 (1), 75–94.

Sakellaropoulos S (2009) The Issue of Globalization through the Theory of Imperialism and the Periodization of Modes of Production. *Critical Sociology,* 35(1), 57–78.

Sakellaropoulos S and Sotiris P (2008) American Foreign Policy as Modern Imperialism: From Armed Humanitarianism to Preemptive War. *Science & Society* 72 (2), 208–35.

Sakellaropoulos S and Sotiris P (2015) From Territorial to Nonterritorial Capitalist Imperialism: Lenin and the possibility of a marxist theory of imperialism. *Rethinking Marxism*, 27 (1), 85–106.

Sjilper F (2013) Guns, Debt and Corruption. Military Spending and the EU Crisis. Transnational Institute.

Vianna, E (2015) Depois de destruir nacionalismo árabe, EUA preparam o bote na América do Sul. Available (consulted in March 30, 2023) at Portal Forum: https://revistaforum.com.br/blogs/escrevinhador/2015/9/10/depois-de-destruir-nacionalismo-arabe-eua-preparam-bote-na-america-do-sul-51693.html.

PART 4

Latin-American Theory on Dependency

CHAPTER 13

The Marxist Theory of Dependency

Contributions of Latin American Marxism to International Relations

Maíra Machado Bichir[1]

1   Introduction

This chapter represents an effort to emphasize the relevance of the theoretical framework produced by the authors of the Marxist Theory of Dependency (MTD[2]) for the field of International Relations, as well as to contribute to a closer dialog between Latin American Marxism and the referred area of knowledge.[3] This initiative is part of a broader movement, namely, the rebirth of studies on dependence in Brazil, especially in its Marxist perspective, which took place in the last decade. Prior to that period, research on the subject of dependence in the country had focused on the analysis of "Dependency and Development in Latin America" by Fernando Henrique Cardoso and Enzo Faletto and Cardoso's production. Although the works of Ruy Mauro Marini, Vânia Bambirra, and Theotônio dos Santos, the main exponents of the Marxist Theory of Dependency, were widely disseminated in Latin American countries between the 1970s and 1980s, among which we can highlight pre-coup Chile and Mexico; in Brazil, his writings would only find acceptance at the beginning of the twenty-first century.[4] The last ten years have been marked by the

---

[1]   Adjunct Professor of the Political Science and Sociology – Society, State, and Politics in Latin America, at the Federal University of Latin American Integration (UNILA). Ph.D. in Political Science at the State University of Campinas (Unicamp).

[2]   The Marxist Dependency of Dependency was the subject of our master's thesis, entitled "The problem of dependency: a study on the Marxist perspective of dependency" (Bichir, 2012), and of our doctoral thesis, "The question of the State in the Marxist Theory of Dependency" (Bichir, 2017).

[3]   Originally published as chapter of the book "Marxism and International Relations": Bugiato C (2021) Marxismo e Relações Internacionais. Goiânia: Editora Phillos Academy. Translated into English by Alberto Resende Jr.

[4]   The main works by Marini, Bambirra, and Dos Santos were published in Spanish since those authors lived, for a long period of their lives, in exile in Chile and Mexico. Despite that fact, many of these works have been published and translated into other languages, including English, Italian, French, and German. In Brazil, the recent dissemination of their works took place through an important initiative by the Institute of Latin American Studies (IELA) at

production of several articles, monographs, master's dissertations, and doctoral theses on the Marxist Theory of Dependency or adopting its theoretical framework, the creation of research groups, and the holding of Congresses, Seminars, and Conferences on the subject.[5]

The Marxist Theory of Dependency, which emerged in the 1960s amid the worsening economic and social contradictions in the Latin American region and the political polarization between revolution and counterrevolution, represented a decisive milestone in the analysis of international relations. Bringing in its theoretical body elements of 'classic' Marxism and a tradition of thought forged in Latin America, concerned with understanding and transforming our reality from their point of view, its authors make explicit the deep hierarchies of power that characterize the international system, highlighting the particular modality of capital accumulation and reproduction in dependent countries, the value transfer mechanisms from dependent countries to imperialist countries and their impacts on the exercise of political power by dependent states. It is in the subversion of the look, the narrative, and the analysis, whose starting point shifts to the Latin American dependent countries, that lies the potentiality of the Marxist Theory of Dependency, both for International Relations and Marxism itself.

Considering the relevance that the theoretical production of those authors acquired in Latin American critical thought and their contributions to the development of Marxism based on their reflections on dependent capitalism, their criticisms of both theories of The Economic Commission for Latin America's (ECLAC) modernization and developmentalism regarding the interpretations and political strategies of Latin American communist parties, we will initially go back to the historical moment in which this current of thought is configured, also indicating the sources and intellectual roots that conform it. Next, we will characterize the constitutive theoretical core of the Marxist Theory of Dependency, highlighting, finally, those contributions that seem central to International Relations.

---

the Federal University of Santa Catarina (UFSC), and the Publisher Insular which, through the collection Pátria Grande – Biblioteca do Pensamento Crítico Latino-americano, published the translation into Portuguese of three of the main works of the Marxist theory of dependency: "Underdevelopment and Revolution", by Ruy Mauro Marini, "Latin American dependent capitalism", by Vânia Bambirra, and "Socialism or fascism: the new character of dependency and the Latin American dilemma", in the years 2012, 2013 and 2018, respectively.

5 We cite some examples: Amaral, 2012; Rocha, 2017; Guanais, 2018; Gouvêa, 2016; Vargas, 2009; Luce, 2011, 2018; Prado, 2015; Carcanholo and Côrrea, 2016. An important mapping of recent production linked to the Marxist Theory of Dependency can be consulted at Castelo and Prado, 2013.

2   The Emergence of the Marxist Theory of Dependency

The constitution of the Marxist Theory of Dependency is inscribed in a historical moment of profound changes in the international system, changes that were concretely manifested both in the political, economic, and social dimensions of Latin America, as well as in the intellectual effervescence produced in that same region. If, on the one hand, the two great world wars and, mainly, the 1929 crisis meant the restructuring of the economies of those countries, on the other hand, they stimulated intense debates about the theme of development/underdevelopment, combining the emergence of a specifically Latin American perspective with the reality that took place during that period. The changes introduced from that period opened a new phase in Latin America, characterized by the industrialization process, which advanced until the mid-1960s, when reconfigurations in the world order, linked to the limits and internal problems of the countries of the region, had a profound impact on crisis of Latin American dependent capitalism.

The profound transformations Latin America underwent in the first half of the twentieth century, whose effects had repercussions on the different and varied dimensions of its concrete reality, were the object of analysis, reflection, and investigation by a very extensive group of Latin American scholars. The industrialization process that began at the end of the nineteenth century in some countries, such as Mexico, Brazil, and Argentina, gained new impetus with the two great world wars and the 1929 crisis, developing in several Latin American countries. In this same process, the Latin American industrial bourgeoisie was consolidated, which, by defending their interests linked to the advance of industrialization, faced the interests of the agrarian-mercantile classes associated with the export sector of Latin American countries, seeking to become hegemonic as the dominant class in those countries.

Even in the face of the conflicts and contradictions of that process, the new position occupied by Latin American countries in the international division of labor was seen by many of those scholars as a real possibility of overcoming the condition of 'underdevelopment' and achieving an autonomous national development. The ECLAC at the end of the 1940s, whose emergence had redimensioned studies on development in the region, embodied the interests of the ascending industrial bourgeoisie and the state bureaucracy in their studies and reports, defending a development project based on the advancement of industrialization, which should be driven and controlled by the state.

After the World War II, the United States, which experienced an intense economic and military expansion, imposed itself as a new hegemonic force in the world-system amid a process of concentration and centralization of capital perpetrated by multinational companies. Such movements gave rise to investments in the industrial sectors of Latin American dependent countries, a fact that introduced substantial changes in the economic, social, and political dynamics of those countries. The penetration of foreign capital into the region's economies, while enabling the continuity of their import substitution processes, meant the subordination of their political and economic decisions to the plans of foreign countries and companies, as well as the failure of 'national projects' of the Latin American industrial bourgeoisie. Circumscribed to that conjuncture is the crisis of Latin American dependent capitalism, which was revealed politically in the antagonism between revolution and counterrevolution.

It is precisely in this context of changes in economic and social reality and political polarization that debates and criticisms of developmentalism take place in the field of Latin American thought, an ideology produced within ECLAC and shared by Latin American industrial bourgeoisie, which starts to suffer severe attacks, being questioned politically and intellectually. The possibility of an autonomous national development is frustrated by the world monopoly integration, in which Latin America is inserted, and industrialization, previously seen as a solution to the obstacles to the region's development, starts to represent a new phase of dependence on the Latin American countries.

The conjunction of those elements gave rise to a profound crisis of dependent capitalism in the 1960s, which opposed, on the one hand, the dominant classes, eager to maintain their power, and, on the other, the dominated classes, who yearned for better living conditions. That opposition is radicalized in two major movements: insurrections and popular uprisings in different regions of Latin America and the formation of coups and military dictatorships in Latin American countries, a fact that is recorded by Marini:

> [...] the rise of social struggles in the region was recorded uninterruptedly, causing a political radicalization that crystallized, at one pole, in the Cuban Revolution, at the end of the decade and, at the other, in the military dictatorship that, from the military coup of 1964 in Brazil, were implanted in various countries.
> MARINI, 1999 [1994]: 12

As for the political radicalization of the Latin American popular classes, the Cuban Revolution in 1959 represented a dividing point in the social and political struggles of the Latin American continent. The anti-imperialist struggle and the subsequent anti-capitalist character assumed by the Cuban revolutionary process meant for the left and the Latin American working class the possibility of breaking with the established order, with the capitalist economic-social system. Under the impact of the Cuban political movement, Latin American countries were involved in a strong rise of the mass movement. Theotônio dos Santos highlights the various dimensions assumed by the Latin American political struggle:

> At the political level, an explosive situation is created where the tendencies to question the current system seek radical forms of expression, either through explosive mass rebellions or through organized forms of mass struggle such as general strikes or the electoral support for political forces that are presented as a denial of the existing system. This questioning does not yet have a clear political form but is rather the expression of a general radicalization and an inability of the current system to offer convincing solutions to the serious crisis in progress.
> DOS SANTOS, 1972 [1971]

In the midst of the complex situation that Latin America was experiencing, marked by possibilities and uncertainties, and the political-theoretical discussions that emerged from it, analyzes were developed on the problem of dependency, which become a major concern of social scientists, economists, and historians of the region in the 1960s and 1970s. What are the roots of 'underdevelopment' in Latin American countries? What are the prospects for their economies and societies? Would the social upheavals that multiplied since the end of the 1950s lead to the structuring of a new Latin American order? These and several other themes involved the minds of those who focused on the analysis of the reality that surrounded them, motivating heated intellectual and theoretical discussions and, even more, strong political clashes.

3   The Encounter between Marxism and the Latin American Thought

Reflections around dependency have their emergence anchored in Chile, in Santiago, a city where institutions such as ECLAC, the Latin American Institute of Economic and Social Planning (ILPES), an ECLAC body, and university centers such as the Center for Socioeconomic Studies (CESO), the Institute of Economics and the Institute of Sociology, at the University of Chile, where scholars from different Latin American[6] countries gathered, allowing for an expanded intellectual exchange and political-social experiences (Faletto, 1998). Chile's[7] role in this process is highlighted by Ruy Mauro Marini:

> From 1968 onwards, concomitantly with the generalization of military coups and the advance of repression in the continent, left-wing intellectuals began to converge on Chile, which kept its democratic regime intact and which ended up becoming the privileged *locus* of elaboration of the new theory.
> MARINI, 1992: 88

The 'Dependency Theories' understood as an integral part of the history of Latin American ideas (Faletto, 1998: 109) and as a 'structured current of thought' were constituted from a set of works formulated or published between the years 1964 and 1967, which triggered an intense intellectual debate in the region (Marini, 1992: 88). Authors such as Vânia Bambirra, Theotônio dos Santos, Ruy Mauro Marini, André Gunder Frank,[8] Orlando Caputo, Roberto Pizarro, Sérgio Ramos, CESO[9] members, as well as Fernando Henrique Cardoso, Aníbal Quijano, Enzo

---

6 Many of these scholars had been exiled from their countries, as was the case of Ruy Mauro Marini, Theotônio dos Santos and Vânia Bambirra, all exiled after the 1964 military coup in Brazil.

7 Although Chile constitutes the epicenter of debates on dependency reflections, and contributions on this theme were also developed in Venezuela, with the works of Héctor Silva Michelena, in Mexico, with the writings of Alonso Aguilar, Pablo González Casanova, and Fernando Carmona, in the Caribbean, from the works of Norman Girvan, in Colombia, by Mario Arrubla, and in Uruguay, within the Institute of Economics of the *Facultad de Ciencias Económicas y de Administración de la Universidad de la República Oriental de Uruguay* (Bambirra, 1978: 24–25). It is also worth highlighting Florestan Fernandes' production on the issue of Latin American dependency, discussed in his *work* "Dependent capitalism and social classes in Latin America", from 1973.

8 Although André Gunder Frank, a German intellectual, who dedicated a large part of his research to the study of Latin America, influenced the writings of Bambirra, Marini, and Dos Santos, especially from his formulation regarding the 'development of underdevelopment', we do not consider him as a representative of the Marxist theory of dependency, considering that the author himself does not inscribe his analyzes in the Marxist theoretical-methodological field (Frank, 1996). It should be noted, however, that the political orientation underlying their analyzes converge, to a great extent, with the understanding that the Marxist theory of dependency has of Latin American political processes since they are marked by the confrontation with imperialism, a phenomenon to which dependency was intrinsically connected, and by the commitment with the rupture of the capitalist order (Frank, 1973a; 1973b).

9 A study on the trajectory of Bambirra, Dos Santos, and Marini at CESO can be found in the monograph work by Mateus Filippa Meireles (2014), "Origins of the Marxist Theory of

Faletto, Edelberto Torres, Francisco Weffort, Tomás Amadeo Vasconi, who were members of ILPES, actively took part of this construction. (Bambirra, 1978: 23). It is possible to distinguish from the studies and works produced by these authors two groups of scholars who, throughout their trajectory, distanced themselves and opposed each other in heated discussions about the character and ways of overcoming Latin American dependency. On the one hand, the Brazilians Theotônio dos Santos, Vânia Bambirra, and Ruy Mauro Marini, members of CESO, gathered around a research[10] group and published the results of their investigations regarding dependence on works such as "Socialism or Fascism: The Latin American Dilemma", from 1968, "The Latin American Dependent Capitalism", from 1972, "The Dialectics of Dependency,"[11] from 1972, and, on the other hand, the Brazilian Fernando Henrique Cardoso and the Chilean Enzo Faletto, members of ILPES, synthesized their interpretation of Latin American economic development in the work "Dependency and

---

Dependency: the Center for Socioeconomic Studies (CESO) of the University of Chile and the practice of Ruy Mauro Marini, Vânia Bambirra and Theotônio dos Santos (1966–1973)".

10 Formed in 1967, the group of researchers was composed of the Brazilians Vânia Bambirra and Theotônio dos Santos, Chileans Sérgio Ramos, Orlando Caputo, and Roberto Pizarro, as well as Peruvian José Martínez. The research was organized around two main themes, "The crisis of the theory of development and dependency relations" and "The historical evolution of dependence", coordinated by Theotônio dos Santos, and contained three lines of research, 1) "The world integration process and Latin America", coordinated by Theotônio dos Santos and Sérgio Ramos; 2) " Dependency relations and capital movement in Latin America", whose coordination was in charge of Orlando Caputo and Roberto Pizarro; and 3) "Dependent structures in the world integration phase ", under the responsibility of Vânia Bambirra and José Martínez (Dos Santos et al., 1967: 3 apud Meireles, 2014: 76–77). Ruy Mauro Marini joined this group in 1970, proposing, during his stay at CESO, a research seminar entitled "Marxist theory and Latin American reality" (Marini, 2005 [1994]). Although it was a collective effort, with the participation of seven researchers (with the arrival of Marini), it was the works of Bambirra, Dos Santos, and Marini that gained greater diffusion, either due to the theoretical breadth of their works or due to the diaspora played by such authors, who after the Chilean military coup in 1973, migrated to Mexico, where they resided for a long period.

11 The three works were originally published in Spanish and only translated into Portuguese in the 2000s. A study on the diffusion of the Marxist Theory of Dependency in Brazil and on the boycott suffered by the works of Vânia Bambirra, Ruy Mauro Marini, and Theotônio dos Santos in that country can be found in Prado (2011). In that text, Correa Prado links the restricted penetration from MTD thought in Brazil not only to the censorship of the Brazilian military dictatorship but, above all, to the effort undertaken by some authors, with special emphasis on Fernando Henrique Cardoso, to disqualify the works of the author(s) of the MTD, based on their criticisms. A significant example of this boycott can be seen in the article criticizing Ruy Mauro Marini's perspective, written by Cardoso and José Serra (1978), which was published in Brazil by the Brazilian Center for Analysis and Planning (CEBRAP), without a response from Marini (1978).

Development in Latin America", written between 1966 and 1967, as a product of their research carried out within the scope of ECLAC.

Although those groups have competed in their studies of the Latin American economic, political and social reality, both concerning the methodological option and the political implications of their theses, both have taken a critical position about ECLAC thinking to the extent that they emphasized that industrialization in Latin American countries had not been consolidated as the matrix of an autonomous national economic development, and, even more, it would have deepened the ties of dependence of the region in relation to the developed center (Cardoso and Faletto, 2004 [1970]; Marini, 2007 [1972]). The contact with their works shows, however, that it is not possible to classify them as belonging to the same school of thought.

While in the theoretical-methodological field, the analyzes are sometimes linked to eclecticism and sometimes to Marxism, in the political dimension, two distinct postures can be identified in the face of dependence: the first is associated with interdependence, and the second, with an anti-imperialist posture and anti-capitalist, with socialism as its political horizon. Fernando Henrique Cardoso and Enzo Faletto share a theoretical-methodological eclecticism and characterize the integration between Latin American economies and the international market, in the 1960s, as interdependent. Such eclecticism is attributed to those authors given the preface to the English edition of "Dependency and development in Latin America", written by Cardoso and Faletto in 1976, in which both provide an extensive explanation of the method they used in the referred work. In it, the authors refer to three distinct traditions of social thought: Weberian, Marxist, and structuralist (ECLAC). At the same time that they emphasize their attempt to reestablish the intellectual tradition based on comprehensive social science, they claim to use the dialectical approach to the analysis of society, its structures, and its processes of change. They also make explicit, through the option for the historical-structural method, their approach to ECLAC structuralism (Cardoso and Faletto, 1979 [1976]).

From a political perspective, Cardoso and Faletto suggest the possibility of consolidating a relationship of interdependence between Latin American countries "capitalistically more advanced" and the international market, in which there would be room for a "associated development-capitalist" of Latin American economies (Cardoso and Faletto, 2004 [1970]: 196). The interdependence category, introduced as a possibility to "boost the industrialized and dependent nations of Latin America" (Cardoso and Faletto, 2004 [1970]: 186), added to the assertion of the authors about the solidarity of foreign industrial investments with the economic expansion of the domestic market in Latin

American countries, demonstrate a dilution, or even concealment of the phenomenon of imperialism in the dynamics of Latin American countries, which distances them from the authors of the Marxist Theory of Dependency.

Ruy Mauro Marini, Theotônio dos Santos, and Vânia Bambirra, in turn, are affiliated with Marxism by adopting Historical Materialism as a theoretical-methodological reference in their interpretations of the concrete Latin American reality, and show, in their works, postures anti-imperialists and anti-capitalists, since they consider that overcoming Latin American dependence could only happen through a socialist revolution. Faced with the context of a new international order and restructuring of the international division of labor, in which the phenomenon of the internationalization of capital gains dimension, these authors analyze the impacts of those transformations on Latin American reality and draw attention to the change in the orientation of flows of foreign investment in Latin American economies, which, from the 1950s onwards, began to focus on the sphere of industrial production. Those transformations impute, according to those authors, a new character to Latin American dependency, conditioning in an even more extreme way the pattern of development of those economies and deepening the overexploitation of labor in those countries and the contradictions of capitalism dependent.

From Karl Marx's theory of value, passing through the theories of imperialism by Vladimir Ilitch Lenin, Rosa Luxemburg and Nicolai Bukharin, and by the joint writings of Karl Marx and Friedrich Engels, the Marxist heritage was present both in his works and in his postures in the face of reality, characterizing, moreover, their political praxis. Such influence is made explicit in the analyzes produced by them, which claim Historical Materialism as a method for apprehending concrete reality and particularly in Marini's thesis about the overexploitation of work, a thesis developed essentially from Marx's theory of value (2013 [1867]), as well as the critical appropriation that these authors made of studies on imperialism carried out by Lenin (1982 [1917]), Luxemburg (1985 [1912]) and Bukharin (1986 [1915]). As Theotônio dos Santos states:

> The study of the development of capitalism in the hegemonic centers originated the theory of colonialism and [of] imperialism. The study of the development of our countries [Latin American countries] should give rise to the dependency theory. For this reason, we must consider limited the approaches of the authors of the theory of imperialism. Lenin, Bukharin, Rosa Luxemburg, and the main Marxist theorists of the theory of imperialism, as well as a few non-Marxist authors who dealt with him, such as Hobson, did not approach the issue of imperialism from the point of view of the dependent countries. Although dependency must

be situated in the global context of the theory of imperialism, it has its reality, which constitutes a concrete legality within the global process and which acts on it in this concrete way. Understanding dependency, conceptualizing it, and studying its mechanisms and historical legality, means not only expanding the theory of imperialism but also contributing to its reformulation.

DOS SANTOS, 1973 [1970]: 38

The Marxist Theory of Dependency, at the same time, can be analyzed as an offshoot of the imperialism theory, as it starts from the same issues that guided those analyzes and configures an original perspective, either by deepening and developing some issues or by the inauguration of a new approach – the imperialist phase of capitalism seen from the perspective of dependent countries, from the theoretical category of dependency. Although the notion of dependency was already present in Lenin's[12] writings to describe the power relations between States in the imperialist stage, it is within the scope of dependency theories that this phenomenon will gain a more precise definition. In the case of MTD, we find two coincident definitions, that of Theotônio dos Santos and that of Ruy Mauro Marini, according to which dependency is understood as a relationship between countries/nations. While Dos Santos states that this is "a situation where the economy of a certain group of countries is conditioned by the development and expansion of another economy, to which that one is subject" (Dos Santos, 1973 [1970]: 42), Marini points out that dependency should be understood as "a relationship of subordination between formally independent nations, in which framework the production relations of subordinated nations are modified or recreated to ensure the expanded reproduction of dependency" (Marini, 2007 [1972]: 102).

Concerned with the formulation of a Latin American thought from the perspective of dependent capitalism, which deeply marked the economies of the countries of that region, such scholars sought, based on Historical Materialism, to develop reflections about the particular Latin American reality, in which perspectives of transformation and overcoming their dependence were inscribed, both linked to the socialist revolution. According to Marini, the greatest merit of the 'Dependency Theory'[13] "was to replant the interpretation

---

12 Although Bambirra, Marini, and Dos Santos recognize the contributions of Bukharin and Luxemburg to the analysis of imperialism, it is mainly Lenin's writings that guide their conceptions on the subject.

13 We maintain here the terminology used by Marini, but we add quotation marks, as we understand that the divergences existing within studies on dependence do not allow framing them as parts of the same theory.

of Latin American reality from Marxism, opening the way for it to progressively assume a character of centrality in the intellectual and political scenario of the region" (Marini, 1999 [1994]: 13).

In this sense, the authors of the Marxist Theory of Dependency must also be understood as important representatives of Latin American Marxism, insofar as, like authors such as Julio Antonio Mella, José Carlos Mariátegui, Cyril Lionel Robert James, Caio Prado Jr., were able to give life to a Marxism rooted in the issues and problems of our Latin American[14] societies, in an original and creative way, thus valuing one of the richest elements of Marxism, its method, and thus contributing to the development of Marxism itself.

From this Marxist heritage and their political militancy,[15] Bambirra, Marini, and Dos Santos engaged in a critical debate both with national-developmental thought, whose stronghold was identified in ECLAC, and with the strategies and tactics defended by sectors of the Latin American left, particularly the communist parties. Marini, Bambirra, and Dos Santos's thought, although related to one of the main explanatory references of ECLAC – the concept of center-periphery – represented a criticism of the analyzes and responses offered by that institution to the 'underdevelopment' of the countries in the region. Such authors recognized in their writings ECLAC's efforts to build a perspective that reflected the Latin American view of its reality, as well as its advances concerning classical economic theories[16] and theories of development, formulated, for the most part, in the United States and Europe,[17] but drew attention to the limits of its conception. They emphasized

---

14 Bernardo Ricupero proposes an interesting analytical key to discuss the thinking of Caio Prado Jr., a Marxist and militant of the Brazilian Communist Party (PCB), that is, the 'nationalization of Marxism' in Brazil (Ricupero, 2000). Following this same key, we could say that the thought of the Marxist Theory of Dependency would have operated a 'Latin-Americanization of Marxism'.

15 Bambirra, Dos Santos, and Marini participated in the foundation of the Marxist Revolutionary Organization – Politics of the Workers (POLOP), in 1961 in Brazil, and, during the period in which they were exiled in Chile, they approached political parties and movements during the government of Salvador Allende. Marini joined the Revolutionary Left Movement (MIR), Dos Santos joined the Chilean Socialist Party, and Bambirra was a member of the Chilean Socialist Party without, however, joining.

16 We refer here mainly to the formulations of David Ricardo (1996 [1817]) through his theory of comparative advantages.

17 In the literature on development, there are different denominations attributed to authors who debated this theme during the 1950s and 1960s. Sometimes they have grouped around the broad umbrella 'theories of development', as Dos Santos, Marini, and Bambirra do, or 'theories of modernization' (Chirot and Hall, 1982), insofar as their works share the same object of concern, that is, the passage from traditional, archaic, or underdeveloped societies to modern or developed societies, sometimes they are gathered from the field

that transfers from peripheral countries to central countries, characterized by ECLAC as income transfers, also represented transfers of value and, therefore, of added value. They also questioned the industrialization strategy advocated by ECLAC, stating that it would not lead to the breaking of Latin American dependence but rather to its recrudescence. For MTD, dependency would constitute an intrinsic element of the capitalist system and, more than that, necessary for its development and reproduction. Thus, its overcoming could only be associated with overcoming the very logic of the accumulation of the capitalist mode of production.

Concerning the communist parties in the region, by revealing the implications of the deep penetration of foreign capital in the industrial production of the countries of the region and the associated character of the Latin American industrial bourgeoisies with imperialism, which was manifested in the deep ties existing between the ruling classes of dependent states and the ruling classes of imperialist states, the Marxist Theory of Dependency shed light on the impossibility of configuring autonomous capitalist development in Latin American economies. Faced with this assessment, the political alliance between the bourgeoisie and the Latin American working classes toward national development was no longer justified. As a response to the processes that took place in Latin American countries at that historical moment, Bambirra, Marini, and Dos Santos strongly affirm in their works the urgency of the protagonism of the working classes in the construction of a revolutionary alternative for the Latin American reality. The compromise of the analysis produced by the Marxist Theory of Dependency with the popular struggle is explained by Marini:

> (...) Dependency theory was, above all, a movement of ideas that tried to respond to the concerns and hopes that mobilized broad popular sectors of Latin America: workers, peasants, students, and professionals, to offer them an alternative to a capitalist development whose subordinate and exclusive character made it less and less capable of guaranteeing attention to the essential needs of the population.
> MARINI, 1999 [1994]: 13

---

of knowledge, 'development economics', 'sociology of development' or 'sociology of modernization'.

4   The Construction of a New Perspective on the International System

The existence of a similar narrative about the issue of dependency, the criticism of ECLAC developmentalism and the interpretations and strategies of sectors of the Latin American left, and the Marxist theoretical-methodological framework are some of the elements that justify the classification of the author(s) of MTD as a current of thought. It should be noted, however, that the bibliographical production of the three authors regarding dependence does not represent a homogeneous whole, and it is even possible to discern nuances and particularities in their interpretations of the concrete Latin American reality, which are due more to the differences in objective and focus adopted by each author, rather than the analytical and interpretative divergences between them.

While Marini dedicates himself to revisiting Marx's theory of value to characterize Latin American dependent capitalism, scrutinizing the fundamental contradiction on which dependence is based, namely the transfer of value and the overexploitation of work, Dos Santos focuses on the characterization of the general frameworks on which dependency relations between Latin American countries and imperialist countries develop, giving greater attention to the period of world monopoly integration, a moment in which Latin American dependency takes on a new character, as well as employs efforts in the sense of constructing a systematic definition of dependence and conforming it as a theoretical body. Bambirra, in turn, focuses on the work of building a typology of dependent societies and highlighting the political dimension of social struggles in the region, directing her gaze to the struggles carried out by the popular classes, as well as to Latin American leftist organizations. Such differences, instead of questioning the elements of unity that engender the core of the three authors' analyzes, affirm their complementary nature. Given the purposes of this chapter, we will shed light on relevant contributions of MTD to International Relations, which can contribute towards indicating paths and potential for dialog.

In "The Dialectics of Dependency", Marini aims, starting from Marx's theoretical construction of Capital, particularly his theory of value, to undertake analysis at an intermediate level of abstraction, which would allow him to understand the dependent character of Latin American economies and their specific legality (Marini, 2005 [1994]: 90). The route followed by the author in his argument consists of identifying, initially the form and nature of the integration of those economies into the world market, highlighting their role in the industrialization process in European countries, and then explaining the impacts that this integration had in those economies. Without disregarding the relevant role played by Latin American economies in the formation of the world capitalist economy in the sixteenth, seventeenth, and eighteenth centuries, as a producer of precious metals and 'exotic' genres, Marini states that it was only in the nineteenth century, after 1840, that their articulation with the world economy is fully realized, already as formally politically independent countries, with the establishment of the international division of labor. For the author, it is only from that moment on that one could speak of dependence. Understood as "a relationship of subordination between formally independent nations, in which framework the production relationships of subordinated nations are modified or recreated to ensure the expanded reproduction of dependence" (Marini, 2007 [1972]: 102), the dependence is explained by the author based on the contradictory character that marks the participation of Latin American economies in the world market, which is based on the transfer of value, which is why such economies seek to compensate for the resulting losses by resorting to overexploitation of labor, within the scope of its internal production, which is reflected in a particular form of the cycle of dependent economies, which reproduces these mechanisms.

In that way, Latin American countries, disadvantaged by unequal exchange, instead of seeking to correct the imbalance between the prices and values of their products generated from international trade, seek to compensate their losses through the increase in worker exploitation within the scope of its internal production, which takes place through mechanisms such as the increase in the intensity of work, the extension of the working day and the expropriation of part of the work necessary for the worker to replenish his workforce. While the first two, by forcing them to overspend their workforce, causing its premature exhaustion, deny the worker the necessary conditions for them to replace the wear and tear of their workforce, the last removes the possibility for the worker to consume what is strictly indispensable to keep their workforce in a normal state (Marini, 2007 [1972]: 116). Such mechanisms, employed to increase, through an increase in surplus value, the appropriated value (and even the value produced when using the increase in labor intensity), as well as the profit rate of the Latin American dominant classes, compensating for the transfer of value resulting from an unequal exchange, imply remuneration of workers below their value (Marini, 2007 [1972]: 113–120). That would consist, according to Marini, of the super-exploitation of work.

Having explained the foundation on which dependency is anchored, we now turn to the articulation that the Marxist theory of dependency builds between the national matter and the class matter.

Similar to Lenin, Bambirra places the national matter at the level of class struggle. According to the author, how the class struggle manifests itself makes explicit the links between the national and class dimensions. In that sense, there would not be, in her perspective, a contradiction or ambiguity in the analytical framework from which the Marxist theorists of dependency depart.

> Marxists must know that the class struggle within an oppressed nation goes through the class struggle at the international level and, even though it takes place specifically in the sphere of national societies – which strongly raises the problem nationally – is not isolated from the characteristics and dynamics assumed by the struggle between the oppressed nation and the oppressor. Therefore, it is necessary to elucidate the confusion that can be generated on the one hand by isolating and privileging the 'greater contradiction' of class, to the detriment of the contradiction between the oppressed and oppressor nation and, on the other, the underestimation of the national factor, that is, how the contradictions between the antagonistic classes manifest themselves at the level of a national society. Dialectical reasoning determines the close link between the two levels of the class struggle.
>
> BAMBIRRA, 1978: 54

If in the previous passage, the author's argument is located on a more abstract plane, in the following one, Bambirra offers a more concrete analysis of the interconnection between the two dimensions, emphasizing the articulation established between imperialism and the dominant classes of the dependent countries, in the function of the control of the axis of accumulation of those economies by the imperialist capitals, whose impact is deeply felt in the political power of those countries.

> Today, when dependency relations have already assumed their specific character, through which imperialist capitals come to control the central axis of the accumulation process – the manufacturing industry – and to be a constitutive part of the economy at the national level, with all the implications that this entails in regards to *its indirect but live interference in political power*, when this domination even permeates the origins of the oppressed nations, imperialism becomes the enemy of the peoples in the last instance, since the bourgeoisie are intimately associated with it. In such conditions, the 'greatest contradiction' of classes is, at the same time, the contradiction between the interests of the proletariat and its allies, that is, the dominated classes against the bourgeois-imperialist domination. All the great revolutions that until today have led the people towards socialism have had to face, before or after the triumph, direct, cruel imperialist aggression on their territory.
>
> BAMBIRRA, 1978, p 56, emphasis added

Based on Bambirra's arguments and the writings of Marxist dependency theorists, we identified that national States are taken as a unit of analysis in the study of dependency relations, however, those same States are not understood as monolithic blocks or as abstract entities. Understood as the center of political power, the State, from the perspective of Marxist dependency theorists, is the representation of class domination underlying such social formations. The imbrication between the national issue and the class issue acquires concreteness in the dependent States from the conformation of the power bloc[18] in those States through the participation of foreign dominant class fractions. Dependence, in this sense, at the same time that it constitutes a relationship between States, gains political effectiveness through class relations that are configured at national and international levels.

The Marxist dependency theorists, in addition to emphasizing the class character of the State, draw attention to the hierarchy of power among capitalist states – imperialist and dependent states – that engenders the international system. We recover, at this moment, the formulations developed by Jaime Osorio, an important Chilean Marxist and scholar of the theme of power and the State, who was part of the research group coordinated by Dos Santos at CESO and whose works are inscribed in the field of the Marxist theory of dependency. In his books, "The State at the Center of Mundialization" (2004); "Redoubled exploitation and actuality of revolution" (2009); "State, biopower, exclusion" (2012); "State, reproduction of capital and class struggle" (2014a), "Marxist Theory of Dependency" (2016), the author introduces fundamental contributions to the understanding of the theme of the dependent capitalist state, which represent, in our perspective, the most advanced development carried out in this field within the scope of the MTD.

---

18   The concept of power bloc, is developed by Nicos Poulantzas, a Greek Marxist philosopher and sociologist, to explain how the dominant classes exercise power in the capitalist state. According to Poulantzas, it is the "[...] particular contradictory unity of the politically dominant classes or class fractions, in their relationship with a particular form of the capitalist state" (Poulantzas, 1977 [1968]: 229, original italics). In an obvious counterpoint to the idea that the ruling class would constitute a monolithic bloc, the Greek Marxist draws attention to the existence of important divisions and contradictions within the bourgeoisie in its different fractions, which are expressed in its relationship with the state. Amid such divisions and contradictions present within the bourgeois class, the hegemony of a bourgeois fraction is imposed, which guarantees the political domination of the class as a whole.

In dialog with the Marxist debate on the State, especially in the figures of Lenin, Gramsci, and Poulantzas, Osorio advances in the characterization of the State in contemporary society and dedicates a large part of his effort to the integration between the Marxist theory of the State and the Marxist Theory of Dependency. In this sense, in addition to pointing out the main traits of the State in capitalism, he highlights the hierarchy of power that marks the state system and the existing differences between imperialist states and states in dependent capitalism, a theme that has been very little developed in the field of political studies and Latin American studies.

Osorio points out two central elements that characterize states in Latin American dependent capitalism. The first is the restricted sovereignty of those states. In a world-system characterized by the unequal exercise of state sovereignty, the states of dependent capitalism can be defined as sub-sovereign. That does not mean, according to the author, that this State lacks something, but rather that its actions are subordinated to the operations and decisions of the imperialist centers. The conditions of reproduction of the local dominant social classes are conditioned by imperialist capital and its projects, which reproduce dependence and subordination. The other element is the particularity of exploitation in dependent societies, which is based on the super-exploitation of the workforce, that is, on the structural and permanent violation of the value of the workforce and the conversion of part of the consumption and life fund of workers in capital accumulation fund. According to Osorio, this process implies the development of capitalism that sharpens the elements of barbarism and reduces the field of the dominant classes to establish modalities of domination sustained by stable forms of consensus, which explains the democratic instability in the Latin American region, always threatened by processes that weaken it and by authoritarian trends in the history of the region (Osorio, 2014b).

The author indicates, however, that the limitation of Latin American sovereignty did not prevent the exercise of political power by the ruling classes of such countries to boost their projects precisely because those classes have strong ties with the interests of the ruling classes of imperialist countries. At the same time, he stresses that state heterogeneity in the world-system is "consistent with the logic of expropriating the value of some regions and states over others, of the hierarchical structures of dominion that such a process claims and of the differentiated exercise of state sovereignties that this entails" (Osorio, 2004: 150, original emphasis).

Considering the production of the authors of the Marxist Theory of Dependency, we identified important contributions of this theoretical current to International Relations, as well as a broad field of research to be explored by those who study this knowledge area. In light of this thought, it is understood that dependency constitutes a fundamental and structuring object of the international system, articulating and conditioning the relationship between states and between social classes, explaining the intersection between those two dimensions, national and class, and highlighting the links that are built from the exercise of political power. By adopting dependency as a focus and Latin America as a starting point, they shift the analysis and, therefore, the explanatory framework since the perspective becomes that of the dependent States, a change that produces implications both in terms of epistemological as well as political. This movement reconstitutes the conformation of dependent capitalism as a specific modality of accumulation, reproduction of capital, and exploitation of labor, it makes explicit the role played by Latin America in the international division of labor from the moment of its integration into the international market to the imperialist phase of capitalism, thus problematizing explanations that naturalized the 'development/underdevelopment' dyad or that highlighted the interdependent nature of the international system. Such a perspective reveals the asymmetries, inequalities, and contradictions that mark international relations. In these elements reside some of the main contributions of the Marxist Theory of Dependency to International Relations, which indicate open paths for an interlocution to be built.

References

Amaral S (2012) Teorias do imperialismo e da dependência: a atualização necessária ante a financeirização do capitalismo. Unpublished doctoral thesis. University of São Paulo, São Paulo.

Bambirra V (1978) *Teoría de la dependencia: una anticrítica*. México, D.F.: Era.

Bichir M (2012) A problemática da dependência: um estudo sobre a vertente marxista da dependência. Unpublished master thesis. University of Campinas, Campinas.

Bichir M (2017) A questão do Estado na Teoria Marxista da Dependência. Unpublished doctoral thesis. University of Campinas, Campinas.

Bukharin N (1986[1915]) *A economia mundial e o imperialismo: esboço econômico*. São Paulo: Nova Cultural.

Carcanholo M and Corrêa H (2016) Uma teoria da superexploração da força de trabalho em Marx? Um Marx que nem mesmo ele tinha percebido. *Revista da Sociedade Brasileira de Economia Política*, n. 44, June-September., 10–30.

Cardoso FH and Faletto E (1979 [1976]) *Dependency and development in Latin America*. Berkeley: University of California Press.

Cardoso FH and Faletto E (2004 [1970]) *Dependência e Desenvolvimento na América Latina*. 8. ed. Rio de Janeiro: Civilização Brasileira, 2004 [1970].

Cardoso FH and Serra J (1978) Las desventuras de la dialéctica de la dependencia. *Revista Mexicana de Sociología*, vol. 40, Extraordinary Number, 9–55.

Castelo R and Prado F (2013) O início do fim? Notas sobre a teoria marxista da dependência no Brasil contemporâneo. *Pensata*, v. 3, n. 1, Dezember, 1–29.

Chirot D and Fall T (1982) World-system theory. *Annual Review of Sociology*, v. 8, August, 81–106.

Dos Santos T (1972 [1971]) *La crisis norteamericana y América Latina*. Buenos Aires: Periferia.

Dos Santos T (1973 [1970]) *Dependencia y cambio social*. Santiago, Chile: CESO, 1973 [1970].

Falleto E (1998) Los años 60 y el tema de la dependencia. *Revista Estudos Avançados*. São Paulo, vol.12, n. 33, May, 109–117.

Fernandes F (1993 [1973]) *Capitalismo dependente e classes sociais na América Latina*. Rio de Janeiro: Zahar.

Frank AG (1973a) *América Latina: subdesarrollo o revolución*. México: Era.

Frank AG (1973b) *Capitalismo y subdesarrollo en América Latina*. Buenos Aires: Siglo veintiuno.

Frank AG (1996) *The Underdevelopment of Development*: essays in honor of André Gunder Frank. Sage publication.

Gouvêa M (2016) Imperialismo e método: Apontamentos críticos visando a problemas de tática e estratégia. Unpublished doctoral thesis. Federeal University of Rio de Janeiro, Rio de Janeiro.

Guanais J (2018) *Pagamento por produção, intensificação do trabalho e superexploração na agroindústria canavieira brasileira*. São Paulo: Outras Expressões/ FAPESP.

Lenin V (1982 [1971]) *Imperialismo, fase superior do capitalismo*. São Paulo: Global.

Luce M (2011) A teoria do subimperialismo em Ruy Mauro Marini: contradições do capitalismo dependente e a questão do padrão de reprodução do capital. A história de uma categoria. Unpublished doctoral thesis. Federeal University of Rio Grande do Sul, Porto Alegre.

Luce M (2018) *Teoria Marxista da Dependência: problemas e categorias – uma visão histórica*. São Paulo: Expressão Popular.

Luxemburgo R (1985 [1912]) *A acumulação do capital*. São Paulo: Nova Cultural, 1985 [1912].

Marini R (1978) Las razones del neodesarrollismo (respuesta a F. H. Cardoso y J. Serra). *Revista Mexicana de Sociología*, vol. 40, Extraordinary number, 57–106.

Marini R (1992) *América Latina: independência e integração*. São Paulo: Brasil Urgente.

Marini R (1999 [1994]) Presentación. In: Marini R and Millpan M (eds.) *La teoria social latino-americana – Tomo II Subdesarrollo y dependencia*. México: El Caballito.

Marini R (2005 [1994]) Memórias. In: Traspadini R and Stédile J (eds.) *Ruy Mauro Marini, vida e obra*. São Paulo: Expressão Popular.

Marini R (2007 [1972]) Dialéctica de la dependência. In: Martins C (ed.) *América Latina, dependencia y globalización*. Buenos Aires: CLACSO-Prometeu.

Marx K (2013[1867]) *O capital*. São Paulo: Boitempo.

Meireles M (2014) Origens da Teoria Marxista da Dependência: o Centro de Estudos Socioeconômicos (CESO) da Universidade do Chile e a práxis de Ruy Mauro Marini, Vânia Bambirra e Theotônio dos Santos (1966–1973). Unpublished graduation monograph. Federeal University of Rio Grande do Sul, Porto Alegre.

Osorio J (2004) *El Estado en el centro de la mundialización*. México, D.F.: Fondo de cultura económica.

Osorio J (2014a) *Estado, reproducción del capital y lucha de clases*. México, D.F.: Universidad Nacional Autónoma de México, Instituto de Investigaciones Económicas.

Osorio J (2014b) *O Estado no centro da mundialização*. São Paulo: Outras Expressões.

Poulantzas N (1977 [1968]) *Poder político e classes sociais*. São Paulo: Martins Fontes.

Prado F (2011) História de um não-debate: a trajetória da teoria marxista da dependência no Brasil. *Comunicação&política*, v.29, n.2, 68–94.

Prado F (2015) A ideologia do desenvolvimento e a controvérsia da dependência no Brasil contemporâneo. Unpublished doctoral thesis. Federeal University of Rio de Janeiro, Rio de Janeiro.

Ricardo D (1996 [1817]) *Princípios de economia política e tributação*. São Paulo: Nova Cultural.

Ricupero B (2000) *Caio Prado Jr. e a nacionalização do Marxismo no Brasil*. São Paulo: Departamento de Ciência Política da Universidade de São Paulo; Fapesp.

Rocha M (2017) Capitalismo dependente e Serviço Social: Crítica à Formação Social Brasileira na produção teórica do Serviço Social e outras Contradições. Unpublished doctoral thesis. Federeal University of Rio de Janeiro, Rio de Janeiro.

Vargas T (2009) Particularidades da formação do capitalismo dependente brasileiro – O debate entre Cardoso e Marini. Unpublished graduation monograph. University of Campinas, Campinas.

CHAPTER 14

Imperialism and Dependence vs. Interdependence
The Muted Side of a Theoretical Clash

Rejane Carolina Hoeveler[1]

1   Introduction

> For the weaker developing countries, interdependence appears as a system of dependence.[2] Hence the appeal of theories which stress elements of *dependencia* in the world economy, including multinational corporations, and which underlie much of the rhetoric, if not the political strategy, of many developing countries.
>
> COOPER et al., 1977: 191

The term 'complex interdependence', coined in the early 1970s, is probably one of the most current terms in the International Relations (IR) area around the world. Although some of the ideas that laid the foundation of its dissemination have been reviewed by its very authors, Joseph Nye and Robert Keohane, it is still part of a renowned theoretical framework that is read within the field, as opposed to what happens regarding the theories of dependence and imperialism developed in the 1960s and 1970s.

This chapter seeks to understand the theory of interdependence from its historical contextualization and internal analyzes of its arguments, seen as a development of the functionalist and liberal theory within IR, contrasting it to the theory of dependence in its various origins, based on the Marxist Theory of Dependency (MTD).

Our goal is to show that, although the interdependence authors did not mean to address the dependence theoreticians (at least not explicitly), but rather the 'realistic' tradition of International Relations, such theory constitutes an invalidation of the dependence theories, in its Marxist and non-Marxist variants,

---

1   PhD in Social History at the Fluminense Federal University; post-doctoral student in Social Work at the Federal University of Alagoas (UFAL) and a collaborating professor in UFAL's Postgraduate Program in Social Work.
2   Originally published as article in the Brazilian journal "Estudos Internacionais", v.5 n.3, 2017. Translated into English by the author.

due to their deep influence over the social movements and the 'third-worldly' and anti-imperialistic political propositions as a whole in the early 1970s.

We also aim to demonstrate, from the Gramscian theoretical framework, that those who suggest the theory of dependence, as it is commonly known, may be seen as organic intellectuals, co-developers of a collective understanding linked to class fractions organized in certain private hegemonic apparatuses.

In the first part of the chapter, we briefly summarize the theories of dependence so that we may subsequently address the theory of interdependence, initially contextualizing it through Nye's and Keohane's intellectual and political paths, and then contrasting both theories. In the fourth part, we highlight some convergences and divergences between the ideas of these authors and those of Zbigniew Brzezinski, intending to clarify their political partnership in initiatives such as the Trilateral Commission.

2 The Theories of Dependence and the Anti-imperialism

Formally founded in 1948, in Chile, CEPAL (Economic Commission for Latin America and the Caribbean) aimed at addressing the economic and social specificities of Latin America, initially from the paradigm of the theory of dependence or modernization, whose 'underdevelopment' concept essentially meant 'lack of industrialization'. This theory suggested the 'modernization' of economic, social, institutional, and ideological structures until the point when the country would reach what was known as 'take of', i.e., when the country would be capable of self-supported development.

Although our goal does not comprise a thorough and complex description and history of the theory or theories of dependence in their different origins, a summary is necessary. To do so, we are going to rely on Ruy Mauro Marini's perspective (1992), one of the main theoreticians of the Marxist Theory of Dependency (MTD), and on Adrián Sotelo Valencia's most recent work.

CEPAL's original project, according to Marini, was an attempt, undertaken by the 'developed countries', to institutionally and theoretically respond to the unrest displayed in newly-decolonized countries and Latin America – unrest over internal social inequalities and historical inequalities in economic relations and international policies (Marini, 1992: 67–74).

In addition to the considerable impact of the "Economic Survey on Latin America 1949", issued in 1950, the works of Raul Prebisch (Argentina), the main author of the report, Aníbal Pinto (Brazil), and Victor Urquidi (Mexico) – all of whom had political offices in their countries' societies at some point – could not be ignored in the Latin American debate (Gurrieri, 1982).

Despite being far from a theory of imperialism, the Cepaline theory introduced key criticism to major liberal ideas regarding international trade: instead of ideas derived from 'comparative advantages', inspired by David Ricardo, CEPAL would seek to show a tendency to the deterioration of the terms of trade, which would always be prejudicial to the exporting countries of primary goods. Therefore, it highlighted the existence of an income transfer that implied wealth extortion from 'underdeveloped' to 'developed' countries. The theory of unequal exchange explicitly stated that the "underdevelopment" of most of the world was a 'necessary condition' for the 'development' of wealthy countries (Marini, 1992).

In the early 1960s, CEPAL changes its position, initially aligned with the theory of development, giving more emphasis to structural reform. Essentially, it was an inflection motivated by the economic crises that arose in countries like Brazil, which had received substantial foreign investment and advanced the industrialization process, neglecting, however, the concentration of land ownership and the overexploitation of labor. According to Marini, this crisis, responsible for inflationary spirals that devoured the already scarce actual wages of Latin American workers, contributed to a new cycle of social struggle, bolstered by the victory of the Cuban Revolution in 1959. When the avalanche of military coups begins, Cepaline developmentalism would suffer a crisis, opening the way to theories that, although stemming from Cepaline thinking, criticized it.

The theory of dependence, as it is known, initially appears in a group of works published between 1964 and 1967, in an extremely substantial Latin American debate, contradictorily fostered by the exiles induced or forced by the military coups. Nevertheless, this debate reverberated in the United States, as André Gunder Frank shows in his criticism of some of Celso Furtado's theses. Gunder Frank's central argument was that capitalist developmentalism in dependent countries would always lead to more dependence, and not independence (Furtado, 1961; Frank, 1966). Celso Furtado's work was already known in several countries, including the United States, as well as Fernando Henrique Cardoso's and Enzo Falleto's, whose most important work was written in Chile, between 1964 and 1967 (Cardoso and Faletto, 1977 [1967]).

In summary, the theory of dependence, as Marini explains,

> led to the rejection of the idea of autonomous capitalist development, dear to Cepaline ideologists, and to the assumption that dependence could not be overcome under the capitalist framework.
> MARINI, 1992: 89

Although not a Marxist theory *per se*, the theory of dependence in its most widespread versions stated that 'imperialism' permeated all dependent economics, constituting a structuring and determining element, though neither unique nor univocal, of the State and social, political, and cultural relations as a whole. In all its variants, the theory of dependence's underlying concern was the consolidation, in the wake of the World War II, of a hegemonic system whose center was the United States of America. In its turn, the Marxist Theory of Dependency (MTD) arose as an updated theory of imperialism, under the new conditions generated by the second post-war era – even though the matter of dependence would still be placed within a wider historic framework. Brazilian authors Ruy Mauro Marini, Vânia Bambirra e Theotônio dos Santos[3] theorized about the specificity of Latin American dependence relationships, understanding that the extreme poverty of popular masses would only be overcome under the socialist framework.[4] The renovation of the Marxist debate about imperialism in the English-speaking world was also noteworthy in the 1960s. During this period, economist Hugo Correa identifies three groups of theoretical contributions: in addition to the theory of dependence and, in parallel, to the 'third-worldly' thought, it is worth mentioning the debates published in the "Monthly Review" magazine, initiated by Paul Sweezy, Paul Baran e Harry Magdoff; and also, the Trotskyist current, basically through Ernest Mandel (Corrêa, 2012: 157).

And this imperialist-centered conversation in the Anglo-Saxon world was not accidental: social mobilization throughout the world set the scene for it. According to literary critic Fredric Jameson, the 1960s began with the Cuban Revolution and the first sit-ins in the United States, in 1959, reaching another peak in 1968, considerably strong in so-called Third World countries (Jameson, 1992; Ali, 2005). Besides that, the late-1960s historical context defines a renovation of the international political alignment of the 'Third World'.[5] In the left-wing sphere, in 1966, the Tricontinental Alliance had been created in Cuba, a solidarity organization among the anti-colonial/anti-imperialistic movements

---

3 First Brazilian author to critically analyze the Trilateral Commission and the foreign policy of Carter's administration in a book published in Portuguese in 1979 (Assman et al., 1979).
4 Marini's original contribution was essential to the MTD, with the concepts of super-exploitation of labor force and 'sub-imperialism', in which he anticipated a thorough analysis of a phenomena that would expand considerably in the following decades: the exportation of Brazilian-generated capital to other dependent countries (Marini, 2012a, 2012b; Luce, 2011).
5 This term is being used in a descriptive, non-analytical way. For a critical perspective on the Three Worlds Theory, it is essential to refer to Ahmad, 2002: 170–176.

of Latin America, Africa, and Asia, in which context the revolutionary leader Che Guevara gave his famous speech claiming for two, three, many Vietnams.

In 1973, at the core of the Israeli assault in the Middle East, OPEC (Organization of the Petroleum Exporting Countries) imposes an embargo on the sale of oil, followed or preceded by the constitution of a series of mineral producers organizations, such as the International Bauxite Association – a movement described by liberal intellectuals as 'old-fashioned', 'destabilizing', 'nationalist', and 'protectionist' (Bergsten 1974). Then, the revindication for a 'New International Economic Order' in multilateral forums, such as the UN, becomes significantly internationally important.[6]

In addition to that, an overproduction crisis starts to arise at the end of the 1960s, leading to increasing commercial deficits in central imperialistic countries, such as the United States, and the incitement of inter-imperialistic conflict between the United States, Western Germany, and Japan (Block, 1977).

In the United States, the book "Age of Imperialism", by Harry Magdoff (1969), became a best-seller and a solid cornerstone for many American protesters who were against their country's imperialistic policies and sympathetic to Third World revindications (Magdoff, 1978). As noted by John Bellamy Foster, Magdoff's work was considerably attacked by the establishment and, at the same time, was highly inspirational to those who protested against the war and the country's participation in Latin American dictatorships (Foster, 2002; Green, 2009).[7] Other critical works, although non-Marxist, such as Sidney Lens' "The Forging of American Empire", originally published in 1971, challenged and rejected the 'myth of morality' of American interventions throughout the world (Lens, 2006), achieving considerable political impact.

Going directly against this movement, American and European intellectuals built alternative theories, implicitly or explicitly opposed to the idea of imperialism being central to International Relations analysis. This is the case of Nye and Keohane's 'interdependence'; although it was focused on the 'realistic' ideas in IR, it was built around the denial of structural relationships of dependence between countries. Let us see how this theory emerged in the intellectual journey of these two important authors.

---

6 The "New International Economic Order" was a group of propositions prepared in the United Nations General Assembly, throughout 1974, fostered by Third World countries aiming to assure improved negotiation conditions with central countries in several areas, such as stability of raw material price, access to the developed countries' markets, technological transfer, regulation of transnational corporations, among others.

7 Indeed, Magdoff's book in the only Marxist work mentioned by Nye and Keohane, and Brzezinski.

3 The Position of Interdependence in the Intellectual Journey of Nye and Keohane

Joseph Nye, who graduated in Political Science from Harvard University, becomes a professor in the same institution in 1964, later holding several important positions in the renowned John F. Kennedy School of Government, of which he would be the director in 1995. In his first publications, still in the early 1960s, he used the concept of 'regional integration' and carried out some case studies about East Africa (Kenya, Uganda, and Tanganyika – current region of Tanzania) and Central America (Nye, 1965, 1968). These studies included the formation of common markets, which Nye analyzed through an explicitly neofunctionalist model (Nye, 1970).

Neofunctionalist author Ernest Haas was an important reference to Nye and Keohane in the 1970s. In general, functionalism argued that a better action of international organizations would lead to a 'compartmentalization' of matters, as organizations 'technical' or specific organizations would work better than the ones with broad or general goals, such as the League of Nations. It was peace by pieces, as the educational pun would teach.

The functionalist approach introduced the idea that cooperation – as preferable to competition due to its greater efficiency in achieving these benefits – would generate a gradual 'overflowing' effect, in which how one succeeds in a goal or function would flow to other areas (the famous spill-over effect) in a process coming from functional, and not political, efficiency (Nogueira and Messari, 2005: 78). One of Haas' greatest contributions to this line of reasoning was the incorporation of the political scope, even if in the strict sense of state decision, to the understanding of international institutions. A key idea in his work was the importance of the 'values' and 'education' of bureaucratic and governmental elites that constitute the international institutions (Nogueira and Messari, 2005; Herz, 1997).

The regional integration theory, as it was developed by functionalist authors, was used as a theoretical tool by Nye in his comparisons between different processes of regional integration, such as the European Economic Community and the Central American Common Market. In his studies, the author presented explanatory models about how the integration processes expanded from small economic to big political and institutional matters, distinguishing 'economic microregions' from 'economic macroregions'. Although integration is seen as essentially good, the author also mentions its 'limitations' and 'problems'. In this work, Nye aligned explicitly with the 'liberal' (IR) traditions, conceptualizing the regional integration theory as intrinsically linked to it (Nye, 1971).

In 1972, the Harvard professor organized, alongside his reference author, Ernest Haas, a book about conflict management through international organizations, a work that gathered data about 146 conflicts worldwide that were managed by regional and international organizations between 1945 and 1970 (Nye et al., 1972).

Robert Keohane, who was also a political scientist and a professor at Princeton University, was the editor of the prestigious periodical International Organization (1974–1980) and a member of the National Science Foundation's Political Science panel. It is worth noting that, before his works alongside Nye, Keohane studied the constitution of pressure groups over small countries in the United Nations General Assembly, a phenomenon that, since the 1960s, had increasingly become a concern to the imperialistic potencies (Keohane, 1967, 1969, 1971, 1977). Afterward, Keohane would be the president of the renowned American Political Science Association (APSA).

Nye and Keohane's first work together was "Transnational Relations and World Politics", initially published as an article in the academic journal "International Organization" (1971) and, soon after, as a book. In this work, they strongly criticized what they referred to as the 'state-centric' paradigm, which, according to them, relegated a secondary role to 'intersocietal interactions' (Keohane and Nye, 1972). Thus, they engaged in close dialog with two other future members of the Trilateral Commission, Karl Kaiser e Richard N. Cooper – the latter, a well-known economist who, in a study commissioned by the Council on Foreign Relations, used the interdependence concept in his international economics analyzes, especially directed to monetary and foreign investment matters (Cooper, 1968).

In "Transnational Relations and World Politics", Nye and Keohane listed the effects brought forth by the multiplication of transnational and non-state interaction: 1. Changes in the citizens' attitudes; 2. International pluralism (the connection between national interest groups in transnational structures, often coordinated by transnational organizations); 3. Increase in the constraints on the States; 4. Increase in some governments' ability to influence others; and 5. The emergence of autonomous actors, with private foreign policies that may deliberately oppose or collide with state policies (Keohane and Nye, 1971: 337).

According to Stephen Gill, the English writer Anthony Hartley was the first one to, in an article in "Interplay" journal, propose the idea of 'interdependence'. "Interplay" was founded in 1967 by American diplomat Gerard Smith (main American negotiator in the SALT I agreement) and ideated as a magazine about Europe-United States relations. As shown by Gill, during its brief existence, until 1971, the magazine published a broad range of articles within what is known as 'Atlanticism', and would be the model for one of the Trilateral Commission publications, created in 1973[8] (Gill, 1990: 138–9).

The term 'interdependence' would be central in Nye and Keohane's most famous work, "Power and Interdependence" (1977), in which the authors stated that they not only rejected 'political realism' – understood as a perspective controlled by the constant fear of military conflicts – but also set themselves apart from those who they considered 'popularizers of economic interdependence', writers who saw a nearly total eclipse of nation-state by 'non-territorial' agents, such as multinational corporations and transnational social movements.

Later, Nye and Keohane would stress that the complex interdependence was less of a theory and more of a Weberian 'ideal type', i.e., an abstract construction with certain characteristics. In fact, according to the authors, both "complex interdependence" and "realism" would have self-explanatory capacities in accordance with the kind of situation being analyzed, as real-world relations are always somewhere between the "realist model" and the "complex interdependence model". While relations in the Middle East, for example, would be closer to the "realist model", the relations between Canada and the United States would be closer to the "complex interdependence model" (Nye, 2009: 264–265).

As Nye himself recently defined,

> As an analytical word, *interdependence* refers to situations in which actors or events in different parts of a system affect each other. Simply put, interdependence means mutual dependence.
> NYE, 2009: 256

This way, States are acknowledged to remain as the main actors in the international system, but their 'interaction' with 'non-State actors' (multinational corporations, NGOs, and various transnational movements, such as environmentalism) is considered. In this theory, other interests, such as 'economic well-being', are added to the security and survival of the State, which, according to the realist theory, should be its sole goals.

Nye and Keohane's analysis in "Power and Interdependence" had, essentially, 3 themes: a political analysis of the interdependence policy, based on

---

8 The Trilateral Commission, founded in 1973 by major entrepreneurs, politicians, and intellectuals from the United States, Europe, and Japan (the 'three sides' represented in every meeting and publication). The 'Trialogues' are quarterly reports issued by the Trilateral Commission about the main American, European, and Japanese concerns.

the bargaining theory[9]; an ideal type analysis, which the authors defined as 'complex interdependence' and the impact of the processes it comprised; and an attempt to explain the changes in international regimes – which were defined as 'set of governing arrangements that affected relationships of interdependence'.

What the authors argue in "Power and Interdependence" was that the use of force had become increasingly costly for the more powerful States as a result of 4 conditions: the risk of nuclear escalation; the 'resistance by people in poor, weak countries'; the 'uncertain and possibly negative effects on the achievement of economic goals'; and 'domestic opinion opposed to the human costs of the use of force'. Although these 4 conditions had a reduced impact on the policies of authoritarian or totalitarian governments, the net effect of these trends would be the 'erosion of hierarchy based on military power'. This is an overly explicit reference not only to the vague anti-war mobilization but also to its effects on the military structure of the United States.

Writing about "Power and Interdependence" 10 years later, Nye and Keohane stated that

> Our [1977] analysis linked realist and neorealist analysis to concerns of liberals with interdependence. Rather than viewing realist theory as an alternative to liberal 'interdependence theory', we regarded the two as necessary complements to one another. This approach was analytically justified, in our view, because realism and liberalism both have their roots in a utilitarian view of the world, in which individual actors pursue their own interests by responding to incentives. Both doctrines view politics as a process of political and economic exchange, characterized by bargaining. Broadly speaking, both realism and liberalism are consistent with the assumption that most state behavior can be interpreted as rational, or at least intelligent, activity. Realism and liberalism are therefore not two incommensurable paradigms with different conceptions of the nature of political action.
>
> KEOHANE AND NYE, 1987: 728–729[10]

---

9   The 'bargaining theory', substantially influential among funcionalist authors, defines the 'bargaining situation' as one in which two or more players have a common interest in cooperation, but face conflicts of interests concerning how this cooperation would be conducted (the players may be individuals, firms, countries, or organizations). Bargaining could define any process, be it in the political, economic, or international arena, where the interested parties try to reach a deal (Muthoo, 2000).

10 The authors' defense against liberal and realist criticism, that their analyzes of both traditions were incomplete, was that their intention had not been to develop a historical

According to the authors themselves, the result of their analytical synthesis in "Power and Interdependence" would have been "to broaden neorealism and provide it with new concepts" (Keohane and Nye, 1987: 733). This is a symptomatic assessment of the inflections in Nye's and mainly Keohane's thoughts since the 1980s.

The 'revisited version' of the 1977's classic work, from which the excerpt above was taken, was written in the Reagan administration context – which, to many observers, was marked by force and security concerns, leaving behind the 'decade of interdependence', which would have been the 1970s. This did not mean, however, the rejection of this concept, whose development was retaken by Nye in the 1990s and has still been present in his intellectual production to date (Nye, 2005, 2009).

4 An 'Interdependence' to Discredit 'Dependence'?

As we have seen, complex interdependence, according to Nye and Keohane, referred to a situation in a series of countries in which various linking channels connect societies (i.e., states do not monopolize these contacts); in which there is a hierarchy of matters, and military force is not used by one government against the other. Interdependence could bring forth several benefits, but at a high price, which could be measured in 'sensitivity' (degree of impact that, in the short term, an event in one country would project over the others) or 'vulnerability' (which comprises the costs of changing the structure of a given interdependence system).

Well, following this line of thought, the advantages and disadvantages of the interdependence relationship are classified in terms of 'symmetry' or 'asymmetry' and would, nonetheless, have nothing to do with reducing interdependence merely to relationships in which there is 'equal dependence'. Thus, "manipulating interdependence asymmetries may be a source of power in foreign politics" (Nye, 2009: 256). A certain kind of interdependence could interfere with negotiations that comprise another kind, undermining a given asymmetry. The authors, therefore, linked interdependence to the properly political scope only when manipulating an 'asymmetrical interdependence' can be seen as a way to constitute a source of power[11].

---

analysis of these traditions, but to assess some of their fundamental assumptions concerning the interdependence matter (Keohane and Nye, 1987, p. 729).

11 This idea, according to Nye and Keohane, is first developed by Hirschman, 1945; and can also be found in Kenneth Waltz (1970)'s work (Kindleberger, 1970).

In 1971's "Transnational Relations and World Politics", it had become explicit that the authors' choice of using the term 'asymmetrical interdependence relationship' was directly linked to a total rejection of the idea of imperialism. In their words, the term 'imperialism' was not only 'old' but also rather 'ambiguous', being capable of defining virtually any relationship across state boundaries among unequals that involves the exercise of influence – what would comprise the majority of global politics. Thus, the concept of imperialism would have no heuristic value at all, even in a stricter meaning, when referring to, for example, a relationship in which an uneven power is used to achieve 'unfair value allocations'.

Nye and Keohane argued that in addition to "fairness" being an extremely difficult concept to agree on, "some transnational relationships" would be "imperialistic" and others would not; therefore, the ambiguity of the term would still be present, being thus preferable to use the terms "asymmetry" or, at most, "inequalities". (Keohane and Nye, 1971: 346). Well, by these criteria, the interdependence concept should also be rejected. The central matter is the rejection of not only the term 'imperialism' but also of the very idea of dependence and any reference to a structural relationship of domination between countries.

While terms such as 'imperialism', 'imperial', and others disclose a relationship of domination, the term 'asymmetry' conveys an idea of imperfection, a deviation from the standard, which may be specific and conjunctural, in the relationship between essentially equal countries. The idea of 'interdependence' with 'asymmetries' alludes directly, though not explicitly, to the idea of comparative advantages, initially developed by David Ricardo. Each country would politically and economically exploit its various resources aiming to maximize its earnings both in the market and in international politics. At its core, it is a benevolent perspective of the empire.

Nevertheless, as Franz Hinkelammert's pioneering essay points out, the concept of interdependence is not static, as in neoclassic economic theory, but rather a dynamic concept, "of a process with future projection", something that even reaches the condition of historical subject, even if through certain men. The advancement of interdependence (as it would be presented in the 1990s globalization) would be an inexorable historical process, but this would also include the need to 'manage' it, for it would bring forth, according to its authors, new problems to the management of the international system – and managing the new situation meant coordinating "the maximum of interdependence with the minimum of social justice" (Hinkelammert, 1979: 85). Nye and Keohane's collaboration with 'interdependence management' projects in the Trilateral Commission can be seen as evidence. Another piece of evidence would be the non-accidental convergence in thought between them and another important International Relations theoretician of that time, 'realist' Zbigniew Brzezinski, a matter we are going to address in the following section.

5   Congruence with Brzezinski

The idea of interdependence and the rejection of the imperialism or dependence categories were present in many authors before Nye and Keohane. In his 1969 work, "Between Two Ages", the Polish Sovietologist Zbigniew Brzezinski addressed the matter of how economic power would be becoming increasingly depersonalized through the emergence of a 'high complexity interdependence' between governmental institutions (including the military institution), scientific establishments, and industries (Brzezinski, 1971 [1969]). Although Brzezinski's words referred to the relations between institutions and spheres within a society rather than between societies, the coincidence of terms is noteworthy.

Going back to Hinkelammert once again, to the Trilateral thought, in the rising 'technetronic era' (a term coined by Brzezinski), States are no longer bearers and protectors of national interests, but rather "geographical places where interdependence happens"; this implied, among other things, the rejection of national policies, such as full employment, that arose as forms of social contention and capitalist development in the post-war decades (Hinkelammert, 1979: 93).

According to Brzezinski, the influence of innovation and the economic presence of the United States – or its encouragement – would be taking the place of the "informal imperial system" consolidated by the USA, especially during the II World War and the beginning of the Cold War, a period when the American military bases were spread throughout the world (Brzezinski, 1971: 45).

Marxist analyzes of imperialism, according to Brzezinski, would be wrong to "disregard" this new kind of relationship with the world, as they would consider imperialism merely as an "expression of an imperial impetus", ignoring the dimension of the scientific-technological revolution that would impel backward countries to copy the more advanced ones, stimulating the exportation, from the latter to the former, of organization techniques and skills (Brzezinski, 1971: 45).

In this excerpt, the Sovietologist deliberately omitted the works of Marxists such as V.I. Lenin (and Marxists who saw imperialism as a phase of capitalism) or L. Trotsky, whose theory of unequal and combined development, written still at the beginning of the twentieth century, had been an attempt to understand the mechanisms through which "backward" countries, under the perspective of capitalist development, "skip stages" and, therefore, acquire peculiar political, social, and economic aspects (Trotsky, 1967 [1932]: 23–32). It is evident the omission or caricatural representation of Marxist thought.

In Brzezinski's words, "asymmetrical relationships" between countries could even exist, but the content of this "asymmetry" cannot be "branded as imperialism" (Brzezinski 1971: 45). It is worth noting this coincidence of terms used by Brzezinski and Nye/Keohane.

Although the similarities between Brzezinski's and Nye and Keohane's theories go so far as this, it is a fact that the guiding theses of the previously mentioned Trilateral Commission's works during the 1970s constituted a synthesis of the two schools of thought. The pivotal matters of this synthesis can be systematized in the following way: a) the idea that there was a decrease in the USA's capacity of controlling the international system, along with an increase in the economic power of other potencies, such as Japan and Germany, anachronizing the political outlines of the Kissinger years and demanding the construction of a 'shared hegemony'; b) the perception that the Third World, in the formation of regional alliances and/or specific interests, such as oil exporters, could cause severe economic turbulences in central countries, demanding some kind of counter-coalition, beginning with the coordination of the 'trilateral countries'; and c) the emphasis on the need for creating and strengthening international institutions, especially (pretentiously) 'depoliticized' and 'technical' institutions (detailed and emphatic recommendations present in several reports issued by the commission).

The reports of the Trilateral Commissions during the 1970s would reflect both Nye and Keohane's and Brzezinski's theories, three characters who, however different, were very active in its constitution. The Trilateral Commission is founded in 1973 from a project developed within the Council on Foreign Relations (CFR), having Brzezinski as its main organizer (Gill, 1990; Sklar, 1980; Maira, 1982). The participants included politicians from various parties (from Republican to Democrat 'liberals', German social-democrats), entrepreneurs (its overwhelming majority being huge American transnational organizations and, in a smaller proportion, Japanese, German, English, Belgian, and Italian organizations), and the heads of important international organisms, such as Robert McNamara, then CEO of the World Bank. It is worth noting that 'interdependence' became a key term in 1978's World Development Report (WDR), the first of a series of reports that would become the World Bank's main publication – what shows that, far beyond a theory, 'interdependence' was on its way to becoming part of a political action program made by multilateral organizations.[12] In this way, we cannot but address its authors' political activity alongside various organizations, which enables us to call them 'organic intellectuals'.

6   Organic Intellectuals and Private Hegemonic Apparatuses

The 1974 Council on Foreign Relations' (CFR)[13] annual report detailed a new program, whose title was "1980s Project" and whose objective would be to "help transform the political and economic system (...) in a process of accelerated changes since the end of the 1960s (...) by the impact of competition within the advanced capitalist world, by the Vietnam War (...) by the revolutionary processes in the Third World and by the international monetary system crisis" (Shoup and Minter, 1977: 254).

At that point, scholar Joseph Nye was the director of the Committee for Economic Development (CED). Founded in 1942, the CED, similar to the CFR, was an association constituted by great entrepreneurs and scholars, initially formed by an initiative of the Department of Trade. It constituted, like the CFR, a private hegemonic apparatus (Gramsci, 2007; Liguori, 2017: 44–45) that intended to "rescue the businessman from his own intellectual neanderthalism" and, at the same time, "bring scholars and theories for free association with men who reached leading positions in industry and business through their own effort" (Dreifuss, 1987: 42). This kind of private organization allowed, in the words of historian Virgínia Fontes, the

> much broader and farther-reaching *cosmopolite diffusion* of certain interests, certain action patterns, and certain ways of thinking than if they were bound by international political deals or national legislations that regulated directly economic activities, effective for the establishment of companies.
>
> FONTES, 2010: 174–5

---

12   According to Mendes Pereira, the report had already recommended changes in the profiles of Third World debts', with longer due dates, in a clear concern to manage the ungoverned process of external indebtedness incurred by many of these countries (Pereira, 2010: 232).

13   Founded in 1921 and responsible for the prestigious "Foreign Affairs" journal, the CFR is the most traditional USA's foreign policy think-tank.

During the 1970s, CED, alongside their international counterparts, promoted studies and events about the international monetary crisis and the relationships between transnational corporations and the Third World (Dreifuss, 1987: 80). Therefore, Nye's invitation to join the exclusive CFR's "1980s Project Coordinating Group" is not a surprise.

The "1980s Project Coordinating Group" mostly comprised university professors, among them economists Richard N. Cooper and Carlos Diaz-Alejandro, from Yale; Harvard professors Harvard Stanley H. Hoffman and Samuel Huntington; Richard Falk, from Princeton; environmental studies professor Gordon J. MacDonald, from Dartmouth; and Michigan University political science professors Ali Mazrui and Alan S. Whiting.[14] But it also included three corporate members: W. Michael Blumenthal, director of Bendix; Stephen Stamas, vice-president of Exxon; Edwin K. Hamilton, president of Griffenhagen-Kroeger Inc; and Bruce K. MacLaury, president of Federal Reserve Bank, Minneapolis.

"1980s Project" coordinating group included 3 future members of the Trilateral Commission: Richard Cooper, Bruce K. MacLaury, and Joseph Nye himself. Besides them, 8 CFR directors became part of the Trilateral Commission since its foundation, among them Brzezinski, Gerard Smith, George Franklin, and David Rockefeller, then CEO of the Chase Manhattan Bank and heavily active in political-diplomatic matters, responsible for a great amount of the funds raised to start the entity (Rockefeller, 2002: 444–447).

"1980s Project's" first publication, signed by economist Miriam Camps, led to the suggestive title of "The management of Interdependence: A Preliminary View". The book/report was concluded after two years of study group meetings about the subject of "1980s Project", between 1971 and 1973 (Camps, 1974). In the report, it was stated that no nation could ever play the role the USA had played in the past and that, given this, it was indispensable that the advanced capitalist industrial powers should manage a "collective administration" (Shoup and Minter, 1977: 265–7).

Nye and Keohane's more active participation in the Trilateral Commission's works occurred in the task-force reports (TFRS) concerning international institutions and would take up a significant part of the Commission's efforts between 1976 and 1978, with 3 detailed deports written with the consultation

---

14 Whiting and MacDonald were consultants for the State Department, and the latter for the Department of Defense. Huntington was the editor of the newly-founded "Foreign Policy" journal, in whose editorial board Falk, Cooper, Nye, and Hoffman participated (Shoup and Minter, 1977: 257–258).

Nye, Keohane, and many other academic intellectuals from the United States, West Europe, and Japan.

In the Commission's first task-force report (TFRS), named "The Reform of International Institutions", signed by C. Fred Bergsten, Georges Berthoin, and Kinhide Mushakoji, written in 1976 with Robert Keohane's consultation, "independence" is a key term as the cornerstone for multilateral organizations reform propositions, such as the UN (Bergstein, Berthoin and Mushakoji, 1976).[15] The proposition was to essentially remove the UN's deliberative capacity, as it was considered an overly 'political' organization, and transfer it to more 'technical' and decentralized organisms, where 'more effective deals' could be closed.

The term 'complex interdependence' would be profusely cited in another TFR, named "Towards a Renovated International System", written by Richard Cooper, Karl Kaiser, and Masataka Kosaka, who were advised by 22 consultants, Joseph Nye being one of them (Cooper et al., 1977).[16] It is in this document that one can find the symbolic excerpt, the epigraph of this chapter, one of the rare direct mentions to the theory of dependence:

> For the weaker developing countries, interdependence *appears as* a system of dependence. Hence the appeal of theories which stress elements of *dependencia* in the world economy, including multinational corporations, and which underlie much of the rhetoric, if not the political strategy, of many developing countries.
>
> COOPER et al, 1977: 191, bold added

The report, written, according to the authors themselves, in collaboration with Joseph Nye, was a sheer mockery of the ideas defended by the theoreticians of dependence, characterizing it as a 'late economic nationalism', as a form of 'protectionism' that should be abolished so that countries could have a good relationship, such as the defense of selfish interests responsible for the incitement of international conflicts, instead of their resolution. It was a matter of developing a sophisticated strategy to fight anti-imperialist policies, whether informed or not by theories of dependence and for this the theory of interdependence was a perfect fit.

In this way, we can state that the theses developed by Nye and Keohane were not in any way disconnected from class organization forms in civil

---

15   The report is available (consulted in September 28, 2023) at: https://www.trilateral.org/publications/task-force-report-11-the-reform-of-international-institutions/.

16   Available (consulted in September 28, 2023) at https://www.econbiz.de/Record/towards-a-renovated-international-system-cooper-richard/10002025471.

society – which we may understand, based on Antonio Gramsci, as private hegemonic apparatuses. On the contrary, they were intimately linked to certain policies defended by certain class fractions organized into these apparatuses – in the Trilateral case, it was specifically the monopolist capital that constituted the transnational corporations originated in central imperialist countries. In light of this, we can once again based on Gramsci understand them as 'organic intellectuals' (Gramsci, 2007; Voza, 2017: 430–431).

Nye's subsequent path would be marked by some degree of action within the political society (state *strictu sensu*) in the United States, more notably in Democrat administrations. Between 1977 and 1979, during the Carter administration, he had a position at the Undersecretary of State for Security Assistance, Science, and Technology, and presided over the National Security Council Group for the non-proliferation of nuclear weapons, for which he would receive the Distinguished Honor Award from the State Department in 1979.

In 1993 and 1994, in the Clinton administration, Nye would be nominated director of the influential National Intelligence Council, an organ that answered directly to the President; and in 1994, he would become Assistant Secretary of Defense for International Security Affairs, receiving state awards for both offices. In October 2014, he was nominated by the Obama administration's Secretary of State, John Kerry, for the Foreign Affairs Policy Board, a group that would meet regularly to discuss strategic matters and report back to the Secretary of State.

In addition to these state offices, Nye would be part of a series of private research organizations and institutions intimately linked to the state, *strictu sensu*, including think tanks for rendering 'consulting' services. Some examples are the Project on National Security Reform (PNSR), founded in 2006, which formally studies forms of reorganization of the national security State structure in face of the new threats, such as terrorism, transnational crime, among others, and the Center for a New American Security (CNAS), founded in 2007.[17] His works in the Trilateral Commission have been continuous and since 2008 Nye has been the entity's American director.[18]

---

17 Founded in 2007, CNAS, according to its own description, deals with national security matters, such as terrorism and irregular war, with the future of United States Armed Forces, the implications for national security of the consumption of natural resources, among other issues. See CNAS – Who we are – Mission, available (consulted in September 28, 2023) at: https://www.cnas.org/mission.

18 See Trilateral Commission. Available (consulted in September 28, 2023) at: https://www.trilateral.org/about/members-fellows/.

Following a different path, Keohane did not have significant offices in political societies – which certainly did not mean a distance from the circles of power or exemption from State policies.

7 Final Considerations

At the beginning of the 1970s, the theory of dependence exceeded the Latin American intellectual debate, where it had already reached great notoriety, and spread to American and European intellectual centers, flowing into the profitable Marxist debate in progress as part of the renovation of the theory of imperialism, constituting a political and theoretical challenge faced by intellectuals such as Brzezinski, Nye, and Keohane.

As we sought to demonstrate, the theory of interdependence constituted a conceptual framework that inspired private and State political strategies, driven forward by dominant fractions of the dominant classes in central imperialist countries. Debated in and incorporated into private hegemonic apparatuses, such as the Council on Foreign Relations (CFR), the Committee for Economic Development (CED), and the Trilateral Commission, the theory of interdependence was the cornerstone of propositions, made by these entities, for the reformation of international institutions, monetary policies, foreign policies, international "economic aid" policies, among many others. Such a framework clashed with the theory of dependence, which, in its many variants, understood imperialism and international political and economic domination as key determiners of international relations.

With undeniable recognition in the IR field, the theory of interdependence is far more well-known in the area than the theories of dependence. Bringing the latter back to the debate and identifying all authors within their political positions is essential for International Relations students to have access to the sort of theoretical antithesis they have been denied for far too long.

References

Ahmad A (2002) *Linhagens do presente*. Ensaios. São Paulo: Boitempo.
Ali T (2005) *O poder das barricadas*. São Paulo: Boitempo.
Assman H, Dos Santos T and Chomsky N (1979) *A Trilateral – nova fase do capitalismo mundial*. Petrópolis: Vozes.
Bergsten C (1974) The new era in the world commodity markets. *Challenge*, September-October.

Bergsten C, Berthoin G ans Mushakoji K (1976) The reform of international institutions. *Trilateral Commission*, Task-Force Report n.11.

Block F (1977) *The origins of International Economic Disorder. A study of United States International Monetary Policy from World War II to the present*. Berkley/Los Angeles: University of California Press.

Brzezinski Z (1971 [1969]) *Entre duas eras. América: Laboratório do mundo*. Rio de Janeiro: Artenova.

Camps M (1974) *The Management of Interdependence:* a preliminary view. New York: Council on Foreign Relations.

Cardoso FH and Faletto E (1977 [1967]) *Dependência e desenvolvimento na América Latina*: ensaio de interpretação sociológica. Rio de Janeiro: Zahar.

Cooper R (1968) T*he economics of interdependence: economic policy in the Atlantic Community*. New York: McGraw-Hill Book Co.

Cooper R, Kaiser L and Kosaka M (1977) *Towards a renovated international system Trilateral Commission*, Task-Force Report n.14.

Corrêa H (2012) *Teorias do imperialismo no século XXI*: (in) adequações do debate no Marxismo. Unpublished doctoral thesis. Fluminense Federal University, Niterói.

Dreifuss R (1987) A *internacional capitalista. Estratégias e táticas do empresariado transnacional (1918-1986)*. 2nd edition. Rio de Janeiro: Espaço e Tempo.

Fontes V (2010) *O Brasil e o capital-imperialismo*. Teoria e História. Rio de Janeiro: EPSJV/ UFRJ.

Foster J (2002) The Rediscovery of imperialism. *Monthly Review*, vol.54, November.

Frank AG (1966) The development of underdevelopment. *Monthly Review*, vol. 18, n.4, September.

Furtado C (1961) Celso. *Desenvolvimento e subdesenvolvimento*. Rio de Janeiro: Fundo de Cultura.

Gill D (1990) *American Hegemony and the Trilateral Commission*. Cambridge: Cambridge University Press.

Gramsci A (2007) *Cadernos do Cárcere*. Volumes 3, 4 and 5. Rio de Janeiro: Civilização Brasileira.

Green J (2009) *Apesar de vocês. Oposição à ditadura brasileira nos Estados Unidos, 1964-1985*. São Paulo: Companhia das Letras.

Gurrieri A (1982) *La obra de Prebisch en la Cepal*. México: Fondo de Cultura Económica.

Herz M (1997) Teoria das Relações Internacionais no Pós-Guerra Fria. *Dados*, Rio de Janeiro, vol.40, n.2, January.

Hinkelammert F (1979) O credo econômico da Comissão Trilateral. In: Assman H, Dos Santos T and Chomsky N (eds.) *A Trilateral – nova fase do capitalismo mundial*. Petrópolis: Vozes.

Hirschman A (1945) *National Power and the Structure of Foreign Trade*. Berkeley: University of California Press.

Jameson F (1992) Periodizando os anos 60. In: Hollanda H (ed.) *Pós-modernismo e política*. Rio de Janeiro: Rocco.

Keohane R and Nye R (1977) *Power and Interdependence: world politic in transition*. Boston: Little, Brown and Company.

Keohane R (1971) The Big Influence of Small Allies. *Foreign Policy*, no. 2, spring.

Keohane R (1969) Institutionalization in the United Nations General Assembly. *International Organization*, vol. 23, no. 4, autumn.

Keohane R (1967) The Study of Political Influence in the General Assembly. *International Organization*, vol. 21, no. 2, spring.

Keohane R and Nye J (1971) Transnational Relations and World Politics: an introduction. *International Organization*, vol.25, n.3, summer, 329-349.

Keohane R and Nye J (1972) *Transnational Relations and World Politics*, Cambridge, Massachussets: Harvard University Press.

Keohane R and Nye J (1987) Power and Interdependence revisited. *International Organization*, vol. 41, n.4, autumn, 725-753.

Kindleberger C (ed.) (1970) *The international Corporation*. Cambridge: MIT Press.

Lens S (2006 [1971]) *A fabricação do império americano. Da revolução ao Vietnã: uma história do imperialismo dos Estados Unidos*. Rio de Janeiro: Civilização Brasileira.

Liguori G (2017) Aparelho hegemônico. In: Liguori G and Voza P (eds.) *Dicionário Gramsciano (1926-1937)*. São Paulo: Boitempo, 44-45.

Luce M (2011) A teoria do subimperialismo em Ruy Mauro Marini: contradições do capitalismo dependente e a questão do padrão de reprodução do capital: a história de uma categoria. Unpublished doctoral theseis. Universidade Federal University of do Rio Grande do Sul, Porto Alegre.

Magdoff H (1978 [1969]) *A Era do Imperialismo*. São Paulo: Hucitec.

Maita L (1982) *America Latina y La crisis de hegemonia norte-americana*. Lima, Peru: Desco/Centro de Estudios y promocion del desarrollo.

Marini R (1992) *América Latina*: Dependência e integração. São Paulo: Editora Página Aberta.

Marini R. (2012a [1977]) A acumulação capitalista mundial e o subimperialismo. In: *Outubro*, São Paulo, n.20, 32–70, 2012.

Marini R (2012b) *Subdesenvolvimento e revolução*. Florianópolis: Insular.

Muthoo A (2000) A non-technical introduction to bargaining theory. *World Economics*, vol. 1, n.2, April-June.

Nogueria J and Messari N (2005) *Teoria das Relações Internacionais*: correntes e debates. Rio de Janeiro: Elsevier.

Nye J (1965) *Pan africanism and East African integration*. Cambridge: Harvard University Press.

Nye J (1968) A Latin Example for African Regionalists. *Africa Report*, April.

Nye J (1970) Comparing Common Markets: A Revised Neo-Functionalist Model. *International Organization*, autumn.

Nye J (1971) *Peace in Parts: Integration and Conflict in Regional Organization*. Boston: Little Brown and Company.

Nye J, Hass E and Butterworth R (1972) *Conflict Management by International Organizations*. New Jersey: General Learning Press.

Nye J (2009) *Cooperação e conflito nas Relações Internacionais. Uma leitura essencial para entender as principais questões da política mundial*. São Paulo: Editora Gente.

Nye J (2005 [2002]) *O paradoxo do poder americano. Por que é que a única superpotência mundial não pode actuar isoladamente*. Lisboa: Gradiva.

Pereira J (2010) *O Banco Mundial como ator político intelectual e financeiro (1944-2008)*. Rio de Janeiro: Civilização Brasileira.

Rockfeller D (2002) *Memórias*. Rio de Janeiro: Rocco.

Shoup L and Minter W (1977) *Imperial Brain Trust. The Council of Foreign Relations and the United States Foreign Policy*. *Monthly Review Press*.

Sklar H (1980) *Trilateralism*: managing dependence and democracy. Boston: South and Press.

Trotsky L (1967 [1932]) A *história da revolução russa*. Rio de Janeiro: Saga.

Voza P(2017) Intelectuais orgânicos. In: Liguori G and Voza P (eds.) *Dicionário Gramsciano (1926-1937)*. São Paulo: Boitempo, 430-431.

Waltz K (1970) The myth of National Interdependence, In: Kindleberger C (ed.) *The international Corporation*. Cambridge: MIT Press.

CHAPTER 15

Brazilian Sub-imperialism and Peripheral Development

A Critique of the Marxist Dependency Theory

Tiago Soares Nogara[1]

1   Introduction

Throughout the twentieth century, the assimilation and development of Marxist political ideologies and methods of analyzing Brazil's political and social issues have occurred nonlinearly.[2] In particular, the Communist Party of Brazil (PCB)[3] hegemonized the Marxist political, ideological, and theoretical spheres until 1964, with the defense of bourgeois-democratic revolution and narrative on feudal remnants in the Brazilian socioeconomic system. However, the defeat of the PCB's theory of an alliance of laborers with the nationalist bourgeoisie in 1964 boosted revisionist and dissident currents, both those that opted for armed struggle and those already skeptical of the communist orientations.

---

1   Tiago Soares Nogara is currently affiliated with the College of Liberal Arts at Shanghai University (上海大学). He holds a PhD in Political Science from the University of São Paulo (USP), a MA in International Relations from the University of Brasília (UnB), and a BA in Social Sciences from the Federal University of Rio Grande do Sul (UFRGS). For inquiries, he can be contacted at: tiagosnogara@gmail.com.
2   Originally published as a chapter of the book "Theory of International Relations: Marxist contributions". Reference: Pautasso D and Prestes A (2021) Teoria das Relações Internacionais: contribuições marxistas. Rio de Janeiro: Contraponto. Translated into English by the author.
3   In 1962, a schism emerged within the ranks of the Communist Party of Brazil (PCB), which was established in 1922. The primary factions within the party diverged on several key issues at the time, including global ideological disputes (Stalinism versus revisionist Khrushchevism), approaches to the socialist revolution in Brazil (armed revolt versus peaceful reforms), and strategies for political alliances (advocating political isolation and immediate socialist revolution versus aligning with reformist governments to pursue a bourgeois-democratic program). The party leadership, led by Luiz Carlos Prestes, leaned towards revisionism and peaceful methods by collaborating with the reformist factions of JK and Jango. Conversely, their adversaries opted to break away from Prestes' leadership (who, in an effort to legalize the party, renamed it the "Brazilian" Communist Party while retaining the acronym PCB) and reverted to the original name of Communist Party of Brazil, under the acronym PCdoB.

With the legal prohibition of the PCB and the defeat of leftist guerrilla organizations on the one hand and the rise of the democratic front and the Workers' Party (PT) on the other hand, revisionist and liberal tendencies were affirmed. Members of the revisionist camp were critical not only of the narratives that emanated from the communist ranks but also of the developmentalist and national-developmentalist prescriptions linked to those they called 'populists', just like Vargas and their successors. In the wake of these political developments, centers of academic thought and policymakers from leftist organizations adhered to narratives that were critical of assumptions that were previously held to be hegemonic, such as the alliance with the industrial bourgeoisie in Brazil, the exaltation of nationalism, anti-imperialism, and the need to dominate the so-called feudal remnants that supposedly prevailed in agrarian production and relations. Among these, the dependency theories would acquire singular importance with their liberal and Marxist emphasis on the limits of peripheral industrial development.

In this chapter, we discuss some of the main trends of the so-called Marxist Theory of Dependency—which was expounded by the Brazilian Ruy Mauro Marini, one of its greatest exponents—and its basic tenets, including the denial of developmentalism and the bourgeois-democratic strategy of the PCB. In particular, we analyze the concept of sub-imperialism and how it has influenced the analyzes of Brazilian international insertion under the former military regime and the later PT government, especially during the administration of Luiz Inácio Lula da Silva from 2003 to 2010. The construction and meaning of this concept demonstrate its understanding of issues such as the economic development of peripheral countries, how they articulate their domestic and foreign policies, the reasons for the emergence of a theory of socialist revolution that is distinct from that which is held by communist parties or nationalist movements in Latin America, the organization of industrial production on a global scale, and how countries dealt with each other in international relations.

This analysis addresses issues pertinent to Marxism and its treatment of themes linked to international relations. It emphasizes that the so-called theories of imperialism, which were the focus of profound debate in Marxist analyzes for decades, have been replaced by the canonization of post-Marxist, post-colonial, or liberal ideologies. Leading textbooks and courses claimed these ideologies as exponents of Marxism in mainstream theories on international relations. When debates on theories of imperialism appear in writings and narratives on schools of thought, the concept of sub-imperialism usually becomes particularly relevant.

The twenty-first century's first decade was marked by an increase in Brazil's participation in multilateral initiatives at regional and global levels. It played a leading role in developing regional and intercontinental integration and hosted essential forums to discuss changes in the balance of power in international relations. Although these initiatives by Brazil were viewed as positive developments by several studies, they did not escape criticism over their shortcomings or for their supposedly hegemonistic motivations. This last criticism was highlighted by the concept of sub-imperialism, often cited by critical interpretations of Brazilian international insertion.

Although the bibliography on sub-imperialism is relatively extensive, few texts have criticized it. This article aims to fill this gap by reviewing the primary texts that have charged Brazil's foreign policy based on the concept of sub-imperialism, debating their analyzes, and contrasting them with the reality they claimed to define. The hypothesis is that sub-imperialism has limitations that prevent it from categorizing Brazil's foreign policy of the period, which reinforces a systemic vision that is abstracted from the material conditions that constitute the current global order and reaffirms structures that discursively claim to antagonize by denying peripheral countries the ability to formulate national strategies to overcome underdevelopment.

Thus, we divide this chapter into four sections to discuss the concept, its application, and its validity. In the first section, we address the idea of sub-imperialism based on the assumptions of the Marxist dependency theory while paying close attention to the observations of Ruy Mauro Marini and his followers. Next, based on the concept of sub-imperialism, we examine the main criticisms of Brazil's foreign policy in South America during the Lula administration from 2003 to 2010—when the country reached the apex of regional leadership at the beginning of the twenty-first century—by highlighting its similarities and innovations with Marini's ideas. In the last two sections, we compare the concept to the theories it advocates, specifically the Leninist theory of imperialism, and analyze Brazil's foreign policy toward South America, particularly in regional integration and bilateral relations with South American countries.

2 Ruy Mauro Marini's Perspective on Brazilian Sub-imperialism

Based on Marxist theory and the classical theory of imperialism, the Marxist Theory of Dependency states that the dependent condition of peripheral societies results from capital reproduction practiced by the global capitalist economy (Carcanholo, 2013). The idea emerged in the mid-1960s and represented a theoretical effort to understand the limits of late economic development. It was critical of both the developmentalist theses and Marxist views that valued a policy of alliance with the national bourgeoisie. This theory is not the same as that of the Economic Commission for Latin America and the Caribbean (ECLAC) or the associated dependency theory pointed out by Bresser-Pereira (2010) as the other strands of the dependency theory. The leading exponents of the Marxist Theory of Dependency in Brazil included Ruy Mauro Marini, Theotônio dos Santos, and Vânia Bambirra. The concept of sub-imperialism was a theoretical construct developed by Marini, who refined its definition in his book "Subdesarrollo y Revolución".

In their interpretation of dependency as a condition that is inherent in a peripheral country within the capitalist system—that is, immutable within the laws of capital reproduction—Marini and the Marxist dependentists reached a consensus that the only way to overcome this dependency is a social revolution that would strip local and imperialist elites of their command in a country to allow a broad reorganization of the productive system that will prioritize the needs of the local population. Consequently, agrarian reform and cessation of overexploitation of labor would expand the domestic market and create new possibilities for national development. This led him to establish the Marxist Revolutionary Organization–Workers' Policy (ORM–POLOP) on the eve of the 1964 coup, which pitted itself against the alliance of the PCB with sectors of the national bourgeoisie and called for popular mobilization for the seizure of power. After he was exiled to Chile, Marini pursued a similar political course when he approached the *Movimiento de la Izquierda Revolucionaria* (MIR) and urged the party to contest the policy of alliance between the *Partido Socialista* (PS) and the *Partido Comunista de Chile* (PCC) with Christian Democracy and to propose armed struggle, which was represented by the main slogan of MIR as 'people, conscience, and rifle'.

For Marini (1974), the reproduction cycle of capital in Brazil was supported by two pillars before the *coup d'état* of 1964: progressive increase in productivity and constant depression in the remuneration of the great masses of workers. The rise in profit was attributed to the use of new technologies and suppression of wages by workers, who were subjected to what Marini described as 'super-exploitation' of labor. These trends created an impasse by flattening the domestic market and generated problems for the realization of capital in Brazil. This contradiction led to the development of the concept of sub-imperialism by Marini and his vision of the political situation in Brazil.

To overcome the limitations of the domestic market, the military governments acted on two fronts: promoting public consumption and opening overseas markets (Marini, 1971). However, the expansion of consumption did not focus on increasing the purchasing power of the lower classes of society but rather on boosting sectors linked to luxury goods production. For overseas markets, the governments focused on those capable of absorbing Brazil's surplus goods, raising its economy's competitiveness, and ensuring conducive political conditions to access these markets (Marini, 1974).

However, far from being just a strategy to increase the export of products and capital or reproduction of the theory of imperialism, the concept of sub-imperialism by Marini aims to represent a more complex dimension that would lead Luce (2014) to characterize it as a 'superior stage of dependent capitalism'. From a strictly economic point of view, sub-imperialism is defined along two structural axes: (1) the effects of the new global division of labor, which led to the transfer of less advanced industries from major capitalist countries to peripheral countries and (2) the laws of the cycle of reproduction in dependent capitalism, which created problems for the realization of capital through the super-exploitation of labor and gave rise to extreme monopolization that favors the production of luxury goods as well as the progressive integration of national wealth into foreign capital (Marini, 1974).

Although the concept was not only endowed with economic dimensions, Marini has affirmed their preponderance through his depiction of Brazil as a sub-imperialist country. The sub-imperialist status of Brazil was a result of the integration of its production systems, which had evolved to become a monopoly on reaching the stage of financial capitalism. It constituted an intermediate point in the organic composition of capital at a global level (Marini, 1974). Consequently, the political dimension of sub-imperialism emerged through the internal contradictions within the reproduction cycle of capital. To increase local companies' competitiveness and expand their overseas markets, a sub-imperialist country would practice a policy of 'antagonistic cooperation' with the central imperialist core, such as the US (Marini, 1974).

Marini (1971) cited the Brazilian government's development of a national nuclear program as an example to illustrate the contradictions in the cooperation between sub-imperialist Brazil and the imperialist US. This determinant of antagonistic cooperation would appear as a *sine qua non* condition to qualify a dependent capitalist nation as a sub-imperialist country, as well as the globalization of its economy to address internal problems in capital realization. Therefore, a dependent country can practice an expansionist policy that is relatively autonomous of the objectives of the imperialist center, which would define—beyond the economic determinants of the export of products and capital—the phenomenon of sub-imperialism. It was for this reason that Marini had, at the time, designated Brazil as the only sub-imperialist country in Latin America, even though Argentina and Mexico had shared some of its characteristics (Marini, 1971). After all, sub-imperialism could take shape not only through exporting capital and manufactured products to weaker countries but also through strategic political moves to ensure its practice and domination over countries with less robust economies. The sum of economic (export of goods and capital) and political (strategies to achieve hegemony over weaker countries) conditions would lead to a sub-regional division of labor that could replicate, on a regional level, the asymmetries in the global division of labor:

> Not all the new economic sub-centers that reached an average organic composition and became exporters of manufactured goods and, to a lesser extent, of capital were able to impose a sub-regional division of labor to benefit their internal bourgeoisie. In Latin American capitalism, only Brazil became a sub-imperialist social formation.
> LUCE, 2014: 52

In the writings of Marini, sub-imperialism appears as a hierarchy of the world-system and as a development stage in dependent capitalism (Luce, 2014). The phenomenon that gives it an impetus is the contradictions of dependent economies with significant industrial development. This is because they are faced with the opposing needs to expand their domestic markets—as a condition for the realization of capital—and to flatten the purchasing power of their popular masses, which are subjugated by the predominance of super-exploitation of labor. This contradiction could have led to an intensification of the class struggle. In Brazil's case, it resulted in an alliance between sectors of foreign capital and the upper strata of the Brazilian bourgeoisie to curb social demands and reaffirm the super-exploitation of labor, even as its military dictatorship expanded its overseas markets and increased production of luxury goods to solve the impasse of capital realization.

Marini has used the example of political interference in Latin American countries' domestic affairs by Brazil's military dictatorship as proof of sub-imperialism. In his view, it would ensure the supremacy of Brazilian investments in those countries. With the progressive weakening of dictatorships in Latin American countries and the rise of re-democratization processes, the theme of sub-imperialism in Marini's writings has diminished. However, it is mentioned occasionally, and several authors have used it in contexts different from Marxism. In the twenty-first century, however, it has frequently appeared in analyzes of Brazil's foreign policy toward regional integration in South America.

3   Brazilian Sub-imperialism in the Twenty First Century

As the biggest market for Brazilian exports of manufactured goods, South America accounted for 18.4% of total Brazilian exports in 2010, and 84% of products exported to the region were manufactured goods (Couto, 2013). Since South America is a strategic market for Brazil, regional relations are a high priority for its foreign policy. During the Lula administration from 2003 to 2010, Brazil's foreign policy aimed to establish a dialog with its neighbors to develop regional statehood and diplomacy (Vaz and Nogara, 2020). Consequently, its goal was to improve the workings of the Southern Common Market (MERCOSUR) and shape the South American Community of Nations (CASA) and, later, the Union of South American Nations (UNASUR). The leading role played by Brazil in the region soon reignited the interest of researchers in the Marxist Theory of Dependency, who, once again, viewed Brazil's foreign policy toward the region as sub-imperialist.

Luce (2014) has maintained Marini's theoretical framework and attributed Brazilian deindustrialization to the predominance of a new pattern in the export of production specialization: the decline of the manufacturing industry and the rise of extractive industries, with raw materials making up a dynamic sector. Thus, agribusiness and sectors linked to mineral extraction would drive efforts to diversify its overseas market, thereby giving meaning to the foreign policy strategy of the Lula administration. In updating Marini's concept, Luce went even further than him by designating other rising regional powers as sub-imperialists. He even mentioned multilateral arrangements on South-South cooperation as sub-imperialist tools.

In his observations of the bilateral relations between Brazil and some countries in South America, Luce has highlighted the asymmetries generated by the globalization of Brazilian companies. In the case of Bolivia, he highlighted the disruptions caused by the investments of Petrobras in the country, which took advantage of the privatization of local companies to consolidate its interests in the production of gas and reap profits from its economic surpluses instead of using them to benefit the Bolivian population (Luce, 2007). He also highlighted the investments of Brazilian companies in Argentina, Ecuador, Paraguay, Peru, and Uruguay due to the dissociation between commodity production and the needs of the people in these countries. Hence, the priority given to Brazil's overseas search for surpluses would be based on the prevalence of the contradiction between production and the demands of the population in a dependent economy (Luce, 2014).

Luce (2011) has also discussed the reasons for regional integration. For him, promoting the Initiative for South American Regional Integration (IIRSA) and establishing CASA and UNASUR have supported Brazil's sub-imperialist strategy. In addition, IIRSA would intensify productive specialization in the region and aims to meet a global division of labor that goes against the development needs of a country. This would lead to a strengthening of the bourgeoisie while at the same time denying the workers essential living and working conditions (Luce, 2014).

Fontes (2013) has strengthened this view by portraying Brazilian international insertion as a capital-imperialist. For him, Brazil's capitalist development had led the country to join other capital-imperialist countries from around the world, even when it maintained a subordination facing the more developed nations such as the US. The export of Brazilian capital and goods and the globalization of local companies are also proof of the supposedly Brazilian hegemonistic predatory behavior, which has turned capital-imperialist; even Canada is included as a victim of these policies (Fontes, 2013).

However, Zibechi (2013) indicated a need to update Marini's concept to ensure that it is compatible with Brazil's international insertion in the twenty-first century. According to him, the current ruling elites in Brazil have expanded their room for political maneuvers. They have colluded with the military and the bourgeoisie to establish a powerful strategy capable of elevating the country to the ranks of a superpower. In this strategy, Brazil's neighbors in South America are seen as its backyard, with relations remaining extremely asymmetrical. He suggested that the concept of imperialism, rather than sub-imperialism, would better describe Brazil's actions.

To support his thesis, Zibechi has produced an extensive and exhaustive survey on the process of capital export and globalization of Brazilian companies. The Brazilian elites held this strategy to build a new military and industrial complex inspired by the National Defense Strategy (END). In his analysis of real-life cases, Zibechi highlighted events such as the presence of the *Brasiguayos* in Paraguay, the behavior practiced by Brazil in its distribution of profits from the Itaipu hydroelectric plant to Paraguay, the ostensive influence of Petrobras and Brazilian farmers in Bolivia, the incisive insertion of Odebrecht and Petrobras in Ecuador, and the respective social and political conflicts that resulted from them. Consequently, Zibechi called on the countries and peoples of the region to halt the advance of Brazilian imperialism (Zibechi, 2013).

Although Zibechi's (2013) criticism is similar to the Marxist dependency theory, it is also opposed to the notion of economic development and the extractive practices that support it. This is also why his criticism was directed at Brazilian enterprises that did not have a significant impact on neighboring countries, such as Belo Monte, as it was aimed at the entire model of exploitation of natural resources from around the world. Although it is distinct from the ideas of Marini and other authors linked to the Marxist Theory of Dependency, this environmentalist or post-colonial approach echoes the main arguments of the Marxist Theory of Dependency, which have also attacked the IIRSA projects in the same way.

López and Lima (2016) have also identified sub-imperialist tendencies in the regional foreign policy of Brazil. They described the pattern of relations between Brazil and Bolivia as a flagrant example of meeting the multiple interests of the Brazilian bourgeoisie, such as using a neo-developmentalist project to establish its hegemony in the region. In the case of Paraguay, they also emphasized the alleged damage caused by the exploitation of the Itaipu hydroelectric plant to supply cheap energy to Brazil at the expense of the Paraguayans.

A feature of Brazil's foreign policy has been its support of regional integration. Carcanholo and Saludjian (2013) have highlighted the liberal profile of its economic features and its tendency to deepen productive specialization in South America, especially with progressive Chinese penetration into regional trade relations. For them, these relations would contribute to the technological impoverishment of exports from South American countries. In his analysis of IIRSA, Borón (2013) also endorsed their reading of the consolidation of productive specialization. However, he has designated it a caudate of American interests to revive the Free Trade Area of the Americas (FTAA).

Generally, not all authors have viewed Brazil's foreign policy under the Lula administration as sub-imperialist based on the concept by Ruy Mauro Marini and the Marxist dependency theory. For example, Fontes had called it capital-imperialist. Although Zibechi has used a part of Marini's theory, he has rejected extractivist development policies in his thesis and has instead aligned himself with Gudynas' (2012) criticism of neoextractivism.

These theories have demonstrated an understanding of the role that the globalization of local companies and the export of goods and capital in Brazil play in shaping its relations with countries in Latin America and Africa with less economic and political importance. The growing influence of Brazil on their economies is seen as part of its sub-imperialist, imperialist, or capital-imperialist strategy to wield political dominance over them. This could lead to a sub-regional division of labor which can create relations of power that are typical of the global capitalist system. In the following sections, these interpretations will be analyzed in light of the political and economic realities they aim to elucidate and questions their propositions.

4 Some Aspects of the Dependentist Thesis and Their Implications

After grasping the Leninist theory of imperialism, proponents of sub-imperialism found it useful for analyzing Brazil's foreign policy under the Lula administration. Drawing from a hierarchical perspective of the global system, which delineates major capitalist countries from dependent ones, these theorists sought out middle powers capable of proposing a sub-regional division of labor to align with their theory. In examining Brazil's leadership in formulating regional integration in South America, they utilized the concept to unveil what they perceived as opportunistic motives veiled beneath a facade of cooperation.

Revisiting the concept of sub-imperialism, we observe its affirmation of product and capital export due to a domestic market demand deficiency, stemming from the super-exploitation of labor, indicating an imbalance in the national production system. However, these conditions only partially result from a sub-imperialist policy if the country engages in antagonistic cooperation with major capitalist nations. Nevertheless, with autonomy over its foreign policy, it can assert the dominance of its investments in weaker nations that import its products and capital. As previously highlighted, other elements also align with this phenomenon, including the consolidation and monopolization of capital and the continual influx of imperialist foreign capital into the dependent economy of the sub-imperialist country itself. These elements fulfill the primary conditions for applying the concept of sub-imperialism and were utilized to analyze Brazilian international insertion at the outset of the twenty-first century.

Recognizing the constraints of the sub-imperialism concept in explaining Brazil's foreign policy in the twenty-first century, this chapter does not solely address the disparities between its application and the events of the period. It also aims to scrutinize any theoretical inconsistencies. While not a direct replica of imperialism as delineated by Lenin, sub-imperialism was conceived by Marini to address gaps in the Leninist approach, affirm its core tenets, and integrate specific concepts pertinent to so-called dependent capitalism. However, despite their foundation in the Leninist theory of imperialism, proponents of dependency theory have inverted some of its principal assertions:

> Contrary to the interpretation that ended up predominating in the approaches of the so-called Latin American dependency theory in the 1960s and 1970s, the concept of 'uneven development' formulated by Lenin did not point to the continuous deepening of asymmetries between the center and the periphery in the world capitalist economy – what

> Gunder Frank called 'the development of underdevelopment -, but the opposite: the structural tendency towards the erosion of the power of the dominant center in the face of the rise of new poles of greater economic dynamism in areas of later capitalist development in the center itself or on the periphery of the system.
>
> FERNANDES, 2017: 58

By reversing the understanding of uneven development, capital export and its consequences, proponents of dependency theory have utilized this phenomenon to elucidate the existence of a hierarchy among nations in the international system. In this view, countries with a greater capacity to export high-value goods and capital to peripheral countries constitute the imperialist center of the world economy. Meanwhile, middle powers capable of enforcing a sub-regional division of labor form the second group of dependent countries with a sub-imperialist status and engage in antagonistic cooperation with the imperialist center.

However, contrary to the claims of the dependentists, Lenin (2011) has pointed out the imperialist effect of unequal development as a reason for the tensions between countries, as capital tends to migrate from more advanced economies to peripheral nations. This would guarantee higher profit levels and lead to the development of productive forces and capitalist production relations, as well as the creation of new social contradictions that could lead peripheral nations to aspire to join the imperialist center, thereby leading to wars for hegemony. Hence, major capitalist countries would be progressively consumed by the dominance of financial capital in their economies that—based on a rent-seeking and parasitic logic—profits from speculation and is sustained by surpluses generated by productive activities performed outside the imperialist center (Fernandes, 2017). Rather than complete stagnation in peripheral economies, the contradictions of imperialism—an elevated form of capitalism—would, instead, create opportunities for developing new dynamic polarities depending on how they were inserted into this intricate network of relations.

In an anti-dialectical perspective, dependency theorists argue that capital exports from countries in the imperialist center solely fuel underdevelopment in peripheral countries, without considering the effect of sharpening contradictions resulting from the development of productive forces and capitalist relations of production. Politically, Marini and his adherents have consistently advocated for mass mobilization to initiate a revolution as the primary alternative to addressing national issues. They recognize that the overexploitation of labor sustains capitalist development in peripheral countries, leading to underconsumption—a crucial element that, despite a contracting market, ensures profits for a national bourgeoisie subservient to the interests of global capitalism. A social revolution is deemed the sole means to break this cycle, as the bourgeoisie would never enact policies that enhance labor remuneration or agrarian reforms that challenge the status quo. Instead, a social revolution led by popular forces against the national and global bourgeoisie is perceived as the only viable solution. On the brink of military coups in Brazil and Chile in 1964 and 1973, Marini's political groups in both countries—ORM–POLOP and MIR, respectively—attacked the formation of alliances between leftists with centrist and bourgeois sectors, such as the Social Democratic Party (PSD) and Christian Democracy, that were part of João Goulart and Salvador Allende coalitions. They advocated for an immediate severance of ties with these sectors, thereby inadvertently aiding the success of the subversive strategies employed by their opponents:Parte superior do formulário

> The radicalization, fueled by militants from the MIR, the left wing of the PS, and other radical factions—chanting slogans like 'crear, crear, poder popular' and 'trabajadores al poder'—precipitated a situation in Chile akin to the events leading to General Francisco Franco's uprising against the republican government in Spain in 1936. They acted similarly to the militants of the Spanish Socialist Workers Party (PSOE), who called for the formation of a proletarian government and a people's army, waving red flags and displaying portraits of Lenin, Stalin, and Francisco Largo Caballero. They envisioned Madrid as if it were Petrograd on the eve of the Bolshevik insurrection in 1917. However, neither in Spain in 1936 nor in Chile in 1973 did the army disintegrate as it had in Russia, where demoralized and exhausted troops, defeated in the war against Germany, mutinied and ultimately joined and supported the revolution led by Vladimir Lenin and Leon Trotsky. Simultaneously, the accelerated process of expropriations, occupations, requisitions, and interventions, affecting both industrial companies and agricultural establishments, contributed to the disorganization of the economy, decreased productivity, and exacerbated shortages and inflation. Since the workers were not trained to administer companies and manage the problems generated by the abrupt nationalization of several productive sectors, this situation favored the application of the formula for chaos, implemented by the CIA. This occurred amid general strikes and terrorist attacks that the CIA encouraged and financed, while the psychological war, reviving the specter of communism, increasingly pushed the middle classes into opposition, along with the officialdom of the armed forces.
>
> BANDEIRA, 2008: 592

In March 1964, Cabo Anselmo—a CIA agent who had infiltrated leftist movements in Brazil (Almeida 2010)—led a revolt by sailors advocating for radical reforms. Such action, reminiscent of tactics used by the labor movement in the Bolshevik Revolution, had a significant impact on national public opinion, affecting the government's strategy of conciliation with centrist sectors of parliament and loyalists within the Armed Forces (Bandeira, 2010). Similarly, in Chile, the centrist Christian Democrats wielded influence over parliament and high-ranking military officials. The CIA's strategy aimed to radicalize the left wing to prevent centrist sectors in parliament and the military from supporting the government.

In addition to the political strategies employed by Marxist movements and parties, the dependentist paradigm has also influenced the analysis of international insertion by Latin American countries. Observations of the structures governing asymmetrical relations in the global system have elucidated the mechanisms and dynamics contributing to the ascent and stagnation of various nations within the system. As we delve deeper, the trajectory of this theory unfortunately ended up bolstering certain contentions within the field that sought to foster antagonism.

5 Foreign Policy and Peripheral Development

As previously demonstrated, Brazilian products with higher added value are primarily exported to countries in South America. However, a significant disparity exists between the importance of these markets for Brazilian products and their consideration as part of a sub-imperialist policy or as an obstacle to the development of neighboring economies. In fact, neighboring countries' criticisms of Brazil stem much more from its reluctance to bear the costs of its regional leadership (i.e., to contribute more investments to regional cooperation projects) than from any alleged undue interference in the politics or economies of other countries (Malamud, 2011). To address this criticism, Brazil bolstered infrastructure integration in South America through its National Bank for Economic and Social Development (BNDES)[4], given its consistent annual trade surpluses with every country in South America except Bolivia (Couto, 2013).

---

4 For further details, see Bugiato (2017).

Some simplified arguments reveal their limitations when attempting to explain nations' behaviors and leadership regarding the asymmetries in the global division of labor. If the international division of labor is perceived as static, what other factors could elucidate the cyclical rise and fall of global and regional powers?

Between the 1960s and the 1980s, the organization of a sub-regional labor division that orbited around the Japanese economy had served as a springboard for developing countries in Asia, such as communist China and the Four Asian Tigers (Hong Kong, Singapore, South Korea, and Taiwan). They had projects that claimed assertive international insertion. The Four Asian Tigers' capitalist state was based on dictatorial political regimes that planned essential aspects of the economy and actively intervened by indirectly nationalizing or controlling several sectors, especially the financial sector (Visentini, 2012). Export revenue was used to promote industrialization, and protectionist measures were implemented to protect the domestic market and avoid losing foreign exchange. The state, associated with private companies, invested massively in technology and labor force training. Companies were also organized into business conglomerates with a solid oligopolistic character in strategic sectors of the economy, which are called chaebols in South Korea. At its height, the right-wing governments in Seoul and Taipei carried out radical agrarian reforms to modernize agriculture and accumulate capital which contained elements borrowed from the policies of their communist rivals (Visentini, 2012). After Japan embarked on the Third Industrial Revolution by concentrating its production in the computer, automotive, robotics, and high-technology sectors, other Asian economies also reaped absolute gains in their development projects:

> The Asian Tigers, both by their actions and as a result of the new conjuncture, developed the second step of the former Japanese way of development, with steel, naval production, automobiles, engines, electric electrical, and other technological goods. China, in turn, joined this movement, receiving Japanese and Western investments and industrial plants. It played an economic role similar to the Asian Tigers, exploiting their comparative advantages and competing in some fields. The difference was that China had military power, territorial, population size, and political autonomy (including its entry into the UNSC), getting more international relevance than the Asian Tigers.
>
> VISENTINI, 2012: 65

Today, Asian economies are gravitating toward the Chinese economy, a role reminiscent of the position held by the Japanese economy in the region several decades ago (Brautigam, 2020; Pautasso et al., 2019, 2020). While the exports of most Asian economies consist of products with lower technological content compared to those exported by China, this structure enables them to generate surpluses that, when utilized coherently within their national development strategies, could potentially alter their trade relations in the future (Pautasso et al., 2020). Similar dynamics of asymmetry can be observed in the export patterns of South American countries, including the relationship between Brazil and China:

> It is also worth noting that deindustrialization cannot be reduced to faces of the same coin: the growth of exports of minerals and agricultural products to meet Chinese demand in no way hurts the core of the concept; it could be seen as an opportunity and not as a threat if it were inserted into a development project or strategy. The hegemony of the primary sector in the exports, thus, does not necessarily mean deindustrialization, even because Brazil has a robust domestic market, and the foreign surplus generated by the export of commodities could, in an eventual project, become a relevant variable to leverage the growth of high-tech sectors or more equitable income distribution.
> FONSECA, 2015: 50

This brief description of Asian economic development highlights the contradictions in the argument that an eventual sub-regional division of labor in South America could reaffirm relations of dominance. If the development projects of countries are always determined by the asymmetric economic ties in which they are inserted, there would be no basis for changes in disputes in the global system. After all, there would be no room for politics, strategy, and planning to direct economic forces. Thus, a process that can lead to a reversal in the relations between Brazil and China would be inexplicable. In the 1980s, the Chinese sold oil to Brazil and bought manufactured products with higher technological content from Brazil. By using the asymmetries in trade and investment relations between nations to depict their standings in the global system, the dependency theory ossifies the hierarchical status quo of the international order by amplifying the laws of reproduction of capital in the imperialist center and peripheral nations.

Since every description of sub-imperialism by Marini has focused on the reasons that contributed to the realization of capital beyond national borders, he has paid little attention to the relationship between the so-called sub-imperialist countries and those that are immersed in the sub-regional division of labor. When he did so, he alluded to the interventions by the military government in Brazil in the domestic politics of neighboring countries, which were guided by ideologies and alignment with US interests to combat communism and the leftist movement during the Cold War.

However, in the twenty-first century, the relations established by Brazil with its strategic neighbors are different from the interventions taken by its military dictatorship previously. In their case studies, the dependentists cited the example of the globalization of Brazilian companies and their defense by the government as irrefutable proof of the existence of sub-imperialism in Brazil. For instance, just as Brazil was hesitant to relinquish Petrobras assets acquired in Bolivia, Bolivia would likewise resist any disruption to the operations of GasBol.In the dependentist critiques, Brazil was the only sub-imperialist country in South America. However, it is worth noting that toward the end of the Lula administration, Brazil did not make it to the list of the five most prominent foreign investors in any country except Uruguay.[5] Cited by dependentist literature as one of the victims of Brazilian sub-imperialism, Bolivia had received more direct investments from Colombia than from Brazil (Couto, 2013). Likewise, its claim that Brazil's foreign policy was influenced by the eager desires of the bourgeoisie to control South American markets has no basis in reality. It was the state that had awarded incentives to the national bourgeoisie to strengthen its investments in neighboring countries:

> Private enterprise does not follow the prioritization of the diplomatic agenda. The breath and the business stakes go beyond the political choices of the State. Despite being an explicit priority of Brazilian diplomacy, South America does not exert the same power of attraction to national economic agents, who do not seem to faithfully follow state induction or orientation in the molds designed by the Logistical State. (…) The expansion of exports to the region, which follows the pace of the increase in Brazilian sales to the world as a whole – since South America

---

5 According to ECLAC data, between 1999 and 2009, Brazil was the country with the highest volume of direct overseas investment in South America. However, Brazil was not part of the top five countries with the most investments in South America. Uruguay was the only country in which Brazil ranked as one of its five most prominent investors. Chile, in turn, appeared as one of the five largest investors in Argentina and Peru, which are its preferred countries for investments. Meanwhile, Colombia was listed as one of the largest investors in Bolivia and Venezuela in the 2000s (Couto, 2013).

does not increase its share in the country's exports – is not offset by the importing mood or the flow of foreign investment out of the country.

COUTO, 2013: 200

Berringer (2013) pointed out that Brazil's foreign policy under the PT government had led to the rise of the bourgeoisie within the ruling power bloc in the country. Even then, there were disagreements over some of the policy decisions that were made as they did not favor the interests of the bourgeoisie. As for South America, although the government had received support for much of its effort to strengthen regional integration, it was, however, confronted with questions on issues such as Venezuela's entry into MERCOSUR, the Petrobras imbroglio in Bolivia, and the revision of the Itaipu Treaty with Paraguay (Berringer, 2017).

However, the analyzes of Couto (2013) emphasized that these differences failed to address the real issues and that the trade and investment priorities of the national bourgeoisie were on scenarios other than South America. Hence, the country's long-term national policy contributed to the significant presence of Brazilian economic agents in its neighboring countries. With the current decline in Brazil's international insertion, it has become even more challenging to attribute Brazil's diplomacy to a consideration of the economic interests of the national bourgeoisie:

> The application of the sub-imperialism thesis faces substantial obstacles, such as the irrelevance of FDI supported by the state in the set of investments abroad, the absence of an internationalization support policy during most of the expansion cycles of Brazilian companies abroad, dismantling of the current destruction of institutional arrangements (BNDES closed all offices abroad and halted all disbursements of Finem internationalization and Exim for works in other countries) created to stimulate internationalization, the relative loss of importance of Brazil in FDI flows in Latin America and also the more significant percentage expansion of Chile and Colombia on this topic when compared with Brazil.
>
> SANTOS, 2018: 133

In light of these contradictions, several unanswered questions persist. As Marini proposed, a socialist revolution could potentially accelerate industrialization and development in a country like Brazil. Would this not create a situation in which Brazil would tend to export capital and higher-value-added products to markets with lower productive capacity? Consequently, would socialist Brazil still be perceived as sub-imperialist?

The existence of asymmetries in the international order is not exclusive to the capitalist mode of production. This is because asymmetrical relations shape the market itself. They would not cease to exist even if a socialist revolution did take place in Brazil, just as the former USSR did not cease to interact with the global market after the Bolshevik Revolution in 1917. If industrialization and income redistribution were merely an expression of rulers' political and ideological will, rationing would have never taken place in socialist countries, and neither would Lenin have resorted to the New Economy Policy to strengthen the USSR in the years following the 1917 revolution. The mistakes made by the dependentists between the market and capitalism, as well as asymmetries and domination, have created confusion that makes it challenging to elucidate the rise and decline of powerful nations in the vast international chessboard. Consequently, in line with Trotskyist traditions, they tend to resort to subterfuges—such as the betrayal of ideals (Losurdo, 2003)—to analyze the reality of socialist countries that adopt heterodox strategies, which does not aid in a metaphysical understanding of socialism.

When Brazil emphasizes the need to deepen South American integration, this need is aligned with its interests in safeguarding its national security and guaranteeing export markets for its products and capital. When facing this situation, the political calculation of neighboring countries is not made with any other procedure than that of Brazil, with adaptations to their respective realities. The asymmetry of political and economic relations is not a static variable. Hence, not only Brazil's proposals for South American integration but also the Bolivarian Alliance for the Peoples of Our America (ALBA) and the Pacific Alliance have grown during this period.

Rather than posing a problem, Brazil's greater political and economic capacities have been leveraged by neighboring countries to their advantage, as evidenced by Uruguay and Paraguay's success in establishing Convergence Fund of the Southern Common Market (FOCEM), Paraguay's successful renegotiation of the Itaipu hydroelectric plant terms, and the Petrobras conflict in Bolivia (Nogara, 2022).

Brazil's relations with Paraguay and Bolivia over the management of the Itaipu hydroelectric plant and Gasbol, respectively, could be characterized as interdependency rather than subservience to one country by another. The Brazilian economy is also dependent on neighboring countries to guarantee electricity and gas, which can be perceived in the stalled negotiations with Paraguay over the price of energy (Ricupero, 2017). Furthermore, Brazilian behavior diverges completely from that associated with the major imperialist powers, as imperialism "presupposes the capacity to use military force to compete for markets," and Brazil "does not utilize these to aid its economic expansion" (Bugiato and Berringer, 2012: 39). The portrayal of a sub-imperialist or imperialist Brazil, dominating its smaller and defenseless neighbors, does not accurately reflect reality. It is a depiction that bears little resemblance to the complexities of the decision-making processes involved in international politics.

The discussion of this concept by academia and militant circles has shaped the theoretical and political debate on its themes. Theoretically, by proposing an update of Marxist and Leninist thought for an understanding of international relations, the Marxist Theory of Dependency and the concept of sub-imperialism have sustained deterministic structuralism by inverting the meaning of critical concepts—such as unequal development—and affecting the ability of Marxists to align their perspectives with current events in international relations. Politically, they have encouraged leftist movements in peripheral countries to adopt antagonistic orientations to the class alliances, leading them to prefer political isolation[6] and to distance themselves from debates on national development since they are against state policies that raise the profile of their countries on the global stage.

As highlighted by Costa (2008), the history of the twentieth century in countries such as Germany, Japan, the US, and the USSR was marked by the success of state interventionism and government planning as engines of development, which presupposed the control of economic systems by political forces. By proposing a systemic conceptual framework that conditions economic development to the inevitability of a socialist revolution, the dependentists invert the meaning of uneven development and defend that nothing beyond the socialist revolution could help peripheral countries to change the static structure of the international system.

The confusion created by the dependentists has prevented Marxist dependency theory from explaining issues related to the great dispute currently taking place at the global level: the intention by great Western powers to reclaim their global political influence and weaken the recent rise of peripheral

---

6 Reflecting on the criticism by leftist movements of the alliances forged by class alliances, the Argentine Marxist historian Rodolfo Puiggrós (1986: 131) argued decades ago against the political isolation adopted by these groups: "In our nations, the national anti-imperialist revolution compels social classes with divergent interests to unite, some aiming for capitalism and others pursuing socialism, and it is within this multi-class movement that the working class must assert its leadership. By disengaging from broader class alliances (or worse, opposing them), they consign themselves to isolation and ineffectiveness."

countries (Visentini, 2019). Instead, the dependency theory tends to focus on the designation of new regional power blocs as part of a cycle to strengthen imperialism by the central powers. Thus, there is little debate within this political-ideological strand on how Brazil could position itself as an interested third party in the tremendous systemic dispute between China and the US (Pautasso and Nogara, 2023), which is perhaps one of the most relevant issues that can define Brazil's foreign policy. While adopting a revisionist and assertive stance in the international system may be crucial for a nation's ascent, it does not inherently ensure the ongoing sustainability of its development:

> When analyzing historical contexts, it becomes evident that maintaining a stance of non-involvement in mediation often proves advantageous and strategically sound. Such a position aligns with that of an interested third party, offering the freedom to navigate within the dialectic established between the center and periphery, culture and barbarism. The role of an interested third party allows for a nuanced approach, neither assuming the central position nor relegating to the periphery, not characterized by cultural refinement but also not labeled as barbaric. This apparent neutrality, positioning oneself as a third pole, mitigates the impact of direct confrontation, potentially positioning this party as an alternative sought by other actors. In the trajectory of civilization, while contestation is deemed necessary, it remains insufficient. Having an engaged participant who directly assumes the role of the primary contender is often preferable.
> COSTA, 2008: 427

Instead of clarifying the potential variations in the ascent and decline of great and middle powers, the Marxist dependency theory has reinforced a metaphysical conception of the structures of the global order. From a conservative standpoint, José Guilherme Merquior (cited by Hage, 2013) has characterized the dependency theory as a byproduct of cultural underdevelopment in Latin America, an overstated argument that adds little to its accurate characterization. Nevertheless, there is no doubt that the theory contains elements that reaffirm the existing hierarchical *status quo*, even though it aims to subvert the global order. This emphasis on the inevitability of hindrances to development by peripheral nations and a disdain for alternative power structures in the international system are notable features of the theory.

6 Conclusion

In this chapter, we have examined the origins of the concept of sub-imperialism in the dependency theory and how it was rescued from contemporary analyzes of Brazil's foreign policy. In particular, a discrepancy was observed in applying the concept in the real world, even though most of the authors cited in the second half of this chapter had claimed a continuity in the central assumptions of the Marxist Theory of Dependency. Consequently, this analysis has revealed differences in the theoretical beliefs of dependentists over the years. Whereas early followers of the dependency theory had drawn their political conclusions from a complex conceptual framework with clear limitations, younger followers have taken the opposite path by viewing Brazilian sub-imperialism as wishful thinking to overcome their disillusionment with the PT governments. However, it is undeniable that both groups remained skeptical of other means—other than a socialist revolution—to develop peripheral societies and forge political alliances by leftist parties and organizations.

In the second half of this chapter, the discussion of the concept was widened to include the debate on imperialism and unequal development by Marxist theories, especially Leninist theory, and the rise of peripheral countries in the international system in the twentieth and twenty-first centuries. It highlights the limitations of the concept, which includes negating and contradicting the fundamental beliefs in the Leninist theory of imperialism that it claims to uphold. It also questions the concept's usefulness in understanding worldwide nations' rise, decline, and stagnation. Finally, it outlines the political implications of adopting the dependency theory.

In Brazil, dependency theories were born through the harsh leftist criticism of developmentalist and communist ideals strategies. The adherence of the military regime to the developmentalist ideology—albeit in a twisted way, by depriving it of its social-reformist dimension and mixing it with the doctrines of national security typical of the Cold War—had accentuated the rise of these revisionist doctrines in the leftist movement. Thus, its liberal wing, with exponents such as Fernando Henrique Cardoso, and its Marxist wing, with Marini, aligned themselves in their criticism of developmentalism and national-developmentalism. They emphasized the limits of the strategies for peripheral development and the worker's alliance with the national bourgeoisie in Brazil. Subsequently, both wings took divergent paths. The liberal wing progressively adhered to the defense of neoliberal initiatives and the subordinate integration of Brazil into the international system. The Marxist wing, however, radicalized its demands for a socialist revolution without any mediation with the centrist sectors or the national bourgeoisie.

The liberal dependentists implemented a part of their political program after their primary mentor, Fernando Henrique Cardoso, was elected President of Brazil. However, this contributed to the dilapidation of the national patrimony inherited from the developmentalist era through the progress and mistakes that were made between the 1930 Revolution and the 1980s. The Marxist dependentists also exercised their influence more in the theoretical and academic domains than in politics. Nevertheless, they are still far from attaining the scale of political achievements that their original opponents—orthodox communists, "populists," and authoritarian nationalists—have accomplished. Even Theotônio dos Santos and Vânia Bambirra, prominent leaders within the Marxist dependency theory framework, disregarded certain differences emphasized during the pre-1964 period against the nationalist "populists" and opted to assist Leonel Brizola in forming the Democratic Labor Party (PDT).

However, contrary to its founders, the new generation of Marxist dependency theorists chooses to revive outdated notions such as Brazilian sub-imperialism and a strategy of political isolation and sectarianism, which ends up keeping them away from the primary leftist decision-makers in the country. Instead, they have aligned themselves with the liberal and reactionary critics against developing national projects. Far from contributing to the revolution, they deny the achievements and progress made by the former developmentalist strategies and focus their efforts on obstructing and countering measures that favor the resumption of development in peripheral societies.

References

Almeida AS (2010) *Todo o leme a bombordo: marinheiro e ditadura civil-militar no Brasil, da rebelião de 1964 à anistia*. Dissertação, Niterói, UFF.

Bandeira M (2010) *O governo João Goulart: as lutas sociais no Brasil (1961–1964)*. São Paulo: Editora UNESP.

Bandeira M (2008) *Fórmula para o caos: a derrubada de Salvador Allende (1970–1973)*. Rio de Janeiro: Civilização Brasileira.

Berringer T (2017) A burguesia interna brasileira e a integração regional da América do Sul (1991–2016). *Oikos* 16 (1): 15–29.

Berringer T (2013) A tese do sub-imperialismo em questão. *Crítica Marxista* 36: 115–127, 2013.

Brautigam D (2020) A critical look at Chinese 'debt-trap diplomacy': The rise of a meme. *Area Development and Policy* 5(1): 1–14.

Borón A (2013) *América Latina en la geopolítica del imperialismo*. Buenos Aires: Ediciones Luxemburg.

Bresser-Pereira L (2010) As três interpretações da dependência. *Perspectivas* 38: 17–48.

Bugiato C (2017) A importância do BNDES na política externa do governo Lula. *Cadernos do Desenvolvimento* 12 (21): 43–69.

Bugiato C and Berringer T (2012) Um debate sobre o Estado logístico, subimperialismo e imperialismo brasileiro. *Em Debate* 7: 28–44.

Carcanholo M (2013) O atual resgate crítico da teoria marxista da dependência. *Trabalho, Educação e Saúde* 11 (1): 191–205.

Carcanholo M and Saludjian A (2013) Integración latinoamericana, dependencia de China y sub-imperialismo brasileño en América Latina. *Mundo Siglo XXI* 29 (8): 43–62.

Costa D (2008) *Fundamentos para o estudo da estratégia nacional*. Rio de Janeiro: Paz e Terra.

Couto L (2013) Relações Brasil-América do Sul: a construção inacabada de parceria com o entorno estratégico. In: Lessa A and Altemani H (eds.) *Parcerias estratégicas do Brasil: os significados e as experiências tradicionais*. Belo Horizonte: Fino Traço.

Dos Santos T (2000) *A teoria da dependência: um balanço histórico e teórico*. Rio de Janeiro: Civilização Brasileira.

Dos Santos T (2007) Subdesarrollo y dependencia. In: Lowy M (2007) *El Marxismo en América Latina*. Santiago: LOM Ediciones.

Fernandes L (2017) *A revolução bipolar: a gênese e derrocada do socialismo soviético*. São Paulo: Anita Garibaldi.

Fernandes L (2000) *O enigma do socialismo real: um balanço crítico das principais teorias marxistas e ocidentais*. Rio de Janeiro: Mauad.

Fonseca P (2015) Desenvolvimentismo: a construção do conceito. *IPEA – Texto para discussão* 2.103: 1–67.

Fontes V (2013). A incorporação subalterna brasileira ao capital-imperialismo. *Crítica Marxista* 36: 103–113.

Gudynas E (2012) O novo extrativismo progressista na América do Sul: teses sobre um velho problema sob novas expressões. In: Léna P and Do Nascimento E (eds.) *Enfrentando os limites do crescimento: sustentabilidade, decrescimento e prosperidade*. Rio de Janeiro: Garamond.

Hage J (2013) A teoria da dependência: uma contribuição aos estudos de relações internacionais. *Revista Política Hoje* 22 (1): 106–136, 2013.

Lenin V (2011) *O imperialismo: etapa superior do capitalismo*. Campinas (SP): Navegando.

López F and Lima R (2016) Ruy Mauro Marini y el sub-imperialismo brasileño en Bolivia y Paraguay en el siglo XXI. *Cadernos Cemarx* 9: 69–88.

Losurdo D (2003) History of the Communist Movement: Failure, Betrayal, or Learning Process? *Nature, Society and Thought* 16 (1): 33–124.

Luce M (2011) *A teoria do sub-imperialismo em Ruy Mauro Marini:* contradições do capitalismo dependente e a questão do padrão de reprodução do capital. Rio Grande do Sul: Universidade Federal do Rio Grande do Sul.

Luce M (2014) O sub-imperialismo, etapa superior do capitalismo dependente. *Tensões Mundiais* 10 (18): 46–65.

Luce M (2007) O sub-imperialismo brasileiro revisitado: a política de integração regional do governo Lula (2003-2007). Unpublished master's thesis, Universidade Federal do Rio Grande do Sul, Porto Alegre.

Marini R (2017) A dialética da dependência. *Germinal: Marxismo e educação em debate* 9 (3): 325–356.

Marini R (1971) El sub-imperialismo brasileño. *Centro de Estudios Socio-Económicos (CESO)*: 1–11.

Marini R (1965) Eje militar Brasil-Argentina y sub-imperialismo. *Arauco* 71: 19–25.

Marini R (1974) *Subdesarrollo y revolución*. Buenos Aires: Siglo XXI Editores.

Nogara T (2022) South American regionalism between Brazil and Venezuela: Divergences during the Lula and Hugo Chávez administrations. *Contexto Internacional* 44 (3): 1–21.

Oliveira H (2012) *Brasil e China*: cooperação sul-sul e parceria estratégica. Belo Horizonte: Fino Traço.

Pautasso D, Nogara T, Colório A and Wobeto V (2019) O cerco multidimensional à Teerã e a aproximação sino-iraniana. *Tensões Mundiais* 15 (29): 165–182.

Pautasso D, Nogara T and Doria G (2020) A Nova Rota da Seda e o projeto chinês de globalização. *Insight Inteligência* 90: 106–115.

Pautasso D, Nogara T, Ribeiro E (2020) A Nova Rota da Seda e as relações sino-indianas: o desafio do colar de pérolas. *Mural Internacional* 11: e50594.

Pautasso D and Nogara T (2023) The Belt and Road Initiative's Security Challenges. In: Duarte PAB, Leandro FJBS and Galán EM (org.). *The Palgrave Handbook of Globalization with Chinese Characteristics*. Palgrave Macmillan Singapore.

Puiggrós R (1986) *Historia crítica de los partidos políticos argentinos II: las izquierdas y el problema nacional*. Buenos Aires: Hyspamérica Ediciones Argentinas.

Ricupero R (2017) *A diplomacia na construção do Brasil, 1750–2016*. Rio de Janeiro: Versal.

Santos L (2018) BNDES: internacionalização de empresas e o sub-imperialismo brasileiro. *Geousp – Espaço e Tempo (Online)* 22 (1): 115–137.

Vaz A and Nogara T (2020) Evolución y ejes de la política exterior brasileña contemporánea. *Anuario Internacional CIDOB*: 248–256.

Visentini P (2012) *As relações diplomáticas da Ásia:* articulações regionais e afirmação mundial (uma perspectiva brasileira). Belo Horizonte: Fino Traço.

Visentini P (2015) *O caótico século XXI*. Rio de Janeiro: Alta Books.

Visentini P (2019) Axes of World Power in the 21st Century: An Analytical Proposal. *AUSTRAL: Brazilian Journal of Strategy & International Relations* 8 (15).

Zibechi R (2013) *Brasil potencia: entre la integración regional y un nuevo imperialismo.* Lima: Programa Democracia y Transformación Global.

Index

accumulation 6, 8, 20, 61, 65, 68, 111, 114, 116, 118, 144, 145, 153, 156, 157, 158, 159, 160, 161, 161n6, 162, 162n8, 163, 164, 165, 167, 167n11, 168, 175, 184n15, 185, 188, 191, 195, 205, 216, 219n13, 220, 221, 228, 248, 251, 254
Africa 55, 69, 144, 220, 223, 261, 262, 277, 286
America 37, 38, 63, 64, 65, 68, 69, 73, 121, 122, 123, 126, 134, 203, 211, 220, 223, 228, 237, 237n3, 238, 239, 240, 241, 242n7, 242n8, 243n10, 244, 248, 254, 258, 260, 261, 262, 276, 279, 280, 281, 282, 283, 284, 285, 286, 292, 293, 293n5, 294, 295
Amin, Samir 36, 60, 61, 61n8, 69, 70, 73, 144
anarchy 12, 24, 78, 89, 90, 97, 100n34, 180, 214, 215, 224
Anderson, Perry 103, 104, 150, 154, 191
Angola 37
Arendt, Hannah 36, 44, 99, 99n32, 102
Aron, Raymond 35
Arrighi, Giovanni 36, 42, 44, 62, 73, 145, 167
Asia 60, 64, 144, 149, 164, 202, 223, 228, 261, 291
Austria 93

Baran, Paul 59, 60, 73, 144, 196n6, 260
bourgeois 5, 21, 37, 38, 52, 55, 56, 76, 76n4, 84, 87, 89, 91n22, 92n24, 105, 106, 108, 108n4, 108n5, 108n6, 109, 110, 111, 115, 116n14, 117, 123, 159, 175, 178n10, 187, 188n19, 203, 206, 209, 212, 224, 225, 251, 252n18, 278, 279
bourgeoisie 51, 56, 87n15, 91, 93, 124, 125, 179, 195, 196, 202, 204, 205, 206, 209, 216, 220, 223, 225, 226, 239, 240, 248, 251, 252n18, 278, 279, 281, 283, 285, 286, 293, 294, 298
Brazil 37, 69, 73, 124, 126, 142, 142n2, 146, 149, 224, 228, 237, 237n4, 239, 240, 242n6, 243n11, 247n14, 247n15, 258, 259, 278, 279, 280, 281, 282, 283, 284, 285, 286, 292, 293, 293n5, 294, 295, 297, 298, 299
Bukharin, Nikholai 36, 50, 52, 53, 144, 186, 210, 213, 214, 215, 217, 230, 231, 245, 246n12, 254
Bulgaria 40

Buzan, Barry 44, 146, 154

Cabral, Amílcar 38
capital 50, 51, 53, 54, 55, 56, 57, 58, 59, 61, 65, 67, 68, 69, 90n20, 124, 126, 144, 145, 146, 150, 152, 154, 157, 158, 159, 160, 161, 161n7, 162, 162n8, 163, 164, 165, 167n12, 168, 175, 177n8, 179, 179n12, 180, 182, 187, 190, 192, 194, 196, 197, 198, 199, 200, 201, 202, 203, 204, 205, 206, 207n10, 208, 209, 210, 212, 213, 214, 215, 216, 216n9, 217, 219, 220, 221, 222, 223, 224, 225, 226, 227, 230, 232, 233, 238, 240, 243n10, 245, 248, 252, 253, 254, 255, 256, 260n4, 273, 275, 276, 280, 281, 282, 283, 285, 286, 288, 291, 292, 295, 300, 301
Capital 73, 74, 163, 169, 170, 179n12, 180n13, 181, 192, 193, 209n11, 214, 216n7, 225, 226, 231, 232, 249
capital accumulation VIII, 61, 66, 111, 113, 118, 162, 164, 201, 207n10, 212, 215, 221, 222, 224, 238, 253
capitalism VII, IX, X, 3, 5, 6, 7, 8, 9, 9n9, 10, 13, 22, 37, 39, 43, 51, 52, 53, 54, 55, 56, 57, 58, 59, 60, 61, 66, 70, 76, 80, 83, 86, 88, 89, 98, 101, 105, 111, 112, 113, 118, 119, 144, 152, 156, 157, 158, 159, 160, 160n5, 161, 162, 163, 164, 165, 166, 168, 173, 174, 175, 176, 177, 178, 178n10, 179, 179n11, 179n12, 181, 182, 183, 184n15, 185, 186, 186n17, 187, 187n18, 188, 188n19, 190, 191, 194, 196, 198, 199, 200, 204, 206, 207n10, 209n11, 211, 212, 213, 214, 215, 216, 217, 218n12, 219, 219n13, 220, 221, 222, 222n15, 223, 224, 224n17, 225, 227n20, 228, 230, 233, 238, 238n4, 239, 240, 242n7, 245, 246, 249, 253, 254, 268, 282, 283, 288, 295
capitalist 39, 40, 41, 42, 43, 51, 54, 56, 57, 58, 59, 61, 64, 66, 67, 68, 81, 85, 86, 90, 97, 144, 156, 157, 158, 159, 160, 161, 161n6, 162, 162n8, 163, 164, 165, 167n11, 168, 175, 175n4, 177, 177n8, 178, 178n10, 179, 179n12, 181, 182, 184, 184n15, 186, 187, 190, 191, 195, 199, 200, 201, 202, 203, 203n9, 204, 205, 206, 207n10, 208, 209n11, 211, 214, 214n4,

capitalist (cont.)
215, 216, 216n9, 217, 218n12, 219, 220, 221, 222, 223, 224, 225, 226, 227, 229n23, 231, 232, 233, 241, 242n8, 244, 248, 250, 252, 252n18, 259, 268, 269, 270, 271, 280, 281, 282, 285, 286, 287, 288, 291, 295

capitalist state 90, 108n4, 111, 190, 201, 203, 203n9, 207n10, 209n11, 221, 222, 252, 252n18, 291

capitalist states 252

Cardoso, Fernando Henrique 122n3, 237, 242, 243, 243n11, 244, 254, 255, 256, 259, 275, 298, 299

Carr, Edward 35, 79, 80, 80n7, 81, 83, 84, 84n10, 85, 86, 87, 88, 89n19, 90, 91, 92, 92n23, 93, 93n25, 94, 95, 98, 101, 102, 104, 177n7

Castro, Fidel 38

China 36, 37, 39, 42, 62, 64, 65, 66, 69, 73, 149, 150, 152, 153, 165, 229n22, 231, 291, 292, 297, 300, 301

class 50, 51, 52, 56, 61, 62, 66, 71, 86, 86n13, 87, 88, 89, 97, 98, 101, 123, 125, 128, 134, 146, 151, 153, 154, 159, 160, 162, 163, 164, 165, 166, 178n10, 180, 197, 200, 201, 205, 206, 209, 210, 219, 220, 223, 224, 227, 231, 232, 239, 241, 250, 251, 252, 252n18, 254, 258, 272, 283, 296, 296n6

class struggle 33, 61, 71, 86n13, 88, 90, 98, 105, 106, 107, 134, 146, 151, 153, 206, 210, 223, 224, 231, 250, 251, 252, 283

Clausewitz, Carl von 35

colonialism XV, 51, 66, 71, 144, 146, 150, 159, 160n5, 162n8, 180, 197, 222, 245

communism 26, 293

Communist Manifesto IX, 3, 5, 6, 7n5, 8, 8n7, 9, 109, 179n11, 225

Constructivism VII, 35

crise 74, 120, 155, 211

critical theory 178n10

Cuba 36, 39, 150, 199, 227, 260

Czechoslovakia 40

democracy 18, 41, 65, 67, 86, 89, 91n22, 103, 124, 128, 131, 132, 135n12, 137, 138, 139, 140, 147, 148, 149, 221, 222, 277, 281

dependence IX, 20, 36, 50, 55, 57, 67, 112, 115n13, 117, 119, 126, 149, 178, 188, 196, 197, 204, 206, 208, 209, 210, 237, 240, 243, 243n10, 244, 245, 246, 246n13, 248, 249, 250, 252, 253, 257, 258, 259, 260, 261, 264, 266, 267, 268, 272, 274, 277

dependency IX, XV, 9, 112n10, 112n9, 113, 118, 187, 196, 216n8, 237n1, 238, 238n4, 241, 242n7, 242n8, 243, 243n10, 245, 246, 248, 249, 250, 251, 252, 254, 279, 280, 281, 285, 286, 287, 292, 296, 298

dictatorship 41, 69

diplomacy 84, 86, 91, 198, 284, 293, 294

domination 34, 36, 55, 58, 62, 63, 67, 68, 71, 134n11, 142, 143, 144, 147, 151, 152, 154, 159, 162, 163, 175, 175n4, 176, 182, 188, 195, 196, 198, 201, 204, 208, 209, 216, 220, 224, 251, 252, 252n18, 253, 267, 274, 283, 295

empire 14, 15, 16, 16n3, 20, 21, 23, 25, 26, 28, 29, 30, 31, 32, 81, 87n16, 103, 112, 143, 145, 146, 147, 150, 162, 175, 195n5, 198, 207n10, 208, 211, 213, 218, 218n11, 220, 221, 223, 230, 233, 261, 267

Engels IX, 1, 5, 7, 8, 9n9, 13, 14, 15, 16, 17, 18, 18n4, 20, 21, 22n6, 25, 26, 27, 28, 29, 29n8, 31, 32, 33

Engels, Friedrich 36, 50, 84n10, 102, 178n10, 179, 179n11, 180n13, 181, 192, 203n9, 212, 233, 245

England 55, 56, 57, 60, 178n10

Espinosa 35

Ethiopia 37, 40

Europe 37, 40, 60, 63, 64, 65, 68, 69, 86, 87, 92, 149, 159, 178n10, 189, 197, 198, 199, 201, 202, 203, 204, 207n10, 208, 209, 210, 211, 217, 228, 229, 230, 232, 247, 263, 264n8, 272

exploitation 144, 147, 161n7, 162, 173, 178, 198, 205, 216, 220, 225, 226, 231, 250, 252, 253, 254, 260n4, 281, 282, 283, 286

fascism 105, 233, 243

Fichte, Johann G 36, 143

finance capital 11, 55, 114n12, 144, 165, 187, 214

financial 50, 54, 55, 56, 57, 58, 60, 61, 67, 70, 71, 72, 73, 76, 126, 159, 182, 187, 188, 205, 217, 219, 223, 224, 226, 228, 282, 288, 291

foreign capital 115, 115n13, 116, 117, 118, 163, 198, 204, 205, 206, 240, 282, 283

INDEX

foreign policy   XII, XVII, 17, 18, 19n5, 21, 22, 27, 43, 44, 63, 65, 110, 195, 196n6, 197, 198, 229, 260n3, 270n13, 280, 283, 284, 286, 293, 294, 297, 298
France   56, 60, 91n22, 135, 140, 184n15, 203n9, 229
Frank, Andre Gunder   144, 242, 242n8, 242n8, 255, 259, 275, 288
Fred Halliday   4, 119
Friedrich Engels   VII, 5, 15, 18, 33
Fukuyama, Francis   44

Germany   40, 52, 56, 60, 61, 84n11, 88n17, 91, 91n21, 91n22, 99, 100, 184n15, 261, 269, 296
global   39, 42, 43, 64, 65, 68, 71, 76, 101, 122, 142, 144, 145, 146, 148, 149, 151, 151n4, 152, 155, 163, 164, 165, 167, 179n12, 189, 191, 192, 193, 196, 201, 207n10, 210, 212, 218, 219, 220, 221, 223, 225, 225n18, 227n20, 230, 231, 233, 246, 267, 279, 280, 282, 283, 285, 286, 292, 295, 296
globalisation   213, 217, 219, 220, 221, 222, 225, 225n18, 227, 231
globalization   XII, 5, 8, 10, 13, 43, 59, 62, 70, 118, 142, 143, 145, 153, 165, 184, 188, 220, 225, 233, 267, 282, 284, 285, 286, 293
government   52, 55, 66, 70, 72, 88n17, 91n22, 124, 145, 150, 225, 227, 231, 247n15, 266, 279, 282, 293, 294, 296
Gramsci   XV, 13, 13n14, 111n8
Gramsci, Antonio   60n6, 60n7, 63, 63n9, 67, 68, 74, 129, 134, 136, 139, 151, 167n11, 203n9, 253, 270, 273, 275
Great Britain   147, 153
Greece   230
Guevara, Che   38, 261

Halliday, Fred   34, 36, 37, 39, 42, 43, 44, 76, 101, 103, 142, 154, 225, 232
Harvey   IX, 65, 69, 74, 145, 156, 157, 158, 159, 160, 160n5, 161, 161n6, 161n7, 162, 162n8, 163, 164, 165, 166, 166n10, 167, 167n11, 168, 169, 170, 183, 192, 213, 223, 232
Hegel   27
Hegel, Georg W F   36, 143, 160n5
hegemony   VII, 50, 58, 61, 62, 63, 64, 67, 68, 69, 70, 72, 73, 106, 110n7, 111n8, 113, 117, 124, 126, 127, 129, 130, 132, 134, 135n12, 138, 167, 167n11, 168, 189, 201, 206, 208, 217, 220, 228, 252n18, 269, 283, 286, 288, 292
Hilferding, Rudolf   36, 50, 53, 74, 144, 186, 213, 214, 214n4, 214n5, 214n6, 215, 216, 216n7, 216n9, 217, 219, 230, 231, 232
Historical Materialism   34, 36, 43, 49n2, 166n9, 169, 210, 231, 232, 233, 245, 246
Historical Sociology   42
Hobbes, Thomas   35, 135
Hobsbawm, Eric   37, 79, 80n6, 81, 103
Hobson, John A   36, 50, 53, 55, 74, 89, 90n20, 191, 216n10, 217n10, 245
Hume, David   35
Hungary   40, 87, 93

Idealism   35, 95, 96, 101, 104
ideology   9, 62, 87n15, 107, 124, 129, 147, 240, 298
imperialism   VIII, IX, XV, 7, 36, 38, 41, 49, 50, 51, 52, 53, 55, 56, 57, 58, 59, 60, 61, 62, 63, 64, 65, 66, 67, 68, 69, 70, 71, 72, 73, 83, 86, 88, 89, 90n20, 94, 102, 105, 106, 111, 113, 114, 115, 116, 116n14, 117n16, 118, 119, 142, 143, 144, 145, 146, 147, 148, 150, 151, 152, 153, 156, 157, 158, 160n5, 161, 162n8, 163, 164, 168, 173, 174, 175, 176, 178, 180, 182, 183, 183n14, 185, 185n16, 186n17, 187, 188, 189, 190, 191, 194, 195, 195n5, 196, 197, 198, 199, 201, 202, 203, 204, 205, 206, 207, 207n10, 208, 210, 211, 212, 213n3, 214, 214n6, 215, 216, 216n10, 217, 218, 219, 221, 222, 223, 223n16, 224, 225, 226, 229n23, 230, 231, 232, 233, 234, 242n8, 245, 246, 246n12, 248, 251, 257, 258, 259, 260, 260n4, 261, 267, 268, 269, 274, 275, 278, 279, 280, 281, 282, 283, 285, 288, 292, 293, 294, 296, 297, 298
India   150, 220
intellectuals   129, 186, 242, 258, 261, 264n8, 270, 272, 273, 274
interdependence   106, 244, 257, 258, 261, 262, 263, 264, 265, 266, 266n10, 267, 268, 269, 272, 274, 275
international   34, 34n2, 35, 36, 37, 38, 39, 40, 41, 42, 43, 49, 49n1, 50, 51, 52, 56, 58, 59, 61, 62, 63, 64, 65, 67, 68, 72, 73, 76, 76n1, 76n3, 77, 78, 79, 79n6, 80, 80n6, 82, 83, 84, 84n11, 85, 86, 86n13, 99, 88, 89, 90, 91, 92, 92n23, 94, 95, 99, 100, 101,

international (cont.)
102, 103, 104, 124, 142, 142*n*1, 143, 145, 146, 147, 148, 149, 150, 151, 152, 153, 156, 156*n*2, 156*n*3, 156*n*4, 157, 163, 164, 165, 166, 167, 168, 173, 173*n*2, 174, 175, 176, 176*n*7, 177, 178, 179, 179*n*12, 180, 182, 183, 188, 189, 190, 190*n*20, 191, 194*n*2, 194*n*3, 195, 197, 198, 199, 199*n*7, 200, 201, 202, 203, 205, 206, 207, 207*n*10, 208, 210, 212*n*3, 214*n*5, 215, 216, 216*n*9, 218, 221, 222, 223, 224, 225, 226, 227, 228, 229, 230, 231, 233, 237, 238, 239, 244, 245, 253, 250, 251, 252, 253, 254, 257, 258, 259, 260, 261, 261*n*6, 262, 263, 264, 265, 265*n*9, 267, 268, 269, 270, 271, 272, 273, 274, 275, 276, 277, 279, 280, 285, 291, 292, 294, 295, 296, 298

system   VII, IX, 3, 4, 5, 7, 10, 11, 12, 13, 16, 17, 18*n*4, 23, 24, 25, 26, 31, 115, 117, 119

International Political Economy   43, 142, 146, 168, 173*n*2, 212*n*3

International Relations   34, 34*n*2, 35, 36, 37, 38, 41, 42, 43, 49, 49*n*1, 50, 51, 59, 63, 67, 76, 76*n*1, 82, 84, 88, 102, 103, 104, 142, 142*n*1, 143, 146, 150, 153, 156, 156*n*2, 156*n*3, 156*n*4, 166, 167, 168, 173, 173*n*2, 174, 175, 176, 176*n*7, 177, 178, 179, 180, 182, 183, 189, 190, 190*n*20, 191, 194*n*2, 194*n*3, 195, 198, 202, 205, 207, 207*n*10, 210, 218, 237, 238, 249, 253, 254, 257, 261, 268, 274, 279, 280, 296

international system   34, 35, 37, 42, 43, 61, 62, 72, 146, 173, 175, 177, 190, 195, 212*n*3, 223, 225, 227, 229, 230, 231, 238, 239, 252, 254, 264, 267, 269, 275, 296, 298

IR   76, 76*n*4, 77, 78, 79, 79*n*5, 80, 81, 82, 83, 84, 84*n*10, 86, 87*n*16, 89, 90, 91, 92, 93, 94, 94*n*26, 95, 96, 99, 100*n*34, 101, 102, 142, 143, 145, 146, 166, 257, 261, 262, 274

Iran   36, 37, 64, 153, 227, 229*n*22

Italy   230

Japan   39, 60, 63, 65, 69, 199, 208, 261, 264*n*8, 269, 272, 291, 296

Karl Marx   VII, 14, 15, 33

Kautsky   51, 52, 56, 74, 80, 106, 144, 177, 177*n*8, 180*n*13, 185, 186, 194*n*4, 195*n*5, 198, 204, 207, 207*n*10, 210, 212, 213, 215, 216, 216*n*10, 216*n*7, 216*n*8, 217, 219, 230, 232

Keohane, Robert   35, 76*n*4, 103, 257, 258, 261, 261*n*7, 262, 263, 264, 265, 266, 266*n*11, 267, 268, 269, 271, 272, 274, 276

Kindleberger, Charles   35, 266*n*11, 277

Kissinger, Henry   41, 44, 269

Laclau   IX, 121, 122, 126, 127, 127*n*7, 128, 129, 130, 131, 133, 134, 135, 136, 138, 139, 140

Latin America   69, 73, 239, 243*n*10, 254, 258

Lenin   IX, 3, 11, 11*n*11, 13, 13*n*14, 14, 111

Lenin, Vladimir   36, 49, 50, 51, 52, 53, 53*n*4, 54, 55, 56, 57, 58, 59, 60, 63, 66, 67, 70, 74, 75, 80, 86*n*12, 87, 87*n*16, 91*n*22, 94*n*27, 129, 144, 151, 162, 177, 177*n*8, 185, 186, 194, 194*n*4, 195, 203*n*9, 204, 207, 207*n*10, 207*n*10, 210, 212, 213, 219, 222*n*15, 224, 224*n*17, 225, 226, 227, 227*n*20, 230, 232, 234, 245, 246, 246*n*12, 250, 253, 255, 287, 288, 295, 300

Liberalism   VII, 9, 34, 35, 93, 143, 150

Losurdo   IX, 69, 71, 75, 142, 143, 146, 147, 148, 149, 150, 151, 151*n*4, 152, 153, 154, 155, 229*n*23, 232

Lukács   17, 52, 53*n*4, 75

Luxemburg   IX, 52, 64, 76, 76*n*1, 77, 78, 80, 80*n*6, 81, 81*n*8, 83, 84, 85, 86, 87, 87*n*14, 87*n*15, 87*n*16, 88, 89, 90, 91, 91*n*21, 91*n*22, 92, 92*n*23, 93, 94, 94*n*26, 94*n*27, 95, 95*n*28, 96, 96*n*29, 97, 98, 99, 99*n*31, 99*n*32, 100, 101, 102, 103, 104, 144, 162, 162*n*8, 170, 198, 232, 245, 246*n*12, 299

Machiavelli, Niccolo   35, 67

Magdoff   106, 195, 195*n*5, 196, 196*n*6, 201, 204, 207*n*10, 208, 209, 210, 260, 261*n*7, 276

Mandel   106, 195, 195*n*5, 199, 199*n*7, 201*n*8, 202, 203, 204, 207, 207*n*10, 209, 210, 211, 260

Manifesto   192, 212, 233

Mao Zedong   38, 71, 151

Marini   112*n*9, 120, 193, 237, 237*n*4, 240, 242, 242*n*6, 242*n*8, 242*n*9, 243, 243*n*10, 243*n*11, 244, 245, 246, 246*n*12, 246*n*13, 247, 247*n*15, 247*n*17, 248, 249, 250, 255, 256, 258, 259, 260, 260*n*4, 276, 279, 280, 281, 282, 283, 284, 285, 286, 292, 298, 300, 301

INDEX   307

market   38, 39, 56, 60, 69, 85, 123, 125, 143,
         145, 146, 148, 157, 165, 167, 167n12, 175,
         179, 179n11, 179n12, 180, 181, 188, 190, 196,
         198, 202, 205, 206, 215, 217, 218, 220, 244,
         249, 254, 267, 281, 284, 291, 292, 295
Marx   IX, XIII, 1, 3, 4, 5, 6, 7, 8, 9, 10, 11, 12,
         13n14, 14, 15, 16, 17, 18, 18n4, 20, 21, 22,
         22n6, 23, 24, 25, 26, 27, 28, 29, 29n8, 31,
         32, 32n9, 33, 109, 115
Marx, Karl   35, 36, 44, 45, 50, 53, 74, 87,
         96n29, 97, 150, 154, 155, 157, 159, 160n5,
         161n7, 168, 170, 178, 178n10, 179, 179n12,
         180, 180n13, 182, 190, 192, 193, 203n9,
         209n11, 212, 216n7, 218n12, 224, 226, 227,
         232, 233, 245, 249, 254, 256
Marxian   76n4, 157, 159, 160, 160n5, 178n10,
         179, 179n12, 181, 182, 186, 232
Marxism   34, 36, 37n3, 38, 41, 42, 43, 50, 76,
         84n10, 101, 102, 121, 129, 131, 138, 140, 142,
         156, 169, 170, 175, 177, 178, 183, 186n17,
         190, 191, 195, 203n9, 217, 226, 233, 234,
         237, 238, 241, 244, 245, 247, 247n14,
         279, 283
Marxist   34, 35, 36, 40, 43, 49n1, 76, 76n4, 77,
         79, 79n5, 80, 80n6, 82, 83, 84, 84n10,
         84n11, 86, 86n12, 87, 87n16, 89, 90, 94,
         101, 102, 122n3, 123, 129, 130, 133, 134, 136,
         138, 142, 142n1, 143, 144, 145, 146, 156, 157,
         162n8, 166, 167, 168, 169, 178, 182, 183,
         184, 184n15, 185, 187, 188n19, 189, 190,
         191, 192, 194, 195, 196n6, 203, 203n9, 207,
         208, 208n10, 210, 211, 212, 213n3, 214, 215,
         216n8, 221, 222, 223, 225, 231, 237, 237n1,
         238, 238n4, 239, 242n8, 242n9, 243n10,
         243n11, 244, 245, 246, 247, 247n14,
         247n15, 248, 249, 250, 251, 252, 252n18,
         253, 257, 258, 260, 261, 261n7, 268, 269,
         274, 278, 279, 280, 281, 284, 285, 286,
         296, 296n6, 298, 299
Marxist theory   157, 184n15, 194, 195, 203,
         203n9, 208n10, 210, 212, 221, 222, 237,
         238, 238n4, 242n8, 243n10, 245, 247,
         247n14, 248, 250, 252, 253, 258, 260, 280
Minh, Ho Chi   38
mode of production   5, 6, 7, 11, 107, 108, 111,
         113, 159, 175, 177, 178, 180, 181, 187, 190,
         199, 204, 218n12, 224, 248, 295

monopoly   51, 53, 54, 55, 57, 59, 60, 61, 67, 69,
         71, 144, 148, 158, 177, 177n7, 187, 196, 199,
         200, 202, 204, 214, 214n4, 219n13, 224,
         240, 249, 282
monopoly capital   11, 113, 114, 200
Morgenthau, Hans   35, 90
Mouffe   IX, 121, 122, 128, 129, 130, 131, 132,
         132n8, 132n9, 133, 134, 135, 137, 138,
         139, 140
Mozambique   37

national   38, 39, 42, 43, 51, 58, 62, 63, 70, 71,
         72, 73, 83, 87, 87n16, 91, 122, 123, 124, 125,
         126, 143, 145, 146, 150, 151, 151n4, 152, 160,
         161n7, 162, 163, 175, 176, 181, 188, 194, 196,
         197, 199, 200, 201, 202, 203, 204, 205,
         206, 209, 213, 215, 216, 218, 219, 219n13,
         220, 221, 222, 225, 225n18, 226, 230, 239,
         240, 244, 247, 248, 250, 251, 252, 254,
         263, 268, 270, 273, 273n17, 279, 280, 281,
         282, 292, 293, 294, 295, 296, 298, 299
national state   7, 9, 11, 15, 16, 32, 33, 43, 202,
         206, 220
nationalism   35, 38, 52, 81, 87, 151, 202, 203,
         272, 279
nation-state   40, 67, 175, 211, 217, 219, 223,
         226, 264
nation-states   7, 208, 220
neoliberalism   61, 62, 125, 150, 157, 164, 167,
         167n12, 168
Neorealism   35
North Korea   36, 39, 149
Nye, Joseph   35, 64, 75, 257, 258, 261, 261n7,
         262, 263, 264, 265, 266, 266n11, 267,
         268, 269, 270, 271, 271n14, 272, 273, 274,
         276, 277

paradigm   34, 35, 64, 78, 138, 186, 191, 230,
         258, 263
periphery   VII, IX, 36, 38, 39, 40, 41, 42, 43,
         49, 50, 59, 61, 65, 66, 106, 144, 145, 187,
         195, 203, 247, 287
Poland   91n21, 149, 226
political economy   X, XII, XIII, XVI, 12, 13,
         34, 74, 103, 144, 168, 169, 170, 179, 181,
         184n15, 185, 191, 199n7, 202, 209n11, 210,
         231, 232, 233

Political Science   36, 41, 80, 121n2, 237n3, 262, 263
populism   121, 122, 122n3, 123, 124, 125, 126, 127, 128, 129, 134, 136, 137, 138, 139
Portugal   57, 211
Poulantzas   IX, 105, 105n1, 105n3, 106, 107, 108, 109, 110, 111, 111n8, 112, 112n9, 113, 114, 114n11, 114m12, 115, 116, 116m14, 117, 117n16, 118, 119, 195, 203, 203n9, 205, 207, 207n10, 209, 210, 211, 227, 233, 252n18, 253, 256
power   34, 35, 37, 44, 50, 51, 54, 56, 62, 63, 64, 65, 66, 67, 68, 69, 70, 71, 72, 73, 73n12, 84, 85, 86, 89, 90, 91, 94n26, 98, 122, 124, 125n5, 126, 129, 131, 132, 135, 135n12, 142, 145, 146, 147, 149, 150, 153, 154, 157, 158, 159, 160, 161, 162, 163, 164, 165, 166, 167n12, 175n4, 177, 184n15, 187, 194, 195, 196, 199, 200, 201, 205, 206, 208, 209, 218, 218m12, 219, 220, 223, 226, 227, 228, 229, 238, 240, 246, 251, 252, 252n18, 253, 254, 265, 266, 267, 268, 269, 274, 280, 281, 283, 286, 288, 291, 293, 294, 297
powers   40, 42, 44, 58, 60, 62, 77, 81, 83, 86, 93, 94n26, 101, 125, 126, 144, 150, 151, 153, 165, 174, 195, 201, 203, 206, 212, 215, 216, 217, 221, 222, 223, 224n17, 227, 228, 228n21, 229, 229n22, 229n23, 230, 271, 284, 296
primitive accumulation   157
production relations   61, 107, 108, 108n4, 108n5, 109, 110, 174, 178, 182, 188, 246, 288
productive forces   5, 106, 111, 144, 152, 163, 180, 199, 218, 227, 288
proletariat   5, 38, 67, 80n6, 87n15, 88, 89, 99, 99n31, 107, 121, 138, 251
property   39, 67, 97n30, 159, 231

Realism   VII, 34, 35, 62, 89, 150, 265
relations of production   5, 111, 180, 182, 288
republic   88n17
revolution   16, 18, 19, 34, 35, 36, 38, 39, 41, 42, 43, 50, 51, 52, 77, 80n6, 92, 92n23, 95, 96, 97, 98, 99, 99n31, 123, 151, 161, 199, 210, 238, 240, 245, 246, 252, 268, 278, 279, 281, 295, 296, 298, 299
Revolutions   34, 34n1, 35, 36, 37, 38, 39, 40, 41, 42, 43, 44, 45
Rosenberg, Justin   36

Rousseau, Jean J   35
ruling class   22, 25, 26, 32, 62, 73, 87n16, 89, 91, 110, 111n8, 115, 117, 118, 158, 194, 195, 197, 206, 225, 248, 252n18, 253
Russia   39, 50, 51, 52, 55, 64, 84n11, 129, 149, 228, 229, 229n22, 231
Russian Revolution   VII, 17, 40, 51, 129, 197

Second International   80, 177
Skocpol, Theda   41, 45
Smith, Adam   169, 232, 233, 263, 271
social class   XII, 32, 105, 106, 107, 109, 110, 115, 119
social classes   63, 176, 242n7, 253, 254
socialism   VII, 11, 22, 26, 38, 39, 84n10, 87n14, 87n15, 87n16, 88, 89, 92, 93, 97, 97n30, 98, 105, 105n3, 119, 130, 142, 143, 145, 146, 153, 214n6, 217, 244, 251
Socialism   38, 40, 44, 97, 102, 125n5, 232, 238n4, 243
socialist   37, 38, 40, 58, 77, 80n6, 84, 84n10, 84n11, 86m12, 87n16, 91, 91n22, 96, 97, 97n30, 98, 99, 99n31, 100, 146, 151, 153, 187, 197, 199, 202, 245, 246, 260, 279, 295, 296, 298
socialist revolution   296
sovereign   7, 10, 11, 12, 23, 43, 181, 253
sovereignty   127, 135, 137, 138, 139, 144, 149, 150, 152, 218, 229, 230, 253
Soviet Union   11, 40, 44, 184, 187
Spain   230
Stalin, Joseph   99n32, 155
State   34, 35, 37, 39, 42, 44, 51, 58, 60n6, 61, 66, 69, 71, 72, 76n3, 102, 104, 123, 124, 129, 137, 146, 173, 173n2, 178, 179, 179m12, 184, 184n15, 187, 187n18, 188, 189, 190, 190n20, 191, 192, 198, 201, 202, 206, 209, 209n11, 215, 233, 237n1, 237n3, 239, 252, 252n18, 253, 260, 262, 264, 271n14, 273, 274, 293
state system   69, 70, 72, 111, 115, 144, 191, 196, 253
states   50, 51, 57, 62, 63, 65, 72, 73, 86, 87n14, 90, 91, 92, 94n26, 95, 151, 157, 160, 161, 163, 164, 190, 194, 196, 197, 199, 200, 201, 203, 204, 205, 206, 207n10, 208, 209, 213, 214n4, 216, 216n9, 217, 218, 219, 221, 223, 225, 226, 227, 228, 229n23, 230, 238, 245, 246, 248, 250, 253, 280

INDEX 309

sub-imperialism   152, 279, 280, 281, 282, 283, 285, 298
supremacy   63, 64, 70, 72, 147, 149, 152, 198, 201, 204, 206, 207n10, 208, 217, 283

Third World   35, 37, 38, 39, 44, 203, 260, 261, 261n6, 269, 270, 270n12, 271
Thucydides   35
Toynbee, Arnold   41, 45
trade   39, 62, 67, 90n20, 123, 125, 147, 179n12, 181, 197, 198, 200, 203, 250, 259, 286, 292, 294
transition   37, 38, 42, 53, 62, 123, 173, 180, 183, 186, 187, 188, 204, 214n6, 231
transnational   34, 36, 42, 145, 162, 209, 213, 218, 219, 220, 221, 232, 261n6, 263, 264, 267, 269, 271, 273
Trotsky   9, 14, 80, 87n16, 91n22, 99n32, 151, 268, 277
Turkey   228

underdevelopment   67, 112, 239, 241, 242n8, 247, 254, 258, 259, 275, 280, 288
uneven development   61, 67, 106, 113, 157, 213, 227, 229, 287, 296
Union of Soviet Socialist Republics   VII
United States   39, 56, 60, 61, 86, 92, 187, 197, 198, 201, 207n10, 208, 209, 210, 217, 218, 219, 222, 223, 227, 228, 229, 229n22, 230, 231, 232, 239, 247, 259, 260, 261, 263, 264, 264n8, 265, 268, 272, 273, 273n17, 275, 277

USSR   VII, 58, 65, 209, 217, 295, 296

Vattel, Emmerich   35
Vietnam   36, 37, 39, 65, 153, 270

Wallerstein, Immanuel   36, 42, 61, 69, 75, 144
Waltz, Kenneth   42, 76n3, 90, 104, 266n11, 277
war   35, 36, 39, 40, 50, 51, 52, 58, 60, 60n7, 62, 66, 68, 70, 72, 77, 78, 79n6, 80, 81, 81n8, 82, 83, 84, 85, 86, 86n12, 88, 88n17, 89, 89n18, 90, 91, 92n23, 94, 94n26, 95, 96, 98, 99, 99n31, 100, 101, 102, 123, 146, 148, 149, 150, 152, 153, 154, 177n7, 189, 194, 196n6, 199, 202, 215, 216, 217, 219, 225, 228, 231, 260, 261, 265, 268, 273n17
wealth   50, 142, 145, 150, 151, 153, 212, 259, 282
western powers   20, 26, 28, 29, 30
workers   50, 97, 99, 99n31, 123, 125, 128, 159, 162, 218n12, 248, 250, 253, 259, 281, 285
working class   IX, 83, 88, 159, 162, 248
world market   4, 8, 9, 179, 181, 250
World War I   VII, IX, 39, 40, 52, 78, 84, 94, 102, 129, 142, 176, 194, 196, 207n10
World War II   VII, 40, 58, 59, 60, 70, 78, 113, 186, 194, 195, 196, 197, 202, 204, 207, 207n10, 217, 218, 221, 222, 239, 275
world-system   4, 9, 35, 36, 37, 43, 61, 62, 70, 77, 145, 189, 195, 196, 198, 208, 239, 253, 283
World-system   36, 39, 40, 43

www.ingramcontent.com/pod-product-compliance
Lightning Source LLC
Chambersburg PA
CBHW070611030426
42337CB00020B/3747